Complete French

Gaëlle Graham

Advisory editor
Paul Coggle

For UK order enquiries: please contact Bookpoint Ltd, 130 Milton Park, Abingdon, Oxon OX14 4SB. *Telephone:* +44 (0) 1235 827720. *Fax:* +44 (0) 1235 400454. Lines are open 09.00–17.00, Monday to Saturday, with a 24-hour message answering service. Details about our titles and how to order are available at www.teachyourself.com

For USA order enquiries: please contact McGraw-Hill Customer Services, PO Box 545, Blacklick, OH 43004-0545, USA. *Telephone:* 1-800-722-4726. *Fax:* 1-614-755-5645.

For Canada order enquiries: please contact McGraw-Hill Ryerson Ltd, 300 Water St, Whitby, Ontario L1N 9B6, Canada. *Telephone:* 905 430 5000. Fax: 905 430 5020.

Long renowned as the authoritative source for self-guided learning – with more than 50 million copies sold worldwide – the *Teach Yourself* series includes over 500 titles in the fields of languages, crafts, hobbies, business, computing and education.

British Library Cataloguing in Publication Data: a catalogue record for this title is available from the British Library.

Library of Congress Catalog Card Number: on file.

First published in UK 1998 by Hodder Education, part of Hachette UK, 338 Euston Road, London NW1 3BH.

First published in US 1998 by The McGraw-Hill Companies, Inc.

This edition published 2012; previously published as Teach Yourself French.

The *Teach Yourself* name is a registered trademark of Hodder Headline.

Advisory Editor: Paul Coggle, University of Kent at Canterbury

Typeset by Integra Software Services Pvt. Ltd., Pondicherry, India.

Illustrated by Barking Dog Art, Sally Elford and Stephanie Strickland.

Printed and bound in Dubai for Hodder Education, an Hachette UK Company, Carmelite House, 50 Victroria Embankment, London EC4Y 0DZ.

The publisher has used its best endeavours to ensure that the URLs for external websites referred to in this book are correct and active at the time of going to press. However, the publisher and the author have no responsibility for the websites and can make no guarantee that a site will remain live or that the content will remain relevant, decent or appropriate.

Hachette UK's policy is to use papers that are natural, renewable and recyclable products and made from wood grown in sustainable forests. The logging and manufacturing processes are expected to conform to the environmental regulations of the country of origin.

Impression number	15	14	13
Year	2023	2022	2021

Contents

BEGINNER

ADVANCED BEGINNER

INTERMEDIATE

ADVANCED

Meet the author

Gaëlle Graham was born in Brittany, France, and went to University at La Sorbonne in Paris where she studied English. On moving to England, Gaëlle taught French in London comprehensive schools for 25 years. She now works for the National Union of Teachers. She has a Master's degree in Applied Linguistics from the University of Kent at Canterbury. She is a regular contributor to France Inter, the French national radio, about English educational news.

Gaëlle enjoys travelling back and forth from London to Paris and to her beloved Brittany. She never travels without her camera and tries to capture the changes she observes in the course of her frequent visits to France. She believes the Vélib', a system of bike rental using a swipe card at bike stations dotted all over Paris, is the best way to appreciate the capital.

Gaëlle's other great loves are cinema and reading. She sticks to a very strict self-imposed reading pattern of alternating French and English books.

Gaëlle has been contributing to the Teach Yourself French course since 1984 and is always searching for new ways of making the course accessible and informative to learners. She endeavours to share with the readers the latest cultural, political or social developments and hopes therefore that you will enjoy having her as your guide as you embark on your study of French.

Welcome to Complete French!

THE AIM OF THIS BOOK

If you are an adult learner with no previous knowledge of French and studying on your own, then this is the course for you. Perhaps you are taking up French again after a break from it, or you are intending to learn with the support of a class? Again, you will find this course very well suited to your purposes.

The language you will learn is introduced through everyday situations. The emphasis is first and foremost on using French, but we also aim to give you an idea of how the language works, so that you can create sentences of your own. The course covers all four of the basic skills – listening and speaking, reading and writing. If you are working on your own, the recording will be all the more important, as it will provide you with the essential opportunity to listen to French and to speak it within a controlled framework.

The course also provides information on various aspects of everyday life such as the level of formality that is appropriate when you talk to strangers, and how the health service works if you should fall ill.

FRENCH IN THE MODERN WORLD

According to a 2010 study by the *Organisation Internationale de la Francophonie*, there are approximately 220 million French speakers throughout the world, with 115 million claiming French as their first language. Outside France, French is the first language for large communities in Belgium, Luxembourg and Switzerland. France also has five overseas **départements** which come under French administration and are part of the French Republic: Guadeloupe, Martinique, Réunion, Guyane and Mayotte (one of the Comoro Islands, situated in the Indian Ocean, north of Madagascar). Until 2011 Mayotte was one of two **collectivités territoriales**, the other one is St-Pierre-et-Miquelon. France has other overseas territories which include Polynésie française, Nouvelle-Calédonie, Wallis-et-Futuna, terres Australes et Antarctiques (terre Adélie, Kerguelen, Crozet, St-Paul).

French is also spoken in countries that have been under French rule in the past. In North Africa, French is the second language after Arabic in Tunisia, Algeria and Morocco. The same applies to many west and central

African countries such as Senegal. There is still an ageing population that speaks and understands French in Vietnam. In North America, Louisiana still has some vestiges of the French language. In Canada, in the province of Quebec, French is spoken by many people as their first language. French in Quebec has developed differently from the French spoken in France. The accent and the intonations are very different and it has more or less become a language in its own right although its speakers can understand and communicate with French people without difficulty.

How the book works

The course book contains 25 units that need to be taken in order, as the language builds up on the French from previous units. There is one **Unité de révision** (*Review unit*) to recycle the main language points from units 1-25.

Each unit contains most or all of the following:

What you will learn

A set of learning objectives identifies what you will be able to do in French by the end of each unit.

Culture point

An opening passage about a cultural aspect related to the unit theme introduces key words and phrases.

Vocabulary builder

This section, along with its accompanying audio, previews the key vocabulary and expressions you will hear in conversations.

Conversations

The language is presented in manageable chunks, building carefully on what was learned previously. Model conversations between native speakers, but also reading passages or narratives, are presented in the book and on the audio. **Insight** boxes provide further assistance with relevant language or cultural information. **Comprehension questions** accompany each conversation to help focus your listening.

Language Discovery

Questions guide you to consider the key language points from the conversations. Look to the light bulb icon to discover how French works, whether it is a rule or just a way of saying things.

Learn more

This section contains the nuts and bolts of the language you need to construct your own sentences correctly.

Practice

A variety of exercises, including speaking activities and role plays give you a chance to 'pull it all together' and use your French meaningfully. Exercises are graded so that activities which require mainly recognition come first. As you grow confident in manipulating the language forms you will be encouraged to write and speak the language independently.

Pronunciation

The best way to acquire good pronunciation and intonation is to listen to the native speakers on the audio CDs and to try to imitate them. However, as certain sounds in French are very unfamiliar we include specific advice on pronunciation within the unit themselves.

Test yourself

Will help you asses how much you have learned. **Self-check** lets you see what you can do in French. When you feel confident that you can perform the language functions correctly, move on to the next unit.

Study the units at your own pace and remember to make frequent and repeated use of the audio.

Symbols

To make your learning easier and more efficient, a system of icons indicates the actions you should take:

 Read a culture vignette

 Play the audio track

 Listen and pronounce

 Figure something out for yourself

 Learn key words and expressions

 Practise what you have learned

 Write or make notes

 Read an authentic French text

 Speak French out loud or role-play

 Check your French language skills

Consult and return to **Learn to learn** at the beginning of the book. As you progress through the course, you will become more comfortable with studying on your own.

And at the back of the book, you will find these reference sections:

▶ **Transcripts** of all the listening comprehension activities which are not given in print.
▶ **Key to the exercises** to check your answers to all the activities and self-tests in the units.
▶ A **Quick guide to French pronunciation.**
▶ A **Grammar summary**: reference notes about the main language structures covered in the course.
▶ **Verb tables** show the conjugations of 30 useful verbs.
▶ An **English-French vocabulary** list, which includes most of the words used in the course.

Learn to learn

There are lots of approaches to language learning, some practical and some quite unconventional. Perhaps you know of a few, or even have some techniques of your own. In this book we have incorporated the **Discovery Method** of learning, a sort of DIY approach to language learning. What this means is that you will be encouraged throughout the course to engage your mind and figure out the language for yourself, through identifying patterns, understanding grammar concepts, noticing words that are similar to English, and more. This method promotes language awareness, a critical skill in acquiring a new language. As a result of your own efforts, you will be able to better retain what you have learned, use it with confidence, and, even better, apply those same skills to continuing to learn the language (or, indeed, another one) on your own after you've finished this book.

Everyone can succeed in learning a language – the key is to know how to learn it. Learning is more than just reading or memorizing grammar and vocabulary. It's about being an active learner, learning in real contexts, and, most importantly, using what you've learned in different situations. Simply put, if you **figure something out for yourself**, you're more likely to understand it. And when you use what you've learned, you're more likely to remember it.

And because many of the essential but (let's admit it!) dull details, such as grammar rules, are taught through the **Discovery Method**, you'll have more fun while learning. Soon, the language will start to make sense and you'll be relying on your own intuition to construct original sentences independently, not just listening and repeating.

Enjoy yourself!

BECOME A SUCCESSFUL LANGUAGE LEARNER

1) Make a habit out of learning

Study a little every day, between 20 and 30 minutes if possible, rather than two to three hours in one session. Give yourself **short-term goals**, e.g. work out how long you'll spend on a particular unit and work within the time limit. This will help you to **create a study habit**, much in the same way you would a sport or music. You will need to concentrate, so try to **create an**

environment conducive to learning which is calm and quiet and free from distractions. As you study, do not worry about your mistakes or the things you can't remember or understand. Languages settle differently in our brains, but gradually the language will become clearer as your brain starts to make new connections. Just **give yourself enough time** and you will succeed.

2) Maximise your exposure to the language

As part of your study habit you could try listening to radio and television or reading articles and blogs. Remember that as well as listening to online radio live you can use catch-up services to listen more than once. Perhaps you could find information in French about a personal passion or hobby or even a news story that interests you. In time you'll find that your vocabulary and language recognition deepen and you'll become used to a range of writing and speaking styles.

3) Vocabulary

▶ To organise your study of vocabulary, group new words under:

  a generic categories, e.g. food, furniture.

  b situations in which they occur, e.g. under restaurant you can write waiter, table, menu, bill.

  c functions, e.g. greeting and leave-taking, giving thanks, apologizing.

▶ Say the words out loud as you read them.
▶ Write the words over and over again. Remember that if you want to keep lists on your smartphone or tablet you can usually switch the keyboard language to make sure you are able to include all accents and special characters.
▶ Listen to the audio several times.
▶ Cover up the English side of the vocabulary list and see if you remember the meaning of the word.
▶ Associate the words with similar sounding words in English, e.g. **parler** *(to speak)* with **parlour**, a room where people chat, or **Parliament**, an institution where debates take place.
▶ Create flash cards, drawings and mind maps.
▶ Write words for objects around your house and stick them to objects.
▶ Pay attention to patterns in words, e.g. adding **bon** or **bonne** to the start of a word usually indicates a greeting, **bonjour**, **bonsoir**, **bonne nuit**.
▶ Experiment with words. Use the words that you learn in new contexts and find out if they are correct. For example, you learn in Unit 5 that one of the meanings of **passe** means *go* in the context of time,

e.g. **le week-end passe trop vite** (*the week-end goes too quickly*). Experiment with **passe** in new contexts, e.g. **les vacances** (*the holidays*) **passent trop vite**; **la semaine** (*the week*) **passe ...** . You can also play around with words and expressions e.g. compare **le temps passe** (*time goes*) and **un passe-temps**, literally a pass-time. Check the new phrases either in this book, a dictionary or with French speakers.

▶ Make the best of words you already know. When you start thinking about it you will realise that there are lots of French words and expressions which are commonly used in English: **apéritif**, **Art Déco**, **c'est la vie** (*that's life*), **cuisine, déjà vu** (*already seen*), **rendez-vous**, **tête à tête** and many more.

4) Grammar

▶ To organise the study of grammar write your own grammar glossary and add new information and examples as you go along.

▶ Experiment with grammar rules. Sit back and reflect on the rules you learn. See how they compare with your own language or other languages you may already speak. Try to find out some rules on your own and be ready to spot the exceptions. By doing this you'll remember the rules better and get a feel for the language.

▶ Try to find examples of grammar in conversations or other articles.

▶ Keep a 'pattern bank' that organises examples that can be listed under the structures you've learned.

▶ Use old vocabulary to practise new grammar structures.

▶ When you learn a new verb form, write the conjugation of several different verbs you know that follow the same form.

5) Pronunciation

▶ When organising the study of pronunciation keep a section of your notebook for pronunciation rules and practise those that trouble you.

▶ Repeat all of the conversations, line by line. Listen to yourself and try to mimic what you hear.

▶ Record yourself and compare yourself to a native speaker.

▶ Make a list of words that give you trouble and practise them.

▶ Study individual sounds, then full words.

▶ Don't forget, it's not just about pronouncing letters and words correctly, but using the right intonation. So, when practising words and sentences, mimic the rising and falling intonation of native speakers.

6) Listening and reading

The conversations in this book include questions to help guide you in your understanding. But you can go further by following some of these tips.

▶ Imagine the situation. When listening to or reading the conversations, try to imagine where the scene is taking place and who the main characters are. Let your experience of the world help you guess the meaning of the conversation, e.g. if a conversation takes place in a snack bar you can predict the kind of vocabulary that is being used.

▶ Concentrate on the main part. When watching a foreign film you usually get the meaning of the whole story from a few individual shots. Understanding a foreign conversation or article is similar. Concentrate on the main parts to get the message and don't worry about individual words.

▶ Guess the key words; if you cannot, ask or look them up.
When there are key words you don't understand, try to guess what they mean from the context. If you're listening to a French speaker and cannot get the gist of a whole passage because of one word or phrase, try to repeat that word with a questioning tone; the speaker will probably paraphrase it, giving you the chance to understand it. If for example you wanted to find out the meaning of the word **voyager** (*to travel*) you would ask **Que veut dire voyager?** Or **Que signifie voyager?** This second example demonstrates how much you already know (*signify* and *voyage*) and this makes the guessing much easier.

7) Speaking

Rehearse in the foreign language. As all language teachers will assure you, the successful learners are those students who overcome their inhibitions and get into situations where they must speak, write and listen to the foreign language. Here are some useful tips to help you practise speaking French:

▶ Hold a conversation with yourself, using the conversations of the units as models and the structures you have learnt previously.

▶ After you have conducted a transaction with a salesperson, clerk or waiter in your own language, pretend that you have to do it in French, e.g. buying groceries, ordering food, drinks and so on.

▶ Look at objects around you and try to name them in French.

▶ Look at people around you and try to describe them in detail.

▶ Try to answer all of the questions in the book out loud.

▶ Say the dialogues out loud then try to replace sentences with ones that are true for you.

▶ Try to role-play different situations in the book.

8) Learn from your errors

▶ Don't let errors interfere with getting your message across. Making errors is part of any normal learning process, but some people get so worried that they won't say anything unless they are sure it is correct. This leads to a vicious circle as the less they say, the less practice they get and the more mistakes they make.

▶ Note the seriousness of errors. Many errors are not serious, as they do not affect the meaning; for example if you use the wrong article (**le** for **la**), wrong pronouns (**je l'achète** for **je les achète**) or wrong adjective ending (**blanc** for **blanche**). So concentrate on getting your message across and learn from your mistakes.

▶ As you progress you will also become aware of **faux-amis** *(false friends)*. These are words which look or sound like English words, but may have a very different meaning, e.g. **la librairie** is not *the library,* but *the bookshop.* In French **la bibliothèque** is *the library.* The most important thing to remember though is BE BOLD! Getting it wrong at times is a huge part of your learning process and success.

9) Learn to cope with uncertainty

▶ **Don't over-use your dictionary.**
When reading a text in the foreign language, don't be tempted to look up every word you don't know. Underline the words you do not understand and read the passage several times, concentrating on trying to get the gist of the passage. If after the third time there are still words which prevent you from getting the general meaning of the passage, look them up in the dictionary.

▶ **Don't panic if you don't understand.**
If at some point you feel you don't understand what you are told, don't panic or give up listening. Either try and guess what is being said and keep following the conversation or, if you cannot, isolate the expression or words you haven't understood and have them explained to you. The speaker might paraphrase them and the conversation will carry on.

▶ **Keep talking.**
The best way to improve your fluency in the foreign language is to talk every time you have the opportunity to do so: keep the conversations flowing and don't worry about the mistakes. If you get stuck for a particular word, don't let the conversation stop; paraphrase or replace the unknown word with one you do know, even if you have to simplify what you want to say. As a last resort use the word from your own language and pronounce it in the foreign accent.

Salutations
Greetings

In this unit you will learn how to:
- ▶ *say hello.*
- ▶ *use greetings for different times of the day and special occasions.*
- ▶ *talk about a few places in town.*
- ▶ *talk about food and drinks.*
- ▶ *use gender and number references.*

CEFR: *Can recognize familiar words and basic phrases (A1); Can use basic greeting and leave taking expressions (A1); Can handle numbers and quantities (A1); Can understand news items (A2); Can ask how people are and react to news (A1); Can write short, simple notes (A1)*

Hello and Goodbye

When you are in France, you will find that conversations start with a greeting and finish with a farewell. As you get into a taxi, go into a shop or order a meal, you will exchange a **bonjour** (*good morning and good afternoon*), **bonsoir** (*good evening*) or a **bonne nuit** (*good night*) depending on the time of day. You can add **salut** (*hi*) to give a more informal greeting. When meeting friends and relatives, you may exchange two, three, or even four **bisous** (*kisses*), depending on the region you are in.

Likewise, when it's time to get out of the taxi, leave the shop or restaurant..., you will exchange a farewell. This could be **au revoir** (*goodbye*), **à bientôt** (*see you soon*) or **à plus tard** (*see you later*). Amongst young people speaking more casually, you will notice **à plus** is frequently used instead of **à plus tard**.

a   If someone says to you bonjour, what are you going to say?
b   What are you doing when you say "bonne nuit"?

Vocabulary builder

GREETINGS

 1 01.01 **Listen to the greetings and repeat.**

Bonjour!	*Hello! (in the day time)*
Salut!	*Hi!*
Au revoir!	*Goodbye!*
Bonjour monsieur!	*Hello! (to a man)*
Bonjour Madame Martin!	*Hello! (to a woman, Mrs. Martin)*
Salut Dominique!	*Hi!/Hello! (to a friend or acquaintance, Dominique)*
Au revoir mademoiselle!	*Goodbye (to a young, unmarried woman)*

Note that the term 'mademoiselle' is no longer in official usage (for example in government paperwork).

> **INSIGHT: LANGUAGE**
> If you know someone's name, for example a neighbour's, you greet them with their full name. Otherwise you greet them as **Madame**, **Monsieur** or **Mademoiselle**. You usually use first names for family and close friends only.

 3 01.02 **In addition, you need to know the correct greeting for each time of day. Listen and complete the English translations.**

    a À bientôt! À tout à l'heure!   *See you soon!*
    b Bon après-midi!   *Good afternoon!*
    c Bonsoir!   _____ *evening!*
    d Bonne nuit!   _____ *night!*

 4 01.03 **Bonjour! Say the appropriate greetings to the people. Then listen and check your answers.**

    a *Hello* to Madame Corre
    b *Goodbye* to Marie-Claire
    c *Good night* to Paul
    d *Good afternoon* to a young woman at the cash desk in the supermarket
    e *See you soon* to Monsieur Jarre

5 01.04 **Listen to some more greetings and match them to the correct English expressions.**

a Allez, bon voyage!

b Bon week-end!

c Allez, bonne route!

d Bonnes vacances!

e Bonne Année!

f Bon anniversaire!

1 *Have a good weekend!*

2 *Happy birthday!*

3 *Have a good journey!*

4 *Happy New Year!*

5 *Have a safe journey!*

6 *Have a good holiday!*

A VOTRE SANTÉ! *(TO YOUR GOOD HEALTH!)*

1 01.05 **French people always find a good reason to drink a toast. Listen to the following toasts and repeat.**

Said to a group or a person addressed formally	
A votre santé!	To your (good) health!
A la vôtre!	To yours!
Said to one person informally	
A ta santé!	To your (good) health!
A la tienne!	To yours!
Santé!	Good health! Cheers!

NEW EXPRESSIONS

Look at the expressions that are used in the next conversations. Note their meanings.

Conversation 1

Allez, à bientôt!	*Oh well, see you soon!*
Allez, bon appétit!	*Oh well, have a good meal!*
Allez, bonne pêche!	*Oh well, have a good catch!**

*Note: *usually said to someone fishing, but here as an expression of encouragement to say Oh well, I'll leave you to it!*

Conversations 2, 3 and 4

Vivent les mariés!	*Long live the bride and groom!*
Vive le marié!	*Long live the groom!*
Vive la mariée!	*Long live the bride!*

Conversations 5, 6 and 7

S'il vous plaît. (SVP)	*Please.*
Merci.	*Thank you.*
Merci bien.	*Thanks a lot.*
C'est combien?	*How much is it?*
L'addition s'il vous plaît!	*The bill, please!*

Conversations

 1 01.06 **Listen to the conversation between two neighbours and answer the question.**

a *Is it daytime or evening?* _____

Conversation 1

Madame Lebrun	Bonjour Monsieur Blanchard, comment ça va?
Monsieur Blanchard	Ça va bien merci, et vous Madame Lebrun?
Madame Lebrun	Oh, comme ci, comme ça! Allez, au revoir Monsieur Blanchard.

---

b *Now answer the questions about the conversation.*

1 *Who is feeling fine?* _____

2 *Who is feeling 'so-so'?* _____

 2 01.07 **Listen to the audio and answer the question.**

a *What are the people doing?* _____

> **INSIGHT: LANGUAGE**
> When hearing **Comment ça va?** most people reply **Ça va, ça va!** or **Ça va bien merci!** If someone replies **Comme ci, comme ça!** it indicates that all is not well, things could be better.

Conversation 2

Man 1:	Bonne Année!
Woman 1:	À votre santé!
Man 2:	Santé!
Woman 2:	À la vôtre!

Conversation 3

Woman 1:	Bon Anniversaire Françoise!
Man 1:	À la santé de Françoise!
Man 2:	À la tienne Françoise!
Woman 2:	À la vôtre!

Conversation 4

Man 1:	À la santé des mariés!
Woman 1:	À la santé d'Estelle et Paul!
Man 2:	À la vôtre!

b Quelle est la fête? *What is each group celebrating?*

1 **In Conversation 2 they are celebrating ...**
   a *a good holiday.*   **b** *a wedding.*   **c** *the New Year.*

2 **In Conversation 3 they are celebrating ...**
   a *a good journey.*   **b** *a birthday.*   **c** *a good holiday.*

3 **In Conversation 4 they are celebrating ...**
   a *a wedding.*   **b** *an anniversary.*   **c** *the New Year.*

3 01.08 **Look at the illustrations and listen to the three short conversations. Then answer the questions.**

> **Conversation 5**
> **Woman 1:** Taxi! Taxi! La gare du Nord s'il vous plaît!
> **Man 1:** Oui madame!
> **Conversation 6**
> **Man 1:** Un café, une bière et un sandwich au fromage, s'il vous plaît.
> **Man 2:** Oui monsieur.
> **Man 1:** L'addition s'il vous plaît.
> **Conversation 7**
> **Woman 1:** Une baguette, un camembert et un kilo de pommes s'il vous plaît.
> **Man 1:** Oui mademoiselle!
> **Woman 1:** Merci bien. C'est combien?
> **Man 1:** Cinq euros, mademoiselle.

Conversation 5
Are the people   **a** at home?   **b** at a grocery shop? **c** in the street?

Conversation 6
Are the people   **a** in church?   **b** in a café?   **c** at a grocery shop?

Conversation 7
Are the people   **a** at the station? **b** in the street?   **c** at a grocery shop?

4 **Now read the conversations and find the French expressions which mean:**
   a *a kilo of apples* _____
   b *five euros* _____
   c *a cheese sandwich* _____
   d *a beer* _____
   e *the station* _____

1 *Salutations Greetings*   **7**

Language discovery

Look at the conversations and complete the expressions. Notice the three different ways of spelling the word for good.

a _____ voyage!

b _____ année!

c _____ vacances!

Learn more

Noun genders and adjectives

In French, nouns (words which represent objects, people or ideas) have a gender; they can be either feminine or masculine. **Un voyage** *(a journey)* is masculine, **une année** *(a year)* is feminine, **des vacances** *(holidays)* is feminine but also plural. The gender of nouns does not follow any logical pattern so you will need to be aware of the gender of every noun you learn.

Bon, bonne and **bons, bonnes** are four forms of the same adjective (a word which describes a noun). In French, adjectives take the same gender as the nouns they describe, so we have masculine and feminine adjectives that can both be singular (one item) or plural (more than one item).

French adjectives are spelt differently according to their genders. Generally (but not always) an **-e** at the end of an adjective is for feminine, an **-s** is for plural and the base form is for mansculine.

	Masculine	Feminine
Singular	**un bon raisin** (*a good grape*)	**une bonne pomme** (*a good apple*)
Plural	**des bons raisins** (*good grapes*)	**des* bonnes pommes** (*good apples*)

* **des** = *some/more than one*

> ### LANGUAGE TIP
>
> In the plural form, most French speakers use **des** in front of a noun preceded by an adjective (e.g. **des bons fruits)** in everyday conversation. You might also hear the **s** of **des** dropped in more formal French.
>
> **Il y a de jolis villages en France.** *(There are some pretty villages in France.)*
>
> **Grand-mère fait de délicieuses confitures avec de bons fruits.**
>
> *(Grandma makes delicious jams with good fruit.)*

Practice

Look at the examples in *Learn more* and find the right word to describe the villages, your grandmother's jam, the apples and the wine:

    a J'admire les _____ villages français
    b J'adore la _____ confiture de Grand-mère
    c J'aime les _____ pommes
    d J'adore le _____ vin

 PRONUNCIATION

01.09 **Read the pronunciation explanations. Then listen to the words and repeat.**

▶ **Ça va** – The letter **c** with a cedilla (ç) sounds like an **s**. It is only used in front of **a**, **o** and **u**: ça [sa], ço [so] and **çu** [su]. Note that there is no cedilla in **merci** and that in **comme ci, comme ça** only **ça** needs a cedilla.

▶ **Comment** – the **t** at the end is silent and **en** is pronounced in a nasal fashion.

▶ **Année, santé, enchanté, présente, appétit** all have an **e** with an acute accent. It changes the neutral **e** sound into one close to the sound in the first syllable of 'ready'.

01.10 **Grand-mère** *(Grandmother)* **is telling les enfants** *(the children)* **what to say. Listen and respond as if you were the children.**

Grand-mère	Dites bonjour à Elise.
Les enfants	Bonjour Elise!
Grand-mère	Dites au revoir à Papa.
Les enfants	Au revoir Papa!
Grand-mère	Dites bon anniversaire à Maman.
Les enfants	Bon anniversaire Maman!
Grand-mère	Dites bonnes vacances à Mademoiselle Lapierre.
Les enfants	Bonnes vacances Mademoiselle Lapierre!
Grand-mère	Dites bonne fête à Catherine.
Les enfants	Bonne fête Catherine!

SPEAKING

The word **dites** comes from the verb **dire** (*to say*).

dites-le avec...	*say it with...*
des fleurs	*flowers*
des chocolats	*chocolates*
un livre	*a book*
une carte	*a card*

WRITING

Make your own *liste de provisions (shopping list)* using all the words for food and drinks in the unit.

> 1 kilo de pommes
> _____
> _____
> _____
> _____
> _____

Go further

01.11 **Listen to some people asking how to get to various places around town. After each one, speak in the pause and practise asking for directions.**

Exemple: Pardon madame, la boulangerie s'il vous plaît?
(*Excuse me, where is the baker's please?*)

   a Pardon monsieur, la poste s'il vous plaît?
   b Pardon mademoiselle, l'office du tourisme s'il vous plaît?
   c Pardon madame, le supermarché s'il vous plaît?
   d Pardon madame, le garage Citroën s'il vous plaît?

> **SPEAKING TIP**
> If you want to know where places are, the important thing is to know what to ask for, then people will point you in the right direction. Practise your questions.

❓ Test yourself

1 Put the following five expressions in chronological order.

a *Bonsoir* _____

b *Bonjour* _____

c *Bon après-midi* _____

d *Bonne nuit* _____

2 Choose the best expression or greeting for each of the following situations.

1 *to people having a picnic*
   a *A la vôtre!*   b *L'addition SVP!*   c *Bon appétit!*

2 to a shopkeeper
   a *Bon appétit!*   b *C'est combien?*   c *L'addition SVP!*

3 at someone's birthday party
   a *Bon anniversaire!*   b *L'addition SVP!*   c *Vive la mariée!*

4 in a restaurant
   a *L'addition SVP!*   b *Bon anniversaire!*   c *Vive la mariée!*

5 *at a wedding*
   a *Vive la mariée!*   b *Bon anniversaire!*   c *C'est combien?*

3 Pick words from the box to complete the following expressions (think feminine / feminine + plural and masculine / masculine + plural)

pain (masc - bread)   fêtes (festivities)   appétit   fruits   bière

a bonnes ...

b bon ...

c bon ...

d bonne ...

e bons

SELF CHECK

I CAN. . .

⬤	. . . say hello.
⬤	. . . use greetings for different times of the day and special occasions.
⬤	. . . talk about a few places in town.
⬤	. . . talk about food and drinks.
⬤	. . . use gender and number references.

Premiers contacts
Meeting people

In this unit you will learn how to:
▶ *give and understand information about marital status, family links, age and profession.*
▶ *use numbers up to sixty-nine.*
▶ *use these four verbs: être (to be), parler (to speak), s'appeler (to be called), avoir (to have).*

CEFR: *Can ask and answer questions about personal details (A1); Can handle numbers (A1); Can produce phrases to say where one lives and people one knows (A1)*

 ## French etiquette

When meeting someone in France for the first time if formally introduced, the standard response is to shake hands and say **enchanté(e)** (*Nice to meet you*). Within a family or close circle of friends, people are likely to kiss three times on the cheeks even if they have not met before. They will be on first name terms immediately. For older generations, there may still be a more formal **"Bonjour Monsieur/ bonjour Madame, enchanté(e)"** (*Hello sir/ma'am, nice to meet you*). Note the term **Mademoiselle** (*miss*) is hardly ever used, except for very young women.

Within a family circle people are likely to use **tu** (*you – informal*) when speaking to one another. When people meet for the first time, they are likely to start with **vous** (*you – formal*) and after a few chats might say **on se tutoie?** (*Shall we use "tu"?*). Older generations are more likely to use the formal **vous** and might find it more difficult to be less formal. An adult can say **tu** to a child but it is not polite for a child to say **tu** to an adult, unless invited to do so.

 a   How do you think a teacher would address a student?
b   How would students address their teachers?

Vocabulary builder

DES NOMBRES ET DES CHIFFRES *(NUMBERS AND FIGURES)*

 1 02.01 **Look at the numbers and listen to how they sound. Then repeat after the speaker.**

0 zéro	10 dix	21 vingt et un
1 un	11 onze	22 vingt-deux
2 deux	12 douze	23 vingt-trois
3 trois	13 treize	30 trente
4 quatre	14 quatorze	31 trente et un
5 cinq	15 quinze	32 trente-deux
6 six	16 seize	40 quarante
7 sept	17 dix-sept	50 cinquante
8 huit	18 dix-huit	60 soixante
9 neuf	19 dix-neuf	61 soixante et un
	20 vingt	69 soixante-neuf

2 **The table above should allow you to work out numbers from 0 to 69. Write out these numbers in French.**

24 _____   52 _____

39 _____   57 _____

43 _____   66 _____

45 _____   68 _____

3 **Look at the KENO® lottery ticket and answer the questions.**
 a For each grid how many numbers can you tick? _____
 b How many winning numbers are drawn every day? _____
 c How much does it cost if you have two draws? If you have one draw? _____

4 02.02 **Listen to the recording. Write down all the numbers you hear and find out if you have any of the winning numbers.**

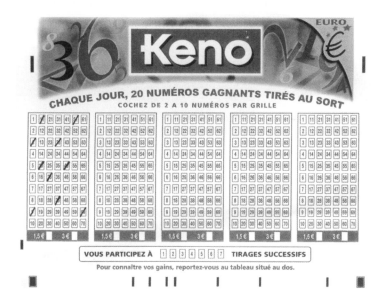

LA FAMILLE *(THE FAMILY)*

 1 02.03 **Look at images and read the sentences. Listen to the audio to practise your pronunciation.**

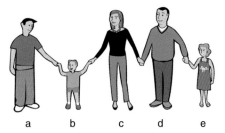

a   b   c   d   e

a Voici Jacques, le frère de Monsieur Norbert.
b Voici Gaétan, le fils des Norbert.
c Voici Madame Norbert.
d Voici Monsieur Norbert.
e Et voilà Joëlle, la fille des Norbert.

2 Qui est-ce? Who is it? Read the explanations below and say what the family link is likely to be:
Your father? Your cousin? Your aunt?
Your brother? Your grandmother?

a C'est la mère de mon père. _____

b C'est le mari de ma mère. _____

c C'est la sœur de mon père. _____

d C'est la fille du frère de ma mère. _____

e C'est le fils de mes parents. _____

NEW EXPRESSIONS

Look at the expressions that are used in the next conversations. Note their meanings.

Conversation 1

un homme	*a man*
une femme	*a woman*
Comment vous appelez-vous?	*What is your name?*
Je m'appelle ...	*My name is ...*
Vous êtes d'où?	*Where are you from?*
moi	*me*

Conversation 2

Je suis ...	*I am ...*
Et vous comment vous appelez-vous?	*And what is your name? (formal)*
Enchantée de faire votre connaissance.	*Pleased to meet you.*
Ah, vous êtes anglaise/ française/etc.?	*Are you English/French/etc.?*
Voici ...	*This is ...*

Conversation 3

la sœur	*the sister*
le frère	*the brother*
moi	*me*
ma sœur	*my sister*
mon frère	*my brother*
toi	*you*

Conversation 4

avec	*with*
à la maison	*at home*
les enfants	*the children*
couramment	*fluently*
mon mari	*my husband*
le professeur	the *teacher*

Conversations

There is a wedding in the family. Isabelle Lejeune and David Miller are getting married in Rouen, Normandy. David is English but works in France. Isabelle is French. At the wedding there are lots of people from both families. Since this is an international marriage, guests have travelled from far and wide to the reception.

 1 02.04 **At the dinner table, two people who have never met before find out each other's names and where they come from. Listen to the recording and answer the question.**

  a What's the man's name? _____

Conversation 1

Homme	*Bonjour, je m'appelle Alain. Et vous, comment vous appelez-vous?*
Femme	*Je m'appelle Claire.*
Homme	*Enchanté de faire votre connaissance, Claire. Vous êtes d'où?*
Femme	*Je suis de Paris. Et vous?*
Homme	*Moi, je suis de Marseille.*

---

  b **Now read the dialogue and answer the rest of the questions.**

   1 What is the woman's name? _____
   2 Where is Claire from? _____
   3 Where is Alain from? _____

2 02.05 **Listen to people introducing themselves at the wedding. Then answer the question.**

a Who is Hélène Lejeune? _____

Conversation 2

Madame Lejeune *Bonjour Madame, je m'appelle Hélène Lejeune. Je suis la mère d'Isabelle. Et vous, comment vous appelez-vous?*

Anne Thompson *Enchantée de faire votre connaissance. Je m'appelle Anne Thompson, je suis la tante de David.*

Madame Lejeune *Ah, vous êtes anglaise?*

Anne Thompson *Non, non, je suis française. Je suis mariée à Mark Thompson, l'oncle de David. J'habite en Angleterre.*

Madame Lejeune *Ah très bien! Enchantée!*

Anne Thompson *Voici mon fils Raphaël et voilà ma fille Sophie. Raphaël, Sophie, je vous présente Madame Lejeune, la maman d'Isabelle.*

Raphaël *Bonjour Madame.*

Sophie *Bonjour.*

---

b **Now read the dialogue and answer the questions below.**
   1 Whose aunt is Anne Thompson? _____
   2 Is Anne Thompson English? _____
   3 What is her husband's name? _____
   4 Where does she live? _____

 3 02.06 **The children at the wedding are getting to know one another. Listen and answer the question.**

a How old are Camille and Sophie? _____

> **INSIGHT: LANGUAGE**
>
> The word for *my* (known as the possessive adjective) changes according to the gender of the thing or person referred to. As a result there are three ways of saying *my*: **mon**, **ma** and **mes** (plural):
>
> **Le** *père* + **la** *mère* = **les** *parents*
> **mon** *père* + **ma** *mère* = **mes** *parents*

b Now, read the dialogue and find the French expressions for these words.

   a I am twelve years old. _____
   b My brother, he is fourteen. _____
   c I don't have a brother. _____
   d Me too! _____
   e How old are you? _____

4 02.07 Still at the wedding, Hélène and Anne discuss which language is spoken in the Thompson household. Listen to the recording and answer the question.

   a Which two languages are mentioned? _____

Conversation 4

Hélène	*Vous parlez français avec les enfants?*
Anne	*Oui, je parle français à la maison. Les enfants parlent couramment les deux langues.*
Hélène	*Et avec Mark?*
Anne	*Avec mon mari je parle français ou anglais, ça dépend. Il parle bien le français, il est professeur de français.*

b Now read the dialogue and answer the questions.

   1 Does Anne speak English or French with Mark, her husband?
   _____
   2 What does Mark teach? _____

c Find the French for the following in the dialogue.

   1 He is a French teacher. _____
   2 It depends. _____
   3 I speak French or English. _____
   4 I speak French at home. _____
   5 The children speak both languages fluently. _____
   6 He speaks French well. _____

Language discovery

1 **Look at Conversation 1 and find the French for the expressions below.**

 a I am from Paris. _____
 b Pleased to meet you. _____

2 **Now read Conversation 2 and try to find out how to say the following in French.**

 a I live in England. _____
 b David's aunt _____
 c And here is my son ... _____
 d My son _____
 e My daughter _____

3 **Look at the exercises above and answer the questions.**

 a Which expression means I am ... ? Je suis   enchanté
 b With which expression can you
   introduce someone nearby? voici   je m'appelle

Learn more

1 SAYING WHERE YOU ARE FROM

To say where you are from you can name a town or a country after the phrase **Je suis de (*I am from*)**. However, you must remember that in French even the names of countries are feminine, masculine or plural.

Masculine	*le Japon, le Portugal, le Mexique*
Feminine	*la France, la Chine, la Russie*
Plural	*les États-Unis*

Masculine	
Je suis du Canada	*I am from Canada*
Je suis du Pays de Galles	*I am from Wales*
Feminine	
Je suis de Chine	*I am from China*
Je suis d'Angleterre	*I am from England*
Plural	
Je suis des Etats-Unis	*I am from the USA*

2 VOICI/VOILÀ *(THIS IS/THAT IS)*

Voici can be used when introducing a first person, standing next to you. **Voilà** is used for introducing a second person, possibly standing further away from you. More generally, **voici** is for pointing out someone or something close by. **Voilà** is for pointing out someone or something slightly further away from you.

3 VERBS

In this unit you have already come across four important verbs (words used indicate an action or state of things). Here is what you have learnt so far:

Être *(to be) (indicating the state of things)*	
Je suis française.	*I am French.*
Je suis mariée.	*I am married.*
Il est anglais.	*He is English.*
Il est professeur.	*He is a teacher.*
Vous êtes anglaise?	*Are you English?*

Avoir *(to have)*	
J'ai trente ans.	*I am (have) thirty (years).*
Il a dix ans.	*He is ten.*
Elle a vingt-cinq ans.	*She is twenty-five.*
Je n'ai pas de frère.	*I don't have a brother.*

S'appeler* *(to be called)*	
Comment vous appelez-vous?	*What's your name? (lit. How do you call yourself?)*
Je m'appelle Anne.	*I am called Anne.*
Comment tu t'appelles?	*What's your name? (when speaking to a child or someone you know well)*

* Note: This a reflexive verb, that is, the subject and the object of the verb are one and the same. Word for word, **s'appeler** means *to call oneself*.

Parler *(to speak)*	
Je parle français.	*I speak French.*
Je parle anglais.	*I speak English.*
Vous parlez français?	*Do you speak French?*
Ils parlent** français.	*They speak French.*

** Note: The -**nt** in **ils parlent** is not pronounced.

Practice

1 02.08 **Listen to the French expressions. Link them to their English equivalents.**

a I am not married.
b What's his name?
c He has a brother and a sister.
d I don't have a sister.
e I don't speak English.

1 Je n'ai pas de sœur.
2 Je ne parle pas anglais.
3 Je ne suis pas mariée.
4 Il a un frère et une sœur.
5 Comment il s'appelle?

2 02.09 **Try talking about age in French. Then listen and check your answers.**

a I am twenty-one years old.
b He is thirty-eight.
c She is sixty-nine.
d He is forty.

PRONUNCIATION

02.10 **Read the explanation. Then listen to hear the correct pronunciation of the bolded expressions.**

In French, words tend to be linked together, particularly when the second of two words starts with a vowel. When saying her age, Camille says **J'ai douze ans.** These four short words are heard as two groups of sounds: [*jai douzan*]. Sophie says of her brother **Il a quatorze ans** which, again, is heard as two sets of sounds: [*ila quatorzan*].

It is important to know how the numbers are spelt because the last letter of the number is always linked with **ans** (*years*) when saying how old you are. Here are some more examples:

> **Isabelle? Elle a vingt-cinq ans. [ella vintcincan]**
> **Danielle? Elle a trente ans. [ella trentan]**

Note that the e at the end of **trente, quarante**, etc. is not heard.

> **Arnaud? Il a neuf ans. [ila neuvan*]**

Note*: an **f** sounds like a **v** when linking two words.

SPEAKING

1 02.11 **You are François or Françoise, a guest at the wedding. You are from Boulogne. Fill in your part of the dialogue.**

Lucien	*Bonjour, je m'appelle Lucien. Et vous, comment vous appelez-vous?*
Vous	**a** *Give your name.*
Lucien	*Enchanté de faire votre connaissance. D'où êtes-vous?*
Vous	**b** *Say where you are from. Say 'And you?' to ask where Lucien is from.*
Lucien	*Je suis de Bruxelles.*

2 Now do the exercise again, using your own identity.

 LISTENING

02.12 **Listen and repeat each family expression. Then look at the words. Which one is l'intrus** (*intruder or odd one out*)? **Why?**

1 Annie, mon amie
2 ma mère
3 ma sœur
4 ma tante
5 mon oncle
6 ma cousine

INSIGHT: CULTURE
In French, first names are often hyphenated compound names.
Boys' names: Jean-Paul; Jean-Pierre; Jean-Marie; Jean-Claude; Pierre-Henri
Girls' names: Marie-Christine; Marie-Pierre; Marie-Chantal; Marie-France; Marie-Claire; Anne-Marie; Anne-Elise

? Test yourself

Qui sont-ils? *Who are they?*

Complete the statements with the words from the box, and for each one, work out who is speaking.

| s' | êtes | de | sont | j' | un | parlent | pas | suis | ma |

1 J'ai douze ans, j'ai _____ frère.

2 Mon oncle et ma tante _____ français et anglais.

3 Mon frère _____ appelle Jacques.

4 Je _____ de Bruxelles.

5 J'ai douze ans et je n'ai _____ de frère.

6 Isabelle est _____ fille.

7 Je suis professeur _____ français.

8 _____ ai trente ans.

9 Mes cousins, Sophie et Raphaël, _____ bilingues.

10 Vous _____ mariée à un anglais

SELF CHECK

I CAN...

○ . . . give and understand information about marital status, family links, age and profession.

○ . . . use numbers up to sixty-nine.

○ . . . use the verbs: **être** (*to be*), **parler** (*to speak*), **s'appeler** (*to be called*), **avoir** (*to have*).

3 On fait connaissance
Getting to know someone

In this unit you will learn how to:
▶ *introduce yourself fully.*
▶ *understand what other people say about themselves.*
▶ *talk and ask about professions, employment and unemployment, leisure activities, likes and dislikes.*
▶ *talk further about marital status and families.*

CEFR: *Can ask and answer questions about personal details (A1); Can describe where he or she lives (A1); Can use a series of phrases to describe family, job, and other lifestyle items (A2); Can give simple presentations in list format (A2).*

Work and leisure

There is a strong work ethos in France and **le chômage,** (*unemployment*) is the top concern of the adult population. **La semaine de travail** (*the working week*), is limited to **trente-huit heures** (*38 hours*), which means that there is a significant amount of time dedicated to **les loisirs** (*leisure*).

Many professions require solid qualifications, namely **les médecins** (*doctors*), **les dentistes** (*dentists*), **les pharmaciens** (*pharmacists*), **les avocats** (*lawyers*), **les ingénieurs** (*engineers*) and **les architectes** (*architects*) among others. A large number of people work **dans l'informatique** (*in IT*), and they are referred to as **les informaticiens** (*information technicians*).

Leisure activities, such as **le cyclisme** (*cycling*), **le football** (*football*), **les sports d'hiver** (*winter sports*), **le camping** (*camping*), or simply watching **la télé** (*TV*), hold an important place in French life. Although people work hard, they always make time to unwind.

a **How many hours a week do French people typically work?**
b **Name the sport that is probably the most popular in France.**

24

Vocabulary builder

EXPRESSING LIKES

03.01 **Here are some expressions for expressing likes. Listen and repeat the words. Then complete the English translations.**

a	J'aime ...	*I like/love ...*
b	J'aime bien ...	*I _____ /I quite _____ ...*
c	J'aime beaucoup...	*_____ like ... a lot*
d	J'adore ...	*_____ adore/love ...*

EXPRESSING DISLIKES

Here are some phrases for expressing dislikes. Complete the English translations.

▶ **a Je n'aime pas (faire le ménage).**
I don't _____ (doing the housework).

▶ **b Je déteste/J'ai horreur de...**
I really don't _____ / _____ hate...

> **INSIGHT: LANGUAGE**
> **Je** becomes **j'** in front of **aime** because **aime** starts with a vowel. The same rule applies with **adore** and with all other verbs starting with a vowel sound . Words beginning with a silent **h** like **habiter** also follow this rule, for example:
> **j'habite ...   j'aime ...   j'adore ...**
> Remember, **e** is the only letter that can be replaced by an apostrophe in front of a vowel.

NEW EXPRESSIONS

Look at some of the words you will hear in Introduction 4. Note their meanings.

avec	*with*
chez	*at*
sauf	*except*
veuve	*widow/widowed (woman)*

Introductions

1   03.02 **A group of people are on un stage** *(a weekend course)* **in Paris preparing for an amateur photography expedition to Vietnam.**

a   Listen to Natalie Le Hénaff introduce herself. Then answer the questions. Try not to look at the text.

> **INSIGHT: LANGUAGE**
> To make a verb negative (the equivalent of adding 'not' in English), use **ne ... pas** (**ne** + verb + **pas**). Here **ne** becomes **n'** before a vowel (**aime**):
> *Je n'aime pas ...*

1 How old is Natalie? _____
2 Is she married?_____
3 How many children does she have? _____
4 Does she speak English? _____
5 Can you tell at least one thing she likes doing?_____

Introduction 1

Natalie   Bonjour! Je m'appelle Natalie Le Hénaff. J'ai trente-six ans.

J'habite à Vannes en Bretagne.

Je suis mariée. J'ai deux enfants, un garçon et une fille.

Je suis professeur d'histoire dans un collège.

Je parle français, anglais et espagnol.

J'aime aller au cinéma, voyager, lire et faire de la photographie.

Je n'aime pas faire le ménage.

---

b **From the text above, can you tell which French expressions Natalie uses to say the following things?**
1 I am a history teacher. _____
2 I love travelling. _____
3 I live in Vannes in Brittany. _____
4 I love going to the cinema. _____
5 I don't like doing the housework. _____

2 03.03 **Now listen to Antoine Durand introduce himself.**

a **Answer the questions as you listen without looking at the text.**
1 How old is he? _____
2 Where does he live? _____
3 What foreign language does he speak? _____
4 What does he like doing best? _____

Introduction 2

Antoine   Alors moi, mon nom c'est Antoine Durand. J'ai vingt-neuf ans.

Je demeure à Paris.

Je suis célibataire.

Je suis ingénieur du son à France 3.

Je parle français et allemand.

J'aime bien regarder des films et le sport à la télé.

J'adore la photographie et les voyages.

J'ai horreur des voitures, alors je vais au travail à vélo.

---

b Use the text above find out what the following expressions are in French.

1 I live in Paris. _____
2 I like watching films on TV. _____
3 I hate cars. _____
4 I go to work by bike. _____

3 03.04 Listen to Monique Duval introduce herself.

a Answer the questions below as you listen. Try not to look at the text.

1 How old is she? _____
2 Who is Pierre? _____
3 Where does she work? _____
4 Does she speak English? _____
5 How does she feel about football on TV? _____

Introduction 3

Monique   *Bonjour, je m'appelle Monique Duval. J'ai quarante-cinq ans.*
Je suis de Dijon.
Je suis mariée à Pierre mais je n'ai pas d'enfants. Pierre a un fils
d'un premier mariage. Il s'appelle Guillaume, il a vingt-cinq ans
mais il ne travaille pas, il est au chômage.
Je travaille à la poste.
Je parle un peu l'anglais et j'apprends le vietnamien.
J'aime beaucoup le sport, les voyages et la photographie.
Je déteste le football à la télévision.

---

b Now read the text and figure out what these expressions are in French.

1 I work at the post office. _____
2 I speak a little bit of English. _____
3 I don't have any children. _____
4 I am learning Vietnamese. _____
5 He is unemployed. _____

4 03.05 Now listen to Pierre Duval introduce himself.

a Answer the questions as you listen without looking at the text.

1 How old is Pierre? _____
2 What is his wife's name? _____
3 Where does he work? _____
4 Where does he live? _____

Introduction 4

Pierre *Alors je me présente: je m'appelle Duval Pierre.*

J'ai cinquante-deux ans. J'habite à Dijon.

Je suis marié à Monique.

Ma mère est veuve et elle habite chez nous.

Je travaille chez Renault.

Je comprends un peu l'anglais.

J'adore les voyages et la lecture.

Je n'aime pas la télé sauf les documentaires sur les voyages.

b Find the French expressions in the text which mean:

1 My mother is a widow. _____

2 I work at Renault. _____

3 She lives with us. _____

4 I love travel and reading. _____

5 I don't like TV except travel documentaries. _____

6 I understand English a little. _____

Language discovery

Look at Antoine Durand's introduction. Find two different uses of alors. Which one means *Well then ...?* Which one means *so*, or *therefore*?

a The first use means _____

b The second use means _____

Learn more

1 SAYING WHERE YOU LIVE OR ARE FROM

To say where we live or where we're from, we use the following expressions:

être de (*to be from*) + name of town / country	**Je suis de Bordeaux**
habiter à / vivre à (*to live in*) + name of town	**J'habite à Bordeaux**
habiter en / au (*to live in*) + name of the region	**J'habite en Bretagne (la Bretagne)**
	J'habite au Pays Basque (le Pays Basque)

2 SAYING WHAT YOUR JOB IS

In French there is no indefinite article (*a* or *an* in English) in front of the name of a profession. In the introductions, Natalie says she is a history teacher in a secondary school.

Je suis professeur d'histoire dans un collège.

The next person, Antoine Durand, says he is a sound engineer for a French TV channel, France 3.

Je suis ingénieur du son à France 3.

The omission of the indefinite article also applies when Antoine says he is a bachelor.

Je suis célibataire*.

*Note: Célibataire is used for both unmarried men and women.

3 ALORS

As soon as you hear French people talking amongst themselves you will hear **alors** or **bon, alors** or **oui, alors**. It loosely means *then* or *so*, similar to someone saying *well / so then...* in English. It is used to fill a gap in the conversation. It also means *therefore*. It can also be used in small talk as an interjection with many expressive meanings:

Eh bien alors, vous en avez de la chance!	*Well, I say, you are lucky!*
Alors vous comprenez...	Then you understand...
Zut alors!	Drat!
Ça alors!	*(to show astonishment)*
Alors ça!	*(to show indignation)*
Et alors!	(to show defiance)

4 QUELLES (QUESTIONS)

There is always more than one way to ask a question. Here are standard questions and answers about personal details.

Topics	Questions	Answers
Name	Comment vous appelez-vous?	Je m'appelle Nathalie.
	Quel est votre nom?	Mon nom c'est Josianne.
Age	Quel âge avez-vous?	J'ai trente-deux ans.
	Vous avez quel âge?	J'ai cinquante ans.
Where living	Où habitez-vous?	J'habite à Nantes.
	Où est-ce que vous habitez?	
	Où est-ce que vous demeurez?	Je demeure à Bordeaux.
Marital status	Vous êtes marié(e)?	Oui, je suis marié(e).
		Non, je suis célibataire.

Profession	Quelle est votre profession?	Je suis dentiste.
	Quel est votre métier?	Je suis dans le commerce.
	Quel travail faites-vous?	
	Où est-ce que vous travaillez?	Je travaille chez Renault.
Languages	Quelles langues parlez-vous?	Je parle français et anglais.
	Vous parlez anglais?	Oui, un petit peu.
Likes	Vous aimez le cinéma?	Oui, j'adore le cinéma.
	Vous aimez le football?	Non, j'ai horreur du football.

The following six interrogative pronouns are likely to be key to your understanding of what is being asked.

Qui êtes-vous?   *Who* are you?

Comment voyagez-vous?   *How* do you travel?

Quand partez-vous?   *When* are you leaving?

Où allez-vous?   *Where* are you going?

Pourquoi?   *Why?*

Qu'est-ce que vous cherchez?   *What* are you looking for?

> **INSIGHT: CULTURE**
>
> A formal way to introduce someone is by giving names in the order **nom, prénom**. Pierre Duval says: **Je m'appelle Duval Pierre.** This is nearly always used for administrative or commercial purposes:
>
> **Monsieur Duval Pierre**
> **16 Avenue de la Gare**
> *DIJON*
>
> This not the usual practice for informal social occasions or in a professional or political context.

Practice

 WRITING

1 **You are a participant on the Paris photography course. Try to write a statement giving the following information:**

> Your name is Anne-Marie Pélerin.
> You are 45.
> You live in Boulogne.
> You are a dentist.
> You speak French, English and German.
> You love football and photography.

2   Look back at the introductions made by the people on the photography course. Enter the missing questions or the missing answers in the table.

Name	Questions	Answers
Natalie	Comment vous appelez-vous?	
Antoine	Quel âge avez-vous?	
Natalie		Je suis professeur d'histoire.
Monique	Où travaillez-vous?	
Pierre		J'habite à Dijon.
Antoine		Je parle français et allemand.
Monique		Oui, j'aime beaucoup le sport.
Pierre	Vous êtes marié?	

3   The following statements are not all accurate. Look back at our four introductions and say which statements are **vrai** *(true)* and which ones are **faux** *(false)*:

   a   Monique apprend le chinois. _____
   b   Pierre et Monique ont deux enfants. _____
   c   Natalie aime aller au cinéma. _____
   d   Antoine est célibataire. _____
   e   Antoine habite à Paris. _____
   f   Pierre travaille chez Citroën. _____

PRONUNCIATION

Look back at what Natalie says and find all the apostrophes. In each case, an apostrophe replaces an **-e** because the word that follows begins with a vowel or an **h**. There is also one example of **de** losing its **e** in front of a vowel sound: **professeur d'histoire**. Here and in **j'habite**, the **h** is silent. All these expressions are pronounced as if they were one word, specifically to avoid a harshness that the repetition of two vowel sounds would create.

1   03.06 **Listen to the expressions and repeat.**

   je mappelle / jai / jabite / jaime / je naime pas / professeur distoire

2 03.07 **Les liaisons** refers to linking words together to give fluidity to the sound. Try these three examples. Then listen to check your pronunciation.

Je suis amoureux/amoureuse. [je suizamoorer / je suizamoorerze]

I am in love.

Bonjour mes amis*. [bonjour mezami]

Hello my friends.

Bon appétit!** [bonappeti]

*Note: The **s** at the end of **amis** is silent.

The **t at the end of **appétit** is silent.

 LISTENING

03.08 **Listen to the recording and say who is the oldest.**

   a Bernard a cinquante-trois ans. _____

   b Sylvie a trente-neuf ans. _____

   c Mona a cinq ans de moins que Sylvie. _____

   d Marc a dix ans de plus que Mona. _____

   e Etienne a trois ans de moins que Bernard. _____

   f Martin a dix ans de plus qu'Etienne. _____

INSIGHT: NEW WORDS

| plus | *more* |
| moins | *less* |

Test yourself

1 **Complete the statements with the words from the box, and using the information about the four course participants work out the answers to Qui êtes-vous?** *Who are you?* **Say who the people are and complete the sentences with the words from the box.**

| mon | utilise | avec | travaille | ans |

   a Je _____ pour une chaîne de télévision française.

   b J'ai trente-six _____ .

   c J' _____ le Vélib' pour aller au travail.

   d Le fils de _____ mari est au chômage.

   e Ma mère habite _____ ma femme et moi.

2 **Complete the statements Marielle Lemaire makes about herself with words from the box.**

> apprends   pharmacien   soixante-cinq
> veuve   son   vivent   regarder

a J'ai _____ ans.

b Je suis _____ et mes deux fils _____ avec moi.

c Mon fils Jérôme est _____ et _____ frère Paul est informaticien.

d J'aime lire et _____ des films à la télé.

e J' _____ l'informatique.

SELF CHECK

	I CAN. . .
⬤	. . . introduce myself fully.
⬤	. . . understand what other people say about themselves.
⬤	. . . talk and ask about professions, employment and unemployment, leisure activities, likes and dislikes.
⬤	. . . talk further about marital status and families.

Un voyage en bateau

A boat trip

In this unit you will learn how to:

▶ *ask where something is situated.*
▶ *understand simple directions.*
▶ *ask if something you need is available.*
▶ *ask most forms of questions.*
▶ *say what you would like to do.*
▶ *count to 101.*

CEFR: *Can handle numbers for costs (A1); Can ask people for things (A1); Can communicate in simple and routine tasks (A2); Can describe something in a simple list of points (A2).*

 Crossing the channel

Visitors going to France from the UK have several travel options to choose from. **Voyager** (*travelling*) *to* France **en bateau** (*by boat*) or **en ferry** (*by cross-channel ferry*), to Caen or St Malo, or if you prefer **traverser la Manche** (*to cross the Channel*) via **Le Tunnel sous la Manche** (*the Channel Tunnel*) the train is a lot quicker.

Le Tunnel sous la Manche is an idea that flourished throughout **le dix-neuvième siècle,** (*the 19th century*). But it was **le 12 février 1986 (mille neuf cent quatre-vingt-six)** (*on 12th February 1986*) when a treaty was signed by **le Président de la république française** (*the President of od French Republic*) and **le Premier Ministre britannique** (*The British Prime Minister*). The project was finally adopted **le 29 juillet 1987 (mille neuf cent quatre-vingt-sept)** (*29th July 1987*) and the inauguration of the **Le Tunnel** took place **le 6 mai 1994 (mille neuf cent quatre-vingt-quatorze)** (*on 6th May 1994*).

 a How would you say 12th century in French?
b How would you say 1990 and 1997?

Vocabulary builder

SUR LE BATEAU *(ON THE BOAT)*

 1 04.01 **Read the names for places on the boat. Then, listen and match the French words to the English translations.**

a	Bureau d'information	**1**	*Self-service restaurant*
b	Bureau de change	**2**	*Baggage room*
c	Sièges inclinables	**4**	*Children's playroom*
d	Local à bagages	**6**	*Information desk*
e	Salle de jeux enfants	**7**	*Shops*
f	Restaurant Self	**11**	*Bureau de change*
g	Salon de thé	**12**	*Reclining seats*
h	Le Bar «Le Derby»	**13**	*Tea shop*
i	Les boutiques	**15**	*Newsagent*
j	Le kiosque	**17**	*'Le Derby' bar*

2 Look at the diagrams. The first one shows a cross section of the boat; the others show various places on Ponts *(decks)* 7, 8 and 9.

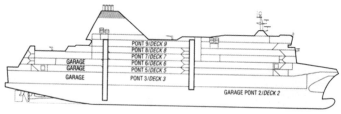

Pont 9

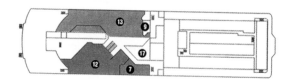

Pont 8

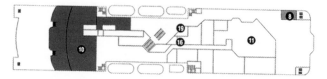

Pont 7

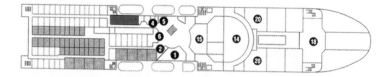

On which deck can you find the following?

1	Bureau d'information	*pont 7*
2	Bureau de change	
4	Sièges inclinables	
6	Local à bagages	
7	Salle de jeux enfants	
11	Restaurant Self	
12	Salon de thé	
13	Le Bar «Le Derby»	
15	Les boutiques	
17	Le kiosque	

NEW EXPRESSIONS

Look at the expressions that are used in the next conversations. Note their meanings.

Conversation 1

la voiture	*the car*
Je ne sais pas.	*I don't know.*
membre de l'équipage	*a member of the crew*
C'est à quel nom?	*Which name?*
l'escalier	*the staircase*
à gauche	*on the left*
Allons-y.	*Let's go.*

Conversation 2

On y va?	*Shall we go?*
Oui d'accord	*Yes O.K.*
Je voudrais + verb	*I would like to...*
Je voudrais voir ...	*I would like to see ...*
salon	*lounge*
salle	*room*
ici	*here*

> **INSIGHT: LANGUAGE**
> **On** *is frequently used in conversation to express a collective action.*
> **On y va?**

Conversations

1 04.02 Sarah Burgess is travelling to France with a French friend, Dominique Périer. They have left their car on **le pont-garage** (the car deck) and are looking for their cabin. Listen to the recording and answer the question.

    a On which deck is their car? _____

Conversation 1

Dominique	Bon, la voiture est au pont cinq. Maintenant allons à la cabine.
Sarah	Où se trouve notre cabine?
Dominique	Je ne sais pas. Allons au bureau d'information au pont sept.
Membre de l'équipage	Bonsoir madame.
Dominique	Bonsoir, j'ai réservé une cabine.
Membre de l'équipage	Oui, c'est à quel nom?
Dominique	Périer, Dominique Périer.
Membre de l'équipage	Oui, alors c'est la cabine 017 au pont huit. Prenez l'escalier à gauche.
Sarah	Allons-y.

---

  b **Now listen again and read the dialogue. Then answer the questions.**

    1 On which deck is their cabin? _____
    2 Where do they go to find out? _____
    3 Is it morning or evening? _____
    4 What is the number of the cabin? _____

2 04.03 Sarah and Dominique are exploring the boat. Listen to the recording and answer the question.

    a What are they looking for? _____

Conversation 2

Sarah	Est-ce qu'il y a un cinéma sur le bateau?
Dominique	Oui, ici au pont 6, il y a deux cinémas. On y va?
Sarah	Oui d'accord!
Dominique	Il y a deux films. À quelle heure?
Sarah	Alors, il y a *Pirates des Caraïbes avec* Johnny Depp à vingt et une heures et à vingt-deux heures trente il y a *Le Come-back avec* Hugh Grant, le film s'appelle *Music and Lyrics en anglais*.

Dominique	Moi j'adore Hugh Grant, et toi?
Sarah	Moi aussi! Je voudrais voir *Le Come-back*. C'est combien?
Dominique	C'est dix euros.

b Now listen again and read. Answer the questions.

1 What film are they going to see? _____

2 Is the film they are going to see at 21.00 or at 22.30? _____

3 How much does it cost to get in? _____

 Language discovery

1 **Look at Conversation 1 and link the English phrases below to the equivalent French expressions.**

a Where is our cabin?

b Let's go to the information desk.

c Take the staircase on the left.

d I have reserved a cabin.

e The car is on deck five.

1 Prenez l'escalier à gauche.

2 J'ai réservé une cabine.

3 La voiture est au pont cinq.

4 Où est notre cabine?

5 Allons au bureau d'information.

2 **Now look at Conversation 2 and link these English phrases to the equivalent French expressions.**

a What about you?

b At 22.30 there is *Le Come-back*.

c What would you like to see?

d Me too.

1 Qu'est-ce que tu voudrais voir?

2 Moi aussi.

3 Et toi?

4 À vingt-deux heures trente il y a *Le Come-back*.

3 **Look at the above exercises and answer the questions below.**

a What expression means Where is...?

b Which expression means on or to?

c Which expression means at?

Où est... ? Qu'est-ce que...?
une   au
à   et

Learn more

1 THE PREPOSITIONS À, À LA, AU, AND AUX

The words **à, à la, au,** and **aux** are all prepositions that indicate directions (e.g., *to, at, in*). All four words mean the same and are placed immediately before a noun. However, they must match the gender (feminine or masculine) and number (singular or plural) of the noun they precede.

à	*before the name of a city*	**Allons à Paris.** *(Let's go to Paris.)*
à la	*in front of a feminine noun*	**Allons à la cabine.** *(Let's go to the cabin.)*
au*	*masculine noun*	**La voiture est au garage.** *(The car is in the garage.)*
aux*	*in front of a plural noun that is feminine or masculine*	**Allons aux jeux vidéo.** *(Let's go to the video games.)*

* **Note: Au** is a contraction of **à + le.**

** **Note: Aux** is a contraction of **à + les.**

2 OÙ SE TROUVE...?/OÙ EST...?

To ask where a place is use either **Où se trouve...?** or **Où est...?** These two expressions are totally interchangeable.

Où se trouve le bar?	*Where is the bar? (lit. Where does the bar find itself?)*
Où est le bar?	*Where is the bar?*

Remember, if a noun is in the plural form, the verb will also be in the plural form:

Où se trouvent les toilettes?	*Where are the toilets?*
Où sont les toilettes s'il vous plaît?	*Where are the toilets, please?*

3 UN PASSAGER, UNE PASSAGÈRE

Nouns finishing with **-er** tend to change to **-ère** in the feminine form.

	masculine	feminine
the baker	**le boulanger**	**la boulangère**
the farmer	**le fermier**	**la fermière**
the butcher	**le boucher**	**la bouchère**

Practice

 ## PRONUNCIATION

04.04 **Read the explanation and practise the pronunciation of the words in bold.**

In French there is a tendency for groups of words to be pronounced as if all the letters were linked up. This applies to the following:

> *Il y a [ilia]   Y a t-il? [iatil]*
> *Est-ce qu'il y a? [eskilia]*

> **INSIGHT: CULTURE**
>
> Nouns for some professions have recently become feminine, as some adjustments have been made by law to reflect the place of women in society. For example in the case of nouns with no feminine equivalent, such as **le professeur** (*teacher*), **l'auteur** (*author*), **le ministre** (the minister), it is now recommended to use **la professeure, l'auteure, la ministre**.

Watch out! Liaising words is not always possible. Although **est** and **un/une** can be linked [***estun/une***], **et** and **un/une** cannot: they must be pronounced separately to avoid ambiguity. For example in **un homme et une femme** (*a man and a woman*), if **et** and **une** are liaised [***etune***] the meaning becomes "a man is a woman!"

 ## SPEAKING

04.05 **Répondez aux passagers. Answer the passengers' questions as if you were a member of the crew.**

Exemple: Passager	Le restaurant self-service, s'il vous plaît?	
Membre de l'équipage	C'est au pont huit, Monsieur.	
a Passager	Pardon, les boutiques s'il vous plaît?	
Membre de l'équipage	_____	
b Passagère	Où est le salon de thé, s'il vous plaît?	
Membre de l'équipage	_____	
c Jeune garçon	S'il vous plaît madame, où sont les jeux pour les enfants?	
Membre de l'équipage	_____	
d Passager	Le bar c'est à quel pont?	
Membre de l'équipage	_____	
e Passagère	Il y a un bureau de change, s'il vous plaît?	
Membre de l'équipage	_____	

> **INSIGHT: LANGUAGE**
>
> **Madame** is used for a woman **passagère** (*passenger*), **monsieur** for a male **passager** (*passenger*).

Go further

1 04.06 **Des nombres et des chiffres de 70 à 101. Look, listen and repeat.**

70 **soixante-dix** [60 + 10]
71 **soixante et onze** [60 + 11]
72 **soixante-douze**
79 **soixante-dix-neuf**
80 **quatre-vingts*** [4 x 20]
81 **quatre-vingt-un**
89 **quatre-vingt-neuf**

90 **quatre-vingt-dix**
91 **quatre-vingt-onze**
92 **quatre-vingt-douze**
99 **quatre-vingt-dix-neuf**
100 **cent**
101 **cent un**

***Note**: Only **quatre-vingts** is spelt with **-s** for plural (four twenties).

2 04.07 **C'est combien? How much is it? Sarah and Dominique are at the shop. They are checking the price of drinks and cigarettes. Listen to the recording and answer these questions.**

a How much is the cognac? _____
b How much is the whisky? _____
c How much are the cigarettes? _____
d How much is the gin? _____

> **INSIGHT: CULTURE**
> In some francophone countries 70, 80 and 90 are said differently:
> 70 is **septante** in Belgium, Switzerland and in the Democratic Republic of Congo.
> 80 is **octante** in Belgium and Quebec.
> 80 is **huitante** in Switzerland.
> 90 is **nonante** in Belgium and Switzerland.

Test yourself

Complete the dialogues below with the appropriate words from the box.

alors	allons-y	pardon	une	sais	merci	bar	commence
bateau	pont	bureau	voudrais	équipage	pas	six	

1. Où se trouve le _____ s'il vous plaît?

Il y a deux bars sur le _____ , un au _____ cinq et un au pont

_____ .

_____ Monsieur !

2. A quel pont est le _____ de change ?

Je ne _____ pas, je ne suis pas membre de l'_____ ,

je suis _____ passagère.

Oh, _____ Madame !

3. Le film _____ à huit heures: _____ !

Je n'aime _____ le cinéma.

Bon, _____ allons à la cabine !

Oui, je _____ lire.

SELF CHECK

I CAN. . .

- ◯ . . . ask where something is situated.
- ◯ . . . understand simple directions.
- ◯ . . . ask if something I need is available.
- ◯ . . . ask most forms of questions.
- ◯ . . . say what I would like to do.
- ◯ . . . count to 101.

5 *On visite la vieille ville*
Visiting the old town

In this unit you will learn how to:
▸ *ask for various places in a town.*
▸ *follow and give directions.*
▸ *count from 102 to 10,500.*
▸ *use some adjectives.*
▸ *use the imperative.*

CEFR: *Can understand directions (A2); Can read basic information (A1); Can handle short social exchanges (A2); Can get simple information about travel (A2); Can ask for and give simple directions on a map (A2).*

 Discovering France

St Malo was founded **au sixième siècle** (*in the 6th century*) by the Welsh monk MacLow. It is **le lieu de naissance** (*the birth place*) of many sailors and discoverers. One of the most famous is Jacques Cartier who discovered **le Canada** (*Canada*) **au seizième siècle** (*in the 16th century*). There are still very strong links between St Malo and Canada, especially with **le Québec** (*Quebec*). It is not unusual to see **le drapeau canadien** (*the Canadian flag*) flying in St Malo.

You may hear references made to **le nord et le sud de la France** (*the north and the south of France*). The dividing line is in fact **la Loire** (*the river Loire*). This geographical divide may be recognisable when **vous traversez la France** (*you travel through France*) by the difference between **les toits des maisons** (*the roofs of houses*): blue slate for the north and red tiles for the south, with the exception of Nord-Pas-de Calais in the northeast, where houses have mainly **des toits rouges** (*red roofs*).

a How would you say "the north of France"?
b How would you say "the English flag"?

Vocabulary builder

DIRECTIONS

 05.01 Read the key directions. Then listen and match them to their English equivalents

a C'est tout droit./ Allez tout droit.

b C'est à droite./ Tournez à droite.

c C'est la première rue à gauche./Prenez la première rue à gauche.

d C'est la deuxième rue à droite./Prenez la deuxième rue à droite.

e C'est la troisième rue sur votre gauche. /Prenez la troisième rue sur votre gauche.

1 It is the second road on the right./Take the second road on the right.

2 It is on the right./ Turn right.

3 It is the third road on your left./ Take the third road on your left.

4 It is straight ahead./ Go straight on.

5 It is the first road on the left./ Take the first road on the left.

ORDINAL NUMBERS

 1 05.02 These are adjectives indicating a ranking position. Listen and repeat.

3rd **troisième**
4th **quatrième**
10th **dixième**
15th **quinzième**

20th **vingtième**
36th **trente-sixième**
100th **centième**
1,000th **millième**

2 Now write out the following ordinal numbers in French.

a 10th _____

b 15th _____

c 34th _____

d 23th _____

e 100th _____

Conversations

*Some tourists have just arrived in St Malo after their crossing on the ferry. They visit the old town, **la Vieille Ville**, which in St Malo is normally referred to as **l'intra muros** (the Latin phrase for "inside the walls").*

 1 05.03 **Listen to a tourist asking for the station. The passer-by is not sure whether she means la gare routière** *(the bus station)* **or la gare SNCF** *(the railway station)*. **Answer the question.**

a Can you tell whether the tourist is looking for:

1 the bus station?

2 the railway station?

Conversation 1

Touriste	Pour aller à la gare s'il vous plaît, madame?
Passante	La gare routière ou la gare SNCF?
Touriste	La gare SNCF...
Passante	Oui, alors vous prenez la première rue à gauche et c'est tout droit.
Touriste	C'est loin?
Passante	Non c'est tout près. C'est à deux cents mètres, au maximum.
Touriste	Merci beaucoup madame.

---

b **Now listen again or read to answer the questions.**

1 Is the railway station:

a the first street on the left and the next one on the right?

b the first one on the left and then straight ahead?

2 How far away is it?

a one kilometre

b one hundred metres

c two hundred metres

d more than two hundred metres

 2 05.04 **As Sarah and Dominique leave the port they decide to visit St Malo before continuing with their journey. They ask for directions. Listen to the recording once through, and answer the question.**

a Who would like to visit the old town? _____

b Now listen again or read to answer the questions.

1 Who do they ask for directions? _____

2 Is the old town far from the port? _____

3 Are there problems with parking? _____

 Language discovery

1 **Look at Conversation 1 and match the English phrases to the equivalent French expressions.**

a At the most	**1** C'est à deux cents mètres.
b Is it far?	**2** C'est tout près.
c It's two hundred metres away.	**3** C'est loin?
d It's straight ahead.	**4** Prenez la première rue à gauche.
e Take the first street on the left.	**5** au maximum
f It's very near.	**6** C'est tout droit.

2 **Now look at Conversation 2 and match the English phrases to the equivalent French expressions.**

a There	**1** Je ne connais pas St Malo.
b At the roundabout	**2** C'est parfait!
c I don't know St Malo.	**3** Demande la direction.
d It's perfect!	**4** pas de problème avec le stationnement

e	Ask the way.	**5**	plusieurs grands parkings
f	no problem with parking	**6**	là
g	several large car parks	**7**	au rond-point

3 Look at the above exercises again and answer the questions.

a What expression means take? **c'est   prenez**

b What ending is added to the adjective grand for a plural masculine noun? **s   e**

c Which expression means know? **connais   demande**

Learn more

1 FEMININE AND MASCULINE ADJECTIVES

You are already aware that there are feminine and masculine nouns in French. Similarly, adjectives describe the nouns they are linked up with and are feminine or masculine according to the gender of the nouns they accompany.

In French adjectives can be placed before or after nouns, although changing the position of an adjective can modify the meaning of the phrase. In many cases **-e** is added for the feminine form of the adjective and **-s** is added for the plural.

Masculine	
un village	*a village*
un joli village	*a pretty village*
des jolis petits villages	*pretty little villages*
un grand château	*a big castle*
des grands châteaux	*big castles*
Feminine	
une ville	*a town*
une jolie ville	*a pretty town*
des jolies petites villes	*pretty little towns*
une grande maison	*a big house*
des grandes maisons	*big houses*

Remember, there are also many adjectives that change more radically from the masculine to the feminine.

Masculine		Feminine	
le vieux port	*the old port*	**la vieille ville**	*the old town*
le premier jour du mois	*the first day of the month*	**la première rue à gauche**	*the first street on the left*

Masculine adjectives ending in **-e** remain the same in the feminine form:

Masculine		Feminine	
le bonnet rouge	*the red hat*	**la fleur rouge**	*the red flower*
le deuxième magasin	*the second shop*	**la deuxième rue**	*the second street*

un beau chêne	*a beautiful oak tree*	**Beau** (*beautiful/nice*),
un bel arbre	*a beautiful tree*	**vieux** (*old*), **nouveau**
un vieux copain,	*an old friend/mate*	(*new*) are three adjectives which change according to
un vieil ami		the masculine noun they
un nouveau copain,	*a new friend/mate*	precede. In front of a vowel
un nouvel ami		they become respectively **bel**, **vieil** and **nouvel**.

2 SAVOIR AND CONNAÎTRE

The verbs **savoir** and **connaître** both mean *to know*, however their meanings are slightly different. **Je sais** means *I know a fact.* **Je connais** means *I know a place, something or someone.*

Je ne sais pas où c'est. (*I don't know where it is.*)

Je ne connais pas la ville. (*I don't know the town.*)

3 GIVING DIRECTIONS IN THE IMPERATIVE AND PRESENT TENSE

Here are some verbs used for directions: **aller** (*to go*), **prendre** (*to take*), **tourner** (*to turn*), **continuer** (*to carry on*). When someone is giving directions or orders, they use a verb form called the imperative (*Go...!, Take...!, Turn...!*).

> **INSIGHT: LANGUAGE**
> **Savoir** is frequently used in general conversation to indicate that you are on the same wavelength.
> **Il est malade, tu sais!**
> (*He is ill, you know!*)
> To which you can reply:
> **Oui, je sais, je sais!**

If the directions are given to a stranger or someone the speaker is not acquainted with, the form of the verb used is different from the form used for family or friends or children. *To an adult, one would say:*

Allez jusqu'au (*as far as*) **château, tournez à gauche puis** (*then*) **prenez la deuxième rue à droite**.

To a child or to an adult you know well, one would say:

Va jusqu'au château, tourne à gauche puis prends la deuxième rue à droite.

It is also possible to use the present tense to give directions:

Vous allez jusqu'au château, vous tournez à gauche puis vous prenez la deuxième rue à droite. (*You go as far as the château, you turn left then you take the second road on the right.*)

4 VOUS AND TU

There are two ways of addressing people in French: **vous** and **tu**. In old French people would use **tu** and **vous** when addressing someone according to moods or occasion. **Vous** would show more respect, but **tu** would express more friendliness or affection. The king would be addressed as **vous** or **Votre Majesté**. Saying **tu** to someone became a sign of lack of respect and **vous** a sign of deference. Servants would be spoken to as **tu,** but would have to address their masters as **vous.**

Today many people use **tu** with peers. There is almost a tacit agreement to **tutoiement** *(calling each other tu)*, and the question to ask is **On se tutoie?** Unless you have misjudged the situation, it is unlikely the other person will say **Non!**

Here are some basic rules:

▶ Use **vous** to individuals who are not friends or relatives, and to more than one person.

▶ Use **tu** to a friend, relative or young child.

> **INSIGHT: LANGUAGE**
> **Vouvoyer** is the verb that describes the action of addressing someone as **vous**. **Tutoyer** is the verb that describes the action of addressing someone as **tu**.

Practice

1 Look back at Conversations 1 and 2 and find:

  a One example of people saying **tu** to one another.

  b One example where someone gives directions using the present tense rather than the imperative.

2 First look at the key words and the map* of St Malo.

  1 la piscine *the swimming pool*
  2 le musée *the museum*
  3 la cathédrale *the cathedral*
  4 le marché aux poissons *the fish market*
  5 le marché aux légumes *the vegetable market*
  6 le château *the castle*
  7 la Grand' Rue *the High Street*
  8 l'Office du Tourisme *the Tourist Office*
  9 les remparts *the ramparts*
  10 le petit aquarium *the small aquarium*

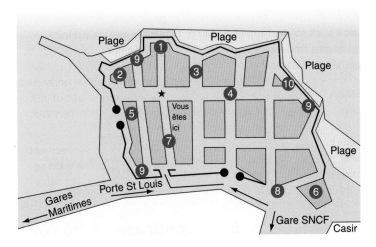

*Note: This is not an accurate map of St Malo.

Now you are standing at the star (vous êtes ici). Choose the correct reply to the questions some.

Question 1 La piscine s'il vous plaît?
Réponse
    a C'est sur votre gauche.
    b C'est à droite.
    c Continuez tout droit.

Question 2 La Grand' Rue SVP*?
Réponse
    a C'est ici la Grand' Rue.
    b C'est à gauche.
    c Prenez la deuxième rue à droite.

Question 3 Pour aller au marché aux poissons SVP?
Réponse
    a Vous prenez la deuxième rue à gauche.
    b Allez tout droit.
    c Vous tournez à droite et c'est la deuxième rue sur votre droite.

*Note: **SVP** stands for s'il vous plaît.

SPEAKING

1 Look back to the map of St Malo. This time you are asking the questions from the same spot. What questions would you ask to get these answers?

Question 1	…
Réponse	Alors vous tournez à droite et vous continuez tout droit. C'est à deux cent cinquante mètres.
Question 2	…
Réponse	Oui, alors tournez à droite et c'est la première rue à gauche.
Question 3	…
Réponse	Tournez à gauche et prenez la deuxième rue à droite.

 2 05.05 It is your turn to answer questions asked by tourists. Before you listen, get your bearings.

a The swimming pool is on the right.

b The museum is 200 metres away.

c The cathedral is very near.

d The tourist office is straight ahead.

e The castle is on the left.

Go further

 1 05.06 Des nombres et des chiffres de 102 à 10500. Look, listen and repeat.

102 **cent deux**

170 **cent soixante-dix**

200 **deux cents**

900 **neuf cents**

926 **neuf cent vingt-six**

1000 **mille**

1900 **mille neuf cents/ dix-neuf cents**

2000 **deux mille**

2020 **deux mille vingt**

10500 **dix mille cinq cents**

2 Now write out these numbers in French.

a 110 _____
b 160 _____
c 280 _____
d 722 _____
e 850 _____
f 1001 _____
g 1300 _____
h 2030 _____
i 10100 _____
j 10634 _____

> **INSIGHT: LANGUAGE**
> Note that when there is more than one hundred, **cent** is spelt with an **s**. However, if another number follows, the **s** is dropped:
> **deux cents** (*200*) **deux cent cinq** (*205*)

Test yourself

Using the definite articles le, la, l', les, test your memory of the gender of nouns you have learnt so far. Use the plural form where appropriate:

1 ___ château
2 ___ ville
3 ___ gare
4 ___ jolis petits villages de ___ région
5 ___ port
6 ___ deuxième rue à gauche
7 ___ piscine
8 ___ aquarium
9 ___ rond-point
10 ___ village

11 ___ pont
12 ___ grandes maisons
13 ___ intra muros
14 ___ directions
15 ___ marché aux poissons
16 ___ vallée de la Rance
17 ___ direction
18 ___ stationnement
19 ___ parking
20 ___ oncle

SELF CHECK

I CAN. . .
. . . ask for various places in a town.
. . . follow and give directions.
. . . count from 102 to 10,500.
. . . use some adjectives.
. . . use the imperative.

6 Où stationner?
Where to park?

In this unit you will learn how to:
▶ *understand parking instructions.*
▶ *use Euro money.*
▶ *use time expressions.*
▶ *talk about daily routines.*

CEFR: *Can understand written directions (A1); Can find specific information in written texts (A2); Can understand public notices (A2); Can describe plans (A2).*

France for free!

In St Malo, like in many French towns, you can buy **une carte prépayée** (*a prepaid card*) for €15 or €40 to use in **les parkings intra muros** (*car parks within the walls*) of the town. **L'horodateur** (*the machine*) also lets you use **pièces de monnaie** (*coins*).

Un bon conseil (*a good piece of advice*): You can **garer votre voiture** (*park your car*) outside the town and use **la navette-bus** (*the park-and-ride system*) to visit St Malo. You have to pay for **le stationnement** (*parking*), but **la navette** is free. **C'est gratuit!** (*It's free!*)

Another tip: since April 2009, everyone **de moins de 26 ans** (*under the age of 26*) from the European Community can visit all French national museums **gratuitement** (*for free*). If you are under 26 and a citizen of a European Union member state, hurry and check these museums out soon!

a What do you think the verb "conseiller" means in English?
b Vous avez vingt-cinq ans et vous visitez le Louvre un jeudi. C'est gratuit?

Vocabulary builder

PARKING EXPRESSIONS

1 06.01 **Listen to the expressions you may see on parking notices and tickets and repeat. Then complete the English translations.**

a	**Stationnement gratuit**	*Free parking*
b	**Stationnement payant**	*Pay-_____*
c	**Stationnement interdit**	*_____ forbidden/No parking*
d	**Stationnement autorisé**	*Parking allowed*

2 Look at the information provided on the car parking leaflet and answer the questions.

> **INSIGHT: CULTURE**
>
> You are likely to hear a lot of French people refer to a car park as **un parking,** but in an effort by various governments to remove the English and American influence on the French language, you will notice that the official name for a car park is **une zone de stationnement**.

a What is the maximum amount of time you can stay in the short-stay car park? _____

b What is the longest time you can stay in the long-term car park? _____

c At what time is parking free? _____

STATIONNEMENT EN FONCTION DE VOS BESOINS.

compagnie Générale de Stationnement

INFORMATIONS ET CONTACTS
• Service du Stationnement.
Horaires d'ouverture:
du lundi au samedi de
9 H à 19 H.

Stationnement payant
de courte durée,
<u>2 H 30</u> maximum.
Tarifs: -1h = 1 €
-2h = 2 €
-2h30 = 2,50 €

NOTA:
Stationnement gratuit
de 19h à 9h

_____

■ Stationnement interdit.
■ Stationnement libre et gratuit. Plusieurs centaines de places.

Stationnement payant
de longue durée,
<u>24 H</u> maximum.
Tarifs: -1h = 1 €
-2h = 2 € 3h = 3 €
-4h = 4 €= -8h = 8 €
-10h = 10 €

---

3 **Look at the information on the car parking card and answer the questions**

   a With this Paris parking card, what is the maximum time a visitor may park when using the card with **un horodateur** (*the car park machine*)? _____

   b Do residents pay the same rate? _____

   c What do you get if you press the **Valider** button? _____

DAYS, MONTHS, AND SEASONS

 1 06.02 **Listen to the days of the week, seasons and months of the year and repeat. Then complete the English translations.**

Les jours de la semaine			
lundi	*Monday*	vendredi	*Friday*
mardi	*Tuesday*	samedi	**b** _____
mercredi	**a** _____	dimanche	*Sunday*
jeudi	*Thursday*		

Les Mois			
janvier	January	juillet	July
février	**c** _____	août	**e** _____
mars	March	septembre	September
avril	April	octobre	October
mai	**d** _____	novembre	**f** _____
juin	June	décembre	December

Les saisons			
le printemps	Spring	l'automne	Autumn
l'été	**g** _____	l'hiver	**h** _____

NEW EXPRESSIONS

Look at the expressions that are used in the next conversations. Note their meanings.

Conversation 1

Tiens!	*Look!*
là-bas	*over there*
C'est tout!	*That's all!*
voilà	*That's*
donc	*therefore*

Conversations

1 06.03 *Dominique and Sarah are trying to find a car park space. They have a guide to all the parking zones in St Malo that they got from l'Office de Tourisme* (the Tourist Office).

Listen to the recording and then answer the question.

a Which type of car park did Sarah and Dominique use?

    1 *long stay*   **2** *short stay*   **3** *free*

Conversation 1

Dominique	Il y des horodateurs comme à Paris mais ici on peut aussi utiliser des pièces de monnaie. A Paris, il faut des cartes de stationnement sauf pour le mois d'août. Au mois d'août à Paris le parking, c'est gratuit!
Sarah	Tiens! Il y a des places au parking là-bas sur le quai.
Dominique	D'accord. C'est une zone de stationnement payant de longue durée. Tu as de la monnaie?
Sarah	Oui un peu. Il faut combien?
Dominique	Je ne sais pas. On reste combien de temps?
Sarah	*Trois ou quatre heures.*
Dominique	Alors quatre heures, cela fait quatre euros. J'ai une pièce d'un euro, une de deux euros et une de cinquante centimes, c'est tout.
Sarah	Pas de problème, moi j'ai une pièce de dix centimes et deux de vingt centimes.
Dominique	Quelle heure est-il?
Sarah	Il est dix heures et quart, donc on a jusqu'à deux heures et quart.
Dominique	Voilà notre ticket. Fin de stationnement autorisé: quatorze heures quinze.

---

b Now listen again or read to answer the questions.

    1 How long did they plan to stay? _____

    2 How much did they pay? _____

    3 How did they pay? _____

    4 Tick the coins they used and say how many of each type they used:

        a 50 centimes _____   **d** 20 centimes _____

        b 1€ _____   **e** 10 centimes _____

        c 2€ _____

2 *Two adults and two children have been asked three similar questions about their **routine quotidienne** (daily routine).*

Questions...	aux adultes	aux enfants
1 At what time do you get up in the morning?	Vous vous levez à quelle heure le matin?	Tu te lèves à quelle heure?
2 At what time do you have lunch?	Vous prenez votre déjeuner à quelle heure?	Tu prends ton déjeuner à quelle heure?
3 At what time do you go to bed?	À quelle heure est-ce que vous vous couchez?	Tu te couches à quelle heure?

 a 06.04 **Listen to their responses and answer the questions.**

1 Who gets up between ten o'clock and half past ten on a Sunday morning? _____

2 At what time does the boy claim he sometimes goes to bed at the weekend? _____

Conversation 2

Femme	En général je me lève à sept heures et demie. Je déjeune à midi et demi et je me couche à onze heures. Le dimanche je me lève entre dix heures et dix heures et demie.
Homme	Je me lève à sept heures. Je prends mon déjeuner entre une heure et une heure et demie. Je me couche vers minuit.
Fille	Alors je me lève à sept heures et quart. Je déjeune à midi et je me couche à vingt-deux heures.
Garçon	Je me lève à six heures quarante-cinq. Je prends mon déjeuner à midi et demi et je me couche à neuf heures. Quelquefois le week-end je me couche à minuit.

b **Now listen again or read to complete the times in the grid.**

	lever	déjeuner	coucher
1 Femme	7.30	_____	_____
2 Homme	_____	1.00–1.30	_____
3 Fille	_____	12.00	_____
4 Garçon	6.45	_____	_____

Language discovery

1 **Look at Conversation 1 and match the following English phrases to their French equivalent.**

- **a** Are there spaces on the quay (or platform)?
- **b** How long will we stay?
- **c** How much do we need?
- **d** What time is it?
- **e** We've got until a quarter past two.
- **f** End of authorized parking.

- **1** Quelle heure est-il?
- **2** Fin de stationnement autorisé
- **3** On a jusqu'à deux heures et quart.
- **4** On reste combien de temps?
- **5** Il y a des places sur le quai?
- **6** Il faut combien?

2 **Look at the previous exercise and answer the questions.**

- **a** What expression means *How much*?   **Il faut   combien**
- **b** What is another word for *we* other than *nous?*   **on   il**

3 **Now look at Conversation 2 and answer the questions.**

- **a** What are the two expressions used for saying *your lunch* (one to an adult and the other to a child)? _____
- **b** What two words do you think the expressions in the answer for 2a are related to?
  - **1** **tu** and **vous**
  - **2** **mon** and **votre**

Learn more

1 MORE NEW VERBS

▶ **Tiens!** is the imperative form for the verb **tenir** to hold but it is frequently used as an expression of surprise, such as Look! or **Tiens! Tiens!** *(Well! Well!)*

▶ **Cela fait deux euros vingt-cinq.** *(That makes it 2,25 €.)* **Fait** is the verb **faire** (*to do/to make*) in the present tense.

▶ **Il faut combien?** literally means *How much is necessary/ required?* but it is best translated as *How much do we need?* The verb **falloir** means *to need/to have to*. It is only ever used with the pronoun il *it* in an impersonal form. **Il faut** could also be translated as *one must*.
  Il faut manger pour vivre.   *One must eat in order to live.*

▶ **Il faut souffrir pour être beau / belle!***   *One must suffer to be beautiful!*
  ***Note: Beau** is masculine and **belle** is feminine.

▶ **Se lever** (*to get up*) and **se coucher** (*to go to bed*) are reflexive verbs. The first reflexive verb you came across in this book was **s'appeler** *to be called* (Unit 2). **Vous vous levez** literally means *you get yourself up*. The subject and the object of the action is the same person (**vous** or *you*, in this case) with reflexive verbs.

▶ **Vous prenez/tu prends** are the present tense of the verb **prendre** *to take*. To say you have a meal in French, you normally say **je prends...**

2 TWO WAYS OF ASKING QUESTIONS

Most everyday conversations between people are informal. This is reflected in the way people ask questions. In all cases the questioning is shown in the tone of voice, which rises on the last syllables.

Question form	Rising intonation
As-tu de la monnaie?	Tu as de la monnaie?
Est-ce que tu as de la monnaie?	
Quelle heure est-il?	Il est quelle heure?
Combien faut-il?	Il faut combien?
Combien de temps reste-t-on?*	On reste combien de temps?

*Note: On is also an impersonal pronoun meaning *one*, but it is frequently used in conversation instead of **nous** (*we*).

3 DES FAUX AMIS (FALSE FRIENDS)

There are a few French words that are deceptively similar to English words, although their meanings are quite different. There are two examples in the dialogue above:

Example 1: rester (*to stay*)
On **reste** combien de temps?   *How long are we staying?*
The verb for *to rest* is actually **se reposer**.
Je me repose.   *I am resting.*

Example 2: de la monnaie (*change*)
Tu as de la **monnaie**?   *Have you got any change?*

Une **pièce de monnaie** is a coin (although **pièce** is usually used on its own). Similarly **un billet** (*a note*) is short for **un billet de banque** (*a bank note*). Money is **de l'argent**. Note that **argent** is also the word for *silver*.

4 L'HEURE– *(THE TIME)*

There is a general tendency to use the 24-hour clock in France. It is used for **les horaires** *(transport timetables)*, **les programmes de télévision** *(TV programmes)*, **les ordinateurs** *(computers)*, **l'Internet** *(the Internet)*, **les horaires de travail** *(working hours)*, **les emplois du temps scolaires** *(school timetables)*, etc. Most people use a mixture of the more traditional way of telling the time and of the 24-hour clock.

Time	Time expression
4h00	il est quatre heures / il est seize heures
4h15	il est quatre heures et quart / il est seize heures quinze
4h30	il est quatre heures et demie / il est seize heures trente
4h45	il est cinq heures moins le quart / il est seize heures quarante-cinq
12h00	**il est midi** *(midday)* / **il est minuit** *(midnight)*

5 TOUT LE, TOUTE LA, TOUS LES, TOUTES LES

In front of nouns these words are adjectives (respectively masculine, feminine, masculine plural and feminine plural, according to the noun they are used with). They mean *all* or *every*.

Il faut visiter toute la ville et toutes les vieilles rues. *(We must visit the whole town and all the old streets.)*

J'adore tout le village et tous les monuments historiques. *(I love the whole village and all the historic monuments.)*

 # Practice

 1 06.05 **Read the times (1-8), then listen and match them with what you hear (a-h). How would you write them down using the 12 hour clock?**

1 1h20 _____

2 23h45 _____

3 17h05 _____

4 12h30 _____

5 8h56 _____

6 11h15 _____

7 3h00 _____

8 6h45 _____

2 **Anyone watching the nature programme on *la Cinquième* can win a prize. Read the competition details and then answer the questions below.**

   a Which TV channel do you have to watch? _____
   b Give the two dates and times when the programme is on. _____
   c What is the Question of the Week? _____

3 **Choose some of the words from Des faux amis to complete the following sentences.**

   a You are in a shop and you would like to get some change.

   J'ai un billet de 50 euros. Vous pouvez me faire la _____ SVP?

   b Je suis fatiguée. Je _____ _____ cinq minutes.

   c On _____ quatre heures ici.

   d Oh le joli bracelet en _____!

   e Oh là là! C'est cent cinquante euros. Je n'ai pas assez d'_____.

LISTENING

06.06 **The distinction a.m. and p.m. has never been used in French. Listen to the recording to hear what people say to make a distinction between morning and afternoon / evening.**

   a What time is it for Jean-Pierre in Paris? _____

   b What time is it for Martine in Sydney? _____

   c What expression is used to say morning? _____

   d What expression is used to say afternoon / evening? _____

Jacques Cartier was a famous sailor from St Malo who discovered
Canada. You can visit *le Manoir de Limœlou* (his manor house),
but when exactly? Look at the leaflet to find out. Then answer the
questions below.

> Visite commentée
> du Manoir de Jacques Cartier
>
> **Musée ouvert toute l'année**
> Accès aux visites guidées
> Tous les jours du 1er juillet au 31 août
> sauf week-end du 1er septembre au 30 juin
> *Horaires des visites*
> du 1er juin au 30 septembre
> de 10 heures à 11 h 30 et de 14 h 30 à 18 heures
> du 1er octobre au 31 mai
> à 10 heures et à 15 heures.
>
> Prix réduit pour écoles
> et groupes de 10 personnes minimum
> *(uniquement sur réservation)*
>
> Gratuit pour :
> Enfants au-dessous de 5 ans.

a Between which dates is it open every day of the week? _____

b Could you have a guided tour the first weekend in September?
_____

c In July what are the opening times? _____

d In May what time of day is it open? _____

e Who can get a reduction? Under what condition? _____

f How much does it cost for a child under the age of five to visit
Jacques Cartier's Manor House? _____

g Find the French expressions for the following:
museum open all year round _____
every day from 1st July to 31st August _____

h Can you spot a difference between French and English in the way
that days and months are written? _____

Go further

06.07 **There are 11 public holidays in France. Listen to them and repeat.**

Les fêtes civiles
1er janvier, Premier de l'an *(New Year's Day)*
1er mai, la Fête du Travail *(Labor Day)*
8 mai, Victoire 1945 *(Victory in Europe Day 1945)*
14 juillet, Fête Nationale *(France's day)*
11 novembre, Armistice 1918, *(Armistice Day 1918)*

Les fêtes religieuses
25 décembre, Noël *(Christmas)*
Lundi de Pâques *(Easter Monday)*
Jeudi de l'Ascension *(Ascencion Day)*
Lundi de Pentecôte *(Pentecost)*
15 août, Assomption *(the Assumption of the Virgin)*
1er novembre, La Toussaint *(All Saints Day)*

🕐 Test yourself

1 Ask a friend the following questions:

  a How much is needed for two hours' parking?

  b Have you got some change?

  c What time is it?

  d At what time do you have breakfast?

  e At what time do you get up on Sundays?

  f Have you got a 10€ bill?

  g How long are we staying?

  h Do you like the old town?

  i Is the museum open all year round?

  j Would you like to have a rest?

2 Complete the following sentences with the correct form of the adjective.

> tout   toutes   toute   tous

  a Il faut manger _____ la soupe.

  b J'adore _____ les vieilles maisons.

  c Le restaurant est ouvert _____ les jours.

  d Je reste à Paris _____ le mois d'août.

  e Elle dit bonjour à _____ mes amis.

  f Il aime _____ les belles villes.

SELF CHECK

	I CAN. . .
⚪	. . . understand parking instructions.
⚪	. . . use Euro money.
⚪	. . . use time expressions.
⚪	. . . talk about daily routines.

7 L'hébergement
Accommodation

In this unit you will learn how to:
▶ *find a hotel.*
▶ *book a hotel room.*
▶ *ask for various facilities.*

CEFR: *Can explain preferences (A2); Can make and respond to suggestions (A2); Can read short and simple texts (A2); Can locate specific information in lists (A2).*

Where to stay - l'hébergement

Most French towns have **un Office de Tourisme** (*a tourist office*). It is the ideal place for you to get **renseignements et conseils** (*information and advice*), whether you are **en vacances** (*on holiday*) or **en voyage d'affaires** (*on a business trip*). They can help you find **où passer la nuit** (*somewhere to stay the night*), **où manger** (*somewhere to eat*) and also **que faire d'intéressant** (*something interesting to do*). Some offices will **faire une réservation** (*make a booking*) for you but if not, they will give you **tous les renseignements** (*all the information*) you need. They deal with **l'hébergement** (*accommodation*), **la restauration** (*where to eat*) and **les loisirs** (*leisure activities*).

Le tourisme (*tourism*) is booming in France . **Il y a un grand choix d'endroits où rester** (*there are lots of places to stay to choose from*). Apart from the traditional range of hotels in towns there is also a much cheaper and sometimes **plus pratique** (*more convenient*) range of accommodation in out-of-town hotels, often in **zones commerciales** (*commercial centres*) or close to **les autoroutes** (*motorways*) **Le camping** (*camping*) is still very popular in the summer **pour les familles** (*for families*). **Pour les jeunes** (*for young people*) there are **auberges de jeunesse** (*youth hostels*), which are not expensive.

You're at the tourist office. Can you say the following?
a I am on holiday.
b I am on a business trip.

Vocabulary builder

HOTEL EXPRESSIONS

1 07.01 **Here are some useful hotel expressions. Listen and match the French and English expressions.**

a une chambre simple

b une chambre double

c une chambre familiale (avec un grand lit + un lit pour enfant)

d une chambre pour personne handicapée

e pension (petit déjeuner + dîner)

f demi-pension (petit déjeuner)

1 full board (breakfast + dinner)

2 a room for a disabled person

3 a single room

4 half-board (breakfast)

5 a double room

6 a family room (with a double bed + a bed for a child)

NEW EXPRESSIONS

Look at the expressions that are used in the next conversations. Note their meanings.

Conversation 2

sans	*without*
la plupart	*most*
de toute façon	*in any case*
disponible(s)	*available*
vérifier	*to check*

> **INSIGHT: CULTURE**
>
> Many French hotels accept dogs. A standard notice reads:
> **Ici on accepte nos amis les chiens.** (*Here dogs are allowed.*)
> In some places you may see:
> **Les chiens ne sont pas admis dans la salle à manger.** (*Dogs are not allowed in the dining room.*)
> **Merci de bien vouloir laisser votre chien au chenil pendant les repas.** (*Thank you for leaving your dog in the kennel during meals.*)

2 07.02 **Now listen and match the names of the hotel facilities and their symbols with their English equivalents.**

a Facilités pour handicapés/pour voyageurs à mobilité réduite

1 Main credit cards accepted

b Ouvert toute l'année

2 Bath and toilets

c Catégorie (une/deux/trois/quatre étoiles)

3 Garage/private car park

d Douches et wc

4 Sea view

e Salle de bain et wc

5 Swimming pool

f Garage/parking privé

6 Children's games

g Restaurant

7 Lift

h Principales cartes de crédit acceptées

8 Facilities for disabled visitors

i TV dans les chambres

9 TV in rooms

j Vue sur la mer

10 Open all year round

k Piscine

11 Category (1/2/3/4 stars)

l Ascenseur

12 Pets welcomed

m Jeux pour enfants

13 Showers and toilets

n Animaux acceptés

14 Restaurant

Conversations

 1 07.03 **Four tourists are at the tourist office. Quickly scan the text and answer the question, then listen.**

a What are the tourists asking about?

1 hotel prices   **2** hotel facilities

Premier touriste	Je voudrais une chambre pour deux personnes, pour une nuit, dans un hôtel trois étoiles, avec vue sur la mer.
Deuxième touriste	J'ai un petit chien alors je cherche un hôtel où l'on accepte les animaux.
Troisième touriste	Je voudrais une chambre pour une personne dans un hôtel pas trop cher, avec restaurant et piscine.
Quatrième touriste	Ma fille est handicapée et elle a un fauteuil roulant. Nous voudrions une grande chambre pour trois personnes dans un hôtel avec ascenseur.

---

b **Now listen again or read to answer the questions below.**

1 The first tourist requires: _____

2 The second tourist requires: _____

3 The third tourist requires: _____

4 The fourth tourist requires: _____

 2 07.04 **After half a day in St Malo, Sarah and Dominique decide to see more of** *la ville et ses environs/ses alentours* **(the town and the area around it). They want to stay for** *quelques jours* **(a few days). Listen to the recording and answer the question.**

a Are the two women likely to find something not too expensive for a few nights? _____

Conversation 2

Dominique	Pardon monsieur, pouvez-vous nous renseigner? Nous passons quelques jours dans la région et nous cherchons un petit hôtel pas trop cher.
Employé	Oui, alors ça devrait être possible. Il y a beaucoup de petits hôtels deux étoiles qui sont très bien. Voici notre brochure Vous voulez un hôtel avec ou sans restaurant?
Sarah	Sans restaurant. Il y a beaucoup de restaurants à St Malo.

Employé	Oh oui, et la plupart des hôtels servent le petit déjeuner de toute façon.
Dominique	Vous vous chargez des réservations?
Employé	Non, je suis désolé madame! Nous ne nous chargeons pas des réservations, mais si vous voulez je peux téléphoner à l'hôtel de votre choix pour vérifier qu'il y a des chambres disponibles.

b Now listen again or read to answer the questions.
1 Would they like a hotel with a restaurant? _____
2 Do most hotels offer breakfast? _____
3 Can they arrange hotel bookings for customers at the Tourist Office? _____

Language discovery

1 **Look at Conversation 2 and find the French for the following expressions.**
   a It must be possible. _____
   b Could you give us some information? _____
   c Do you take care of reservations? _____
   d No, I am afraid not (madame)! _____
   e We are spending a few days in the area. _____

2 **Look at the exercise above and answer the questions.**
   a What word means *must*?   **devrait**   **alors**
   b What expression means *take care of*? **chargez**   **vous**

Learn more

DES VERBES

There are three groups of verbs:
▶ **Group 1:** verbs ending with **-er**. They very nearly all follow a regular pattern (**aller** is an exception).
▶ **Group 2:** verbs ending with **-ir**. Some of them follow a regular pattern.
▶ **Group 3:** mostly verbs ending with **-re/-oir**. They are mostly irregular verbs.

Vouloir *(to want)*

This is a very useful verb to express a wish / something you would like. As in English, it is more polite to use the conditional tense (*I would like*), rather than the present tense (*I want*). *Compare the requests below.*

Je veux une glace!	*I want an ice cream!*
Je voudrais une chambre à deux lits.	*I would like a room with two beds.*
Nous voudrions louer des vélos.	*We would like to hire bikes.*

Note, there is another meaning of the verb **vouloir**.

En vouloir à quelqu'un	*To hold something against someone*
Ne m'en voulez pas trop!	Literally *Don't hold it too much (against me)! / Don't be mad at me!*

An appropriate reply for this is:

Mais je ne vous en veux pas du tout!	*But I don't hold it against you at all!*

Chercher *or* rechercher *(to look for)*

This is an easy verb to use. It is an **-er** verb because its infinitive (basic form) ends with **-er**. It is also a regular verb which means that it should provide you with a good example of how all regular **-er** verbs function.

Look carefully at the table below. It will provide you with some necessary information about French verbs in the present tense:

The present tense forms of chercher	
je cherche	Lit. *I look for* but best translated as *I am looking for*
tu cherches	*you are looking for* (see **tutoyer** Unit 5)
elle/il cherche	*she/he/it is looking for*
on cherche	Lit. *one is looking for* but best translated as *we are looking for*
nous cherchons	*we are looking for*
vous cherchez	*you are looking for* (see **vouvoyer** Unit 5)
ils/elles cherchent	*they are looking for* (pronounced the same way as **il/elle cherche**)

Devoir *(ought to/must)*

▶ In the present tense it mainly means **must**.

Je dois partir. *I must go.*

▶ Just as **je voudrais** is a conditional form of **vouloir**, so **je devrais** *(I ought to)* is a conditional form of **devoir**.

Je devrais téléphoner à ma mère. *I ought to phone my mother.*

▶ In the dialogue **devoir** is used with **cela** (*that / it*) and is often shortened to **ça** as in **ça va?** (See Unit 1).

Cela/ça devrait être bon. *It ought to be good.*

Servir *(to serve)*

Servir is used throughout the unit to talk about what hotels offer. Review the uses below.

Les hôtels servent* le petit déjeuner.   *(Hotels serve breakfast.)*

*Note: The ending **-ent** is the plural form and you cannot hear it. The singular form would be **L'hôtel sert le petit déjeuner à partir de huit heures.** *(The hotel serves breakfast from 8.00 a.m.)*

Vos hôtes vous serviront** un petit déjeuner campagnard. *(Your hosts will serve you a country breakfast.)*

Note: ils serviront *(they will serve)* is the future tense of the verb **servir.

Se charger de *(to take responsibility for something)*

This is a reflexive verb so it must have an object.

Je me charge de tout!   *I'll take care of everything!*

L'Office de Tourisme de St Malo ne se charge pas des réservations.

(best translated as) *St Malo's Tourist Office does not deal with reservations.*

 ## Practice

 1 **Say what accommodation you require. Translate the sentences below.**
   a I am looking for a single room in a hotel with sea view.
   b I would like a double room in a hotel.
   c We are looking for a hotel with a swimming pool. (use **nous**)
   d We would like a hotel room for the weekend. (use **on**)

 2 **Now read the leaflet from Hôtels Campanile and make your own vocabulary list. Find the French words for the following objects:**
   a toothpaste _____
   b baby bottle warmer _____
   c hair dryer _____
   d toothbrush _____
   e shaving cream _____
   f a fax* _____

*Note: This is a different French expression for *fax*, again created in an effort to move away from English and American influence on the French language. However **un fax** is still used most of the time.

Services "Plus" • Service "Extras"

• Dans la plupart de nos hôtels, possibilité de prendre une chambre 24h/24 grâce à notre système de paiement par carte bancaire	24H/24	• In most of our hotels, possibility to take a room 24 hours a day thanks to our automatic payment system operating by credit card.
• Renseignements - réservation de votre prochaine étape chez Campanile		• Information - Booking your next stopover at Campanile
• Envoi d'une télécopie		• Sending a fax
• Vente de boissons (non alcoolisées)		• (Non alcoholic) beverages on sale
• La boutique Campanile : rasoir, crème à raser, dentifrice, nécessaire à couture, brosse à dents...		• The Campanile boutique : razor, shaving cream, toothpaste, sewing kits, toothbrush...
• Prêt d'un fer à repasser, sèche-cheveux, oreillers synthétiques, chauffe-biberon	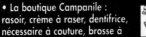	• At your disposal : an iron, hair dryer, synthetic pillows, baby bottle warmer

READING

1 **Read the text and find the French words or phrases for the following:**

  a at farmers' homes _____
  b either for one or several nights _____
  c a country breakfast _____
  d your hosts will serve you _____

HEBERGEMENT
Chambre d'Hôtes à la Ferme

La chambre d'hôtes à la ferme, c'est le 'bed and breakfast' à la française chez des agriculteurs. Que ce soit pour une ou plusieurs nuits, vous serez reçus 'à la ferme'. Le matin, vos hôtes serviront un petit déjeuner campagnard. Dans certains cas, il vous sera  même possible de prendre vos repas chez l'habitant (table d'hôtes). La chambre labellisée 'gîtes de France', c'est l'assurance de bénéficier d'un accueil de qualité dans un cadre chaleureux.

Go further

Look at the information provided by the Hôtel du Palais at St Malo. Then answer the questions.

a Where is l'Hôtel du Palais situated? _____

b How many rooms have they got? _____

c Would you be able to watch East Enders? _____

d What other facilities do they offer? _____

e What is their basic price for a double room? _____

> **INSIGHT: LANGUAGE**
>
> **Héberger** is also a verb which means *to give shelter to.*
>
> **Nous pouvons vous héberger pour la nuit.** (*We can put you up for the night.*)
>
> **Les sinistrés sont hébergés dans des tentes** .(*The victims of the disaster are sheltered in tents.*)
>
> **Un centre d'hébergement pour des réfugiés** (*Refugee shelter*)

HOTEL**
DU
PALAIS

•

Hôtel situé dans la partie haute de la vieille ville: l'Intra Muros. Proche des remparts et de la plage, ainsi que des rues commerçantes très animées tout en restant dans un environnement dégagé et calme. Accès aisé en voiture en toutes saisons.

•

CHAMBRES

18 Chambres – Toilettes, WC – Douche ou bain – Ascenseur
Télévision, Chaînes françaises et anglaises – Petit déjeuner
Prix de base: Chambre double (2 personnes) 45 € à 79 €

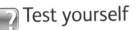 # Test yourself

Using everything you have learnt in this unit and previous units, how would you ask for the following?

1 You and your partner are looking for a hotel room with 2 single beds.

2 You want to know at what time breakfast is served.

3 You want to know if the Tourist Office can reserve room for you.

4 You and your partner want to know if there is a kennel for your dog.

5 You want to know if you can rent a bike.

6 You request for breakfast to be served in your room at 9 a.m.

Can you work out what the following statements mean?

7 C'est plus cher avec vue sur la mer.

8 Nous n'acceptons pas les chèques.

9 La piscine est fermée en hiver.

10 L'ascenseur est réservé pour les personnes handicapées.

11 Il ne reste que des chambres sans salles de bains.

12 Vous devriez téléphoner à la police.

SELF CHECK

I CAN. . .
. . . find a hotel.
. . . book a hotel room.
. . . ask for various facilities.

8 À l'hôtel
At the hotel

In this unit you will learn how to:
▶ *express a preference and make some comparisons.*
▶ *state your room requirements, understand instructions.*
▶ *say the alphabet, use accents and spell names.*
▶ *use du, de la, des.*
▶ *use the pronouns le, la, les.*
▶ *use vouloir, pouvoir, prendre.*

CEFR: *Can ask for everyday goods and services (A2); Can make and respond to suggestions (A2); Can make arrangements (A2); Can complete forms of personal details (A1).*

Choosing a hotel

In France like in any other countries, there is a vast range of hotels to choose from. **Pour la plupart des gens** (*for most people*), the choice is dictated by **le coût** (*the cost*). **Les hôtels cinq étoiles** (*five star hotels*), such as **Le George V** or **le Shangri-La** in Paris, are **des hôtels de grand luxe** (*luxury hotels*) where royal families from all over the world stay when visiting Paris. **Les hôtels-châteaux** (*castle hotels*) in the Loire Valley and all over France were once aristocratic homes.

For most tourists it's important to **trouver** (*find*) a hotel room **selon leurs moyens** (*according to what they can afford*), as long as they can find **le calme, le confort, l'hospitalité et de la gastronomie** (*calm, comfort, hospitality and quality food*).

 La bonne cuisine is always a top priority in France. Which other word is used to describe it in the text?

Vocabulary builder

NEW EXPRESSIONS

**Look at the expressions that are used in the next conversations.
Note their meanings.**

Conversation 1

descendre	*to put up at a hotel**
Descendons à l'Hôtel de la Gare.	*Let's go to the Station Hotel.*

Conversation 2

Vous désirez?	*What can I do for you?*
désirer	*to wish/desire*
Cela s'épelle comment?	*How do you spell it / How is it spelt?*
au bout du couloir	*at the end of the corridor*
la salle à manger	*the dining room*
avoir besoin de...	*to need...*
quoi que ce soit	*whatever it is*
parce que	*because***

* **Note:** **Descendre** usually means *to go down, to alight* but here it *means to put up at a hotel.*

** **Note**: Another word for *because* is **car,** but it is more formal and it is used less frequently in speech and more often in formal, written French.

Conversations

Monsieur and Madame Olivier are having some difficulties choosing a hotel. The choice is between:

L'HÔTEL DE LA GARE **	*(Station Hotel)*
L'HÔTEL DE L'ÉGLISE *	*(Church Hotel)*
L'HÔTEL DU CENTRE ****	*(Centre Hotel)*
L'HÔTEL DES VOYAGEURS ***	*(Travellers' Hotel)*

1 08.01 **Listen once to the recording, then answer the question.**

a *Which hotel does Monsieur Olivier suggest in the first place?*

_____

Conversation 1	
Madame Olivier	*Alors quel hôtel choisis-tu?*
Monsieur Olivier	*Pas de problèmes, descendons à l'Hôtel de la Gare. C'est tout près de la gare. C'est plus pratique, c'est plus facile avec les bagages et c'est l'hôtel le moins cher!*
Madame Olivier	*Oui d'accord, mais il y a aussi l'Hôtel des Voyageurs. C'est aussi tout près de la gare!*
Monsieur Olivier	*Oh je te laisse choisir, c'est plus simple!*
Madame Olivier	*Dans ce cas je choisis l'Hôtel du Centre. C'est plus loin de la gare mais c'est certainement plus confortable!*

b **Now listen again or read to answer the questions.**

1 *Monsieur Olivier gives three reasons for his choice. Name one of them.* _____

2 *Where is l'Hôtel des Voyageurs situated?* _____

3 *Who makes the final choice?* _____

4 *What reason is given for the choice?* _____

2 08.02 **Monsieur and Madame Landré are au bureau de réception** *(at the reception desk)* **of the Beach Hotel. Listen once to the recording and answer the question.**

a *Have Monsieur and Madame Landré reserved a room?* _____

Conversation 2	
Réceptionniste	*Bonsoir monsieur-dame. Vous désirez?*
Madame Landré	*Nous avons réservé une chambre pour deux personnes, pour deux nuits.*
Réceptionniste	*Bien, c'est à quel nom?*
Madame Landré	*Landré, Jacques et Martine Landré.*
Réceptionniste	*Cela s'épelle comment?*
Monsieur Landré	*L-a-n-d-r-e accent aigu.*
Réceptionniste	*Ah oui, voilà. Une chambre double pour deux nuits. Alors vous avez la chambre vingt-cinq au troisième étage. L'ascenseur est au bout du couloir. Voici votre clef. Vous prendrez le petit déjeuner?*
Madame Landré	*Euh oui! C'est à quelle heure?*
Réceptionniste	*Alors le petit déjeuner est servi dans la salle à manger de huit heures à dix heures mais vous pouvez le prendre dans votre chambre si vous voulez.*

Monsieur Landré	*Nous le prendrons dans la salle à manger, merci.*
Réceptionniste	*Très bien. Si vous avez besoin de quoi que ce soit, n'hésitez pas à m'appeler. Si vous sortez, gardez votre clef avec vous parce que la porte de l'hôtel ferme à vingt-trois heures. Bon séjour à l'Hôtel de la Plage, Monsieur et Madame Landré!*
M. et Mme Landré	*Merci bien Mademoiselle. A propos Mademoiselle, nous avons un petit problème. Nous avons un petit chien.*
Réceptionniste	*Pas de problèmes, ici les animaux sont acceptés.*
M. et Mme Landré	*Excellent! Merci Mademoiselle.*

b Now listen again or read and answer the questions.

1 How long do they intend to stay? _____

2 On which floor is their room? _____

3 What is their room number? _____

4 At what time is breakfast? _____

5 At what time does the hotel door close? _____

💡 Language discovery

1 **Look at Conversation 1 and match the following English phrases to the equivalent French expressions.**

a It's further from the station.

b Yes OK, but...

c It's the cheapest.

d It's certainly more comfortable.

e It's more convenient.

f It's easier.

g I'll let you choose.

1 Oui, d'accord mais...

2 C'est plus pratique.

3 C'est plus loin de la gare.

4 Je te laisse choisir.

5 C'est certainement plus confortable.

6 C'est le moins cher.

7 C'est plus facile.

2 **Look at Conversation 2 and match the following English phrases to the equivalent French expressions.**

a on the third floor

b Do not hesitate to call me.

c if you go out

1 si vous sortez

2 Nous avons réservé une chambre.

3 La porte de l'hôtel ferme à...

d Keep your key.	**4** N'hésitez pas à m'appeler.
e Have a good stay!	**5** au troisième étage
f The hotel door closes at...	**6** Gardez votre clef.
g We have reserved a room.	**7** Bon séjour!

3 **Which words convey the notion of *more* or *less* in these sentences?**

   a C'est plus rapide de prendre l'ascenseur.

   b Nous avons trouvé un restaurant moins cher.

Learn more

1 DU, DE LA, DE L', DES

The names of the four hotels in the conversations have been used to show that there are four different ways to say *of the*. Notice the word order in French: *Hotel of the Station* rather than *Station Hotel*. You use **du, de la, de l'** or **des** according to the gender and number of the noun which follows. This can be illustrated with the following names of **rues** (*streets*) or **places** (*town squares*):

Use	Example
De + feminine noun = **de la**	**Rue de la Cité**
De + masculine noun = **du**	**Rue du Port**
De + singular noun beginning with a vowel or mute h = **de l'**	**Rue de l'Europe**
De + plural noun (fem. or masc.) = **des**	**Place des Québécois**

2 MORE ABOUT VERBS

The auxiliary verbs être (to be) and avoir (to have)

In Conversation 2 you have your first few examples of verbs used with the auxiliary verbs **être** (*to be*) and **avoir** (*to have*).

Nous avons réservé une chambre pour deux personnes, pour deux nuits.

Alors le petit déjeuner est servi dans la salle à manger ...

les animaux sont acceptés.

In **Nous avons réservé une chambre**, the verb **avons** (from the base form **avoir**) is used with the verb **réserver** to indicate the past (*we have reserved*). The two examples with **être** are different. In the expressions **Le petit déjeuner est servi** (*Breakfast is served*) and **Les animaux sont acceptés** (*Animals are accepted*), facts are established using **être** plus a verb form functioning as an adjective.

The many uses of the verb descendre

The verb descendre has many uses and meanings. See below for a review of the most common ones.

Nous descendons souvent à l'Hôtel de la Gare.	*We often stay at the station Hotel.*
Je descends l'escalier en courant .	*I run downstairs. (lit. I come downstairs running.)*
Ils habitent à Londres mais ils descendent à Paris plusieurs fois par an.	*They live in London, but they go (down) to Paris several times a year.*
Il s'est fait descendre par la mafia.	*He got himself shot by the Mafia.*

Choisir (to choose)

In Unit 7 you met the verb **chercher**, an **-er** verb with a regular pattern. Similarly **choisir**, which belongs to the second group of verbs (those regular verbs ending in **-ir**), is a useful model for other **-ir** verbs. Unfortunately quite a few verbs ending in **-ir** are irregular and belong to the third group of verbs. The letters underlined below show the pattern of present tense endings.

Choisir *(to choose)*			
je choisis	*I choose/I am choosing*	**nous choisissons**	*we choose*
tu choisis	*you choose*	**vous choisissez**	*you choose*
il/elle choisit	*he/she/it chooses*	**ils/elles choisissent**	*they choose*

Vouloir, pouvoir, prendre, and dire

These four verbs belong to the third group of verbs (mostly irregular which means that they do not all have the same spelling pattern). Here they are in the present tense.

Vouloir *(to want)*			
je veux	*I want*	**nous voulons**	*we want*
tu veux	*you want*	**vous voulez**	*you want*
il/elle/on veut	*he/she/one wants*	**ils /elles veulent**	*they want*
Pouvoir *(to be able to)*			
je peux	*I can*	**nous pouvons**	*we can*
tu peux	*you can*	**vous pouvez**	*you can*
il/elle/on peut	*he/she/one can*	**ils/elles peuvent**	*they can*

Prendre *(to take)*			
je prends	*I take*	**nous pren<u>ons</u>**	*we take*
tu prends	*you take*	**vous pren<u>ez</u>**	*you take*
il/elle/on prend	*he/she/one takes*	**ils/elles pren<u>nent</u>**	*they take*
Dire *(to say)*			
je dis	*I say*	**nous dis<u>ons</u>**	*we say*
tu dis	*you say*	**vous dit<u>es</u>**	*you say*
il/elle/on dit	*he/she/one says*	**ils/elles dis<u>ent</u>**	*they say*

3 *PLUS* (MORE) AND *MOINS* (LESS)

> **INSIGHT: LANGUAGE**
> **C'est à dire** is a useful expression when speaking. It means *That is to say ...*

In order to make a comparison you need at least two comparable things. In Conversation 1, **C'est plus pratique** effectively means that the Station Hotel is more convenient in terms of location than the other three hotels. **C'est plus pratique** is therefore a shortcut for the following:

L'Hôtel de la Gare est <u>plus</u> pratique <u>que</u> l'Hôtel du Centre ....

In more formal speech the sentence would start with **Il est...**

<u>Il est</u> plus pratique de descendre à l'Hôtel de la Gare que de descendre à l'Hôtel du Centre.

Also in Conversation 1, **C'est moins cher** is a short cut for: **L'Hôtel de la Gare est moins cher que l'Hôtel du Centre** (*less expensive than... / cheaper than ...*)

▶ **C'est le moins cher** means *it's the least expensive / it's the cheapest.*

4 PRONOUNS: *LE, LA, LES*

In Conversation 2, the receptionist says:

Vous pouvez le prendre dans votre chambre... *(You can take it in your room...)*

Here, the word **le** refers to **le petit déjeuner** (*breakfast*). **Le** here is a pronoun, a word that stands in for a noun, although not necessarily in the same position. At a later stage you will learn how to use a whole range of pronouns but for the moment it is important to understand the difference between the articles **le, la**, and **les** which mean *the* and come in front of nouns, and the pronouns **le, la** and **les** which replace nouns altogether:

Question	Answer
Vous prendrez le petit déjeuner?	**Oui nous le prendrons.** *(Yes we will have it.)*
Vous gardez la clef?	**Oui je la garde.** *(Yes I am keeping it.)*
Tu gardes les clefs?	**Oui je les garde.** *(Yes I am keeping them.)*

5 VERB + INFINITIVE

In the sentence below, **prendre** is in the infinitive (the basic form of the verb).

Vous pouvez prendre le petit déjeuner dans votre chambre.	*(You can have breakfast in your room.)*

That is simply because when one verb (in this case **prendre**) follows another (in this case **pouvez**), the second one remains in the infinitive. The exception to this rule is after **avoir** (*to have*) and **être** (*to be*) *(see above)*.

Practice

1 **Three suitcases have been left in the corridor. Whose are they? Look at the people and suitcases. Then read the hints and decide whether the following statements are vrai ou faux (*true or false*).**

a   b   c

> Hint #1 — The father works in an office.
> Hint #2 — The mother has an unusual hobby.

a **C'est la valise de la mère.** _____

b **C'est la valise du père.** _____

c **C'est la valise des enfants.** _____

2 Choose the correct words to complete the name of each café:

EUROPE   VIEILLE VILLE   PORT   AMIS *(friends)*

  a Café des _____
  b Café du _____
  c Café de la _____
  d Café de l' _____

3 Find the correct endings for the verbs pouvoir *(can)* and prendre *(to take)*. Match the subject pronouns (I, you, etc.) to the correct parts of the verbs. Note, each pronoun can be linked to more than one verb form.

  a Je
  b Tu
  c Il
  d Elle
  e On
  f Nous
  g Vous
  h Ils
  i Elles

  1 pouvez
  2 prends
  3 prennent
  4 prend
  5 peuvent
  6 peux
  7 prenons
  8 prenez
  9 peut

4 Choose the correct word to complete the sentences.

  a Votre nom **s'appelle / s'épelle** comment?
  b Nous allons **prendre / pouvoir** le petit déjeuner dans notre chambre.
  c Je **pourrais / voudrais** une chambre dans un hôtel à cinq étoiles.
  d Elle **a / est** partie sans payer.
  e Ici **on / ont** accepte les animaux.
  f En général un hôtel à trois étoiles est **plus / moins** cher qu'un hôtel à cinq étoiles.
  g Ils **ont / sont** dit bonjour à la réceptionniste.
  h Si vous **servez / sortez**, gardez votre clef avec vous.
  i Nous **sommes / avons** réservé pour quatre personnes.

5 The name of a café, the name of a hotel and a name for the part of a town are hidden in the grid. Can you find them?

C	Q	A	D	H	B	G	T	I	C	R	V
H	A	P	D	E	O	U	Y	T	N	H	I
S	Q	F	X	G	L	T	W	T	T	Y	E
H	O	T	E	L	D	U	P	O	R	T	I
R	E	G	T	D	F	M	E	D	A	W	L
T	G	H	W	A	E	F	P	F	M	F	L
A	N	G	L	A	I	S	V	I	L	L	E
A	M	G	L	B	I	S	Q	C	R	U	P
B	C	V	N	F	T	H	W	A	Q	S	F

PRONUNCIATION

Monsieur Landré was asked **Cela s'épelle comment?** *(How is it spelt?)*. If you need to spell your name, you will need to know the French alphabet.

1 08.03 **Listen to the alphabet on the recording and repeat.**

> A, B, C, D, E, F, G, H, I, J, K, L, M, N, O, P, Q,
> R, S, T, U, V, W (double V), X, Y (I grec), Z

2 08.04 **In addition to spelling the letters you also need to spell accents and other signs. Listen and repeat.**

> é = e accent aigu
> è = e accent grave
> ê = e accent circonflexe (also â, î, ô, û - often in place of s in earlier language e.g. hostel has become hôtel, paste — pâte, hospital — hôpital)
> ë = e tréma (used to keep two vowel sounds separate e.g. Noël)
> ç = cédille
> Examples of double letters: deux c, deux f, deux m, deux s, etc.

3 08.05 **Listen to the way three different people spell their names and write down what you hear.**

   1 *Sylvie* _____

   2 _____ _____

   3 _____ _____

   4 *Now spell your name in French!*

Go further

French people are very fond of animals, especially small dogs. This has progressively developed in the last 20 years as has a whole business area related to animal care such as dog grooming salons.

 08.06 Listen and read as author Gaëlle Graham interviews Marc Lécaille, an animal groomer. Then answer the questions.

1 Marc grooms pets. Which ones does he mention? _____

2 Is Marc qualified to do this particular job? _____

3 What makes his day? _____

Gaëlle	Marc, vous travaillez avec les animaux. Qu'est-ce que vous faites exactement?
Marc	Je suis toiletteur, c'est à dire que je prends soin de l'hygiène des animaux de compagnie.
Gaëlle	Tous les animaux?
Marc	Non, je m'occupe en particulier du toilettage canin et également de l'hygiène des chats et des lapins.
Gaëlle	Vous aimez votre travail?
Marc	Oui, c'est une passion d'enfance que j'ai réalisé récemment.
Gaëlle	Il faut des diplômes pour exercer ce métier?
Marc	Non, ce n'est pas obligatoire mais dans mon cas j'ai obtenu le brevet de toiletteur canin, et donc c'est un avantage au niveau technique.
Gaëlle	Du point de vue professionel, quel est le meilleur moment de la journée?
Marc	C'est le moment où le client voit son toutou* transformé après le toilettage et sort de chez moi tout fier de son chien.
Gaëlle	Vous avez beaucoup de travail?
Marc	Oui, parce que les Français ont de plus en plus d'animaux de compagnie.
Gaëlle	Alors bonne chance Marc.
Marc	Merci beaucoup.

> **INSIGHT: LANGUAGE**
> **Un toutou** is a slang name for a pet dog.

? Test yourself

1 **What would you like for breakfast? Place the following words in the correct gap:**

> eau minérale   croissants   yaourts aux fruits
> pain   café au lait   confiture

Pour le petit déjeuner je voudrais des _____, du _____, de la
_____, de l'_____ _____ bien fraîche, du _____ _____
_____, et des _____ _____ _____.

2 **Mini dialogues. Questions and answers are listed at random. Pair each question or statement with the only possible reply.**

  a Au cinquième.

  b Non, tu pourrais me faire une tasse de thé, s'il te plaît ?

  c Vous avez choisi le menu?

  d Oui, ma femme a réservé une chambre pour deux personnes

  e Je descends l'escalier avec ma valise.

  f Non, nous descendons souvent au Grand Hôtel. Il est très confortable.

  g Vous avez une réservation ?

  h Vous préférez choisir un autre hôtel ?

  i Oui, je vais prendre une pizza.

  j A quel étage sommes-nous ?

  k Prends l'ascenseur, c'est plus pratique !

  l Tu prends du café ?

SELF CHECK

	I CAN...
○	...express a preference and make some comparisons.
○	...state my room requirements, understand instructions.
○	...say the alphabet, use accents and spell names.
○	...use du, de la, des.
○	...use the pronouns le, la, les.
○	...use vouloir, pouvoir, prendre.

Une si jolie petite ville!
Such a pretty little town!

In this unit you will learn how to:
▶ *talk about places in a town and their location.*
▶ *use more time references.*
▶ *discuss future plans.*
▶ *talk about parts of the day.*

CEFR: *Can understand short, simple texts (A1); Can use simple, descriptive language (A2); Can make arrangements to meet, decide where to go and what to do (A2); Can make and respond to suggestions (A2); Can ask for and give directions referring to a map or plan.*

 French cities

France is known for its many **villes** and **cités** (*cities*). The most popular, of course, is **la capitale** (*the capital*), Paris, with **son histoire** (*its history*), **ses musées** (*its museums*), **ses magasins** (*its shops*), **son architecture** (*its architecture*), **ses cafés** (*its cafés*) and **ses spectacles** (*its events*). All towns have their character and charm. For example, Arles is famous for **ses vestiges romains** (*its Roman remains*) and Rouen for **son histoire**.

If you search **en ligne** (*online*) for «**Les plus beaux villages de France**» (*the most beautiful villages of France*), you can access sites **des 23 régions de France** (*of the 23 regions of France*). You will see **des villages réputés** (*renowned*) for their **maisons fleuries** (*flowered houses*) in Bretagne, Barfleur en Normandie, the ancient **port romain et Viking** (*Roman and Viking port*), and many other unique cities and regions.

a **Which word means *the most*?**	le plus	beaucoup de
b **Which word is a form of *its*?**	son	des

Vocabulary builder

09.01 **Look at the French words and English translations for places around town. Then listen again and repeat as you locate them on the map.**

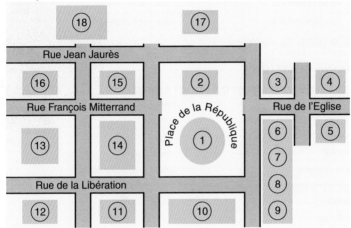

1	**la Place de la République**	*Republic Square*
2	**le Bar-Tabac du Centre (bureau de tabac)**	*bar-tobacconist's*
3	**l'église**	*the church*
4	**la pharmacie**	*the chemist's*
5	**le Commissariat de Police**	*the Police Station*
6	**la Mairie/l'Hôtel de Ville**	*the Town Hall (in smaller/larger towns)*
7	**la bibliothèque municipale**	*the public library*
8	**la boucherie**	*the butcher's*
9	**l'Office de Tourisme**	*the Tourist Office*
10	**la Maison de la Presse**	*the newsagent's + bookshop*

11	le Café de la Poste	*the Post Office Café*
12	l'Hôtel-Restaurant St Jacques	*Hotel-Restaurant St Jacques*
13	l'alimentation (l'épicerie)	*the grocery store*
14	la poste	*the Post Office*
15	la boulangerie–pâtisserie	*the baker's/cake shop*
16	la banque	*the bank*
17	la charcuterie	*the delicatessen*
18	le camping municipal	*the municipal campsite*

ASKING QUESTIONS

 09.02 **Listen and repeat the French expressions.**

Où?	*Where?*
Quand?	*When?*
Comment?	*How?*
demain	*tomorrow*
après demain	*the day after tomorrow*
la semaine prochaine	*next week*
bientôt	*soon*
en voiture	*by car*
par le train	*by train*
à vélo	*by bike*

NEW EXPRESSIONS

Look at the expressions that are used in the next conversations. Note their meanings.

Conversation 1

à côté de	*next to*
en face	*opposite*
derrière	*behind*
entre*	*in between*
au coin de...	*at the corner of/round the corner from*
chacun/chacune	*each one*
de l'autre côté*	*on the other side*
devant*	*in front of...*

Conversation 2

la marée basse	*low tide*
soit... ou bien	*either... or*
beaucoup trop de monde	*far too many people*
aujourd'hui	*today*
demain	*tomorrow*
la marée haute*	*high tide*

*Note: These words are not in the conversations, but are important to the subject.

Conversations

 **1** 09.03 **Sarah and Dominique visit the old town. They each go their own way. Listen to the recording once, then answer the question.**

a What is Sarah going to do? _____

Conversation 1

Sarah	Je vais poster quelques cartes postales. Je vais essayer de trouver un bureau de poste.
Dominique	Regarde, la poste est indiquée sur le plan de la ville, là, PTT. C'est Place des Frères Lamennais. Tiens, regarde, c'est à côté du commissariat de police, en face de la cathédrale.
Sarah	Parfait, j'y vais! Et toi qu'est-ce que tu vas faire?
Dominique	Oh je ne sais pas, je vais peut-être faire un tour des remparts. On se retrouve dans une heure?
Sarah	OK! Où ça?
Dominique	Euh, au bout de la Grand'Rue, derrière la cathédrale, au coin de la rue Porcon de la Barbinais.
Sarah	Au revoir! Bonne promenade!
Dominique	Salut! A tout à l'heure!

b Now listen again or read to answer the questions below.

1 Can the spot Sarah wants to see be found on the map of the town? _____

2 What is Dominique going to do? _____

3 When will they meet again? *In ...*
  a *two hours' time.*   **b** *an hour's time*   **c** *half an hour's time.*

c Vrai ou faux? Say whether the following statements are true or false.

a *Le commissariat de police est derrière la cathédrale.* _____

b *La poste est indiquée sur le plan.* _____

c *Sarah cherche la cathédrale.* _____

d *Dominique va à la poste.* _____

e *Elles (les deux femmes) se retrouvent dans deux heures.* _____

2 09.04 **A family is staying in St Malo for the weekend. The mother, father, daughter and son are planning what they are going to do. Listen once to the recording and answer the question.**

a Who would like to go either to the beach or for a boat trip down the river? _____

Conversation 2	
Maman	Alors, soit on va à la plage et à marée basse on peut aller visiter la tombe de Chateaubriand sur le Grand Bé, ou bien on fait une excursion en bateau sur la Rance jusqu'à Dinan...
Jeune fille	Moi je voudrais aller au Mont Saint Michel!
Maman	Non, il y a beaucoup trop de monde au Mont Saint Michel le week-end!
Jeune garçon	Moi je veux prendre le petit train pour visiter St Malo. C'est moins fatigant et plus amusant!
Maman	Quel paresseux!
Papa	Bon, moi aussi j'ai une idée, on va visiter le barrage de la Rance. Plus de discussion!
Jeune garçon	Dis Papa, et demain qu'est-ce qu'on va faire?

b **Now listen again or read to answer the questions below.**

1 Who would like to go to Mont Saint Michel? _____

2 What would the boy like to do? _____

3 Who puts a stop to the discussion? _____

4 At the end of the discussion what does the boy want to know?
_____

Language discovery

1 Link the following English phrases to the equivalent French expressions from Conversation 1.

a	the police station	**1**	La poste est indiquée sur le plan.
b	The post office is marked on the map.	**2**	Où ça?
c	look	**3**	Bonne promenade!
d	I may go round the ramparts	**4**	On se retrouve dans une heure.
e	What are you going to do?	**5**	le commissariat de police
f	Have a good walk!	**6**	regarde
g	Let's meet again in an hour's time.	**7**	Qu'est-ce que tu vas faire?
h	Whereabouts?	**8**	Je vais peut-être faire un tour des remparts.

2 Link the following English phrases to the equivalent French expressions from Conversation 2.

a	We go to the beach.	**1**	Quel paresseux!
b	I'd like to go on the little train.	**2**	une excursion en bateau
c	What a lazy boy!	**3**	C'est plus amusant!
d	a boat trip	**4**	On va à la plage.
e	It's not so tiring.	**5**	Je voudrais prendre le petit train.
f	It's more fun.	**6**	C'est moins fatigant.

3 Look at the above exercises and answer the questions below.

a	What expression means *you're going?*	**tu vas**	**je vais**
b	What expression means *I'm going?*	**tu vas**	**je vais**
c	Which expression means *fun?*	**fatigant**	**amusant**

Learn more

1 THE VERB *ALLER*

The verb **aller** (*to go*) appears several times in the dialogue. In Unit 7, you learnt that **aller** is the only verb ending in **-er** which does not follow the usual pattern. Here are its present tense forms:

Aller			
je vais	*I go / I am going*	**nous all<u>ons</u>**	*we go / are going*
tu vas	*you go / are going*	**vous all<u>ez</u>**	*you go / are going*
il/elle/on va	*he/she/one goes/is going*	**ils /elles vo<u>nt</u>**	*they go / are going*

2 ALLER + *A SECOND VERB IN THE INFINITIVE*

You can use **aller** followed by another verb to refer to what will happen soon, for example in the next second, minute, hour or day, or even in the next few years in some cases.

Aller + infinitive (future meaning)	
Qu'est-ce que tu vas faire?	*What are you going to do?*
Je vais essayer de trouver un bureau de poste.*	*I am going to try and find a post office.*
Tu vas tomber!	*You are going to fall over!*
Il va pleuvoir.	*It's going to rain.*
Nous allons faire une promenade à vélo.	*We are going to go for a bike ride.*
Avec le nouveau gouvernement tout ça va changer!	*With the new government, all that is going to change!*

*Note: In this example there are two verbs following **aller**. Both of them are in the infinitive.

In most cases the time scale is implicit, but to be more precise use **aujourd'hui** (*today*), **demain** (*tomorrow*), **après-demain** (*the day after tomorrow*), **bientôt** (*soon*).

Qu'est-ce qu'on va faire aujourd'hui?   *What are we going to do today?*
Qu'est-ce qu'on va faire demain?   *What are we going to do tomorrow?*

Aller is also the verb used by supporters in sporting events in expressions such as:
Allez la France!   *Go on France!*
Allez les Bleus!   *Go on the Blues!*
Vas-y Thierry!   (Encouragement shouted to one individual)
On y va!   *Let's go!*
And of course to rally the nation: **Allons enfants de la patrie!**

> **INSIGHT: LANGUAGE**
> **J'y vais.** *(I am going [there].)*
> **Y** is a pronoun standing in place
> of a phrase beginning with **à**. In
> conversation 1, when Sarah says **J'y
> vais**, it is short for **Je vais à la poste.**

3 THE IMMEDIATE FUTURE: PRESENT TENSE

You can also use the present tense to express the immediate future.

The present tense for immediate future	
Qu'est ce que tu fais cet après-midi?	What are you doing this afternoon?
Qu'est-ce que vous faites ce soir?	What are you doing this evening?
Ce midi nous allons au restaurant.	This lunch time we are going to the restaurant.
Cette année nous allons en vacances en Irlande.	This year we are going on holiday to Ireland.

4 *THE ADJECTIVES* **AMUSANT** *(AMUSING/FUNNY)* **FATIGANT** *(TIRING)*

Amuser means *to amuse/to entertain* and the reflexive verb **s'amuser** means *to enjoy oneself.*

Les enfants s'amusent sur la plage. *The children are enjoying themselves on the beach.*

By adding the ending **-ant** in French, we add the equivalent to *-ing* in English. This creates the adjective form of the verb.

C'est un homme vraiment amusant. *He's a really funny man.*

The same goes for the verb fatiguer *(to tire).* When we add **–ant**, it becomes an adjective.

Marcher toute la journée, c'est très fatigant. *Walking all day is very tiring.*

5 MORE VERBS

Trouver/se retrouver *(to find – to meet again)*

The prefix **re-** at the beginning of a verb indicates that the action is being done again, for example, **faire** *(to do)* and **refaire** *(to redo/do again).*
Se retrouver is like a reflexive verb, but here it involves two people; the action is reciprocal. For example, in Conversation 1, Sarah is going to find Dominique again and Dominique is going to find Sarah.

On se retrouve dans une heure? *Let's meet again in an hour's time.*

S'embrasser *(to kiss one another)*

This is another example of a reciprocal action:

Les amants s'embrassent. *The lovers kiss.*

Faire *(to make, to do)*

The expression **faire** is used in a multitude of expressions.

Il fait beau.	*The weather is nice.*
Elle fait du 130 à l'heure.	*She is driving at 130 km/hour.*
Faites attention!	*Be careful!*
Arrête de faire le clown!	*Stop mucking about!*
Ils font de la natation.	*They're swimming.*

6   DIS PAPA! / DIS MAMAN!

Dis papa, dis maman! are children's expressions generally used to attract the attention of adults. **Dis/dites** are the imperative forms of **dire** *(to say)*:

Dis-moi la vérité.	*Tell me the truth.*
Dites-le au maire.	*Tell it to the mayor.*

 ## Practice

1 **Read the statements and look at the map in Vocabulary builder: Around town. What places are they talking about? Write the words.**

a C'est entre la mairie et la boucherie.

   _____

b C'est derrière la poste, entre la banque et le bar-tabac.

   _____

c C'est entre le Café de la Poste et l'Office de Tourisme.

   _____

d C'est devant la bibliothèque et à côté de l'Office de Tourisme.

   _____

e C'est rue François Mitterrand, derrière l'alimentation.

   _____

f C'est à côté de l'église, près du Commissariat de Police.

   _____

g C'est derrière le bar-tabac et à côté du camping municipal.

   _____

2 **Look again at the map from Vocabulary builder: Around town. You are in la Place de la République when a passer-by stops you and asks you two questions. Complete the dialogue. Then practise it aloud.**

Passant	Excusez-moi Monsieur/Madame/Mademoiselle. Pour aller au _____ s'il vous plaît?
Vous	Le _____, c'est derrière la boulangerie et en face de la _____ .
Passant	Merci bien! Et où est la _____ s'il vous plaît?
Vous	C'est à côté de la _____ municipale et en face du Commissariat de Police.

3 **Match the words from all four columns to make complete sentences. Columns A and D are in order; columns B and C are jumbled.**

A	B	C	D
a M & Mme Olivier	allons	visiter	des cartes postales.
b Tu	va	téléphoner	à ton frère.
c Sarah Burgess	vas	choisir	le petit déjeuner au lit.
d Vous	vont	chercher	la vieille ville.
e Je	vont	faire	à St Malo.
f On	allez	rester	du travail.
g Les enfants	va	voir (to see)	une promenade.
h Nous	vais	prendre	le dernier film de Spielberg.

SPEAKING

Where would you tell these people to go? Read the statements. Then practise how you would tell each person where to get what they need (ai besoin de...) or want (voudrais). Then listen to the recording and check your responses.

Exemple: J'ai besoin d'argent. **Vous:** Allez à la banque.

1 Je voudrais du jambon et du pâté.

2 J'ai besoin de médicaments.

3 Je voudrais acheter des journaux.

4 Je voudrais des timbres poste.

5 Je voudrais du pain et des gâteaux.

6 J'ai besoin d'un plan de la ville.

 READING

Read the advert for the little train and answer the questions.

LE PETIT TRAIN DE SAINT-MALO

Visite touristique et commentée de l'intra-muros et de ses alentours

Départ et arrivée : porte St-Vincent au pied du Château

NOCTURNE JUILLET/AOUT

Durée du trajet : 30 minutes

ENGLISH GUIDED TOUR

INFORMATIONS RESERVATIONS GROUPES
Tél. 02 99 40 49 49 - Fax 02 99 40 44 62
BP 173 35408 SAINT-MALO

a *What could you expect to see if you took the little train?*

_____

b *What happens at Porte St Vincent?* _____

c *Could you take a night ride all year round?* _____

⑦ Test yourself

1 **Complete the sentences with the correct form of aller and the most appropriate expression for each activity: intéressant (*interesting*), amusant (*entertaining*) or fatigant (*tiring*).**
   a Demain matin je __ faire le ménage. C'est __ !
   b Dimanche nous __ visiter le musée du Louvre. C'est __ !
   c Les enfants __ aller au cirque mercredi après midi. C'est __ !

2 **Qu'est-ce qu'ils vont faire pendant les vacances de Pâques? What will they do during the Easter holidays? Complete the sentences with the words from the box.**

| où | prochaine | qu'est-ce que | toi | faire | as | y | valise |
| pourrais | pas | réservé | voiture | allons | quand | | |

Gaétan et Hélène parlent de leurs vacances de Pâques :
   a Gaétan : __ tu vas faire pendant les vacances ?
   b Hélène : Je vais __ du ski.
   c Gaétan : __ est-ce que tu vas ?
   d Hélène : Nous __ à Chamonix. Ma sœur a __ un grand chalet.
   e Gaétan: Ah, tu __ de la chance. __ est –ce que tu y vas ?
   f Hélène: La semaine __ . Et __ Gaétan? Tu vas partir en vacances ?
   g Gaétan: Non, je n'ai __ d'argent.
   h Hélène: Tu __ venir avec nous. Nous y allons en __ et il y a de la place dans le chalet. Alors d'accord, on __ va ?
   i Gaétan: Eh bien oui ! C'est formidable ! Je vais faire ma __ .

SELF CHECK

I CAN. . .
● . . . talk about places in a town and their location.
● . . . use more time references.
● . . . discuss future plans.
● . . . talk about parts of the day.

10 Choisir un restaurant
Choosing a restaurant

In this unit you will learn how to:
▶ *talk about eating out.*
▶ *express an opinion.*
▶ *understand the French attitude towards food.*

CEFR: *Can give opinion (A2); Can agree and disagree (A2); Can recognize significant points in straightforward articles (B1); Can briefly give reasons and explanations for opinions and plans (B1).*

Where to eat?

There are numerous types of places in France where you can eat out. They range from master-chefs' restaurants to modest bistrots. You can choose from **la cuisine française traditionelle** (*traditional French cuisine*) or **la cuisine gastronomique** (*gourmet cuisine*).

Les bistrots may vary in quality, but they are **des endroits sans prétention** (*unassuming*). **Le menu du jour** (*the day's menu*) **est écrit sur l'ardoise** (*is written on the board*). **Les meilleurs** (*the best*) **bistrots sont jugés** (*are judged*) **sur l'ardoise et l' ambiance** (*the atmosphere*).

Les brasseries (*breweries*) are traditonnally large cafés selling mainly **de la bière** (*beer*). They serve quick meals, but can also be places **où déguster** (*where to taste*) **de la très bonne cuisine.** On the official site for l'Office de Tourisme de Paris, under «**Les grandes brasseries de Paris**» some are referred to as **incontournables** (*"must-try" places*).

---

a **Dégustation: when travelling through France you may see places advertising their food or wine in vineyard areas. What do you think it means?**

b **How would you say "the dish of the day"? Where is it likely to be written?**

Vocabulary builder

LES HEURES DES REPAS – *(MEAL TIMES)*

 1 10.01 **Listen to the expressions for meal times in French as you match them to their English translations.**

a	**Les repas**	**1**	supper
b	**Le petit déjeuner**	**2**	lunch
c	**Le déjeuner**	**3**	dinner
d	**Le goûter**	**4**	breakfast
e	**Le dîner**	**5**	the meals
f	**Le souper**	**6**	afternoon tea*

*Note: Le goûter (Lit. *to taste*) is a snack given to children when they come home from school. It is never a substitute for a meal in the way that *afternoon tea* can be in England. Adults typically do not eat **le goûter**, they wait for **le dîner**.

LES MOMENTS DE LA JOURNÉE – *(THE TIMES OF DAY)*

 1 10.02 **Listen to the expressions for the times of day in French as you match them to their English translations.**

a	**Le matin**	**1**	later in the evening
b	**À midi (entre midi et deux heures)**	**2**	the afternoon
c	**L'après-midi**	**3**	midday (between noon and two o'clock)
d	**Le soir (vers sept, huit heures)**	**4**	the morning
e	**Plus tard le soir**	**5**	evening (around seven, eight o'clock)

NEW EXPRESSIONS

Look at the expressions that are used in the next conversations and readings. Note their meanings.

Conversation

avoir envie de...	*to long for / to have a craving for/to feel like / to fancy...*
quelque chose	*something*
un verre de vin	*a glass of wine*
pleuvoir	*to rain*

Reading 1

c'est-à-dire	*that is to say*
souvent	*often*
surtout	*above all*
lorsque/quand	*when*
partout	*everywhere*
faire preuve de	*to demonstrate / to show*
s'agir de	*to be a matter of*
la meilleure cuisine	*the best cooking*

Reading 2

bonne nourriture	*good food*
bons repas	*good meals*
le goûter	*afternoon tea*
goûter	*(verb) to taste/to appreciate*
assez léger	*fairly light*
chez eux	*at (their) home (lit. at theirs)*
leur lieu de travail	*their place of work*

Conversation

1 10.03 *Sarah and Dominique are enjoying their stay in St Malo. As well as places to visit, they discuss the restaurants and places where they can have meals.*

Listen to the recording and answer the question.

a What does Dominique suggest they do for lunch? _____

Dominique   *Où est-ce qu'on mange ce midi? On fait un pique-nique?*

Sarah   *Non! Il ne fait pas assez beau. En fait on dirait qu'il va pleuvoir.*

Dominique   *Oui je pense que tu as raison. Alors qu'est-ce qu'on fait? On prend quelque chose de rapide dans une brasserie ou bien dans une crêperie? Qu'est-ce que tu en dis?*

Sarah   *Euh… J'ai envie de manger des moules avec des frites.*

Dominique   *Bonne idée! Tiens, regarde, il y a un petit restaurant de l'autre côté de la rue: repas express, moules-frites plus un verre de vin 10,50 € tout compris.*

Sarah   *C'est parfait. On y va!*

b Now listen again or read to answer the questions.

1 Dominique sees a small restaurant. Where is it?_____

2 How much would they have to pay for mussels, chips and a glass of wine? _____

2 The following statement contains new vocabulary which is essential for slightly more complex conversations. Notice the key words in New expressions, learn them and then read the text.

Reading 1

a Read the text and answer the questions

1 What national trait is mentioned here? _____

2 When is this particular trait mostly evident? _____

> En général les Français sont très chauvins, c'est-à-dire qu'ils font souvent preuve de chauvinisme, surtout lorsqu'il s'agit de ce qu'il y a de plus important: la cuisine française. Pour beaucoup de Français, c'est la meilleure cuisine du monde.

b 10.04 Now listen to the recording. Three people are arguing about the best cooking in the world. What do they say?

1 How many think that French cooking is best? _____

2 What is best about it? _____

3 What other countries are mentioned as possible contenders? _____

4 How many speakers think that the whole issue is a matter of taste? _____

Reading 2

Read this passage – you will understand it all! Then answer the question.

a What do French people like? _____

> Les Français aiment manger. Ils aiment la bonne nourriture et les bons repas. Toute occasion est bonne pour faire un repas de famille ou un repas entre amis: un baptême, une communion ou une confirmation, un mariage, un résultat d'examen, un anniversaire, et évidemment Noël et surtout le premier janvier.
>
> Le midi les Français mangent à la cantine, à la cafétéria, au restaurant ou bien chez eux s'ils habitent près de leur lieu de travail.

Les repas	Les moments de la journée
Le petit déjeuner	Le matin
Le déjeuner	À midi, entre midi et deux heures
Le goûter	L'après-midi (surtout pour les enfants)
Le dîner	Le soir, vers sept, huit heures
Le souper	Plus tard le soir (repas assez léger)

b **Now read the passage again and study the table to answer the questions.**

1 Name at least six occasions that are particularly good pretexts for a family meal or a meal with friends. _____

2 At what time are French people likely to have dinner in the evening? _____

3 Who is **le goûter** mainly for? _____

4 What is the difference between **le dîner** and **le souper**? _____

5 Where do French people eat at midday? _____

Language discovery

1 **Link the following English phrases to the equivalent French expressions from Conversation 1.**

a In fact it looks as if it is going to rain.

b What do you say to that?

c The weather is not good enough.

d Where are we going to eat this lunch time?

e Shall we have a quick meal?

f Ten euros 50 centimes all included.

g I think you are right.

h I fancy eating mussels with chips.

1 Il ne fait pas assez beau.

2 On prend un petit repas rapide?

3 J'ai envie de manger des moules avec des frites.

4 Je pense que tu as raison.

5 Qu'est-ce que tu en dis?

6 Où est-ce qu'on mange ce midi?

7 En fait on dirait qu'il va pleuvoir.

8 10,50 € tout compris.

2 **Which French expression means** *feel like (doing something)* **in these sentences:**

a Sophie a envie d'aller à la mer.

b Vous avez envie de manger des moules?

Learn more

1 EXPRESSING AN OPINION AND SEEKING AN OPINION FROM SOMEONE

To express an opinion you can use **penser** *(to think)* or **croire** *(to believe)*.

Expressing an opinion	
Je pense que / Je crois que	*I think / I believe that...*
Je pense que oui.	*I think so.*
Je crois qu'il est malade.	*I believe he's ill.*

To seek an opinion you can use **penser** and **dire** *to say*:

Seeking an opinion	
Qu'est-ce que tu en* penses?	*What do you think (of it)?*
Qu'est ce que tu en* dis?	*What do you say (about it)?*

*Note: En is a pronoun that replaces whatever has just been said or suggested.

When addressing someone more formally, you will use similar expressions with **vous**.

Qu'est-ce que vous en pensez?

Qu'est-ce que vous en dites?

2 HELPFUL EXPRESSIONS WITH AVOIR, MIEUX / MEILLEUR, AND GOÛTER

Avoir envie de + *verb in the infinitive ... – (I feel like...)*

This is a handy key expression to use in everyday conversation.

> **J'ai envie de rire.** (*laugh*)
>
> **Il a toujours** (*always*) **envie de sortir.** (*go out*)
>
> **Elle a envie de dormir.** (*sleep*)
>
> **Ils ont envie d'aller au théâtre.** (*go to ...*)
>
> **J'ai envie de rester chez moi et de lire un bon livre.** (*stay at home + read*)

Mieux / meilleur – *(best / better)*

In these expressions, mieux is an adverb while meilleur can be an adjective, an adverb or a noun.

J'aime mieux la bière.	*I like beer best.*
Ces pommes sont meilleures.	*These apples are better.*
La viande? C'est meilleur avec du vin rouge.	*Meat? It's better with red wine.*
Beaucoup de gens pensent que les bières d'Alsace sont les meilleures du monde.	*Lots of people think that Alsace beers are the best in the world.*

Goûter

Goûter is both a verb and a noun.

> **le goûter**   (a noun, *taste*)
>
> **goûter**   (a verb, *to taste*)

It can be used in expressions such as the following:

Goûtez mon gâteau, vous m'en donnerez des nouvelles! *Do taste my cake and let me know what you think!*

Alors, il a bon goût, mon gâteau? *So, does it taste good, my cake?*

Pouah! C'est dégoûtant! *Yuck! It's disgusting!*

Practice

1 La dégustation de vin – *Two friends are attending a wine tasting. They are discussing their tastes with an exhibitor.*

Match the questions and answers.

a Qu'est-ce que vous pensez de ce vin, Monsieur?
b Vous croyez qu'il est un peu jeune?
c Et toi Pierre, qu'est-ce que tu en penses?
d Tu aimes mieux les bières belges?
e Il y a une réduction sur le vin aujourd'hui. Ça vous intéresse?

1 Oh moi tu sais... J'aime mieux la bière!
2 Alors je vais en prendre six bouteilles. J'ai envie d'en garder pour Noël.
3 Je le trouve bon.
4 Oui, ce sont les meilleures bières du monde.
5 Non, je ne pense pas. En tout cas vous avez les meilleurs vins de la région.

READING

Look at the advert for a farm in the heart of Brittany – La Ferme des Monts – near an ancient site called La Roche aux fées (Fairies' Rock). Read the text and answer the questions.

RESTAURATION
ILLE-ET-VILAINE

Contact	Descriptif
Jacques RUPIN Les Monts 35150 PIRE SUR SEICHE Tél. 02 97 37 55 92	Au pays de la Roche aux fées, près d l'axe Rennes-Angers, venez visiter les vergers de la ferme des Monts. Vous pourrez découvrir la fabrication traditionnelle du cidre, voir la cave et le matériel utilisé hier et aujourd'hui. Ensuite vous goûterez au jus de pomme, au cidre, aux crêpes et gâteaux maison accompagnés de confitures ou gelées. Vente directe sur place. Ouvert tous les après-midis sur réservation du 1/05 ou 15/09. Hors saison: ouvert sur RDV. Possibilité de recevoir des groupes.

a Name two things you could see or visit at the farm. _____

b What could you drink? _____

c What could you eat with the home-made cakes? _____

d When is the farm open for **le goûter**? _____

e What would you need to do before going there? _____

Go further

1 Look at the following adverts and write the number(s) of the possible places that best fit your requirements. (You can have more than one for each question.)

BAR - LOTO- PMU
4, place de la République - PONT-CROIX
Pizza à emporter ①
non stop, midi à 21 h 30
02 98 70 41 41

②

■ Pleuven :
Au Moulin-du-Pont, ***crêperie « Chez Mimi »***, sur la route des plages Bénodet-Fouesnant. Crêpes traditionnelles, spécialités glaces. Ouverte tous les jours sauf dimanche midi. Recommandée par le Guide du routard. **Tél. 02.98.54.62.02 - fax 02.98.54.69.91**

Crêperie de Pen al Lenn
dans un vieux moulin
avec terrasse couverte côté jardin
sur la route de la Forêt-Fouesnant
Fouesnant - ☏ 02.98.56.08.80

OUVERTE ③
TOUS LES JOURS
en juillet-août
Service continu
de 11 h à 23 h

⑦

Vue panoramique

RESTAURANT
LE SAINT-EVETTE
face à l'embarquadère de l'île de sein

Port de Ste.-Evette - ESQUIBIEN
Tél. 02 98 70 10 29

a You wish to eat seafood. _____
b You would like a meal to take away. _____
c You would like a pancake meal. _____
d You would like a restaurant with a sea view. _____
e You are waiting for the boat to **Ile de Sein**. _____
f You would like a restaurant open every day until late in the summer. _____
g You would like a North African meal. _____

 2 10.05 **Your friend Michel would like to go to the seafood supper at Plovan. Look back at advertisement 6 and listen to the prompts to answer his questions.**

Test yourself

1 **Put the meals in chronological order:**

   a dîner _____

   b déjeuner _____

   c petit déjeuner _____

   d souper _____

   e goûter _____

2 **Complete the sentences with the appropriate word from the box.**

> meilleures   meilleur   goût   dégoûtant   mieux

   a C'est le _____ restaurant de la région.

   b Il est bon ton dessert? Le mien a _____ de vanille.

   c On dit que les bières belges sont les _____. Qu'en pensez-vous?

   d Je n'aime pas la moutarde. C'est _____!

   e Moi, j'aime _____ la cuisine italienne.

2 **How do you say ?**

   a Bordeaux wine is better.

   b There is a reduction if you take six of them.

   c I am thirsty!

   d I feel like drinking a nice Belgian beer.

SELF CHECK

I CAN. . .
. . . talk about eating out.
. . . express an opinion.
. . . understand the French attitude towards food.

11 La pluie et le beau temps!

Rain and shine!

In this unit you will learn how to:
▶ *talk about the weather.*
▶ *talk about the regions of France.*
▶ *express the present and future.*
▶ *understand weather reports on the radio and in the newspaper.*

CEFR: *Can catch the main point in short, clear, simple messages (A2); Can identify the main points of news items, where visual supports the commentary (A2); Can scan longer text to locate information (B1).*

Rain and shine

Le temps (*the weather*) is **un sujet de conversation** (*topic of conversation*) **quotidien** (*daily*) **pour les français** (*for the French*). Not only do people talk about the weather where they are, but about how shocking or how good the weather is in other parts of France: **il pleut toujours en Bretagne** (*it always rains in Brittany*), **il fait toujours beau sur la Côte Méditerranéenne** (*it's always nice on the Mediterranean coast*) et **il n'y a <u>jamais assez</u> de neige en montagne** (*there is <u>never enough</u> snow on the mountains*) **pour les sports d'hiver. Les prévisions météorologiques** (*the weather forecast*), is referred to as **la météo** and often blamed for its lack of accuracy.

a   **What is the word for daily?**
b   **What is the name commonly used for the weather forecast?**

Vocabulary builder

DIRECTIONS

 11.01 Look at the compass points and number the directions in the order you hear them.

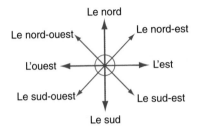

Le nord

Le nord-ouest — Le nord-est

L'ouest — L'est

Le sud-ouest — Le sud-est

Le sud

WEATHER PROVERBS

 11.02 Read the English proverbs and choose the correct French translation. Then listen to check your answers.

a In April do not remove a thread, but in May wear what you will.
1 *Une hirondelle ne fait pas le printemps.*
2 *En avril n'ôte pas un fil, mais en mai mets ce qu'il te plaît.*

b Christmas on the balcony, Easter by the fireplace.
1 *Noël au balcon, Pâques aux tisons.*
2 *S'il pleut à la St Médard il pleuvra pendant quarante jours.*

c In stormy weather the swallow goes up into the clouds.
1 *Par temps d'orage l'hirondelle monte aux nuages.*
2 *Une hirondelle ne fait pas le printemps.*

d A swallow doesn't make it spring.
1 *Hirondelle volant haut le temps sera beau, hirondelle volant bas pluie il y aura.*
2 *Une hirondelle ne fait pas le printemps.*

e If it rains on St. Medard's Day (8 June) it will rain for the next 40 days.
1 *S'il pleut à la St Médard il pleuvra pendant quarante jours.*
2 *Il ne fait jamais mauvais temps pour aller à Paris.*

f If the swallow flies high the weather will be fine, if it flies low there will be rain.

1 *Par temps d'orage l'hirondelle monte aux nuages.*
2 *Hirondelle volant haut le temps sera beau, hirondelle volant bas pluie il y aura.*

g Bad weather is never an excuse not to go to Paris.

1 *Après la pluie, le beau temps!*
2 *Il ne fait jamais mauvais temps pour aller à Paris.*

h After the rain comes good weather./Every cloud has a silver lining.

1 *Après la pluie, le beau temps!*
2 *Noël au balcon, Pâques aux tisons.*

NEW EXPRESSIONS

Look at the expressions that are used in the next conversation. Note their meanings.

le temps	*weather (in the text above) but also time*
le temps est lourd	*the weather is close/muggy*
le ciel	*the sky*
une goutte de pluie	*a raindrop*
les prévisions météo-rologiques/la météo	*weather forecast*
la mi-journée	*midday/lunchtime*
au-dessus	*above*
au-dessous	*below*
pareil	*the same*
prévoir	*to forecast/plan*
comme prévu	*as planned*
mon copain	*my friend/boyfriend*
ma copine	*my friend/girlfriend*

Conversation

11.03 **Sarah et Dominique sont dans leur voiture. Elles vont visiter Dinan, une cité médiévale sur la Rance. Elles parlent de la pluie et du beau temps. Listen to the audio and answer the question.**

a When is it likely going to rain? _____

Dominique	Tu as raison, le temps change...il fait lourd, il va faire de l'orage!
Sarah	Oui, le ciel est couvert. En tout cas il va certainement pleuvoir cet après-midi.
Dominique	Ah oui, voilà les premières gouttes de pluie.
Sarah	Écoutons les prévisions météorologiques.
(Elles écoutent France Inter)	
	...et pour les jours suivants le temps lourd va persister. Il fera encore chaud et ensoleillé. L'évolution orageuse sera plus marquée sur les Pyrénées, les Alpes et sur la Corse. Dans l'ensemble de la France les températures resteront cinq degrés au-dessus des températures de saison. C'était notre bulletin météorologique de la mi-journée. Vous pourrez écouter notre prochain bulletin sur France Inter à seize heures cinquante-cinq. Et voici maintenant notre bulletin d'informations de treize heures...
Dominique	Alors c'est partout pareil en France.
Sarah	Qu'est-ce qu'on fait demain? On va dans le Finistère comme prévu?
Dominique	Oui d'accord, et après cela on commencera à descendre vers Bordeaux en passant par chez moi à St Nazaire et chez mon copain à Nantes.

b **Now listen again to answer the questions.**

1 Why do they turn the radio on? _____

2 The weather forecast mentions storms for at least three French regions. Can you name any of them? _____

c **Now reread the conversation and choose the correct letters to complete the sentences.**

1 The temperatures over France will ...

    a go up.   **b** go down.   **c** be higher than the seasonal norm.

2 The forecast is for ...

   a today only.   **b** tomorrow only.   **c** the next few days.

3 The weather bulletin was ...

   a at 6 a.m.   **b** just before the   **c** at 4.55 p.m.
                            1 o'clock news.

4 Tomorrow Dominique and Sarah ...

   a plan to stay   **b** move on to   **c** get to Bordeaux.
      in St Malo.   Finistère.

5 On their way to Bordeaux they will ...

   a visit Paris.   **b** stop on the way **c** stop to see
                   in St Nazaire.   Dominique's
                                  boyfriend.

 Language discovery

Look at the conversation and complete the sentences:

a Il _____ lourd.

b Il _____ de l'orage!

Look carefully at the verb combinations. What word changes the expression from *It is...* to *It's going to...?*

Learn more

1 QUEL TEMPS FAIT-IL AUJOURD'HUI? *(WHAT IS THE WEATHER LIKE TODAY?)*

French people tend to spend a lot of time talking about the weather. To discuss today's weather they use the present tense and the following structures:

Il fait ...	It is...
beau	*nice*
chaud	*hot*
froid	*cold*
lourd	*muggy*
du soleil	*sunny*
du vent	*windy*
du brouillard	*foggy*
de l'orage	*stormy*

Le temps est....	The weather is...
ensoleillé	*sunny*
nuageux	*cloudy*
brumeux	*misty*
pluvieux	*rainy*
orageux	*stormy*
couvert	*overcast*
Il y a...	There is/are ...
du vent	*wind*
des nuages	*clouds*
de la pluie	*rain*
de la neige	*snow*
General	
Il pleut.	*It's raining.*
Il neige.	*It's snowing.*

2   QUEL TEMPS FERA-T-IL DEMAIN? *(WHAT WILL THE WEATHER BE LIKE TOMORROW?)*

In conversational French you are likely to hear people using the immediate future: **il va** + infinitive to talk about weather.

▶ **Il va faire beau.**
▶ **Il va pleuvoir.** *It's going to rain.*
▶ **Il va faire de l'orage.** *It's going to storm.*

But in more formal situations (forecasts on the radio, TV or newspapers) the verbs are mainly in the future tense.

▶ **Il <u>fera</u> beau.** (**faire** in the future tense)
▶ **Le temps <u>sera</u> orageux.** (**être** in the future tense)
▶ **Le vent <u>soufflera</u>.** *The wind will blow.* (**souffler** in the future tense)
▶ **Il y <u>aura</u>...** (**avoir** in the future tense)
  ▷ **Il y aura des <u>averses</u>.** *(showers)*
  ▷ **Il y aura des <u>éclaircies</u>.** *(bright periods)*
  ▷ **Il y aura de la <u>brume</u>.** *(mist)*
▶ **Il <u>pleuvra</u>.** *It will rain.*
▶ **Il <u>neigera</u>.** *It will snow.*

3 THE FUTURE TENSE

Forming the future tense is simple for most verbs ending with **-er** or **-ir**. Remember the rules below.

▶ When the subject is **il/elle** (*he/she/it*) use the verb (in the infinitive) + ending **-a**:

Le soleil <u>brillera</u>. *The sun will shine.* **(briller + -a)**

▶ When the subject is **ils /elles** (*they*) use the verb (in the infinitive) + ending **-ont**:

Les températures <u>avoisineront</u> les 30 degrés. *Temperatures will be close to 30 degrees.* **(avoisiner + ont)**

▶ Whatever the verb, the endings for the future tense are always the same:

Future tense verb endings			
je	-rai	nous	-rons
tu	-ras	vous	-rez
il	-ra	elles	-ront

4 EN, DANS AND SUR

▶ The preposition **en** is usually used in front of the name of a region or province:

en Bretagne *(in Brittany)*

▶ The preposition **dans** is used in front of a geographical area:

dans le nord-est *(in the north-east)*

▶ The preposition **sur** is used in association with the name of a region mainly with reference to the weather:

sur la Bretagne et la Normandie *(over Brittany and Normandy)*

Practice

PRONUNCIATION

11.04 **Read the pronunciation rules then listen and repeat the bolded words.**

▶ **le sud:** You can hear the **d** at the end of the word but in **le nord** the **d** is dropped.

▶ **le sud-est / le sud-ouest**: Both are pronounced linking the two words. The **-t** at the end of **est** and **ouest** is also pronounced: [**le sudest/le sudouest**].

▶ **le nord-est / le nord-ouest**: Both are pronounced linking the two words but dropping the -d at the end of **nord**. [**le norest / le norouest**]

LISTENING

1 11.05 **Listen to the recording and look at the list of cities and their weather conditions.**

Le temps en villes

Alger Mini 19 Maxi 33	**Dublin** Mini 15 Maxi 21	**Londres** Mini 14 Maxi 26	**Oslo** Mini 12 Maxi 23	**Rome** Mini 20 Maxi 31

Athènes Mini 21 Maxi 29	**Genève** Mini 7 Maxi 12	**Madrid** Mini 20 Maxi 31	**Paris** Mini 18 Maxi 30	**Varsovie** Mini 17 Maxi 25

Now say where the following French people are spending their holidays.

Exemple: 'Bonjour, je m'appelle Étienne. La ville où je suis est ensoleillée et la température est entre 18 et 30 degrés.'

Réponse: Étienne est à Paris.

    a Fabienne est _____.

    b Jérôme est _____.

    c Stéphanie est _____.

    d Alexandre est _____.

2 **Say what the weather is like in the towns where you are spending your holiday.**

    a Vous êtes à Varsovie. Quel temps fait-il? _____

    b Vous êtes à Madrid. Quel temps fait-il? _____

READING

1 11.06 **Look at the weather map. Then listen and read the text. Write where you can find the following weather conditions for the day (in some cases it applies to more than one area).**

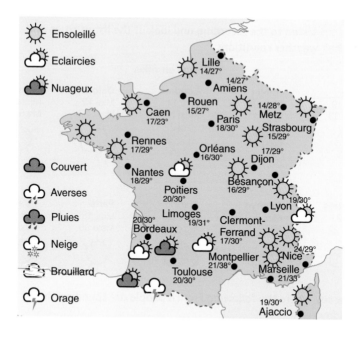

Ensoleillé

Eclaircies

Nuageux

Couvert

Averses

Pluies

Neige

Brouillard

Orage

Lille
14/27°

Amiens
14/27°

Caen
17/23°

Rouen
15/27°

Paris
18/30°

Metz
14/28°

Strasbourg
15/29°

Rennes
17/29°

Orléans
16/30°

Dijon
17/29°

Nantes
18/29°

Besançon
16/29°

Poitiers
20/30°

Lyon
19/30°

Limoges
19/31°

Bordeaux
20/30°

Clermont-
Ferrand
17/30°

Montpellier
21/38°

Nice
24/29°

Toulouse
20/30°

Marseille
21/33°

Ajaccio
19/30°

LE TEMPS AUJOURD'HUI, REGION PAR REGION

Bretagne, Pays de la Loire, Normandie. Sur la Bretagne et la Normandie, le soleil brillera largement toute la journée. Sur les Pays de la Loire, le soleil sera bien présent, mais le ciel se voilera dans l'après-midi. Il fera chaud, entre 24 et 30° du nord au sud.

Nord-Picardie, Ile-de-France. Après quelques brumes matinales, le soleil s'imposera largement. Un léger vent de nord-est soufflera. Le thermomètre indiquera entre 26 et 30° du nord au sud.

Nord-Est, Bourgogne, Franche-Comté. Le temps sera chaud et bien ensoleillé. Les températures avoisineront les 30° soit 5 degrés au-dessus des températures de saison.

Poitou-Charentes, Centre, Limousin. La matinée sera bien ensoleillée mais le temps deviendra lourd et des ondées parfois orageuses se produiront sur Poitou-Charentes et sur le Limousin. Le thermomètre atteindra souvent les 30°.

Aquitaine, Midi-Pyrénées. Dans la matinée, le temps deviendra lourd. Des ondées orageuses se produiront l'après-midi et des orages éclateront sur les Pyrénées dès la mi-journée. Les températures seront comprises entre 27 et 31°.

Auvergne, Rhône-Alpes. En Auvergne, le temps deviendra lourd l'après-midi avec des risques d'ondées orageuses. Sur Rhône-Alpes, le temps sera ensoleillé. Des nuages se développeront sur les Alpes et quelques orages isolés éclateront. Le thermomètre indiquera entre 27 et 31°.

Pourtour méditerranéen, Corse. Sur le Languedoc-Roussillon, la matinée sera assez ensoleillée mais le temps deviendra lourd l'après-midi avec des ondées orageuses. Ailleurs, le soleil brillera largement. Il fera chaud entre 30° sur les côtes et 35° dans l'intérieur.

a Thunderstorms from midday onwards _____

b Sunny all day _____

c Muggy in the afternoon _____

d Morning mist _____

e A light north-east wind _____

f Temperatures ranging from 30° on the coast to 35° inland _____

g Temperatures 5° above the seasonal norm _____

h Cloudy (veiled) sky in the afternoon _____

2 Using the map and the text for information choose the correct statement about what the weather will be like in the various parts of France:

a A Rennes, en Bretagne ...

   1 le ciel sera ensoleillé toute la journée.

   2 les températures maximales seront comprises entre 30 et 33°.

b En Corse, à Ajaccio ...

   1 le soleil brillera largement et il fera chaud.

   2 le temps sera lourd et il y aura des orages.

c A Besançon, en Franche-Comté...

   1 le ciel sera nuageux.

   2 les températures seront 5° au-dessus des températures de saison.

d A Strasbourg, dans le Nord-Est ...

   1 il pleuvra toute la journée.

   2 le temps sera chaud et les températures avoisineront 30°.

e A Toulouse, dans le Midi-Pyrénées...

   1 le temps deviendra lourd et il y aura des orages.

   2 le thermomètre indiquera 35° dans la matinée.

f A Poitiers, en Poitou-Charentes...

   1 les températures minimales seront de 30°.

   2 la matinée sera ensoleillée.

g Dans la région Rhône-Alpes ...

   1 il neigera dans la matinée à Lyon.

   2 il y aura quelques orages isolés sur les Alpes.

Test yourself

For each time frame (part of day, day of the week, season etc.), choose the correct answer to say what the weather is or what it will be. For general weather conditions, use the present tense. Follow the indications in brackets for guidance.

1 Aujourd'hui *(now)*
   a il fera beau.
   b il fait du vent.

2 Généralement en août
   a il va pleuvoir.
   b il fait beau et chaud.

3 Demain matin *(immediate future)*
   a il fera du brouillard.
   b il pleut.

4 L'hiver prochain *(future)*
   a Le temps est brumeux.
   b il fera très froid.

5 Ce matin *(now)*
   a il neige.
   b le ciel sera nuageux.

6 Cet après-midi *(immediate future)*
   a il fait du vent.
   b il va faire de l'orage.

7 En ce moment
   a il va faire chaud.
   b le temps est pluvieux.

8 Généralement à Noël
   a le ciel sera nuageux.
   b il fait froid.

9 Après-demain
   a Le ciel est couvert.
   b il fera chaud

10 Demain soir
   a l y aura des orages
   b il fait du vent.

11 En fin de semaine
   a le soleil brille.
   b il va pleuvoir.

12 A présent
   a Il y a une belle éclaircie.
   b il y aura des averses.

SELF CHECK

I CAN. . .

○ . . . talk about the weather.

○ . . . understand weather reports.

○ . . . understand more about the regions in France.

○ . . . express information about the present and future.

Au restaurant
At the restaurant

In this unit you will learn how to:
▶ *order a drink in a café.*
▶ *read a menu in a restaurant and order a meal.*
▶ *recognize the past tense and express information about the recent past.*

CEFR: *Can order a meal (A2); Can write short simple notes relating to immediate needs (A2); Can write about past events (A2); Can understand phrases and high frequency vocabulary (A2).*

🔘 French cafés

French **cafés**, **bars**, **bistrots** or **brasseries** are all drinking places, but they are only remotely the equivalent of an English or Irish pub. When you enter a French café you may notice there are two different styles of customers, those **accoudés au comptoir** (*elbow resting on the bar*), who are likely to be **les habitués** (*the regulars*), et **les autres** (*the others*), **assis à l'intérieur** (*seated inside*) **du café ou à la terrasse** (*or on the terrace*). **Les fumeurs** (*smokers*) sit on the terrace. **Les habitués** do not need to order, **le Patron** (*the owner*) is likely to say **"Comme d'habitude?"** (*the usual?*) or even serve them as they arrive for **l'apéro** (*short for* **apéritif**). There is no need for **un pourboire** (*a tip*) if you drink at the bar.

L'addition (*the bill*) will be brought with your drink and in busy cafés you may be asked to pay on the spot. You may leave **un pourboire**, but **ce n'est pas obligatoire** (*it is not compulsory*).

a   What is the word for the landlord?
b   You enter a Paris bar for the first time. Are you un habitué?
c   Who usually sits à la terrasse?

Vocabulary builder

RESTAURANT EXPRESSIONS

12.01 **Look at the restaurant expressions. Then listen and repeat as you match them to the English translations.**

a	le menu _____	**1**	*cheese*
b	Prenez votre temps! _____	**2**	*a starter*
c	A la carte ou menu à prix fixe _____	**3**	*a main course*
d	une entrée / un hors d'œuvre _____	**4**	*the bill*
e	un plat principal _____	**5**	*Take your time!*
f	de la viande _____	**6**	*vegetarian*
g	du poisson _____	**7**	*fish*
h	du fromage _____	**8**	*service is included*
i	un dessert _____	**9**	*dessert*
j	végétarien / végétarienne _____	**10**	*the menu*
k	l'addition _____	**11**	*meat*
l	le service est compris _____	**12**	*individual courses or fixed price*
m	le repas	**13**	*meal*

NEW EXPRESSIONS

Look at the expressions that are used in the next conversations. Note their meanings.

Conversation 1

une bière	*a beer*
un panaché	*a shandy*
une glace	*an ice cream*
l'addition	*the bill*
le pourboire	*the tip*
conduire	*to drive*
quelques minutes	*a few minutes*
plus tard	*later*
être au régime	*to be on a diet*
cette fois-ci	*this time*
tout de suite	*right away*
apporter	*to bring*

Conversation 2

la fenêtre	*the window*
convenir	*to suit*
une bouteille	*a bottle*
Je suis désolée.	*I am sorry.*
Cela vous convient?	*Does it suit you?*

Conversations

 1 **Read the paragraph about what Dominique and Sarah are doing now and answer the questions.**

> *C'est le mois de juillet. Nos deux amies, Dominique et Sarah, ont passé le week-end à Quimper pour les Fêtes de Cornouaille. Aujourd'hui elles viennent de visiter des chapelles dans le Pays Bigouden. Maintenant elles sont assises à la terrasse d'un café, Place de l'Église, à Plonéour-Lanvern. Il fait chaud et elles ont très soif.*

1 **The month is:**
   a June   **b** July   **c** January

2 **Our two friends have spent the weekend ...**
   a in Cornwall.   **b** in St Malo.   **c** in Quimper.

3 **They have just visited ...**
   a some chapels.   **b** some castles.   **c** some churches.

4 **They are now ...**
   a in the church.   **b** in a restaurant.   **c** sitting at the terrace of a café.

5 **The weather is ...**
   a muggy and they are tired.   **b** hot and they are very thirsty.   **c** cold.

2 12.02 **Listen to their conversation and answer the question.**

   a Do both women order the same drink?

Conversation 1

Serveur	Bonjour mesdames, qu'est ce que je vous sers?
Sarah	Alors pour moi une bière pression...et toi Dominique?
Dominique	Euh je conduis alors je vais prendre un panaché.
Serveur	Alors une bière pression et un panaché.
Sarah	Et nous allons prendre des glaces aussi?
Serveur	Tout de suite madame, je vous apporte la carte.

(Quelques minutes plus tard)

Sarah	Tu prends une glace Dominique?
Dominique	Non, je suis au régime!
Sarah	Eh bien prends un sorbet; il y a moins de calories.
Serveur	Vous avez choisi?
Sarah	Oui, alors une glace à la fraise et un sorbet au citron. Et l'addition s'il vous plaît.

(Un peu plus tard)

Dominique	C'est moi qui paie cette fois-ci, toi tu as payé la dernière fois! C'est combien l'addition?
Sarah	Ça fait neuf euros cinquante.
Dominique	Dix avec le pourboire.

---

   b Now listen again or read to answer the questions.

   1 Does Sarah order anything else?
   2 Why is Dominique concerned about having more than a drink?
   3 Who asks for the bill?
   4 Who is going to pay? Why?
   5 How much is the bill? Do they leave a tip?

3 12.03 **Didier et Véronique Morin et leurs deux enfants, Armelle et Fabien, passent la nuit à l'Hôtel des Voyageurs. Ils ont décidé de dîner au restaurant de l'hôtel. Listen once to the recording, then answer the question.**

a What seating arrangement does the waitress offer the family?

Conversation 2

Serveuse	Bonsoir Monsieur-dame. J'ai une table pour quatre près de la fenêtre, est-ce que cela vous convient?
Didier	Oui, très bien.
Serveuse	Vous désirez prendre un apéritif?
Didier	Non non, apportez-nous le menu s'il vous plaît.
Serveuse	Vous voulez le menu à la carte?
Didier	Non, nous prendrons des menus à prix fixes. Vous avez un menu pour enfants?
Serveuse	Oui monsieur. Je vous apporte la carte des vins?
Véro	Oui merci.

(Quelques minutes plus tard)

Serveuse	Monsieur-dame vous avez choisi?
Véro	Alors nous allons prendre un menu à 10 €, un menu à 20 €, deux menus pour enfants et une bouteille de Muscadet s'il vous plaît.
Serveuse	Je suis désolée madame mais le menu à 10 € est pour midi seulement.
Véro	Pas de problème, nous prendrons deux menus à 20 € .

b **Now listen again or read to answer the questions.**

1 Do they wish to have an aperitif? _____
2 Apart from fixed price menus, what kind of menu do they ask for? _____
3 Would they like to see the wine list? _____
4 Véro asked for a 10 € menu. Why does the waitress say that she cannot serve it? _____
5 What do they order? _____

Language discovery

1 **Read Conversation 1 and find the French expressions which mean:**

  a *I'll bring you the menu.* _____

  b *Have a sorbet; it's got fewer calories.* _____

  c *A strawberry ice cream and a lemon sorbet.* _____

  d *You paid last time.* _____

  k *a few minutes later* _____

  l *a short while later* _____

Learn more

1 TALKING ABOUT PAST EVENTS

Venir on its own means *to come.* For example:

Venez-vous souvent ici?   *Do you come here often?*

Venir de… indicates that something has just happened or has just been done. To say something has just happened, use **venir** in the present tense + **de** + verb (in the infinitive).

Elles <u>viennent de visiter</u> des chapelles.   *They <u>have just visited</u> some chapels.*

Le bateau <u>vient d'arriver</u> au port. *The boat <u>has just arrived</u> in the port.*

Tu <u>viens de rencontrer</u> le président. *You<u>'ve just met</u> the president.*

The related words **venir** (*to come*), **venir de** (*to have just*), **revenir** (*to come back*), **l'avenir** (*the future*) can also be quite useful.

Viens ici mon Toutou!   *Come here, my doggy!*

Je viens de déjeuner.   *I've just had lunch.*

Je reviens dans cinq minutes.   *I'll be back in 5 minutes.*

À l'avenir tu feras la cuisine!   *In the future you'll do the cooking!*

2 HOW TO FORM THE PERFECT TENSE

The perfect tense is formed with **avoir** or **être** in the present tense + another verb: **j'ai choisi** (*I chose*). **Avoir** and **être** are called auxiliary verbs when they are used in this way. The verb which indicates the event or action which has been completed is in a form called a past participle.

For example, when Jean-Paul discovers that he has won the jackpot he says:

J'ai <u>gagné</u> le gros lot.

Gagné is the past participle of the verb **gagner** *to win*. Verbs which end with **-er** and those which end with **-ir** are very easy to use in past perfect. All verbs ending with **-er** in their basic form (infinitive) have a past participle ending with **-é**. All verbs ending with **-ir** have a past participle ending with **-i**.

-er and –ir verbs in the past perfect	
visiter → visit**é**	finir → fin**i**
passer → pass**é**	choisir → chois**i**
gagner → gagn**é**	servir → serv**i**
aller → all**é*** (though **aller** is used with **être**)	

> **INSIGHT: CULTURE**
>
> This tongue twister contains a verb in the past historic, a written formal and literary equivalent of the perfect tense. It's about the goddess Dido who was said to have dined off the fat backs of ten fat turkeys!
> **Didon dîna dit-on du dos dodu de dix dodus dindons.**

3 C'EST MOI QUI PAIE CETTE FOIS-CI. *(IT'S ME WHO IS PAYING THIS TIME.)*

In Conversation 1, Dominique could have said **Je paie cette fois** *(I am paying this time)* but for emphasis she said **C'est moi qui paie**. In English we would probably use our voice for emphasis, stressing *I'm* paying.

Moi and other pronouns used in conversation to emphasize what is being said can be referred to as emphatic pronouns. In some cases (**elle, nous, vous, elles**) they are the same as subject pronouns, but the masculine singular pronoun is **lui** and the masculine plural pronoun is **eux**:

Emphatic pronouns	
C'est <u>toi</u> qui as gagné?	*Is it <u>you</u> that won?*
C'est <u>lui</u> qui a choisi pas moi!	*He's the one that chose not <u>me</u>!*
C'est <u>elle</u> qui conduit!	*<u>She</u>'s driving!*
C'est <u>nous</u> qui avons visité la Corse.	*<u>We</u>'re the ones who've visited Corsica!*
C'est <u>vous</u> qui habitez à Marseille?	*Is it <u>you</u> that lives in Marseille?*
Ce sont <u>elles</u> qui ont passé l'été en Bretagne.	*<u>They</u>'re the ones who spent the summer in Britanny! (fem. pl.)*
Ce sont <u>eux</u> qui arriveront les premiers.	*It's <u>them</u> who will arrive first. (masc. pl.)*

Practice

1 **Match the words from all four columns to make six complete sentences. Columns A and C are in order; columns B and D are jumbled. Can you say what the full sentences mean?**

	A	B	C	D
1	Je	viennent	d'arriver	un bon film
2	Tu	venez	de finir	le gros lot au Loto
3	Jean-Paul	viens	de gagner	St Malo
4	Nous	vient	de visiter	à Paris
5	Vous	venons	de choisir	tes examens
6	Elles	viens	de voir	un menu

2 **Once again columns B and D have been jumbled. Can you make six correct sentences and say what they mean?**

	A	B	C	D
1	J'	avons	écouté	des moules-frites
2	Tu	ont	fini	les infos à la radio
3	On	avez	mangé	vos cartes postales
4	Nous	a	choisi	ton travail
5	Vous	ai	posté	une cabine
6	Sarah et Dominique	as	réservé	un hôtel pas trop cher

Go further

1 12.04 **Look at the four menus and listen to the recording. Note what Luc and Florence have ordered.**

	Menus (prix)	First course	Second	Cheese	Dessert
Luc	20€				
Florence					

Florence a commandé le menu à 45€. Elle _____

2 12.05 **Now it's your turn to place your order from the 25€ menu. Listen to take part in a conversation with the waitress.**

MENU À 20€

•

ASSIETTE DE FRUITS DE MER

PLATE OF SEAFOOD

OU

COQUILLE SAINT JACQUES À LA BRETONNE

SCALLOPS 'À LA BRETONNE'

BROCHETTE DE JOUE DE LOTTE À LA DIABLE

DEVIL MONKFISH KEBAB

OU

LE COQ AU VIN DU PATRON

COQ AU VIN SPECIAL

OU

CONTREFILET GRILLÉ MAÎTRE D'HÔTEL

GRILLED SIRLOIN STEAK MAÎTRE D'HÔTEL

SALADE DE SAISON

PLATEAU DE FROMAGES OU CHOIX DE DESSERTS

CHEESE PLATTER OR CHOICE OF DESSERTS

•

MENU À 25€

•

ASSIETTE DE FRUITS DE MER

PLATE OF SEAFOOD

OU

SALADE GOURMANDE AUX TROIS CANARDS

GOURMAND THREE DUCK SALAD

OU

6 HUITRES CHAUDES AVEC COCKTAIL D'ALGUES

6 OYSTERS SERVED HOT WITH SEAWEED COCKTAIL

BROCHETTE DE SAINT JACQUES AU BEURRE BLANC

GRILLED SCALLOP KEBAB IN BEURRE BLANC

OU

MAGRET DE CANARD AUX AIRELLES ET AU PORTO

MAGRET OF DUCK IN PORT AND BILBERRY

OU

CHÂTEAUBRIAND AUX CINQ POIVRES

STEAK CHÂTEAUBRIAND SEASONED WITH FIVE PEPPERS

PLATEAU DE FROMAGES

CHEESE PLATTER

CHOIX DE DESSERTS

CHOICE OF DESSERTS

•

MENU À 35€

•

PLATEAU DE FRUITS DE MER

SEAFOOD PLATTER

BROCHETTE DE SAINT JACQUES GRILLÉE, BEURRE BLANC

GRILLED SCALLOP KEBAB IN WHITE BUTTER

ROGNONS DE VEAU BEAUGE AUX MORILLES

VEAL KIDNEYS IN CREAM AND MORREL SAUCE

PLATEAU DE FROMAGES

CHEESE PLATTER

FRAISES MELBA

STRAWBERRY MELBA

•

MENU À 45€

•

PLATEAU DE FRUITS DE MER

SEAFOOD PLATTER

HOMARD BRETON À NOTRE FAÇON

BRETON LOBSTER; CHEF'S SPECIAL

PLATEAU DE FROMAGES

CHEESE PLATTER

DESSERT

CHOICE OF DESSERT

Test yourself

Une carte postale de la Martinique

Chère Sarah,

Je viens d'arriver à l'aéroport Aimé Césaire pour mon voyage de retour à Paris. Je n'ai pas trouvé une seule minute pour t'écrire depuis mon arrivée à la Martinique il y a trois semaines. Mon amie Josiane a pris des vacances pour me faire visiter son île et nous avons fait des choses fantastiques. Elle m'a présentée à toute sa famille, j'ai goûté à la délicieuse cuisine locale, j'ai appris à surfer, j'ai nagé pendant des heures, nous avons fait des balades en mer et je n'ai pas lu une seule ligne du livre que tu m'as prêté. Je le lirai dans l'avion de retour.

Bon, je finis cette carte car mon avion part dans quelques heures. Je te verrai sans doute la semaine prochaine.

Bisous et à bientôt

Claire

1 **Choose the correct answer to each of the questions.**

  a Where is Claire writing from?
    a) Paris   **b)** Fort-de-France   **c)** Josiane's house

  b Claire has been on the island for how long?
    a) 3 weeks   **b)** a fortnight   **c)** a month

  c How long has she been at the airport?
    a) a few hours   **b)** a short while   **c)** not even a minute

  d Who lent her the book she is intending to read in the plane?
    a) Sarah   **b)** Josiane   **c)** Josiane's family

  e What new skill did Claire learn while on holidays?
    a) cooking local dishes **b)** swimming   **c)** surfing

  f What didn't she find time to do?
    a) meeting Josiane's **b)** writing to Sarah   **c)** visiting the island
    family

2 **Read the postcard again and find a phrase meaning:**

  a I learnt to surf _____

  b I didn't read a single line _____

  c I swam for hours _____

  d I tasted local cooking _____

3 **Use what you have learnt and say the following:**

  a You lent me a book.

  b Josiane took 3 weeks of holidays.

  c I have just visited the island.

  d We swam every day.

  e I learnt how to cook.

SELF CHECK

I CAN. . .
○ . . . order a drink in a café.
○ . . . read a menu in a restaurant and order a meal.
○ . . . recognize the past tense and express information about the recent past.

Sur la route
On the road

In this unit you will learn how to:
▶ *talk about French roads and driving in France.*
▶ *communicate at a service station.*
▶ *use the pronouns* y *and* en.

CEFR: *Can deal with most situations likely to arise whilst traveling (B1); Can understand the main point of radio programs (B1); Can comprehend straight factual texts (B1); Can understand short official documents (B1); Can make his or her opinions and reactions understood (B1).*

Rules of the road

Roulez à droite! or **Conduisez à droite!** (*Drive on the right!*), **Serrez à droite!** (*Keep to the right!*), these are the imperative reminders that British motorists cannot avoid noticing as they drive into France. **N'oubliez pas de roulez à droite!** (*Don't forget to drive on the right!*)

You must also be aware of **priorité à droite** (*priority to the right*). Cars have to let vehicles coming from the right go first. This does not apply on **une route prioritaire** (*a main road*). However in small towns, street intersections often have **priorité à droite**. You may notice signs saying **Vous n'avez pas la priorité** (*you do not have priority*). Many **accidents de la route** (*road accidents*) are due to this particular rule being ignored.

L'éthylotest (*the breathaliser*) **est obligatoire** (*is compulsory*) **depuis le 1er juillet 2012**. Drivers must have breathalising equipment in their cars at all times.

 a **What does "depuis" mean in the text?**

Vocabulary builder

PARTS OF A CAR

 13.01 Look at the parts of the car and notice where they are on the vehicle. Then listen and repeat as you fill in the correct articles for each expression.

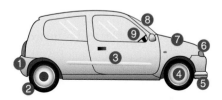

a	_____ coffre		*the boot*
b	_____ pneu		*the tyre*
c	_____ portière		*the door*
d	_____ roue avant		*the front wheel*
e	_____ parechoc		*the bumper*
f	_____ phares		*the headlights*
g	_____ moteur		*the engine*
h	_____ pare-brise		*the windscreen*
i	_____ volant		*the steering wheel*

DRIVING RULES

 13.02 Read the English expressions for the French driving rules. Then choose the correct translations. Listen to check your answers.

a   French speed limits

   1   Cent trente km/h sur les autoroutes sauf s'il pleut

   2   la limitation de vitesse sur les routes françaises

b 50 kph in towns except if some other limit is shown

  1 Cinquante kilomètres/heure dans les villes sauf si une autre limitation est indiquée

  2 Cent dix km/h sur les routes nationales à quatre voies

c 70 or 90 kph on other roads (according to signage)

  1 Soixante-dix ou quatre-vingt-dix km/h sur les autres routes (selon les indications)

  2 La limitation de vitesse sur les routes françaises

d 110 kph on dual carriageways

  1 Cent trente km/h sur les autoroutes sauf s'il pleut

  2 Cent dix km/h sur les routes nationales à quatre voies

e priority to the right

  1 conduisez à droite

  2 priorité à droite

f 130 kph on motorways except in rain

  1 Cinquante km/heure dans les villes sauf si une autre limitation est indiquée

  2 Cent trente km/h sur les autoroutes sauf s'il pleut

g drive on the right

  1 conduisez à droite

  2 priorité à droite

LES PRINCIPALES COULEURS

 13.03 **Match the French words for colours to the English translations. Then listen and check your answers as you repeat.**

a blanc/blanche	**1**	*pink*
b bleu/bleue	**2**	*black*
c noir/noire	**3**	*blue*
d vert/verte	**4**	*red*
e orange	**5**	*orange*
f rouge	**6**	*white*
g rose	**7**	*green*

> **INSIGHT: LANGUAGE**
> Words for colours can be nouns or adjectives. As adjectives, they change according to the gender (unless they end with an **-e**) and number of the noun they are linked to.

NEW EXPRESSIONS

Look at the expressions that are used in the next conversation. Note their meanings.

Zut!	*Drat! (mild expletive)*
en plus	*what's more*
de toute façon	*in any case*
tout de suite	*right here (immediately)*
il vaut mieux	*we'd better*
il faut...	*we must...*
il faut qu'on...	*it's necessary that we ...*
il n'y a presque plus de...	*there is hardly any ...*
gendarmes	*police*

Conversation

13.04 Sarah et Dominique sont en route pour St Nazaire où habite Dominique. Elles sont sur la RN (route nationale) 175. C'est Sarah qui conduit.

> # TRAVAUX SUR RN 175
> # ROUTE BARRÉE À 500M
> # RALENTISSEZ!

Listen to the recording once, then answer the question.

a What's happening on the road? _____

Dominique	Ah zut alors! Tu as vu le panneau? La route est barrée à cinq cents mètres.
Sarah	Oui, il y a une déviation.
Dominique	Il faut passer par Auray. Ralentis un peu. Sarah, regarde le panneau: Travaux. La vitesse limite est de cinquante kilomètres à l'heure. En plus il y a souvent des gendarmes sur cette route!
Sarah	De toute façon il faut qu'on s'arrête à la prochaine station service parce qu'il n'y a presque plus d'essence.

Dominique	Tiens, il y en a une à droite, ici, tout de suite. On devrait aussi vérifier le niveau d'huile et la pression des pneus tant que nous y sommes. Prends la première pompe, là, sans plomb.
Sarah	On fait le plein?
Dominique	Oui, il vaut mieux.

b **Now listen again or read to answer the questions.**
1 What is the speed limit? _____
2 Where are they going to stop next? _____
3 Is the place they are stopping at on the left or on the right? _____

 # Language discovery

1 **Link the English phrases to the equivalent French expressions.**

a *There is a diversion.*

b *Did you see the road sign?*

c *The road is closed in 500 metres.*

d *The speed limit is 50km/h.*

e *We'll have to stop.*

f *We ought to check the tyre pressure.*

g *Shall we fill up?*

h *Slow down a bit, Sarah!*

1 **On devrait vérifier la pression des pneus.**

2 **La vitesse limite est 50km à l'heure.**

3 **On fait le plein?**

4 **Ralentis un peu, Sarah!**

5 **Il y a une déviation.**

6 **Il va falloir s'arrêter.**

7 **La route est barrée à 500 mètres.**

8 **Tu as vu le panneau?**

2 **Which two sentences have a similar meaning? How is the other one different?**
a il faut s'arrêter.
b il va s'arrêter.
c il faut qu'on s'arrête.

Learn more

1 IL FAUT / IL FAUT QUE

The verb **falloir** *(to be necessary)* is only ever used in an impersonal form with subject pronoun **il**: **il faut**. People most often use **il faut** + verb in the infinitive.

Il faut + *verb in the infinitive (one needs to / must / should)*	
Il faut conduire à droite.	*You must drive on the right.*
Il faut se reposer souvent quand on conduit sur de grandes distances.	*You must rest often when driving long distances.*
Il faut manger pour vivre et non pas vivre pour manger.	*One should eat to live, and not live to eat.*
Faut* pas jouer les riches quand on n'a pas le sou (Jacques Brel).	*One mustn't play at being rich when one has no money.*
Faut* pas faire ça!	*Mustn't do that!*
Faut* travailler!	*Must work!*

* Note: In colloquial French, the **il** and the **il ne** are often dropped.

The difference is in the structure: **Il faut manger** *(it is necessary to eat ≈ one must eat)* **(it is necessary + verb in the infinitive).**

Il faut que je mange *(it is necessary that I eat)* **(it is necessary + que + verb in the present of subjunctive).** It is easy for **-er** verbs as in the singular form the present of subjunctive looks like the present tense of regular verbs. (You will learn more about the subjunctive in Unit 18.)

Il faut que + *verb in a present form*	
Il faut qu'on s'arrête à la prochaine station service.	*We have to stop at the next petrol station.*
Il faut que j'achète un litre d'huile.	*I have to buy a litre of oil.*

2 NE ... PLUS / NE ... PAS / NE ... QUE

Use these expressions for forming negative sentences. Use **ne** in front of a consonant and **n'** in front of a vowel.

Negative sentences with ne ... plus / ne ... pas / ne ... que	
Il n'y a plus / il ne reste plus d'essence.	*There is no petrol left.*
Il n'y a presque plus d'essence.	*There is hardly any petrol left.*
Il n'y a pas de station service sur cette route.	*There is no service station on this road.*
Il n'y a pas assez d'huile.	*There is not enough oil.*
Il n'y a que de l'essence super.	*There is only high-grade petrol.*
Il ne reste qu'un billet de vingt euros.	*There is only a 20 € note left.*

3 PRONOUNS Y AND EN

The word **y** *(here/there)* is used frequently in expressions like **il y a** *(there is/there are)*.

Tant que nous y sommes. *While we are about it. (Lit. here)*

The word **en** is used with expressions of quantity and replaces a word already mentioned.

Une station service? Il y en* a une sur la droite. *A service station? There is one on the right.*

Il ne reste plus de bonbons, j'en* achète? *There aren't any sweets left, shall I buy some?*

*Note: The word **en** replaces **une station service** and **bonbons**.

In French, the words **y** and **en** can also be used in negative sentences.

The words y and en *in negative sentences*	
Il reste du pain?	*Is there some bread left?*
Non, il n'y en a plus.	*No, there isn't any (left).*
Tu as du lait?	*Have you got some milk?*
Non, je n'en ai pas.	*No, I haven't got any.*

 Practice

1 **Link the first part of each sentence to the correct ending from the second column. Note that there are two possible ways of ending sentences a and f.**

   a Il n'y a plus d'essence, il faut   **1** en remettre*.

   b Il ne reste que cinquante euros,   **2** j'en achète.
      il faut

   c Je n'ai plus d'argent, il faut que   **3** trouver une station service.

   d Il n'y a pas assez de café, il faut   **4** je trouve du travail.
      que

   e On n'a plus de fromage, il faut   **5** trouver une banque.
      qu'

   f Il n'y a plus d'huile dans le   **6** on en achète.
      moteur, il faut

*Note: The verb **mettre** means *to put* and **remettre** means *to put more / again.*

2 **Look back at Conversation 1. What is the third thing that Sarah and Dominique must do when they get to the petrol station?**

1 Faire le plein d'essence
2 Vérifier le niveau d'huile
3 _____

PRONUNCIATION

13.05 **Read the pronunciation explanations. Then listen and repeat.**

▶ **Il n'y en a** may seem difficult to pronounce, but all the sounds roll into one [**ilniena**].

▶ **Zut!** Getting your **u** right is essential to sounding at all French. You may need to practise in front of a mirror in order to get the correct position for your lips, which should be tightly rounded, as though you are going to whistle. Now try to say **ee** – the result will be a French **u**!

▶ For **i** your lips are straight, but taut. Try saying **i … u … i …u … i … u** several times, alternately stretching **vos lèvres** (*your lips*) and then pursing them.

When you've finished your 'lip exercises' try to repeat the following phrase several times:

Lulu lit la lettre lue à Lili. (*Lulu is reading the letter that was read to Lili.*)

LISTENING

1 13.06 **Read about the types of gas available. Then listen to the recording and say which car each person is driving: 1, 2 or 3.**

> *Choisissez la bonne pompe et le carburant qui convient à votre voiture. Attention! Si vous avez un moteur diesel il faut mettre du gazole/diesel. La plupart des voitures modernes utilisent de l'essence sans plomb.*

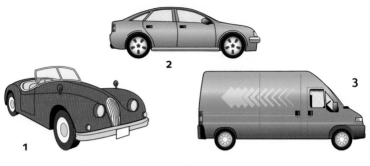

a La première personne conduit la voiture _____.

b La deuxième personne conduit la voiture _____.

c La troisième personne conduit la voiture _____.

S/Plomb 98

S/Plomb 95

Super 97

Diesel

2 What kind of fuel does each of the three drivers ask for?

1 _____, **2** _____, **3** _____.

3 13.07 Listen to a news report following a particularly bad weekend on French roads. Use the grid to note the key information.

Accidents	Type of vehicles involved in the accident	Place where accident occurred	Number of people killed	Number of people injured
a				
b	Bicycle and a car			
c				

1 Read the account of a traffic accident. How many victims were there in total?

Accident mortel sur la Route Nationale 10

Un camion sort d'un chemin privé devant un autocar
bilan:8 morts, 24 blessés

Un accident grave a fait huit morts et vingt-quatre blessés dans la nuit de mardi à mercredi, sur une section dangereuse de la Route Nationale 10 au sud de Bordeaux. Un autocar portugais a percuté un camion qui sortait d'un chemin privé devant l'autocar. Les deux chauffeurs portugais ont été tués. Le chauffeur du camion a été blessé.

---

2 Read the text. Then decide which sentences reflect what is written in the two paragraphs.

INSIGHT: NEW WORDS	
tué	*killed*
mortel	*fatal*
blessé	*hurt*

ZONES A VITESSE LIMITÉE

De nombreuses agglomérations ont vu la création de zones de circulation à vitesse limitée, dites 'Zones 30', à l'intérieur desquelles la vitesse des véhicules est réduite à 30 km/h. En l'absence de panneau, rappelez-vous qu'en agglomération, vous ne devez pas dépasser 50 km/h.

STATION DE GONFLAGE

Cette signalisation annonce une station de gonflage qui vous permettra de vérifier la pression de vos pneus (sans oublier la roue de secours!). Faites-le au moins une fois par mois et surtout avant un départ en vacances. Attention, la pression se vérifie sur un pneu froid ou ayant roulé moins de 15 km. En cas de mesure à chaud, il ne faut pas enlever de pression. N'oubliez pas que la profondeur des rainures ne doit pas être inférieure à 1,6 mm.

a Don't forget to check the spare wheel.

b Most built-up areas do not have speed limit road signs.

c If there is no speed limit sign in a built-up area, the maximum speed is 50 km per hour.

d Check your tyre pressure when your tyres are cold.

e Many built-up areas have ramps to slow down traffic.

f Check your tyre pressure before going on holidays.

g Check your tyres when you have driven less than 15 km.

h Ask someone to measure the grooves in your tyres.

i Check your tyres at least once a month.

j Many built-up areas have 30 km per hour speed limit signs.

Go further

1 The following pictures and explanation from *La prévention routière* talk about the kinds of road signs which are used on French roads. Look at the signs then read the text.

Danger

Obligation

Interdiction

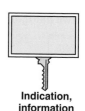

Indication, information

La signalisation routière est une forme de langage très simple; elle peut être comprise par tous.

Il suffit d'en connaître **les clefs**:

▶ La **FORME** permet de reconnaître facilement un panneau.

▶ La **COULEUR** précise la nature exacte du panneau:
  ROUGE = interdiction, BLEU = obligation.

▶ Un **SYMBOLE** facilement identifiable lui donne un sens précis.

▶ Enfin, une **BARRE OBLIQUE** sur un panneau signifiera toujours la fin d'une interdiction, d'une obligation ou d'une indication.

Ces quelques clefs suffisent à comprendre la signification de la plupart des panneaux routiers.

Maintenant vous comprenez les panneaux! Répondez aux questions.

a What does it mean when there is a sign with an oblique line across?

_____

b Which colour indicates that you have to do something? _____

c Which colour sign indicates that something is forbidden? _____

d Which colour and shape gives you some information? _____

INSIGHT: CULTURE

Conduite accompagnée is the equivalent of a red learner's *L*, compulsory when people are learning to drive under supervision in a private car. A red **A** at the back of a car indicates that the driver has passed the driving test less than two years ago. **A** stands for **apprentissage** *(apprenticeship)*.

2 **Use the words below to work out what the signs mean. Match each of the signs to its message.**

un créneau de dépassement	*overtaking lane*
le frein moteur	*engine brake*
le pied	*foot*
briser	*to break (an object)*
la vie	*life*

1 | **Votre sécurité. Créneau de dépassement dans 3 minutes**

2 | **La vie est fragile. Ne la brisez pas!**

3 | **Trop Vite! 90 Levez le pied**

4 | **Merci de votre prudence Bonne route!**

5 | **Utilisez votre frein moteur**

6 | **Merci de ralentir**

7 | **Cédez le passage**

a You are going too fast! The speed limit is 90 kilometres per hour so be sensible, take your foot off the accelerator. _____

b You are not on a priority road so give way. _____

c Thank you for slowing down. _____

d Thank you for being careful. Have a good journey! _____

e You are going down a steep road. Use a low gear to slow down. _____

f Think about safety. Don't overtake now when in three minutes' time you can use the overtaking lane. _____

g Life is fragile. Don't break it! _____

 Test yourself

1 Practise responding in the negative in two steps. Entraînez-vous!

Exemples:

Il y a du pain? **Non, il n'y a pas de pain** → **non, il n'y en a pas.**

Tu as du sucre? **Non, je n'ai pas de sucre** → **non, je n'en ai pas.**

Elle a acheté de l'essence? **Non, elle n'a pas acheté d'essence** → **elle n'en a pas acheté.**

    a Tu as acheté du lait?

    b Il a lu un livre?

    c Ils ont mangé des pommes?

2 Reply in the affirmative.

Exemples:

Il y a du chocolat? **Oui, il y en a.**

Tu veux des pommes? **Oui, j'en veux.**

    a Il faut de l'huile?

    b Il y a du café?

3 The statements below are in the negative. Respond in the affirmative using si.

Exemple:

Il n'y a pas assez de chocolat! **Si, il y en a assez!**

    a Tu ne bois pas assez d'eau!

    b Il ne reste presque plus de vin!

4 **Respond to the statements using il faut and il faut que (note that they are interchangeable here so just add the second alternative)**

Exemple

On n'a plus d'argent! **Il faut qu'on trouve une banque. / Il faut trouver une banque.**

    a J'ai faim! Il faut que tu manges / _____ .

    b Oh le beau château! Il faut qu'on le visite / _____

    c J'ai écris des cartes à mes amis. Il faut les poster / _____

SELF CHECK

I CAN. . .
. . . talk about French roads and driving in France.
. . . communicate at a service station.
. . . use vocabulary related to parts of the car and road signs.
. . . use the pronouns **y** and **en**.

14 On cherche un appartement

Looking for a flat

In this unit you will learn how to:
▶ *talk about housing in France.*
▶ *use language to look for a flat to rent.*
▶ *enquire about a flat on the telephone.*
▶ *use more pronouns.*
▶ *use adjectives ending with –al.*

CEFR: *Can scan longer texts to locate desired information (B1); Can cope with less routine situations about living accommodation (B1); Can obtain more detailed information (B1); Has sufficient vocabulary to express self on most topics (B1).*

Searching for a flat

Si vous cherchez un logement (*somewhere to live*)? **Une maison à louer** (*a house to rent*) **ou à acheter** (*or to buy*) **ou bien un appartement** (*a flat*) you can search **dans les journaux** (*in the newspapers*) under **Annonces Immobilières** (*estate property ads*). You can also go to **une agence immobilière** (*an estate agency*) **et prendre rendez-vous avec un agent immobilier** (*make an appointment with an estate agent*).

There are three indicators to give you an idea of the size of places to rent or buy. The letters F or T indicate the number of rooms . Un T4 has **3 chambres** (3 *bedrooms*), **une salle de bain** (*a bathroom*), **une cuisine** (*a kitchen*) **et un salon** (*a living room*). P shows the number of pièces (*rooms*): 2P/3P, excluding **la cuisine et la salle de bain**.

a   Would un logement T2 be big enough for a family of five?

Vocabulary builder

GETTING AN APARTMENT

14.01 You often need to understand a number of abbreviations and vocabulary when finding an apartment. Read the abbreviations and match them to their meanings. Then listen and check your answers.

a M°

b 12è.

c 2è. étg/der. étg

d c.c./ch.comp

e sdb/wc

f cuis.équip.

g asc.

h ch.perso.

i 10m2 env.

j ref.nf

k chauff.élec.

l rép

1 **cuisine équipée** *(furnished kitchen)*

2 **ascenseur** *(elevator)*

3 **chambre personnelle** *(personal room)*

4 **deuxième étage** *(second floor)*/**dernier étage** *(top floor)*

5 **chauffage électrique** *(electric heating)*

6 **répondeur automatique** *(answerphone)*

7 **douzième arrondissement**** *(Paris district number)*

8 **charges comprises** *(charges included)*

9 **10 m2 environ** *(approximately)*

10 **métro*** *(tube station)*

11 **refait neuf** *(newly decorated)*

12 **salle de bain/wc** *(bathroom/ WC, pronounced les double v c or wouataires)*

*Note: This applies to Paris, Lyon and Marseille only.

**Note: There are 20 districts in all.

14.02 **Listen and number the things in Dominique's apartment in the order you hear them. Then listen again and repeat.**

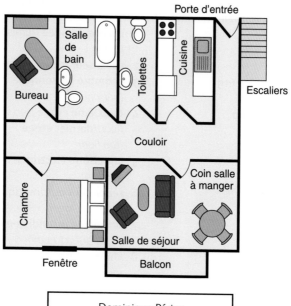

Dominique Périer
5 Avenue de la Vieille Ville
St NAZAIRE 44600

Bureau ❑   Escaliers ❑

Salle de bain ❑   Chambre ❑

Toilettes ❑   Fenêtre ❑

Cuisine ❑   Salle de séjour ❑

Couloir ❑   Balcon ❑

Porte d'entrée ❑   Coin salle à manger ❑

Look at the expressions that are used in the next conversations. Note their meanings.

Conversation 1

Je te préviens.*	*I am warning you.*
déménager	*to move (house)*
louer	*to rent*
les voisins	*the neighbours*
à bout de souffle	*breathless*
un copain	*a friend/boyfriend*
une copine	*a friend/girlfriend*
le tour du propriétaire	*the tour of the property*
le propriétaire	*the owner*
la propriété	*the property*

*Note: Prévenir means *to warn.*

Conversation 2

des meubles	*furniture*
meubler	*to furnish*
une chambre meublée	*a furnished room*

Conversations

1 14.03 **Look at the plan of Dominique's flat as you listen to the recording then answer the question.**

a On which floor is Dominique's flat? _____

Conversation 1

Dominique	Je te préviens, mon appartement est au quatrième étage et il n'y a pas d'ascenseur dans l'immeuble.
Sarah	Tu devrais déménager alors!
Dominique	Non! Je l'adore, mon appartement! Je le loue pour presque rien, il y a une vue magnifique sur les anciens chantiers navals de St Nazaire, et puis mes voisins sont tranquilles. Ouf! Nous y sommes! Je suis à bout de souffle.
Sarah	Ne te plains pas, ma vieille! Monter et descendre les escaliers c'est aussi bien que de faire de l'aérobic, tu sais!
Dominique	Zut! Je ne trouve pas mes clefs. Ah si, les voilà!
Sarah	Oh là là, quel bel appartement! C'est toi qui l'a décoré?

Dominique	Euh ... oui, plus ou moins, avec l'aide de mon copain.
Sarah	Tu me fais visiter?
Dominique	Allons-y pour le tour du propriétaire. Voici la salle de séjour avec le coin salle à manger, sans oublier le balcon. Ici c'est la cuisine, et au bout du couloir il y a ma chambre, et mon bureau. Tu vas dormir là, sur le canapé. Ici, à gauche, il y a la salle de bain et les toilettes.
Sarah	Il me plaît ton appartement. Bon, je m'installe!
Dominique	Tiens, ouvre la fenêtre. Viens voir, en se penchant on aperçoit la mer! Tu la vois?

b **Now listen again or read to answer the questions.**

1 Is there a lift? _____
2 Does she like her flat? Why or why not? Give one reason. _____
3 Why is Dominique out of breath? _____
4 What does Sarah say is as good as aerobics? _____
5 Who decorated Dominique's flat? _____
6 What can they just about see when leaning out of the window? _____

 2 14.04 **Corinne is about to start her first year at university in Paris. She is looking for somewhere to live. Scan the text quickly before you listen and answer the question.**

a Who is Corinne speaking to? _____

Conversation 2

Corinne	Allô Maman, c'est Corinne. Je téléphone pour te dire que je n'ai pas obtenu de chambre à la cité universitaire. Je crois que je vais chercher un studio à louer ou bien un appartement avec une ou deux copines.
Maman	Un studio! Mais c'est beaucoup trop cher! Et puis il faudrait le meubler!
Corinne	Bien sûr, mais je vais travailler pendant les vacances pour acheter des meubles. J'ai besoin d'une table, deux chaises, et un lit ou un sofa, c'est tout!
Maman	Non, il n'en est pas question! Alors tu m'écoutes: il serait beaucoup plus simple de prendre une chambre meublée chez des particuliers, dans une famille. Cherche dans les petites annonces dans le journal demain.
Corinne	OK! Je regarderai dans le journal, en cherchant bien j'arriverai à trouver un studio pas cher!

b   Now listen again or read to answer the questions.

   1   What did Corinne fail to get? _____
   2   What does Corinne want to do? _____
   3   She says that all she needs is a table, two chairs and a bed. How is
   she going to pay for it? _____

Language discovery

1   Now link the following English phrases to the equivalent French expressions from Conversation 1.

a	*There is no lift in the building.*	**1**	**Ouvre la fenêtre.**
b	*I rent it for next to nothing.*	**2**	**la salle de séjour**
c	*going up and down stairs*	**3**	**Ici c'est la cuisine.**
d	*with my friend's help*	**4**	**Tu vas dormir sur le canapé.**
e	*the living room*	**5**	**Je le loue pour presque rien.**
f	*Here is the kitchen.*	**6**	**En se penchant on aperçoit la mer.**
g	*You are going to sleep on the sofa.*	**7**	**monter et descendre les escaliers**
h	*When you lean out you can just about see the sea.*	**8**	**Il n'y a pas d'ascenseur dans l'immeuble.**
i	*Don't complain, old thing!*	**9**	**Viens voir.**
j	*Open the window.*	**10**	**Ne te plains pas, ma vieille.**
k	*Come and see.*	**11**	**avec l'aide de mon copain**

2 **Link the following English phrases to their French equivalent from Conversation 2.**

a *I am going to look for a studio to rent.*

b *I need a table, two chairs and a bed.*

c *I am going to work.*

d *It's out of the question.*

e *I shall look in the newspaper.*

f *by looking thoroughly*

1 **Je vais travailler.**

2 **en cherchant bien**

3 **Je regarderai dans le journal.**

4 **Je vais chercher un studio à louer.**

5 **Il n'en est pas question.**

6 **J'ai besoin d'une table, deux chaises et un lit.**

3 **Pronouns are words that replace nouns, like** *he, she,* **and** *it.* **There are five examples of the pronouns l'/le/la and les in Conversation 1. Find the pronouns that replace the nouns on the right.**

Pronoun	Noun replaced
a **Je l'adore,**	*apartment*
b _____	*apartment*
c _____	*keys*
d _____	*apartment*
e _____	*sea*

Learn more

1 LES PRONOMS: L'/LE/LA/LES

You already know that pronouns (e.g. words like *he, she, it*) are used to replace nouns. In Conversation 1, there are five examples of these pronouns. The first is:

Je l'adore mon appartement!   *I love (it) my flat!*

In this sentence, **l'** replaces **appartement**. This is an example where the pronoun is used first, in anticipation of the noun that comes next. It is used in spoken French to emphasize a point.

Remember that with pronouns and articles the **-e** is dropped in front of a vowel. For example:

Je adore mon appart*! →   **J'adore mon appart!**

*Note: **Appart** is short for **appartement**.

When the pronoun **le** is placed directly in front of the verb, the **-e** of **je** is reinstated and the **-e** of **le** is dropped instead.

Je l'adore mon appartement!

The same process applies with pronoun **la**.

2 LES PRONOMS: ME, TE, LUI, NOUS, VOUS, LEUR

These pronouns are used in front of verbs. At this point you just need to be able to recognize these pronouns rather than use them yourself.

Tu me fais visiter?	*Can you show me round?*
Il me plaît ton appartement.	*I like it. (Lit. It pleases me your flat.)*

You have already met some of them in reflexive verbs, but here their function is slightly different. They are used to target the recipient of an action, for example in **faire visiter sa maison à quelqu'un** *(to show one's home to somebody)*:

Pronoun use with faire visiter à	
tu <u>me</u> fais visiter	*you show me*
je <u>te</u> fais visiter	*I show you (to one person, familiar)*
je <u>lui</u> fais visiter	*I show him or her*
tu <u>nous</u> fais visiter	*you show us*
je <u>vous</u> fais visiter	*I show you (to more than one person or one person you address formally)*
tu <u>leur</u> fais visiter	*you show them*

A slightly different set of pronouns applies with a verb like **prévenir**. **Prévenir quelqu'un** means *to warn someone/to inform someone in advance of an event.* If the verb is followed by **à** (e.g. **faire visiter à**), the above pronouns are used. However, if the verb is not followed by **à** (e.g. **prévenir**), **l', le, la, les** are used for *him, her, it,* and *them.* Compare the two examples:

Je préviens Sarah. *(I warn Sarah.)* → **Je la préviens.**
Je fais visiter à Sarah. *(I show Sarah round.)* → **Je lui fais visiter.**

Examples of pronouns with prévenir	
Tu <u>me</u> préviens s'il pleut, n'est-ce pas?	*You'll let me know if it rains, won't you?*
Je <u>la</u> préviens.	*I am warning her.*
Je <u>le</u> préviens.	*I am warning him.*
Je préviens <u>mes parents</u> de notre arrivée. Je <u>les</u> préviens.	*I'm letting my parents know about our arrival. I'm letting them know.*

3 ADJECTIVES ENDING IN -AL

In the masculine form, most adjectives ending in **-al** have a plural form ending in **–aux**. In the feminine form, all adjectives ending in **-al** take an **-e**, with a plural form ending in **–ales**.

Adjectives ending in -al		
Masculine sing.	**un repas normal**	*a normal meal*
Masculine pl.	**des repas normaux**	*normal meals*
Feminine sing.	**une vie normale**	*a normal life*
Feminine pl.	**des vies normales**	*normal lives*

But there are a few exceptions that you need to know about. In Conversation 1, Dominique says that her flat has a fantastic view over the old shipyards.

Il y a une vue magnifique sur les anciens chantiers navals.

Naval is one of the extremely rare adjectives ending in **-al** that has a plural form with **-s**:

un chantier naval   **des chantiers navals**

Here are more exceptions:

un accident fatal - des accidents fatals *(fatal accident/s)*
un appartement glacial - des appartements glacials *(icy cold flat/s)*
un incident banal - des incidents banals *(banal incident/s)*

This happens with some nouns as well:

un bal → **des bals** *(ball / dance)*,

un carnaval → **des carnavals** *(carnival)*,

4 EN

You already know that in French, the present participle of a verb **-ant** is equivalent to *-ing* in English (see Unit 9). When used with **en** *(when/ while)*, it is a verb form call **le gérondif**, which is referred to as a *gerund* in English.

En se penchant par la fenêtre on aperçoit la mer. *(Leaning out the window one can see the sea.)*

en cherchant bien *(looking thoroughly)*

However, **le gérondif** is not necessarily used in the English equivalent when translated.

Ils sifflent en travaillant. *(They whistle while they work.)*

Corinne fait ses devoirs en écoutant de la musique. *(Corinne does her homework whilst she listens to music.)*

5 MORE VERB USES

Expressions with the verb louer *(to rent / hire)*

Je loue une maison/un studio/une voiture. *(I'm renting a house / studio / car.)*

Depuis Noël j'habite chez mon copain et je loue mon appart à ma sœur. *(Since Christmas I've been living with my friend and renting my flat to my sister.)*

Location de voiture *(Car rental)*

Location saisonnière au mois ou à la semaine. *(Seasonal accommodation by the month or week)*

Appartement à louer *(Flat to let)*

Expressions with the verbs déménager / emménager *(to move out / to move in)* and aménager *(to organize)*, and related nouns

Nous emménageons demain. *(We're moving in tomorrow.)*

Il ne fait pas souvent le ménage. *(He doesn't often do the housework.)*

les travaux ménagers *(domestic chores)*

Je ménage la chèvre et le chou.* *(I spare the goat and the cabbage.)*

l'aménagement du temps scolaire *(organization of the school day)*

*Note: This is an old saying meaning *trying to do one's best for both.*

 # Practice

 ## PRONUNCIATION

14.05 **Read the explanation. Then listen to the pronunciation of the words in bold.**

The verb **apercevoir** *(to perceive/to catch a glimpse)* is one of the many verbs that change **c** to **ç** in order to keep to an original **s** sound. This is necessary if the letter **c** is followed by **a/o/u** when it would normally have a **k** sound. To keep to the **s** sound the letter **c** becomes **ç**.

J'aperçois un ami là-bas. *I can see a friend over there.*

Nous apercevons les montagnes. *We can see the mountains.*

J'ai aperçu la Tour Eiffel. *I glimpsed the Eiffel Tower.*

With other verbs this change does not always occur for the same part of the verb.

Nous commençons à apprendre l'anglais. *We are beginning to learn English.*

Nous recevons des amis pour dîner. *We are having friends over for dinner.*

Il reçoit une récompense. *He gets a reward.*

 SPEAKING

14.06 **You want to rent a studio flat in Paris and plan to phone to ask about advertisement *b* on page 165. The propriétaire's lines are correct, but your lines are jumbled up. Make a conversation and practise it. Then listen to check your answers and pronunciation.**

Propriétaire	Allô, j'écoute!
Vous	1...
Propriétaire	Oui, c'est bien cela.
Vous	2...
Propriétaire	C'est au sixième.
Vous	3...
Propriétaire	Euh, non mais monter et descendre les escaliers est excellent pour la santé!
Vous	4...
Propriétaire	Non, le chauffage est électrique.
Vous	5...
Propriétaire	Oui il y a une cuisine moderne toute équipée.
Vous	6...
Propriétaire	C'est bien cela. Vous pouvez visiter aujourd'hui?
Vous	7...

Your lines

a   Il y a un ascenseur?

b   Je viendrais cet après-midi si vous êtes disponible.

c   C'est bien 400 € toutes charges comprises?

d   Il y a une cuisine?

e   J'ai vu une annonce pour un studio dans Libé. C'est bien ici?

f   Il y a le chauffage central?

g   C'est à quel étage?

Read the article. Then, for questions a-d, choose all the answers that apply.

COMMENT

déménager

SANS SOUCIS

Vous avez trouvé la maison de vos rêves! Votre petite famille aspire à un peu plus d'espace! Bref, vous devez déménager.

Pour déménager, la solution la plus simple reste de faire appel aux copains. On amasse les cartons, on loue une camionnette, on prépare des sandwichs et le tour est joué! Oui mais voilà, tout le monde n'a pas des amis disponibles. A fortiori quand on habite au dernier étage sans ascenseur ou quand le piano à queue pèse trois tonnes! Dans certaines situations, mieux vaut faire appel à des pros.

a Why are you moving?
   1 You are moving because you have got a new job.
   2 You are moving because your family needs more space.
   3 You have found the house of your dreams.

b How are you going to manage it?
   1 It is simpler to do the lot yourself, with the help of your children.
   2 Your friends can help.
   3 You have to hire a van.
   4 You have to make sandwiches for your friends.
   5 You need lots of milk cartons.
   6 You need to collect lots of cardboard boxes.

c **What problems are you likely to face?**
1 You have no friends available for the task.
2 Your friends are a little bit careless.
3 Your friends are not strong enough.
4 Your front door is too narrow.
5 You live on the top floor.
6 Your washing machine weighs a ton.
7 You have a grand piano.
8 There is no lift.

d **What should you do if in doubt?**
1 Decide not to move.
2 Leave the piano in your old flat.
3 Call a professional removal firm.

Go further

Corinne a découpé des petites annonces dans des journaux. Elle n'a pas l'intention de prendre une chambre chez des particuliers. Elle cherche un petit appartement à partager avec une copine ou bien un petit studio pas cher. Elle a 450€ par mois pour payer son loyer.

1 **Look at the adverts Corinne has cut out from the newspaper and answer the questions.**
1 How many studios, flat shares or small flats are within her price range?
2 Which ad is about a furnished studio flat for rent for at least a year?
3 Which ads should she call if she wants to move in immediately or no later than 1 October?
4 How much could she pay for a room in a flat share?
5 Which studio flat is on the 3rd floor and has recently been decorated?

Maisons & appartements

Particuliers
46 € la parution
de 5 lignes
Tél.: 01.44.78.39.51

Studios Location

a) ☐ 14è. M° PLAISANCE Studio
20m2 Refait à neuf, 3è, étage
850 € ccJP2L01.43.35.15.40

b) ☐ 19è.CITE de la MUSIQUE
Studio meublé sympa
imm. très calme, pour 1 an
au moins, loyer 400 € cc.
Gilles 01.40.17.15.35

c) ☐ Paris 3è. Particulier loue
petit 2 P., 25m2, wc, bains,
790 € cc. visite sur place lundi
1er septembre de 12h à 14h
4, RUE BLONDEL. 01.40.60.10.50

d) ☐ 18è.M° Marx-Dormoy
studio 18m2, tbe. coin cuisine
s. de bains, 2è. et dern. étg.
clair, calme sur cour. Chauff.
élec.650 € cc. 01.40.37.71.21

e) ☐ NATION - Studio 25m2
clair, calme, 1er. étg. sur cour,
salle de bain, wc, kitchenette,
680 € cc. Direct propriétaire
01.48.60.60.15

f) ☐ 20è. Pyrénées - Gd. studio
40m2, 6è. étg. asc. beaucoup
de charme, poutres, ref. nf. cuis.
équip. vue dégagée, ds. imm.
PdT.820 € cc 01.43.61.49.37

g) ☐ 2è M° Strasbourg St-Denis
Studio 27m2, séjour + vraie
cuis., sdb.libre le 1er octobre
570 € charges et chauffage
compris - 01.48.02.40.10

h) ☐ 3è. M° Fille du Calvaire
STUDIO MEUBLE
670 € ch. comprises
Tél.: 01.43.65.75.57

Partages

i) ☐ 20è. M° JOURDAIN
100m2 Meublé sympa, sdb. +
chambre perso. 550 € cc.
Tél.: 01.43.65.80.15

j) ☐ 9e. Place Clichy Part. grd
appart. 120m2 Chbre. 400 € .
C.C. Tél.: 01.42.70.60.50

2 Pièces Location

k) ☐ M° LOUIS BLANC
2 Pièces 45m2, cuisine équipée
nombreux rangements,
Libre tout de suite
Tél. 01.43.59.39.32

? Test yourself

The object pronouns le, la, l', les look exactly like the definite articles but they have a different function: they replace the object.

1 Study the examples and answer the questions below.

Elle mange **le gâteau d'anniversaire?** → Oui, elle **le** mange.

J'emprunte **ta voiture?** → Non, tu ne **l'**empruntes pas! (**emprunter** = to borrow)

Tu as compris **le système?** → Oui, je **l'**ai compris! / Non, je ne **l'ai pas compris.**

A vous maintenant! *(your turn)*

    a Vous regardez **la télé** au lit? Oui, nous...
    b Tu achètes **le journal au kiosque?** Oui, ...
    c Il prévient **sa fille** de son divorce? Oui, ...
    d Tu finis de lire **ton livre?** Non, ...
    e Vous connaissez **la route?** Non, on ...

2 C'est Noël. Qu'est-ce que vous offrez à toute la famille? Go back to Learn More if you need to check what you have learnt.

Exemples:

Qu'est-ce que tu offres à ta sœur? **Je lui offre des chocolats.**

Qu'est-ce que vous offrirez à vos parents? **Nous leur offrirons un voyage à Londres.**

A vous!

    a Qu'est-ce qu'on va donner à grand-mère? (say you'll give her a book)
    b Qu'est-ce que ton frère t'a offert l'année dernière? (say he gave you a bracelet)
    c Qu'est-ce qu'elle offre à son mari? (Say she gives him a car)
    d Et à moi, qu'est-ce que tu vas m'offrir? (Say I'll give you a theatre ticket)

3 There are many things that can be done while doing the housework or while driving.

Only choose from the list those activities which are realistic or safe in view of the tasks in hand.

 a Elle conduit sa voiture ...

 b Il fait le ménage ....

en chantant   en écoutant la radio   en regardant la télé
en lisant un livre   en prenant un bain   en faisant son jogging
en surfant sur le web   en mangeant des bonbons
en pensant aux vacances   en faisant bien attention à la circulation
en téléphonant à ses amis

SELF CHECK

I CAN...
⬤ . . . talk about housing in France.
⬤ . . . use language to look for a flat to rent.
⬤ . . . enquire about a flat on the telephone.
⬤ . . . use more pronouns.
⬤ . . . use adjectives ending with **–al**.

Dans les grandes surfaces

At shopping centres

In this unit you will learn how to:
▶ *handle shopping in supermarkets.*
▶ *talk about buying clothes.*
▶ *make comparisons and say something is better or worse.*
▶ *understand sales adverts.*
▶ *use demonstrative pronouns:* celui-ci, celui-là, *etc.*

CEFR: *Can ask someone to verify what was just said (B1); Can express and respond to feelings such as surprise (B1); Can adapt reading style to different texts and purposes (B2).*

Shopping in France

All French towns have out-of-town shopping centres with a vast range of **supermarchés** and **hypermarchés** (*supermarkets and hypermarkets*). They are generally referred to as **grandes surfaces** because of the large space they occupy. Most of them are located in large shopping arcades, with a whole range of smaller shops, boutiques of all sorts and restaurants. In addition to the permanent shopping area, they **fréquemment** (*frequently*) have seasonal products at competitive prices **sous chapiteau** (*under a large marquee*): wines in the autumn, chrysanthemums for All Saints Day on 1 November, oysters for Christmas and the New Year, bedding and furniture in the spring and camping equipment in the summer.

They all compete with one another by having **promotions** (*promotional offers*), **soldes** (*sales*), **affaires du jour** (*bargains of the day*) and **offres spéciales** (*special offers*).

a   What would a French boutique call *the bargain of the week*?
b   Find the French word in the text that is derived from **fréquent** (*frequent*).

Vocabulary builder

SHOPPING EXPRESSIONS

 15.01 **Read the expressions for shopping. Match them to their English equivalents then listen to check your answers.**

a **Super, cette robe! Il faut que je l'essaye!**

b **Bof! C'est une petite taille!**

c **Ouais! J'ai vu mieux ailleurs!**

d **Oh là là! Ça fait ringard!**

e **En plus elle est trop chère!**

f **Essayer des vêtements dans la cabine d'essayage.**

1 *Oh dear! It looks old fashioned!*

2 *Trying on clothes*

3 *Oh! It's a small size!*

4 *What's more, it's too expensive!*

5 *Hm! I've seen better elsewhere!*

6 *This dress is great. I must try it on!*

CLOTHING

 1 15.02 **Look at the French words for clothing. Match them to their English translations, then listen and repeat.**

a **des gants**

b **un pantalon**

c **des chaussures**

d **des lunettes de soleil**

e **un imper***

f **des baskets**

g **une jupe**

h **une doudoune**

i **une chemise**

j **une robe**

k **un pull**

l **un manteau**

m **un maillot de bain**

1 *a dress*

2 *shirt*

3 *padded jacket*

4 *shoes*

5 *sun glasses*

6 *trousers*

7 *pullover*

8 *skirt*

9 *coat*

10 *trainers*

11 *raincoat*

12 *swimsuit*

13 *gloves*

> **INSIGHT: LANGUAGE**
> Here are some interjections you may want to use when shopping.
> **Bof!** To express disappointment
> **Super!** To express admiration
> **C'est trop!** To mean *it's too much / it's perfect!*
> **Ouais!** To express disdain / disapproval
> **Oh là là!** To express surprise (good or bad)

***Note**: This is short for **imperméable**.

1 15.03 **Look at the floor plan of the supermarket. Then listen and write the numbers of the departments you hear. Pause if you need to. Look up any words you don't know.**

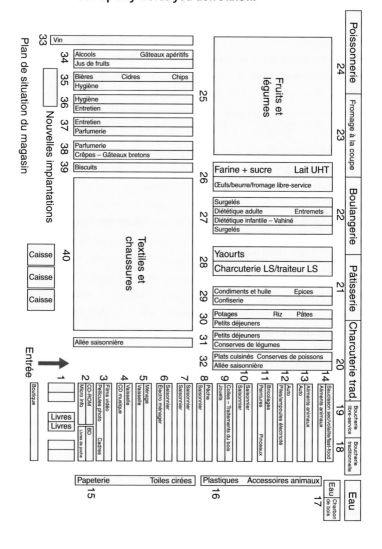

a	_____	f	_____	k	_____
b	_____	g	_____	l	_____
c	_____	h	_____	m	_____
d	_____	i	_____	n	_____
e	_____	j	_____	o	_____

NEW EXPRESSIONS

Look at the expressions that are used in the next conversation. Note their meanings.

le frigo*	*the fridge*
des boîtes**	*tins*
des piles pour ma torche	*batteries for my flashlight*
des vêtements et des chaussures	*clothes and shoes*
le rayon poissonnerie	*the fish counter*
un pull***	*a jumper or pullover*
la taille	*size (for clothes)*
la pointure	*size (for shoes)*
agaçante	*annoying*
un poisson rouge	*a goldfish*

*Note: This is short for **réfrigérateur**.

Note: This is short for **des boîtes de conserve.

***Note: This is short for **un pullover**.

Conversation

15.04 Dominique has come home from her vacation to an empty fridge. She and her friend Sarah decide to go to one of the many out-of-town supermarkets. Listen once to the recording, and then answer the question.

a   Name four items on Dominique's list. _____, _____, _____ and _____.

Dominique	Je n'ai plus rien dans le frigo. Il faut que j'achète de tout.
Sarah	N'oublie pas que tu as fait une liste ce matin.
Dominique	Ah oui, ma liste … je l'ai. Alors lait, fromage, yaourts, beurre, pain, poisson, fruits et légumes, liquide lave-vaisselle, sans oublier des boîtes pour Papaguéno!
Sarah	Pour qui?
Dominique	Papaguéno? C'est mon chat. Ma voisine s'en occupe quand je pars en voyage.
Sarah	Eh bien moi j'ai besoin d'une pellicule pour mon appareil photo, des piles pour ma torche, et puis une bonne bouteille de vin blanc pour boire avec le poisson et un gâteau de pâtisserie pour le dessert.
Dominique	Tu as vu, il y a des soldes de vêtements et de chaussures.
Sarah	J'aime beaucoup beaucoup ces chaussures - il n'y en a qu'une paire. C'est quelle pointure?
Dominique	C'est du trente-huit.
Sarah	Dommage, je chausse du trente-neuf!
Dominique	Regarde, il n'est pas mal ce pull! Et celui-ci est encore mieux!
Sarah	Oui, mais j'ai vu meilleure qualité! Et puis le vert te va mieux que le bleu … Ah non pas le rouge, c'est encore pire!
Dominique	Oh là là, tu es agaçante, tu as toujours raison! Allez viens, on va au rayon poissonnerie acheter du poisson. J'espère qu'ils ne vendent pas de poisson rouge sinon on ne mangera rien ce soir!

b **Now listen again or read to answer the questions.**
   1 Who are the tins for? _____
   2 Who looks after her cat when Dominique is away? _____
   3 Name three items on Sarah's list. _____
   4 Who is the wine for? _____
   5 Dominique noticed that there were sales in the clothes and shoes department. What attracted their attention? _____
   6 Do they buy anything? _____
   7 Which colour suits Dominique best? _____
   8 Which department do they go to? _____

c **At the end of the dialogue Dominique makes a joke which would be meaningless in translation. Why is it a joke in French and not in English?**

 # Language discovery

1 Link the following English phrases from the conversation to the equivalent French expressions.

a	*I have nothing left in the fridge.*	**1**	**Dommage, je chausse du trente-neuf.**
b	*washing-up liquid*	**2**	**pour boire avec le poisson**
c	*My neighbour looks after him.*	**3**	**Il y a des soldes.**
d	*to drink with the fish*	**4**	**Le vert te va mieux que le bleu.**
e	*There are sales on.*	**5**	**Je n'ai plus rien dans le frigo.**
f	*Pity, I take size 39.*	**6**	**du liquide lave-vaisselle**
g	*Green suits you better than blue.*	**7**	**sinon on ne mangera rien ce soir.**
h	*otherwise we won't eat anything tonight*	**8**	**Ma voisine s'en occupe.**

2 Look at the last two exercises and answer the questions.

a	What expression is used to mean *my cat?*	**mieux**	**en**
b	Which expression means *better?*	**mieux**	**en**

Learn more

1 EN

There is a further example of **en** (see Unit 14) in the conversation above.

C'est mon chat. Ma voisine s'en occupe. *It's my cat. My neighbour looks after it.*

Here **en** replaces **de mon chat.**

Ma voisine s'occupe de mon chat. →
Ma voisine s'en occupe.

Elle s'occupe de ma maison. →
Elle s'en occupe.

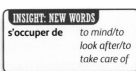

INSIGHT: NEW WORDS

s'occuper de	*to mind/to look after/to take care of*

2 MAKING COMPARISONS

Plus/plus ... que

You have already met **plus ... que** *(more ... than)* and **moins ... que** *(less ... than)*. You can use **plus ... que** with almost all adjectives.

C'est <u>plus cher</u> qu'à Continent. *It's <u>more expensive</u> than at Continent.*

However, **plus ... que** can also be used with adverbs.

Tu marches <u>plus vite</u> que moi. *You <u>walk faster</u> than me.*

Meilleur(e)(s)/mieux

Plus and **plus … que** cannot be used with the adjectives **bon(s)/bonne(s)** which mean *good*. It is better to use **meilleur(e)(s)** here instead.

Les glaces à la fraise sont meilleures (que les glaces à la vanille). *Strawberry ice creams are better [than vanilla ice creams].*

Le climat est meilleur dans le Midi de la France. *The climate is better in the south of France.*

Meilleur can also be used as a superlative for *the best.*

Les vins allemands, les vins italiens sont bons. Mais les français sont les meilleurs vins du monde. *German wines, Italian wines are good, but French ones are the best wines in the world.*

La championne olympique de natation c'est la meilleure nageuse du monde. *The Olympic swimming champion is the best swimmer in the world.*

Plus and **plus … que** cannot be used with the adverb **bien** *(good/well).* **Mieux** *(better)* is used instead.

Le bleu te va bien. *Blue suits you (Lit. Blue goes well with you.)*

Le vert te va mieux que le rouge. *Green suits you better than red.*

Plus mauvais(e)(s) (pire) and plus mal (pis)

Although **plus** and **plus … que** can be used with the adjective **mauvais(e)(s)** *(bad)* and the adverb **mal** *(badly),* you may come across their alternative forms: **pire** and **pis**. **Pis** is not commonly used in comparisons, but you will often hear the expression **Tant pis!** *Too bad! (lit. So much the worse!)*

Celui-ci est encore plus mauvais!/Celui-ci est encore pire! *This one is even worse!*

Marc conduit plus mal que son frère. *Marc's driving is worse than his brother's.*

3 DEMONSTRATIVE PRONOUNS

You can use demonstrative pronouns when you need to refer to something that is present at the time of the conversation.

Demonstrative pronouns				
masc.sing.	**celui-ci**	} this one	**celui-là**	} that one
fem.sing.	**celle-ci**		**celle-là**	
fem.pl.	**celles-ci**	} these ones	**celles-là**	} those ones
masc.pl.	**ceux-ci**		**ceux-là**	

Practice

Choose the correct ending for each of the sentences below.

a	Ce poisson a l'air frais	**1**	mais celles-ci sont meilleures.
b	Cet artichaut est gros	**2**	mais celui-ci sent encore meilleur.
c	Ces pommes sont bonnes	**3**	mais celle-ci est meilleure.
d	Ce melon sent bon	**4**	mais ceux-ci sont meilleurs.
e	Ces gâteaux sont bons	**5**	mais celui-ci a l'air plus frais.
f	Cette bière est bonne	**6**	mais celui-ci est encore plus gros.

 ## LISTENING

1 15.05 **Madame Rouzeau has a long list of delicatessen products she wants to buy au rayon charcuterie (at the delicatessen counter). Listen and identify everything on her list. Then fill in the quantity required for each.**

Item	Quantity
Bayonne ham	
Garlic sausage	
Farmhouse pâté	
Greek mushrooms	
Scallops	

2 Now read the dialogue and check your answers.

Vendeuse	Soixante-quinze? C'est à qui le tour?
Madame R	C'est à moi. Mettez-moi six tranches de jambon de Bayonne, s'il vous plaît.
Vendeuse	Ça vous va comme cela?
Mme R	Oui, c'est bien.
Vendeuse	Et avec ça?
Mme R	Alors il me faut douze tranches de saucisson à l'ail, ... deux cent cinquante grammes de pâté de campagne, ... deux cents grammes de champignons à la grecque, ... et quatre coquilles St Jacques.
Vendeuse	Et avec cela?
Mme R	Ça sera tout, merci!
Vendeuse	Voilà Madame, bonne journée.

Look at the adverts from local papers where local shops have advertised their bargains. Then answer the questions below.

« **L'AFFAIRE DU JOUR!!**
A ne pas manquer. »

OFFRE VALABLE DU 1er AU 3 AOÛT
(le 3 août pour les magasins ouverts le dimanche matin)

NECTARINE BLANCHE

origine France
catégorie 1, calibre B

le kg

CHEZ STOC, UN CLIENT C'EST SACRÉ

stoc SUPERMARCHÉ

FOUESNANT — 4, rue de Kervevelck
CONCARNEAU — 17, quai Carnot
LE GUILVINEC — 1, rue des Moulins
MORLAIX — Rue de Brest
CARANTEC — Kérosquien
PLOUGUERNEAU — Douar Nevez

PRIX FOUS ...

AUJOURD'HUI MERCREDI 6 AOÛT
DERNIER JOUR

FOIRE AUX SOLDES
à PONT-L'ABBÉ

C'est à côté

U.D.C.P.

SOLDES
DERNIERS JOURS

MEUBLES L. Bilien

15, rue du Général-De Gaulle
29750 LOCTUDY

PROMO LITERIE

SOUS CHAPITEAU

GRANDES MARQUES

monsieur meuble
nous sommes bien ensemble!

Route de Quimper
PONT-L'ABBÉ

Par autorisation préfectorale du 30 avril 97

AURAY CENTRE-VILLE • MARDI 12 - MERCREDI 13 AOÛT

GRANDE BRADERIE

Organisation : Auray Préférence
et Rugby Auray Club

CRÉDIT AGRICOLE DU MORBIHAN

OFFRE SPÉCIALE

MOTEUR
135 CV 2L V6
MERCURY
Prix catalogue :
12 600 €

Vendu:
7800 €

BREST NAUTIC
Port du Moulin-Blanc - BREST
02.98.41.43.70

a What is the bargain of the day at STOC?_____

b How long will it last? _____

c What day of the week is 3 August? _____

d Where and when in Auray is the Grande Braderie taking place?
_____

e What is 'Monsieur Meuble' selling Sous Chapiteau? (Clue: first three letters of LITERIE) _____

f How much would one save at Brest Nautic? _____

g When does La Foire Aux Soldes end in Pont-L'Abbé? _____

h What is in the sales at 15 rue du Général de Gaulle? _____

Go further

1 **Dans les paniers de Madame Rouzeau il y a des fruits et des légumes frais. Look in Madame Rouzeau's baskets, and first try learning the words visually.**

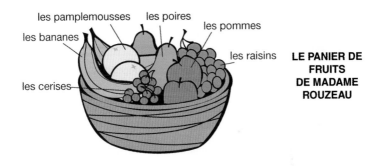

les pamplemousses   les poires   les pommes

les bananes

les raisins

LE PANIER DE FRUITS DE MADAME ROUZEAU

les cerises

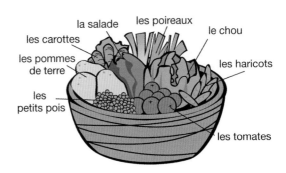

la salade   les poireaux   le chou

les carottes

LE PANIER DE LÉGUMES DE MADAME ROUZEAU

les pommes de terre

les haricots

les petits pois

les tomates

Now find 13 names of fruits and vegetables hidden in the grid.

P	A	C	C	D	M	N	G	H	I	L	P	K
A	D	S	E	A	P	O	M	M	E	S	O	D
M	S	Q	R	D	S	A	T	E	E	G	M	H
P	E	T	I	T	S	P	O	I	S	K	M	K
L	R	G	S	F	T	Y	M	S	E	L	E	H
E	A	P	E	B	A	N	A	N	E	S	S	A
M	I	O	S	D	C	E	T	A	P	A	D	R
O	S	I	Z	A	H	R	E	T	O	L	E	I
U	I	R	C	V	O	B	S	M	I	A	T	C
S	N	E	R	H	U	S	G	D	R	D	E	O
S	C	A	R	O	T	T	E	S	E	E	R	T
E	T	U	Y	U	H	N	F	D	S	V	R	S
S	F	X	J	V	B	C	A	S	W	R	E	M

INSIGHT: CULTURE

Various colloquial expressions in French refer to fruit or vegetables.

Peaches: **Il a la pêche en ce moment!** *(He's in great form at the moment. Lit. He's got the peach...)*

Cabbage: **Mon petit chou!/Mon gros chou!/Mon pauvre chou!** (terms of endearment); **le chouchou de la prof** *(teacher's pet)*

Pears: **Je suis bonne poire, moi!** *(I am too good! Lit. I'm a good pear!)*

Apples: **Elle est tombée dans les pommes.** *(She fainted Lit. She fell into the apples.)*

Mixed: **Quelle salade!** (What a mess! Lit. What a salad!); **Cinq fruits et légumes par jour!** *(Five a day!)*

Test yourself

This one? That one? Which is the best? Is one better than the other?

Find the grammatically correct ending for each sentence:

1 Ce chocolat est plus sucré
2 Ces pommes sont meilleures que celles-ci:
3 Madame Rouzeau est
4 Ce vin n'est pas très bon
5 Cette femme est très belle
6 Pour moi, les meilleurs fruits
7 Celle-ci te plaît?
8 Les baskets de ma sœur sont encore
9 Pouah! Alors celui-là
10 Cette bière a meilleur goût

a plus gentille que son mari.
b plus chères.
c mais je préfère la brune.
d ce sont les poires.
e que celle-là.
f Oui, pas mal!
g c'est le pire de tous.
h mais celui-ci est encore pire.
i que celui-là.
j elles sont plus croquantes.

SELF CHECK

I CAN...
. . . talk about shopping in supermarkets.
. . . buy clothes.
. . . make comparisons.
. . . find bargains in sales adverts
. . . use the demonstrative pronouns **celui-ci**, **celui-là**, etc.

16 À la maison du peuple

At the community centre

In this unit you will learn how to:
▶ *understand a little about multi-ethnic France.*
▶ *talk about young people and out-of-school activities.*
▶ *read an opinion poll about racism.*
▶ *use the perfect tense with être.*

CEFR: *Can verbally obtain more detailed information (B1); Can ask someone to clarify what they have just said (B1); Can identify the main conclusions of argumentative texts (B1); Can explain a viewpoint on a topical issue (B2).*

 ## Diversity in France

France has a strong tradition of **structures d'animation** (*coordination of cultural and sporting activities*). All French towns have places such as **centres socio-culturels** (*sociocultural centres*), **maisons des jeunes** (*youth clubs*) and **maisons de quartier** (*local district clubs*).

As well as these places for young people to go, many towns have **animateurs socio-culturels** who provide leisure, social and cultural activities, clearly distinct from the school system. Their role is vital in local communities. **L'un des buts** (*one of the objectives*) includes **combattre le racisme** (*tackling racism*) in a constructive way.

 a   What are the various roles of animateurs socio-culturels?

Vocabulary builder

POSSESSIVE ADJECTIVES

1 16.01 **Possessive adjectives are words like *my, your,* and *his*. Listen to the possessive adjectives and repeat.**

English	Masculine Sing.	Feminine Sing.*	Plural
my	**mon**	**ma**	**mes**
your (informal)	**ton**	**ta**	**tes**
your (formal)	**votre**	**votre**	**vos**
his/her/its	**son**	**sa**	**ses**
our	**notre**	**notre**	**nos**
their	**leur**	**leur**	**leurs**

*Note: Use the masculine singular form (**mon, ton**, and **son**) instead of **ma, ta,** or **sa** before feminine singular nouns beginning with a vowel or vowel sound . This makes the words flow more smoothly.

2 Now, complete the sentences with the correct possessive adjectives.

   a Djamel est le frère d'Adidja. C'est _____ frère.

   b Sarah est la copine de Claire. C'est _____ copine.

   c Sarah et Josiane sont les cousines de Sophie. Ce sont _____ cousines.

   d Jean-Pierre et Jacques sont _____ cousins.

   e Adidja, c'est _____ sœur.

   f Gildas, c'est _____ collègue.

   g Je suis allé au Maroc plusieurs fois avec _____ parents.

NEW EXPRESSIONS

Look at the expressions that are used in the next conversations. Note their meanings.

Conversation 1

un animateur/une animatrice*	*someone organizing activities, youth worker*
encadrer**	*to provide a framework for activities*
des jeunes maghrébins	*young people with North African origins*
le quartier	*the district / the area*

*Note: The full name for this profession is **animateur socio-culturel**.

Note: The base of this word is **un cadre, which means a frame or support. In a work context it also means a manager.

Conversation 2

arabe	*Arabic*
enrichissant	*to enrich*
ouvert et tolérant	*open and tolerant (to other people and cultures)*

Conversations

 1 16.02 **Dominique and Sarah are on their way to Dominique's parents in Bordeaux. On the way they stop at Dominique's boyfriend's house in Nantes. Read about Dominique's boyfriend. Then listen to the recording once and answer the question.**

Le copain de Dominique s'appelle Gildas Marrec. Il est Directeur de la Maison du Peuple dans un quartier populaire de Nantes.

a Who is Djamel?

   1 Gildas' brother **2** Gildas' colleague **3** Gildas' neighbour

---

Conversation 1

Gildas	Salut! Vous avez fait un bon voyage?
Dominique	Oui, très bien. Gildas je te présente Sarah.
Sarah	Enchantée!
Gildas	Enchanté! Dominique m'a beaucoup parlé de vous. Je vous présente Djamel, un collègue de travail. Djamel, Dominique, ma copine, et Sarah, une amie à elle.
Sarah	(à Djamel) Vous travaillez avec des jeunes aussi?
Djamel	Oui, je suis animateur, c'est-à-dire que j'encadre des jeunes dans de nombreuses activités en dehors du collège.
Sarah	Quel genre d'activités?
Djamel	Oh un peu de tout: du sport, de la photo, de la musique, et même des voyages. Nous avons beaucoup de jeunes maghrébins dans le quartier. Ils n'ont pas grand'chose à faire, à part regarder la télé. Là on vient de rentrer d'un voyage au Maroc.
Gildas	Djamel est formidable avec les gamins.
Dominique	Combien sont allés au Maroc?
Djamel	Dix-huit et on était trois animateurs. On est resté trois semaines. Certains ont logé dans leurs familles.
Sarah	Ils ont rencontré des jeunes marocains?
Djamel	Oui, bien sûr. Ils ont tous fait énormément de découvertes.

---

b Now listen again or read to answer the questions.

1 Djamel works ...

    a *with adults.*   **b** *in a college.*   **c** with young people.

2 What kind of activities does he supervise? _____

3 Where did Djamel and some young people travel to? _____

4 How long did they stay there? _____

5 How many young people and how many adults went on the journey? _____

6 Where did some young people stay? _____

7 Who did they all meet? _____

2 16.03 **Sarah continues the conversation with Djamel. Listen to the recording and answer the question.**

    a What question does Sarah ask Djamel? _____

Conversation 2

Sarah	Et vous, c'est la première fois que vous êtes allé au Maroc?
Djamel	Non, non, je suis né en France mais avec mes parents et mes sœurs nous y sommes allés une dizaine de fois.
Sarah	Vous parlez l'arabe alors?
Djamel	Bien sûr, on parle l'arabe à la maison. Je pense que c'est enrichissant d'avoir une double culture. Je parle trois langues: le français, l'arabe et l'anglais. Je me sens ouvert et tolérant.

---

b Now listen again or read to answer the questions.

1 Where was Djamel born? _____

2 Who did he go to Morocco with? _____

3 How many times have they been there? _____

4 Which language does Djamel speak at home? _____

5 How many languages can he speak? _____

💡 Language discovery

1 **Link the following English phrases to the equivalent French expressions from Conversation 1.**

a *Dominique has told me lots of things about you*

b *Do you work with young people too?*

c *a bit of everything*

d *There aren't many things for them to do.*

e *Djamel is fantastic with kids.*

f *We stayed three weeks.*

g *Some stayed with their own family.*

h *They met young Moroccans.*

1 **Djamel est formidable avec les gamins.**

2 **On est resté trois semaines.**

3 **Ils ont rencontré des jeunes marocains.**

4 **Certains sont restés avec leur famille.**

5 **un peu de tout**

6 **Vous travaillez avec des jeunes aussi?**

7 **Ils n'ont pas grand'chose à faire.**

8 **Dominique m'a beaucoup parlé de vous.**

2 **Look at the exercise above and answer the questions below.**

    a What expression means *met?*   resté   rencontré

    b Which expression means *stayed?*   resté   rencontré

Learn more

THE PERFECT TENSE WITH ÊTRE

Look back at Unit 12 where you met the perfect tense with **avoir**. Since then you have come across many examples of verbs that are formed with **avoir** in the perfect tense.

There are fewer verbs that form the perfect tense with **être** and they function slightly differently from those with **avoir**. They are closer to adjectives and in fact the past participle varies according to the gender and number of the subject in the same way that some adjectives do. For example, in the sentences below, **fatiguée** ends with an **-e** for feminine because it is *she* who is tired. **Allée** also ends with **-e** because it is *she* who went.

Adjective: **Elle est fatiguée.** *(She is tired.)*

Past participle: **Elle est allée en ville.** *(She went to town.)*

The thirteen verbs with **être**

 16.04 **There are only thirteen frequently used verbs which form the perfect tense with être. Listen to them and repeat.**

Base form	Past participle	Base form	Past participle
aller *(to go)*	allé	**naître** *(to be born)*	né
arriver *(to arrive)*	arrivé	**partir** *(to leave)*	parti
descendre *(to go down)*	descendu	**rester** *(to stay)*	resté
devenir *(to become)*	devenu	**sortir** *(to go out)*	sorti
entrer *(to enter)*	entré	**tomber** *(to fall)*	tombé
monter *(to go up)*	monté	**venir** *(to come)*	venu
mourir *(to die)*	mort		

Study the examples below carefully, paying particular attention to the spelling of the past participle:

Je suis <u>allée</u> à la banque. *(a woman speaking)*

Tu es <u>arrivé</u> en retard ce matin, Pierre! *(someone speaking to a young boy)*

Sophie est <u>devenue</u> très sage. *(very well-behaved)*

Mathieu est <u>entré</u> à l'université.

Nous sommes <u>descendus</u> de voiture. *(m.pl. – more than one man or a man and woman)*

Nous sommes <u>entrées</u> à la Samaritaine. *(f.pl. – more than one woman speaking)*

Vous êtes <u>né</u> à Paris, Maurice? *(addressing one male only)*

Vous êtes <u>partis</u> sans moi les garçons! *(m.pl.)*

Ils sont <u>morts</u> dans un accident de voiture. *(Dodi and Princess Diana)*

Elles sont <u>venues</u> à pied. *(f.pl. - They walked here.)*

How to remember the verbs with **être**

The following story is a mnemonic device that you can easily use to remember most of the verbs with **être**. It is the story of Henri, who was born in Marseille, went to Paris, went up the Eiffel Tower, went up to the second floor, stayed there half an hour, came down, came out, went to see la Seine, fell in it and died:

Henri est né à Marseille. À l'âge de trente ans il est venu à Paris. Il est allé à la Tour Eiffel. Il est entré. Il est monté jusqu'au deuxième étage. Il est resté là une demi-heure. Il est descendu. Il est sorti. Il est allé au bord de la Seine. Malheureusement il est tombé et il est mort.

 You may want to write out the story of Henri's twin sister, Henriette to help you remember!

> Henriette est née à Marseille ...
> If you want to write a different version with
> Henri and Henriette both involved, it starts:
> Henri et Henriette sont nés à Marseille ...*

*Note: In groups involving one masculine and one feminine person or thing, use the masculine plural.

Reflexive verbs with **être**

In addition to these specific thirteen verbs, all reflexive verbs form the perfect tense with **être**. When they are not reflexive, they form the perfect tense with **avoir**. For example, **couper** *(to cut)* has the past participle form **coupé**. When using the perfect tense with **avoir**, this sentence means *She cut the bread with a knife.*

Caroline <u>a coupé</u> du pain avec un couteau.

However, when using the perfect tense with **être**, this sentence means *She cut herself with a knife.*

Caroline s'est coupée* avec un couteau.

Note: The reflexive verb has extra **-e** on past participle because Caroline is feminine.

INSIGHT: LANGUAGE

Watch out for little words that sound the same but have very different meanings: **s'est**, **ces**, **sait** and **c'est** all sound the same.

Caroline s'est coupée.	*Caroline cut herself.*
Ces jeunes gens sont allés au Maroc.	*These young people went to Morocco.*
Il ne sait pas où est son père.	*He doesn't know where his father is.*
C'est difficile.	*It's difficult.*

Practice

Make six correct sentences and say what they mean.

a	*Djamel est l'animateur qui s'*	**1**	sont allés au Maroc.
b	*Sarah et Dominique*	**2**	êtes parti avec un groupe de jeunes?
c	*Je*	**3**	est occupé du voyage.
d	*Les jeunes*	**4**	est resté trois semaines au Maroc.
e	*Vous*	**5**	sont arrivées chez Gildas.
f	*Le groupe*	**6**	suis monté(e) à la Tour Eiffel.

16.05 It's your turn to ask questions. You are speaking to Adidja, Djamel's friend, who is also an animatrice socio-culturelle. Listen to the cue and ask the question. Then listen to check your answer and pronunciation.

Vous	**a**	*Ask her if she went to Morocco with the group.*
Adidja		Oui, j'y suis allée.
Vous	**b**	*Ask her how many young people went to Morocco.*
Adidja		Dix-huit. Huit filles et dix garçons.
Vous	**c**	*Ask her how long they stayed.*
Adidja		Nous sommes restés trois semaines.
Vous	**d**	*Ask her if they met young Moroccans.*
Adidja		Oui, beaucoup. C'était formidable.

Est-ce que la France mérite la réputation d'être le pays des droits de l'homme? Lisez les résultats de l'enquête du Nouvel Observateur. Does France deserve its reputation as the country of human rights? Look at the results of a sondage (*opinion poll*) and answer the questions.

Sondage

«Le Nouvel Observateur» vient de publier une enquête sur la façon dont les Français d'origine étrangère jugent la France. Voici ce qu'ils répondent à deux des questions.

– Est-ce que vous avez été personnellement victime de propos ou de comportements racistes?

Oui	65%
Non	32%
Ne se prononcent pas	3%

– Pensez-vous que la réputation de la France comme pays d'accueil et pays des droits de l'homme est tout à fait justifiée, assez justifiée, peu justifiée, ou pas du tout justifiée?

Tout à fait et assez justifiée	50%
Peu et pas du tout justifiée	48%
Ne se prononcent pas	2%

Combien de Français d'origine étrangère...

    a   pensent que la réputation de la France est justifiée? _____

    b   pensent que la réputation de la France n'est pas justifiée?

    _____

    c   ont été victimes de racisme? _____

    d   n'ont pas été victimes de racisme? _____

How to you feel about the article above? Answer the questions in the survey and give reasons for how you feel.

1. Moi, J'ai l'impression que ...
2. _____
3. _____
4. _____

Union européenne
République française

PASSEPORT

 # Test yourself

Une carte postale du Maroc

Salut Gildas,

Juste un petit mot pour te dire que tout va bien. Nous sommes arrivés ici à Marrakech samedi dernier. Les jeunes qui ont des contacts dans la région sont partis visiter leurs familles et sont restés quelques jours mais ils ont maintenant rejoint le groupe; tous sauf Yousef qui est parti chez sa sœur, et Nadima qui s'est installée chez sa tante. La tante est venue la chercher à l'aéroport et la ramènera quelques jours avant le départ.

Donc tout va bien. Pas d'incident à part Saïd qui s'est cassé la figure* en faisant l'idiot mais rien de grave heureusement. Je t'enverrai un mail la semaine prochaine.

A bientôt

Djamel

*Note: se casser la figure (to fall over) (lit. to break one's face)

1. **Choose the correct answer for each of the questions.**

   a Where is Djamel writing from: a) Marrakech b) the airport c) Nadima's house?

   b Who will bring Nadima back to their base: a) Djamel b) her sister c) her aunt?

   c They arrived in Morocco: a) 3 weeks ago b) last Saturday c) yesterday.

   d Some young people did not stay with the group: a) they visited their families b) they went camping as a group c) they visited Saïd in hospital

   e Yousef is staying: a) with his aunt b) in hospital c) with his sister.

2. **Read the postcard again and find a phrase meaning:**
   a I will send you an email.
   b Everything is OK.
   c He fell over while mucking about.
   d Nothing serious.
   e They are now back with the group.

3. **Use what you have learnt and say the following:**
   a They went to visit their families.
   b She will bring her back here.
   c They stayed a few days.
   d We arrived here on Saturday.
   e She settled down at her aunt's house.

SELF CHECK

I CAN...
● ... understand a little about multi-ethnic France.
● ... talk about young people and their activities.
● ... read an opinion poll about racism.
● ... use the perfect tense with **être**.

On cherche du travail

Looking for work

In this unit you will learn how to:
▶ *talk about jobs and professions.*
▶ *look for jobs in the newspaper.*
▶ *express the past with the imperfect tense.*

CEFR: *Can find and understand relvant information in every day material (B1); Can pass on detailed information legibly (B2); Can adapt reading style to different texts and purposes (B2).*

 ## Apprenticeships in France

Lots of young people in France undertake apprenticeships as a way of entering the job market. The national apprenticeship scheme includes **le Dima** (*Dispositif d'Initiation aux Métiers en Alternance*), which is open to young people **à l'âge de 15 ans** (*at the age of 15*) and gives one year of unpaid work experience, at the end of which a one to three year apprenticeship program is offered, depending on the school qualifications that accompany the in-company work. In 2012, **le salaire de l'apprenti** (*the apprentice's salary*) was based on the Minimum Wage, **le SMIC** (*Salaire Minimum Interprofessionnel de Croissance*), but various percentages apply **selon l'âge** (*according to age*) and **le nombre d'années de contrat** (*number of years of contract*). For example anyone **de moins de 18 ans** (*under the age of 18*) and in **leur première année** (*their first year*) of apprenticeship will get 40% of the SMIC, 50% in their second year and 60% in their third and final year **d'apprentissage**.

a   How long is an apprenticeship?

Vocabulary builder

PROFESSIONS

 17.01 Listen and match the French professions to the English translations. Then listen again and repeat.

a	Prof de Philo	1	Editor
b	Professeur de français	2	Wine grower
c	Viticulteur	3	French teacher
d	Pharmacienne	4	German teacher
e	Professeur d'allemand	5	Pharmacist
f	Editrice	6	Philosophy teacher

TASKS FOR PÔLE EMPLOI

 17.02 Pôle emploi is an organization devoted to getting the unemployed back to work. At Pôle emploi a single person is in charge of all aspects of job-seeking. Listen and match the job-seeking tasks in French and English. Then listen and repeat.

a L'accueil et l'inscription des chômeurs
  1 *Welcoming and registering the unemployed*
  2 *Professional training and job-hunting*

b L'indemnisation des chômeurs
  1 *Welcoming and registering the unemployed*
  2 *Unemployment insurance*

c La formation professionnelle et recherche de travail
  1 *Unemployment insurance*
  2 *Professional training and job-hunting*

NEW EXPRESSIONS

Look at the expressions that are used in the next conversations. Note their meanings.

Conversation 1

apprendre	*to learn but also to teach someone something*
dès	*since*
dès que	*as soon as*
enseigner	*to teach (done as a job)*
être à la retraite	*to be retired*
couramment	*fluently*
maison d'édition	*publishing company*

INSIGHT: LANGUAGE

Enseigner refers to teaching, as in at a school.
J'enseigne l'espagnol dans un lycée. *(I teach Spanish in an upper secondary school.)*
Apprendre means *to learn.*
J'apprends la musique. *(I am learning music.)*
Apprendre quelque chose à quelqu'un means *to teach someone something.*
Mon professeur m'apprend à jouer du piano. *(My teacher teaches me to play the piano.)*

INSIGHT: LANGUAGE

More possessive adjectives

My - **mon père, ma mère, mes parents**
Your - **votre / ton père, votre / ta mère, vos / tes parents**

Conversations

1 17.03 **Dominique et Sarah sont arrivées chez les parents de Dominique, Monsieur et Madame Périer, à Pessac, une ville près de Bordeaux.**

a **Listen once to the recording and answer the questions.**

1 What does M. Périer think of Sarah's French? _____

2 What does Dominique say about it? _____

Conversation 1

M. Périer	Mais vous parlez bien le français, Sarah.
Dominique	Sarah est bilingue, Papa!
Sarah	C'est-à-dire que ma mère est française et elle m'a appris le français dès toute petite et le français était la première langue à la maison.
M. Périer	Ah bon! Et qu'est-ce qu'ils font vos parents?
Sarah	Mes parents étaient tous les deux professeurs de langues. Mon père était professeur d'allemand mais il est mort d'un cancer il y a cinq ans. Il parlait couramment le français et l'allemand.
Mme Périer	Je suis désolée. Votre maman va bien?
Sarah	Oui, oui, elle enseigne toujours le français dans une école à Londres.
M. Périer	Et vous, qu'est-ce que vous faites comme profession?
Sarah	Je suis éditrice dans une maison d'édition.
M.Périer	Ah, c'est un métier très intéressant! Dites-moi...
Mme Périer	Voyons François, tu vas fatiguer Sarah avec toutes tes questions. Je vais vous montrer votre chambre.
(Un peu plus tard)	
Sarah	Quelle belle maison! Qu'est-ce qu'ils font tes parents?
Dominique	Oh ils sont à la retraite depuis deux ans. Ma mère travaillait en tant que pharmacienne dans une grande pharmacie de Bordeaux et mon père était viticulteur.

b **Now listen again or read to answer the questions below.**

1 Who spoke French at home when Sarah was a child? _____

2 What happened to Sarah's father? _____

3 How long ago was that? _____

4 How is Sarah's mother? _____

5 Why does Mme Périer interrupt her husband? _____

6 What is she going to show Sarah? _____

7 How long ago did M. et Mme Périer retire? _____

c **Match the names of the people to their professions. Tick the names of those who are still working.**

Noms	Profession/métier
a Dominique	**1** Prof de Philo
b Sarah	**2** Professeur de français
c Mme Périer	**3** Viticulteur
d M. Périer	**4** Editrice
e Mr. Burgess	**5** Pharmacienne
f Mrs. Burgess	**6** Professeur d'allemand

2 17.04 **Three unemployed young people are outside Pôle emploi.**

a **Listen to the recording once, then answer the questions:**

1 What kind of apprenticeship does Raphaël want to do? _____

2 What does Youssef say about his brother Rashid? _____

3 What does Rashid do now? _____

Conversation 2

Raphaël	Salut, vous venez avec moi?
Lætitia	Où ça? A Pôle emploi? Qu'est-ce que tu vas faire?
Raphaël	Je voudrais des renseignements sur l'apprentissage.
Lætitia	Un apprentissage pour faire quoi?
Raphaël	Je ne sais pas moi, je vais demander ce qu'on peut faire.
Youssef	Mon frère Rashid, il était apprenti-boulanger.
Lætitia	Ah oui? Et maintenant qu'est-ce qu'il fait? Des croissants?
Raphaël	Arrête un moment, Lætitia!
Youssef	Maintenant mon frère a un vrai boulot chez un boulanger. L'inconvénient, avant il aimait bien sortir en boîte et tout, et maintenant il ne peut plus parce qu'il commence à travailler à cinq heures du matin.
Lætitia	Bon alors, vous venez? On y va à Pôle emploi mais pas pour devenir apprenti-boulanger! Moi j'aimerais bien travailler dans une pharmacie ou quelque chose comme ça. Alors tu viens Youssef, on va aider Raphaël à choisir son apprentissage.
Raphaël	Ah, non, elle me casse les pieds celle-là! Tu n'as qu'à en choisir un pour toi, d'apprentissage!

b **Now listen again or read to answer the questions below.**

   1 According to Youssef what can't his brother Rashid do any longer? _____

   2 At what time does Rashid start work in the morning? _____

   3 Where does Lætitia say she would like to work? _____

 # Language discovery

1 **Link the following English phrases to the equivalent French expressions from Conversation 2.**

a *Are you coming with me?*	**1** Il commence à travailler à cinq heures du matin.
b *My brother used to be an apprentice.*	**2** quelque chose comme ça
c *He starts work at five in the morning.*	**3** Et maintenant qu'est-ce qu'il fait?
d *What does he do now?*	**4** Vous venez avec moi?
e *something like that*	**5** On va aider Raphaël à choisir.
f *We are going to help Raphaël choose.*	**6** Mon frère était apprenti.

2 **Look at the above exercises and answer the questions below.**

   a Do you use an article like a or an with the structure subject + **être** + profession?   Yes   No

   b Which expression is a form of the verb **être**?   **était**   **fait**

Learn more

1 TALKING ABOUT PROFESSIONS

In Unit 3 you learnt that there is no indefinite article in front of the name of a profession. This applies with the following structure only: subject + **être** + name of profession.

Elle était pharmacienne.	*She used to be a pharmacist.*
Elle est Ministre de l'Environnement.	*She is the Minister for the Environment.*
Il est ingénieur.	*He is an engineer.*
Je suis professeur d'allemand.	*I am a German teacher.*

However, in some structures the definite article is required.

J'avais horreur de la prof de maths.	*I couldn't stand the maths teacher.*

2 ONE MORE WAY TO EXPRESS THE PAST: THE IMPERFECT TENSE

The various past tenses of verbs offer a range of nuances for what happened in the past. The perfect and the imperfect are often used in the same sentence to express how one event occurred in relation to another event.

How to form the imperfect

To form the imperfect tense you need to learn the following endings. They apply to all verbs without exception.

> **INSIGHT: LANGUAGE**
>
> The imperfect tense expressions **Il était une fois...** *(Once upon a time...)* and **il fallait**, the past tense of **il faut** *(from **falloir** must / ought to)* can only be used with the pronoun **il**. Both are impersonal expressions.
>
> **Il était une fois trois petits cochons...** *(Once upon a time there were three little pigs...)*
>
> **Il fallait me le dire!** *(I ought to have been told!)*

Subject pronouns	Verb endings	Subject pronouns	Verb endings
je	-ais	nous	-ions
tu	-ais	vous	-iez
il/elle	-ait	ils/elles	-aient

The four verbs below should provide you with a pattern for all other verbs in the imperfect.

Subject pronouns	Verbs			
	être	parler	finir	prendre
je/j'	étais	parlais	finissais	prenais
tu	étais	parlais	finissais	prenais
il/elle/on	était	parlait	finissait	prenait
nous	étions	parlions	finissions	prenions
vous	étiez	parliez	finissiez	preniez
ils/elles	étaient	parlaient	finissaient	prenaient

When to use the imperfect tense

1 When an action that was continuous or relatively lengthy is interrupted by a shorter one expressed by the perfect.

J'étais aux Etats-Unis quand **j'ai appris** la mort de mon père. (*I was in the US when I learnt of my father's death.*)

In this example, both events took place in the past but the person was in the US longer than the few seconds it took to hear the news.

Nous sommes arrivées au moment où **il prenait** sa douche. (*We arrived just as he was taking his shower.*)

Here, taking a shower is relatively longer than the action of arriving somewhere.

Les jeunes filles travaillaient au café quand <u>la bombe a explosé</u>.
(The girls were working in the café when the bomb went off.)

2 When reminiscing, talking about and describing how things used to be and referring to events which occurred repeatedly in the past.

Quand j'étais petite <u>je passais</u> toutes mes vacances en France.
(When I was little I used to spend all my holidays in France.)

Nous allions chez notre grand-mère en Provence. *(We used to go to my grandmother in Provence.)*

Nos grand-parents s'occupaient bien de nous. *(Our grand-parents took good care of us.)*

Nous travaillions dans les champs tous les étés. *(We used to work in the fields every summer.)*

Nous prenions le goûter tous les après-midi. On mangeait des confitures délicieuses. *(We had tea every afternoon. We ate delicious jams.)*

> ### INSIGHT: LANGUAGE
> A verb in the perfect tense often follows an expression starting with an adverb indicating the past, for example **autrefois** *(in the old days).*
> **Autrefois il faisait toujours chaud en été.** *(In the old days it was always hot in summer.)*
> **Ta grand-mère était très belle autrefois.** *(Your grandmother was very beautiful in the old days.)*

3 A BRIEF INTRODUCTION TO THE CONDITIONAL

The endings of conditionals are similar to the imperfect tense, but the construction is similar to the future tense. Look at the examples in the chart.

imperfect	**Mon grand-père travaillait à l'usine.**	*My grandfather worked at the factory.*
future	**Après ses études ma sœur travaillera à Paris.**	*After her studies my sister will work in Paris.*
conditional	**Elle travaillerait si elle pouvait.**	*She would work if she could.*

Practice

1 Qu'est-ce que vous faisiez quand vous étiez jeune? Answer with the verbs in the imperfect tense. Start your answers with Je/J'.

a danser

b skier

c faire du basket

d aller à la pêche

e faire de la planche à roulettes

f jouer du piano

PRONUNCIATION

1 17.05 **Read the explanation. Then listen and repeat the words in bold.**

In Unit 14 you were given a few examples of verbs where **c** became **ç** in order to keep the same sound. A similar process takes place in the imperfect tense with verbs ending in **-cer** and verbs ending in **-ger**.

▶ **Commencer** *(to begin)*: **je commençais, elle commençait, ils commençaient**

These are all pronounced the same way. With **nous commencions** and **vous commenciez** the cedilla disappears again because it is not required. Remember, **c** followed by **i** sounds like [**s**].

▶ **Manger** *(to eat)*, **nager** *(to swim)*: In order to keep the sound [**je**], verbs ending with **-ger** keep the **e** after the **g**: **Je nageais, elle nageait, ils nageaient**

The **-e** disappears with **nous nagions** and **vous nagiez** because **g+i** has a [**je**] sound.

2 17.06 **Read the explanation. Then listen and repeat the words in bold.**

Because some words tend to be linked up together, you may frequently hear utterances that are not exactly grammatically correct, but are used in everyday conversation.

Tu n'as qu'à en choisir un pour toi! *(You'd better choose one. Lit. You only have to choose one for yourself.)*

The structure is: **ne + avoir + que + à** but in everyday language the ne disappears, even in public talk by most eminent people (on TV, radio etc.). This is high on the list of language used to give advice, for making suggestions in all sorts of circumstances but especially when people suggest what the government should be doing:

Ils n'ont qu'à... *(all they need to do)* becomes **ils ont qu'à... [isonka]**

Tu n'as qu'à ... *(all you need to do)* becomes **t'as qu'à... [taka]**

Il n'y a qu'à... *(all that's needed)* becomes **y a qu'à... [yaka]**

> **INSIGHT: CULTURE**
> You may even see **YACKA** used as the name of bars or cafés, places where people put the world right!

SPEAKING

17.07 **You have decided to choose an apprenticeship. Look at the list of work categories. Tell the employee the categories that interest you. Then listen to confirm your answers.**

Exemple: Say you think you are interested in the building trade.

| Employé | **Quel genre de métiers vous intéressent?** |
| Vous | **Je m'intéresse aux métiers du bâtiment.** |

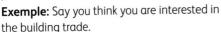

a	**Employé**	Quel genre de métiers vous intéresse?
	Vous	Say you are interested in the hotel industry.
b	**Employé**	Qu'est-ce qui vous intéresse?
	Vous	Say you are interested in photography.
c	**Employé**	Quel genre de métiers vous intéresse?
	Vous	Say you are interested in jobs to do with health.
d	**Employé**	À quoi vous intéressez-vous?
	Vous	Say you are interested in the clothing industry.

Métiers du bâtiment

 Métiers de la chaudronnerie et de la métallerie

 Métiers de bouche

 Métiers de l'hôtellerie et de la restauration

 Métiers de la santé et des soins personnels

 Métiers de l'hygiène et de l'environnement

 Métiers de l'habillement

 Métiers de la photographie et des industries graphiques

 Métiers du commerce et de la distribution

 Métiers du secrétariat et de la comptabilité

 Métiers du secteur agricole

 Métiers de la pierre

READING

Read an excerpt from an apprentice's contract and then answer the questions. You are not expected to understand every word of the text.

LE CONTRAT D'APPRENTISSAGE

LE CONTENU DU CONTRAT

Le contrat d'apprentissage est un contrat de travail de type particulier qui permet au jeune d'acquérir une qualification professionnelle sanctionnée par un diplôme technologique ou professionnel, ou un titre homologué. Ce type de contrat associe une formation en entreprise et des enseignements dans un Centre de Formation d'Apprentis (CFA).

SIGNATAIRES Le contrat d'apprentissage est signé entre l'employeur, l'apprenti et le C.F.A. Il concerne tous les employeurs et tous les jeunes de 16 à moins de 26 ans.

DURÉE La durée d'un contrat d'apprentissage est en général de 2 ans. Elle peut être portée à 3 ans ou réduite à 1 an en fonction du métier, de la qualification préparée et du niveau initial de l'apprenti.

PÉRIODE D'ESSAI Les deux premiers mois constituent une période d'essai pendant laquelle le contrat peut être rompu.

CONGÉS ● L'apprenti bénéficie d'un congé annuel de 5 semaines.

● Au même titre que les autres salariées, l'apprentie peut bénéficier d'un congé maternité (6 semaines avant la date présumée de l'accouchement et 10 semaines après).

● Des congés pour événements familiaux sont également accordés, à savoir :
   4 jours pour le mariage de l'apprenti,
   3 jours pour sa présélection militaire,
   3 jours pour la naissance de l'enfant de l'apprenti,
   2 jours pour le décès du conjoint ou d'un enfant de l'apprenti,
   1 jour pour le décès du père ou de la mère de l'apprenti.

TEMPS DE FORMATION Sur son temps de travail, le jeune suit une formation générale et technologique dans un centre de formation. La durée varie en fonction de la formation choisie (entre 1 à 2 semaines par mois).

a How old do you have to be to sign the contract?
b How long is the apprenticeship for?
c Can it be lengthened or shortened?
d How long is the trial period?
e What can happen during that time?
f How many weeks' holiday does an apprentice have?
g How much maternity leave does a young woman get?
h How many days off do apprentices get:
   1 to get married?
   2 for the birth of a child?
k What kind of course does the apprentice have to lattend?
i What proportion of the time has to be spent on a course?

Go further

Où chercher du travail?
Where to look for work?
Look at the adverts from both a website and a local journal. Then answer questions a–h.

http://www.libération.com

PROFILS NET

Toutes les annonces *d'offres d'emploi* parues dans Libération *depuis* *quinze jours.*
Dès *aujourd'hui* vous pouvez y *répondre* instantanément en laissant *votre CV.*

NOTRE OBJECTIF :

VOUS FORMER À L'INFORMATIQUE DE GESTION

Nous vous proposons une formation de 1200 heures à l'informatique, dans le cadre d'un contrat de qualification.

Dynamique, motivé, âgé de moins de 26 ans, vous êtes diplômé de mathématiques, physique, chimie, sciences économiques, gestion…, l'informatique vous intéresse et vous souhaitez en faire votre métier.

Alors n'hésitez plus, prenez contact avec nous, nous nous ferons un plaisir de vous présenter notre structure et nos projets de développement.

OPPORTUNITES

Des *formations,* des *voyages,* des *services,* des *produits*

Etes-vous prêt à travailler à l'étranger?

Alors consultez sur 3617 TO WORK*, nos centaines d'annonces classées
* "Travailler" en anglais

3617 TO WORK

2000 OFFRES D'EMPLOI
36.17 PLEIN EMPLOI

COMMERCIAL
VENTES

Sté LVG, vins de Bordeaux, recrute **2 VENDEURS** sur votre secteur, clientèle particuliers exclusivement, sur rendez-vous, profil, contact, convivialité, poste stable, débutants acceptés. Formation assurée. Tél. 02.99.55.74.74, pour rendez-vous, de 9 h à 17 h, sauf samedi.

EMPLOIS
DU COMMERCE

Discothèque Finistère-Sud cherche **PORTIER.** Tél. 02.98.70.81.95.

MÉTIERS
DE BOUCHE

Recherche **PATISSIER** sérieux, sachant travailler seul, Pont-de-Buis. Tél. 02.98.73.00.77.

APPRENTISSAGE

Recherche **APPRENTI(E) VENDEUR(SE)**en charcuterie-traiteur. Super U, Plestin-les-Grèves. Tél. 02.96.54.18.18.

GENS DE MAISON

LAVAL : recherche employée de maison, **temps plein,** logée, nourrie, pour s'occuper de deux enfants et entretien maison. Ecrire au Télégramme, 19, rue Jean-Macé, Brest, n° 12.787, qui transmettra.

Recherche DAME pour contrat temps plein, dans appartement centre **QUIMPER,** garde bébé, ménage, repassage. Tél. 02.98.95.28.58.

HOTELLERIE
RESTAURATION

SERVEUSE, 2 ans expérience, recherche emploi **RESTAURATION** traditionnelle ou gastronomique, région Brest ou Quimper. Tél. 02.98.84.64.76.

ADMINISTRATION
COMPTABILITÉ

FEMME, 48 ans, avec expérience, cherche emploi temps partiel, **SECRÉTARIAT, COMPTABILITÉ** ou **COMMERCE,** secteur Quimperlé ou environs. Tél. 02.98.71.86.46.

TECHNIQUE
PRODUCTION

ELECTRICIEN possédant CAP électroménager, bon bricoleur, expérience homme d'entretien, cherche **EMPLOI,** pour toutes propositions, tél. 02.98.96.45.18.

a What can you find on the Internet? _____
b If the advert is one week old, can you still find it? _____
c How and when can you answer the job adverts? _____
d Can you name three jobs which are advertised in the local paper? _____
e Can you give three types of jobs people are looking for? _____
f If you wanted to be trained in information technology for management purposes, how old would you have to be? _____
g Which qualities would you have to demonstrate? _____
h Which background would you need? _____

🕐 Test yourself

1 **Choose the correct answer to complete each of the sentences. Make sure you are using the correct tense and that the complete sentence is meaningful. There may be more than one correct option.**

   a Quand j'étais petite...a) j'habitais à Paris b) nous habiterons à Marseille c) je regarde la télé

b Quand elle est arrivée chez elle...a) la police sera là b) son frère partira c) sa mère était déjà là.

c Il prenait son déjeuner quand ...a) la police est arrivée b) il regardait la télé c) le téléphone sonnera.

d Autrefois...a) nous allions en vacances en Espagne b) nous camperons dans le jardin c) on aimait écouter le Top of the Pop.

e Il était une fois trois petits cochons qui...a) partiront en Angleterre b) voulaient bâtir 3 maisons c) aiment la confiture.

f A Noël...a) j'allais visiter mes grands-parents b) je mangeais trop de chocolat c) mes parents vont aux Jeux Olympiques de Londres.

2 Choose from the list below to complete the sentences:

enseignait   avait   a sonné   travaillait   prenais
prendre   voulions   était (2)   adorions   fallait

a Je _____ ma douche quand le téléphone _____

b Nous _____ réserver des places pour l'opéra mais il n'y en _____ plus.

c Le tsunami au Japon? Je crois que c'_____ le 11 mars 2011.

d Quand ma grand-mère _____ jeune, elle _____ chez un pâtissier à Paris.

e Elle nous _____ l'anglais avec des chansons. Nous _____ cela.

f Il _____ se lever tôt pour _____ le train de 6 heures du matin.

3 Complete the sentences below using the verb in bracket in the perfect tense

Exemple: Il (nager) plus vite que moi.   > il *nageait plus vite que moi.*

a Pendant les vacances nous (nager) tous les jours.

b Il (commencer) à neiger.

c Ils (manger) sans parler.

SELF CHECK

I CAN. . .
. . . talk about jobs and professions.
. . . look for jobs in the newspaper.
. . . express the past with the imperfect tense.

18 On prend le TGV
Catching the high-speed train

In this unit you will learn how to:
▶ *travel by rail and how to buy a ticket.*
▶ *better understand la SNCF and le TGV.*
▶ *use more verbs in the imperfect tense.*
▶ *use the subjunctive.*

CEFR: *Can understand instructions (B1); Can fluently sustain a conversation in a linear sequence of points (B1); Can explain why something is a problem (B1).*

Travelling by train

If you prefer **voyager** (*travelling*) **à travers la France** (*through France*) **par le train** (*by train*), starting or ending your journey in Paris, there are six main line stations which can take you to any corner of France. There are also **liaisons** (*links*) to airports and other major TGV stations around Paris.

Look at the map of Paris above with the six main railway stations: From la Gare Montparnasse, you go **vers l'ouest** (*towards the West*): **la Côte Atlantique, la Bretagne, le sud-ouest** (*the southwest*) et **l'Espagne** (*Spain*). From la Gare St Lazare you can get to **la Normandie.** From la Gare du Nord you can get to **le nord de la France, l'Angleterre et la Belgique.** From la Gare de l'Est you can reach **l'est de la France** (*the east of France*) et **l'Allemagne** (*Germany*). From la Gare de Lyon you can go to **le sud-est de la France, la côte méditerranéenne et l'Italie.** From la Gare d'Austerlitz you can reach **le centre de la France.**

 a **Where can you go to from la Gare Montparnasse?**
b **Which station would you use to get to Brussels?**

Vocabulary builder

ADDITIONAL EXPRESSIONS FOR TIMES OF DAY

 18.01 French uses two words interchangeably for the parts of the day and also for the year. Complete the pairs with the words from the box, then listen and repeat.

un an	une journée	un matin	une soirée

day	**un jour**	a _____
a morning	**b** _____	**une matinée**
an evening	**un soir**	c _____
a year	**d** _____	**une année**

EXPRESSIONS FOR SELF-SERVICE

 18.02 Both the terms automatique and libre-service mean *self-service*. **Listen and choose the correct translation for these self-service expressions.**

a **Une laverie automatique**
   1 self-service laundrette
   2 ATM / cashpoint

b **Un restaurant libre-service (une cafétéria)**
   1 ticket machine
   2 self-service restaurant

c **Un distributeur automatique (de billets; à la banque)**
   1 ATM / cashpoint
   2 ticket machine

d **Une billetterie automatique (à la gare ou à la station de métro)**
   1 self-service laundrette
   2 ticket machine

NEW EXPRESSIONS

Look at the expressions that are used in the next conversations. Note their meanings.

Conversation 1

le TGV: Train à Grande Vitesse	*high-speed train*
tout bonnement/tout simplement	*very simply*
sinon plus	*if not more*
la gare	*the station*
lorsque	*when*

Conversation 2

le suivant	*the next one* (from **suivre**, *to follow*)
la carte Senior	*SNCF concession card for old-age pensioners*
réfléchir	*to reflect/to think back*
la billetterie automatique	*the ticket machine*

Conversations

 1 18.03 *Sarah has spent a week visiting Bordeaux and Les Landes, the vast pine forests south of Bordeaux. She is now planning to travel back to London via Paris.*

a **Listen to the recording once through and answer the questions.**

    1 Why is Sarah leaving the Périers? _____

    2 What does Sarah think of the area? _____

b **Now listen again to answer these questions.**

    1 Where is Sarah going tomorrow? _____

    2 How is she getting there? _____

    3 How long will it take? _____

Conversation 1

M. Périer	Alors Sarah, vous nous quittez déjà?
Dominique	C'est vrai, la semaine est passée très vite! Sarah commence à bien connaître Bordeaux et les Landes, les vins de la région...
Sarah	Oui, j'adore votre région mais il faut que je rentre à Londres, je reprends le travail lundi et j'ai promis à ma sœur de passer quelques jours chez elle à Paris.
M. Périer	Vous prenez le TGV?
Sarah	Oui, c'est très rapide.
Mme Périer	Ça prend combien de temps maintenant pour monter à Paris?
Sarah	Ça dépend des trains mais en choisissant bien c'est faisable en trois heures.
M. Périer	Incroyable! On n'arrête pas le progrès! Savez-vous que lorsque j'étais jeune, j'étais étudiant à Paris, alors je prenais souvent le train pour rentrer. Cela prenait douze heures, sinon plus!
Dominique	Eh oui le progrès! Au fait Sarah, tu as réservé ta place dans le TGV? Tu pourrais le faire sur l'Internet.
Sarah	Non, je te remercie mais je préfère tout bonnement acheter mon billet à la gare. De toute façon on devait aller à Bordeaux cet après-midi, non?
Dominique	Oui bien sûr, c'est comme tu veux. À quelle heure tu pars demain?
Sarah	Je ne sais pas encore mais probablement entre quinze et seize heures: ma sœur viendra me chercher à Montparnasse après le travail, je pensais lui donner rendez-vous vers dix-neuf heures, dix-neuf heures quinze environ.

INSIGHT: LANGUAGE

All the tenses you are likely to need are used in Conversation 1! Here's a quick review.

Present:	**J'adore votre région.**
Perfect:	**J'ai promis à ma sœur.**
Imperfect:	**Je prenais souvent le train.**
Future:	**Ma sœur viendra me chercher.**
Conditional:	**Tu pourrais le faire.**
Subjunctive:	**Il faut que je rentre.**

c **Now listen again or read to answer the questions below.**
   1 How long will it take? _____
   2 How long did it use to take to get to Paris when Monsieur Périer was a student? _____
   3 What could Sarah use the Internet for? _____
   4 At what time is Sarah leaving tomorrow? _____
   5 Who is meeting Sarah on arrival? _____
   6 Name two things which, according to Dominique, Sarah is starting to know well. _____

2 18.04 *Sarah and Dominique are at the ticket office at Bordeaux railway station. An elderly couple is in front of them.*

a **Listen to their conversation, and answer the questions.**
   1 How long does it take to go from Bordeaux to Poitiers? _____
   2 What kind of tickets do the old couple want? Single or return? _____

b **Listen again and answer these questions.**
   1 Which day of the week does the couple wish to travel? _____
   2 One train leaves Bordeaux at 08.26. At what time does it arrive in Poitiers? _____

Conversation 2	
Vieille dame	Nous allons à Poitiers, ça prend combien de temps avec le TGV?
Employée de la SNCF	Voyons, une heure trois quarts environ, madame. Vous voulez réserver?
Vieux monsieur	Deux billets s'il vous plaît.
Employée	Deux billets simples ou deux allers-retours?
Vieille dame	Deux billets allers-retours, s'il vous plaît.
Employée	Quel jour désirez-vous voyager?
Vieille dame	Lucien, nous partons demain n'est-ce pas?
Vieux monsieur	Mais non, Simone, nous allons à Poitiers jeudi, c'est-à-dire après demain.
Employée	Jeudi? Vous prendrez le train de quelle heure?
Vieille dame	À quelle heure y-a-t-il un train dans la matinée?
Employée	Alors jeudi ... il y a un train qui part de Bordeaux à 08.26 qui arrive à Poitiers à 10.09. Le suivant est à 10.37, il arrive à 12.32, et finalement il y a un TGV à 11.59 qui arrive à Poitiers à 13.50.

Vieille dame	Dans ce cas nous prendrons celui de 10.37 et nous arriverons chez ma fille pour le déjeuner...
Employée	Et pour le retour?
Vieux monsieur	C'est-à-dire ... nous ne savons pas encore.
Employée	Ce n'est pas nécessaire de réserver votre retour maintenant, vous pourrez le faire plus tard. Vous avez votre carte Senior?
Vieux monsieur	Simone, c'est toi qui as les cartes Senior?
Vieille dame	Je ne sais pas où je les ai mises ... attendez, il faut que je réfléchisse.
Sarah à Dominique	Tu avais raison, je vais réserver mon billet à la billetterie automatique.

c **Now listen again or read to answer the questions below.**

   1 Which train do they choose in the end? _____

   2 What is the advantage of taking this particular train? _____

   3 Do they need to reserve their return tickets now? _____

   4 What does Sarah decide to do? _____

> **INSIGHT: LANGUAGE**
>
> Note the spellings used for the types of tickets mentioned in Conversation 2. For **deux billets simples**, the adjective (simple) has an added s to reflect the plural of the noun billets. In **deux billets allers-retours** the verb **aller** is used as a noun and therefore both **aller** and **retour** are spelt with and s when there are more than one ticket.

Language discovery

1 **Link the English phrases to the equivalent French expressions from Conversation 1.**

  a *Well, then, Sarah, are you leaving us already?* _____

  b *Sarah is starting to know Bordeaux well.* _____

  c *I am going back to work on Monday.* _____

  d *Incredible! Progress never stops!* _____

  e *I used to be a student.* _____

  1 **Je reprends le travail lundi.**

  2 **J'étais étudiant.**

  3 **Je prenais souvent le train pour rentrer.**

  4 **Alors Sarah, vous nous quittez déjà?**

  5 **Je pensais lui donner rendez-vous vers 7h.**

f *I often took the train to get home.* _____

g *We were going to go to Bordeaux this afternoon, weren't we?* _____

h *I thought I would arrange to meet her around 7 p.m.* _____

6 Sarah commence à bien connaître Bordeaux.

7 Incroyable! On n'arrête pas le progrès.

8 On devait aller à Bordeaux cet après-midi, non?

2 Link the following English phrases to the equivalent French expressions from Conversation 2.

a *Would you like to make a reservation?* _____

b *Which day would you like to travel?* _____

c *We are leaving tomorrow, aren't we?* _____

d *We'll get to my daughter in time for lunch.* _____

e *We don't know yet.* _____

f *Wait, I have to think.* _____

g *I don't know where I put them.* _____

h *You were right.* _____

1 Nous ne savons pas encore.

2 Nous partons demain, n'est-ce-pas?

3 Attendez, il faut que je réfléchisse.

4 Vous voulez réserver?

5 Quel jour désirez-vous voyager?

6 Je ne sais pas où je les ai mises.

7 Tu avais raison.

8 Nous arriverons chez ma fille pour le déjeuner.

3 Reorder the words in these key expressions from Conversation 1 and 2.

a c'est / tu / comme / veux

b combien / temps? / ça / de / prend

c ne / pas / nous / encore / savons

d faut / réfléchisse / je / il / que

Learn more

1 PREPOSITIONS + INFINITIVE

You already know that when two verbs follow one another the second one is in the infinitive form. For example:

On devait aller à Bordeaux.

Verbs following a preposition are also in the infinitive. Prepositions are words which have a constant spelling. They are placed in front of nouns or pronouns or in front of verbs. The following prepositions are frequently used in front of verbs in the infinitive:

à *(at)*   **de** *(to/of)*   **pour** *(for/in order to)*   **sans** *(without)*

pour monter à Paris   *in order to get to Paris*

sans arrêter   *without stopping*

J'ai essayé de ranger.   *I tried to tidy up.*

2 THE SUBJUNCTIVE

The subjunctive is a verb form that is commonly used in French. In fact you have already come across it in Unit 13 in sentences starting with **il faut que**. The subjunctive is a verb form that has its own range of past tenses, although the present tense of the subjunctive is the most used of all. This course will only provide you with examples of the present subjunctive and a few examples of the past form with **avoir** and **être**, as you are not likely to meet other forms when you hear spoken French.

The subjunctive is usually preceded by a verb + **que**. However, there are many verbs with **que** that are not followed by the subjunctive. So this alone is not a guide to whether or not you should use the subjunctive. Instead, look at the meaning of the sentence. The subjunctive is mainly used to express necessity, possibility, doubt, regrets, wishes or fear. The subjunctive is automatically used after the following expressions:

Necessity:
Il faut que je rentre à Londres. *It is necessary that I should go back to London.*

Possibility:
Il est possible que je rentre à Londres la semaine prochaine. *There is a possibility that I shall return to London next week.*

Doubt:
Je doute que je rentre à Londres avant dimanche. *I doubt that I shall be going back to London before Sunday.*

Regrets:
Je regrette qu'elle rentre déjà à Londres. *I am sorry that she is already going back to London.*

Wishes:

Je veux qu'elle rentre à Londres immédiatement. *I want her to go back to London immediately.*

Fear:

J'ai peur qu'elle rentre à Londres sans moi. *I am afraid that she may return to London without me.*

The ending pattern is similar for all verbs in the present subjunctive except for **avoir** and **être**.

Verb endings of the present subjunctive			
je	-e	**nous**	-ions (-yons for avoir and être)
tu	-es	**vous**	-iez (-yez for avoir and être)
elle	-e	**ils**	-ent
Prendre (*to take*)			
que je prenne		que nous prenions	
que tu prennes		que vous preniez	
qu'elle prenne		qu'ils prennent	

Sometimes the subjunctive can be avoided by omitting **que** and using **de** + infinitive; however the sense may be slightly changed.

Subjunctive: **Il est possible que je rentre à Paris la semaine prochaine.**

Infinitive after preposition **de**: **Il est possible de rentrer à Paris la semaine prochaine.**

When you feel ready to use the subjunctive you will find that your French has a slightly more authentic ring to it.

3 UN JOUR/ UNE JOURNÉE, UN MATIN/UNE MATINÉE, UN SOIR/UNE SOIRÉE, UN AN/UNE ANNÉE

As you remember from *Vocabulary builder*, there are two words for each of the following parts of the day and also for the year.

un jour	**une journée**	*a day*
un matin	**une matinée**	*a morning*
un soir	**une soirée**	*an evening*
un an	**une année**	*a year*

There is only a slight difference in meaning between the two forms and indeed that difference is not translatable in English. **Un jour, un matin, un soir, un an** are more likely to describe a portion of time defined by the calendar or the clock (an objective connotation). **Une journée, une matinée, une soirée, une année** have a social connotation and are more likely to express the time experienced by individuals (a more subjective meaning).

Nous partirons dans trois jours.	*We'll leave in three days time.*
Nous avons passé une excellente journée au bord de la mer.	*We spent an excellent day at the seaside.*
Il passe un an à Paris.	*He is spending one year in Paris.*
Bonne année tout le monde!	*Have a good year everyone!*

INSIGHT: LANGUAGE

The following phrase uses **an** and **année** together and is a good example showing how the feminine form is used more to refer to the social aspect of time.

Le 31 décembre à minuit on fête le Nouvel An et on se souhaite une Bonne Année. *(On 31 December at midnight we celebrate the New Year and wish everyone a Happy New Year.)*

 ## Practice

1 **Quel temps? See whether you can identify which tenses are being used in the following sentences. Match the sentence with the correct tense.**

a tu as réservé ta place?

b je te remercie

c je prenais souvent le train

d il faut que je rentre à Londres

e ma sœur viendra me chercher

f tu pourrais le faire par internet

1 present subjunctive

2 perfect tense

3 present indicative

4 imperfect

5 conditional

6 future

2 **Choisissez le bon mot. Choose the correct word (a or b) to complete the sentences.**

a Nous avons passé _____ magnifique chez nos amis. (un soir/une soirée)

b Dans trois _____ il aura cinquante ans. (ans/années)

c Il y a sept _____ dans une semaine. (jours/journées)

d Mon frère a onze _____ de moins que moi. (ans/années)

PRONUNCIATION

18.05 **Read the explanation and then listen and repeat the bolded words.**

▶ **C'est faisable.** *(It's feasible.)* Here, **-ai-** has a neutral sound similar to the **e** of **je** [je].

▶ **On n'arrête pas le progrès. On arrête la voiture.** There is no difference in sound between the two phrases here. But the listener knows that the first example is a negative sentence because of **pas** after the verb.

SPEAKING

18.06 **You are in Bordeaux and want to reserve a single ticket on the TGV travelling tomorrow. You want to get to Paris by 11 a.m. Look at the train timetable and decide on a train.**

Arcachon → Bordeaux → Paris / Ile de France

| PRIX | | | | TGV vert: toutes les réductions (minimum 15%) sont calculées sur le prix normal de niveau **1** | Pour connaître le prix de votre billet, consultez - Si vous voyagez en 1ᵉ classe la page 46 - Si vous voyagez en 2ᵉ classe la page 47 |

N° du TGV		8402	8404	8410	8410	8412	7850	8414	7860(1)	8518	8420	8420
Restauration												(4)
Arcachon	D					a	b	b	b	b		
Facture	D					a	b	b	b	b		
Bordeaux	D	4.59	6.01		6.08	6.42	6.46	7.05	7.59	8.22		8.26
Libourne	D	5.18			6.27			7.26				
Angoulême	D	6.03		7.10	7.10			8.11	8.58		9.25	9.25
Ruffec	D			e					c		c	e
Poitiers	D	6.47		7.55	7.55		8.28	8.56	9.43		10.09	10.09
Châtellerault	D	7.04		8.12	8.12						10.25	10.25
Saint-Pierre-des-Corps	D						9.08	9.37	10.23		10.54	10.54
Massy TGV	D						9.58		11.13			
Marne la Vallée Chessy	D						10.34		11.53			
Aéroport Ch.de Gaulle TGV	D						10.49		12.06			
Paris-Montparnasse 1-2	D	8.20	9.00	9.30	9.30	9.40		10.35		11.25	11.50	11.50

Now listen to the recording and respond to the employee's questions.

a	**Vous**	Say you would like to reserve a ticket to Paris, please.
	Employée	Vous voyagez aujourd'hui?
b	**Vous**	Say no, you are travelling tomorrow.
	Employée	Vous prenez le train de quelle heure?
c	**Vous**	Say you take the 7:05 train.
	Employée	Vous prenez un billet aller-retour?
d	**Vous**	Say no, you would like a single. Ask the price of the ticket.

LISTENING

18.07 **Look at the map and listen to the recording. Find out how long it takes to get from Paris to other cities.**

INSIGHT: LANGUAGE

Remember that you can say **un nouveau livre** but you cannot use **nouveau** before a noun starting with a vowel. You have to say **le nouvel an, un nouvel ami, un nouvel appartement.**

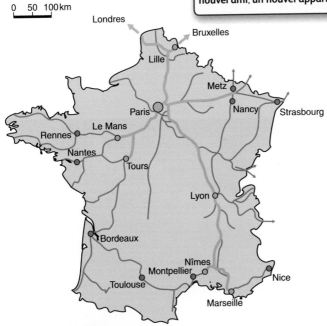

0 50 100 km

Londres
Bruxelles
Lille
Metz
Paris
Nancy
Strasbourg
Le Mans
Rennes
Nantes
Tours
Lyon
Bordeaux
Nîmes
Montpellier
Toulouse
Nice
Marseille

―― Ligne à Grande Vitesse
― "Ligne TGV" d'après les documents de la SNCF à destination du grand public
◎ "Ville de la Grande Vitesse"
● Métropoles régionales accessibles en TGV

©Bouron, 2005–2008 www.geotheque.org

Exemple: Marseille　　　2 hours 55 minutes

  a Nantes _____　　2 hours

  b Toulouse _____　　5 hours

  c Lyon _____　　1 hour 55 minutes

  d Lille _____　　1 hour exactly

READING

Read the information about buying tickets in the leaflet entitled SNCF - Les points de vente. Then decide whether the following statements are **vrai ou faux** (true or false).

a You cannot buy your tickets more than two months in advance at the ticket office. _____

b All stations have a special ticket office for advance booking. _____

c At the ticket machine you can only buy your ticket 61 days in advance of travelling. _____

d If you use the ticket machine you can use up to 15 € in coins. _____

e You won't get any change. _____

f You can use your credit card for any journey. _____

g You can get your meal reservation from the machine too. _____

Les points de vente HABITUELS

LES POINTS DE VENTE

Tous les billets sont vendus dans les gares, les boutiques SNCF et les agences de voyages.

Achetez-les à l'avance, ils sont valables 2 mois.

Que vous prépariez votre voyage ou soyez en instance de départ, tous les guichets délivrent, en principe, l'ensemble des prestations.

Certaines grandes gares disposent de guichets vous permettant de préparer votre voyage à l'écart des flux de départs immédiats.

LES BILLETTERIES AUTOMATIQUES

Ce sont des guichets en libre service qui vous permettent d'acheter un billet pour un trajet en France ou à destination de l'étranger (principales relations):

- de 61 jours à quelques minutes avant votre départ (sauf train autre que TGV avec réservation)
- avec ou sans réservation
- avec supplément éventuellement.

Vous pouvez également y réserver vos titres repas ou y retirer vos commandes passées par téléphone.

Comme moyen de paiement, la billetterie automatique accepte à partir de 2 € les cartes Bleues, Visa françaises ou étrangères, Eurocard/Mastercard, American Express et Diner's Club International.

La billetterie automatique accepte les pièces jusqu'à un montant total de 15 € et rend la monnaie.

> La billetterie automatique vous permet d'éviter les files d'attentes aux guichets.

[www.sncf.com]

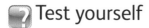 Test yourself

The present subjective is used to express facts, fear, regrets, anxiety, doubt: ideas and thoughts which are uncertain but not impossible or unrealisable. How is it used? In many cases in ready-made structures with **il faut que..., je doute que..., quoi que....**

J'ai peur que..., avant que, are followed by a negative structure when they express fear or anticipation.

1 **Choose an appropriate ending for each of the sentences. Make sure you are using the correct tense and that the complete sentence is meaningful. There may be more than one correct option.**

a Il faut que...
   a) *nous sommes arrivés...*
   b) *nous arrivions...*
   c) *nous arrivons... ...à Paris à quatorze heures.*

b J'ai bien peur qu'elle...
   a) *ne prenne le train pour Londres.*
   b) *a oublié de téléphoner.*
   c) *mangera assez pendant le voyage.*

c Quoi qu'...
   a) *il arrive...*
   b) *elle disait...*
   c) *elles en pensent .... je pars en vacances.*

d Nous regrettons que...
   a) *tu as perdu ton billet de train.*
   b) *nous devons rentrer.*
   c) *tu partes.*

e Appelle la police avant qu'...
   a) *il ne cause un accident.*
   b) *elles vont faire du shopping.*
   c) *ils sont partis.*

f Je doute qu'...
   a) *il arrive aujourd' hui.*
   b) *il y a un train ce matin.*
   c) *elle s'intéresse aux Jeux Olympiques.*

2 Complete these sentences with the right word: **à, de, pour, sans.**

   a Il a traversé la rue _____ regarder.

   b J'ai un train _____ prendre à huit heures.

   c J'ai acheté des fleurs _____ offrir à ma mère.

   d Ce n'est pas poli _____ partir _____ dire merci!

3 Complete the sentences below using the verb **prendre** in the correct form.

   a Hier nous avons _____ le métro.

   b Il faut que nous _____ le train pour aller à Paris.

   c Vous _____ votre petit déjeuner à quelle heure demain matin?

   d Elle va _____ l'avion à quelle heure ?

   e Tu _____ le bus scolaire pour aller au collège quand tu étais jeune?

SELF CHECK

	I CAN...
○	... talk about travelling by rail and buy a ticket.
○	... understand more about **la SNCF** and **le TGV**.
○	... use more verbs in the imperfect tense.
○	... use the subjunctive.

19 À l'hôpital
At the hospital

In this unit you will learn how to:
▶ *better understand public transport.*
▶ *express yourself at the hospital if you have a minor injury.*
▶ *recognize indirect object pronouns.*
▶ *use the subjunctive in more situations.*

CEFR: *Can keep up with animated conversation between native speakers (B2); Can follow detailed directions (B1); Can understand descriptions of feelings (B1); Can engage in extended conversation (B2).*

 ## At the GP or at the pharmacy?

In France people tend to have a good relationship with their **pharmacien ou pharmacienne** (*pharmacist*). For many, **la pharmacie** (*the pharmacy*) is the first port of call in case of **des petits maux et blessures** (*minor ailments and wounds*) or for **un conseil de santé** (*an advice on their health*). **La Sécurité Sociale** is France's national health service.

Going to **votre médecin traitant** or **généraliste** (*your general practitioner*) means you have to pay **le prix de la consultation** (*the full price of the visit*) on the spot. **Les honoraires** (*the fees*) are in principle regulated by the government. In 2012 **le tarif de base était de 23€** (*the basic cost was 23 €*), but it is more expensive **chez un spécialiste** (*with a specialist*). **Certains généralistes et certains spécialistes** work on the basis of **honoraires libres**, (*their fees are not fixed*) by la Sécurité Sociale.

 What is the name of France's national health system?

Vocabulary builder

BODY PARTS AND HEALTH PROBLEMS

 19.01 **Look at the picture as you listen and repeat the words.**

LES PARTIES DU CORPS

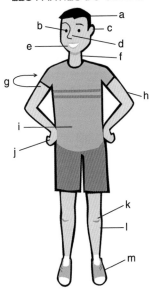

1 **Listen again and complete the body parts with the articles you hear: *l'*, *le*, or *la*.**

a ___ tête

b l'oeil, ___ yeux

c ___ oreille, les oreilles

d ___ nez

e ___ bouche

f ___ cou

g ___ dos

h ___ bras

i ___ ventre

j ___ main

k ___ genou

l ___ jambe

m ___ pied

2 19.02 **Listen to the health problems and match the English and French expressions.**

a	J'ai mal à la tête.	**1**	*I have a headache.*
b	J'ai mal au ventre.	**2**	*I've broken my leg.*
c	Je me suis coupé.	**3**	*I have got sunburnt.*
d	Je me suis brûlé.	**4**	*I cut myself.*
e	Je suis blessé.	**5**	*I burnt myself.*
f	J'ai une insolation.	**6**	*I can't breathe properly.*
g	J'ai pris un coup de soleil.	**7**	*I am injured.*
h	J'ai de la fièvre.	**8**	*I have a stomach ache.*
i	J'ai du mal à respirer.	**9**	*I have sunstroke.*
j	Je me suis cassé la jambe.	**10**	*I have got a high temperature.*

PHARMACIST TASKS

19.03 **In France pharmacists are generally well disposed towards their clients. Listen and choose the correct translations for the types of services they provide.**

a Ils donnent des conseils.
  1 *They give advice.*
  2 *They give information.*

b Ils donnent des renseignements.
  1 *They treat minor ailments and wounds with medicines and bandages.*
  2 *They give information.*

c Ils soignent les petits maux et blessures avec des médicaments ou des pansements.
  1 *They treat minor ailments and wounds with medicines and bandages.*
  2 *They give advice.*

EXPRESSIONS WITH UNE GARANTIE (GUARANTEE)

19.04 **Read about the various forms of the word garantie. Then choose the correct form to complete the sentences. Listen to check your answers.**

noun	**une garantie**	*guarantee*
adjective	**garantie** (f.) / **garanti** (m.)	*guaranteed*
verb	**garantir**	*to guarantee*

a **J'ai un bon de _____**
   pour ma montre.

      I have a certificate of
      guarantee for my watch.

b **Ma montre est _____**
   pour deux ans.

      My watch is guaranteed for two years.

c **Je te garantis _____**
   c'est vrai!

      I promise you it's true!

NEW EXPRESSIONS

Look at the expressions that are used in the next conversations. Note their meanings.

Conversation 1

téléphone portable/ **un portable/un mobile**	*mobile phone*
emmener	*to take someone/something somewhere*
rejoindre	*to rejoin/to meet someone somewhere*
un point de suture	*a stitch (medical)*
une piqûre	*an injection/insect bite*
J'ai perdu	*I have lost*
Qu'est qu'il lui est arrivé?*	*What's happened to her?*
Ouf!	*Phew! (sigh of relief)*

* Note: This is for recognition only at this stage, but you need to understand how this structure has been arrived at:

Il est arrivé quelque chose à Marie → à elle

Something has happened to Marie.

à + elle is contracted to → **lui**

Il lui est arrivé quelque chose.

Something has happened to her.

Qu'est ce que + il ...?

que + il is contracted to → **qu'il**

Qu'est ce qu'il lui est arrivé?

> **INSIGHT: LANGUAGE**
>
> **Quelque chose can mean both**
> *something* or *anything*:
> **Je cherche quelque chose...**
> *I'm looking for something...*
> **Vous avez mangé quelque chose?**
> *Have you had anything to eat?*

Conversation 2

pleurer	*to cry*
vomir	*to vomit*
montrer	*to show*
garder	*to keep*

Conversations

1 Read the passage and information about la SNCF. Then answer the questions below.

> *Le train de Bordeaux arrive à Montparnasse à dix-neuf heures quinze, avec dix minutes de retard. Sarah descend, mais ne voit pas sa sœur sur le quai. Elle attend quelques moments puis elle décide de téléphoner chez sa sœur. Elle a son téléphone portable dans son sac.*

Did you understand? Then answer these questions.

1 At what time does Sarah's train arrive in Paris? _____

2 What was the scheduled arrival time? Will Sarah get any compensation? _____

3 Can she see her sister on the platform? _____

4 What does she decide to do after a few moments? _____

5 What has she got in her bag? _____

ET TOUJOURS: L'HORAIRE GARANTI

Depuis le 1er septembre 1996, la SNCF s'engage à offrir une compensation dès qu'un train Grandes Lignes est en retard d'au moins 30 minutes.

Cette compensation représente:

– 25% du prix du billet du trajet concerné lorsque votre retard à destination est de 30 minutes à 1 heure,

– 50% du prix du trajet si le retard est supérieur à 1 heure.

Elle est réalisée sous forme de bons d'achat trains ('bons Voyage'). Pour en bénéficier, il est nécessaire d'avoir acquitté et effectué un parcours d'au moins 100 kilomètres en train Grandes Lignes.

2 19.05 *Sarah parle au téléphone à son beau-frère, Guillaume.*

a **Listen to the conversation and answer the questions.**

    1 What does Sarah think she has lost? _____

    2 What is the telephone number that Sarah has just dialed? _____

b **Now listen again and answer these questions.**

    1 Where is Marie-Claire? _____

    2 How did she cut herself? _____

    3 Does Guillaume think it is serious? _____

Conversation 1

Sarah	Zut! J'ai perdu mon portable! Ouf! le voilà! Alors ... zéro un, quarante-huit, zéro cinq, trente-neuf, seize. Bon ça sonne! Allô!
Guillaume	Allô oui?
Sarah	Guillaume, ici Sarah. Tu sais où est...
Guillaume	Ah Sarah! Encore heureux que tu aies téléphoné! J'étais inquiet...
Sarah	Qu'est-ce qu'il se passe?
Guillaume	Marie-Claire a eu petit accident, elle est aux urgences à l'hôpital.
Sarah	Quoi? Qu'est-ce qu'il lui est arrivé?
Guillaume	Rien de grave ... elle s'est coupée en ouvrant une boîte pour le chat. La voisine l'a emmenée à l'hôpital.
Sarah	Tu veux que j'aille la rejoindre à l'hôpital?
Guillaume	Non, non, ça ne devrait pas prendre longtemps ... juste quelques points de suture et une piqûre anti-tétanique, c'est tout!
Sarah	Et les enfants? Où sont Ariane et Pierre?
Guillaume	Ici, avec moi. Ecoute ... je suis désolé ... prends un taxi.
Sarah	Non! Je connais bien le trajet en métro: je vais jusqu'à Châtelet, je change et je prends la direction Château de Vincennes et je descends à Nation.
Guillaume	Oui, c'est cela mais si tu as beaucoup de bagages un taxi sera plus pratique.
Sarah	Bon d'accord, j'arrive!

---

c **Now listen again or read to answer the questions.**

    1 Who are Ariane and Pierre? _____

    2 What does Guillaume suggest Sarah should do? _____

    3 Why does he say that a taxi may better than the métro? _____

3 19.06 *C'est le mois d'août. A l'Hôpital d'Arcachon il y a beaucoup de personnes avec des maux et blessures en tous genres qui attendent de voir un docteur. A doctor is now seeing to a little girl called Magalie Dumas.*

a **Listen to the conversation and answer the questions.**
   1 Is Magalie still crying? _____
   2 Where does it hurt? _____

b **Now listen again and answer these questions.**
   1 What is her temperature? Is it very high? _____
   2 What is Magalie's mother worried about? _____

Conversation 2

Dr Lebrun	C'est bien Magalie, tu ne pleures plus, tu es une grande fille. Alors montre-moi où ça fait mal.
Magalie	Là. Oh! Oh! J'ai mal au ventre.
Dr Lebrun	Ça fait mal quand je touche ici?
Magalie	Non. Aïe! Ici ça fait très mal!
Dr Lebrun	Elle a un peu de température, 38.2°C.
Madame Dumas	Vous croyez que c'est une crise d'appendicite, Docteur?
Dr Lebrun	Non, je ne pense pas. Est-ce qu'elle a mangé ce midi?
Madame Dumas	Non, elle n'a rien mangé depuis le petit déjeuner. Elle a vomi vers dix heures ce matin.
Dr Lebrun	Nous allons la garder en observation cette nuit. Si tout va bien elle pourra sortir demain matin.

c **Now listen again or read to answer the questions.**
   1 What did she have for lunch? _____
   2 What meal did she last eat? _____
   3 When was she sick? _____
   4 What does the doctor say should happen tonight? _____

Language discovery

1 **Link the following English phrases to the equivalent French expressions from Conversation 1.**
   a *I was worried.*   **1** **Ça ne devrait pas prendre longtemps.**

   b *What is happening?*   **2** **Elle s'est coupée.**

c *What happened to her?*

d *nothing serious*

e *She cut herself.*

f *The neighbour has taken her to hospital.*

g *It should not be long.*

h *I get out at Nation.*

3 La voisine l'a emmenée à l'hôpital.

4 J'étais inquiet.

5 Qu'est-ce qu'il lui est arrivé?

6 Je descends à Nation.

7 Qu'est-ce qu'il se passe?

8 rien de grave

2 Now link the following English phrases to the equivalent French expressions from Conversation 2.

a *You are not crying any more.*

b *Show me where it hurts.*

c *She has a bit of a temperature.*

d *She has eaten nothing since breakfast.*

e *We are going to keep her tonight for observation.*

f *She was sick at about 10 a.m.*

1 Montre-moi où ça fait mal?

2 Elle a vomi vers dix heures.

3 Tu ne pleures plus.

4 Elle a un peu de température.

5 Elle n'a rien mangé depuis le petit déjeuner.

6 Nous allons la garder en observation cette nuit.

3 Look at the above exercises and answer the questions below.

a What expression means *her?*   lui   qu'il

b What other expression means *her?*   à   l'

Learn more

1 INDIRECT OBJECT PRONOUNS

You have already come across the whole range of pronouns but there are still some complexities that need to be explained. In the conversation Sarah says:

Qu'est-ce qu'il lui est arrivé?   *What has happened to her/him?*

The model for the structure in this particular example is:

Il est arrivé quelque chose à quelqu'un.   *Something has happened to someone.*

Qu'est-ce qu'il est arrivé à Marie-Claire?   *What has happened to Marie-Claire?*

When the object (here Marie-Claire) is linked to the verb by a preposition (here **à**), this object is called an indirect object. When a personal pronoun (here **lui**) is used to replace the indirect object, it is referred to as an indirect object pronoun. The plural form of **lui** is **leur**. The other object pronouns **(me, te, nous, vous)** are the same whether the object is direct or indirect. This can be more easily demonstrated in simpler examples, using the present tense.

Noun		Indirect object pronoun	
Je donne les fleurs à ma mère.*	*I give the flowers to my mother.*	**Je lui donne les fleurs.***	*I give her the flowers.*
Je donne les chocolats à mes parents.*	*I give the chocolates to my parents.*	**Je leur donne les chocolats.***	*I give them the chocolates.*
J'ai réservé une place pour ma mère.	*I've reserved a place for my mother.*	**Je lui ai réservé une place.**	*I've reserved her a place.*
Tu as écrit à tes parents?	*Have you written to your parents?*	**Non, je ne leur ai pas écrit.**	*No, I haven't written to them.*

* Note: In the first two examples, there are two objects after **donne** and it is possible to use two pronouns side-by-side to replace them, but taking one thing at a time, **à ma mère** is replaced by **lui** and **à mes parents** is replaced by **leur**.

2 EMPHATIC PRONOUNS

These are generally used after prepositions like the ones below.

à	*at*	**dans**	*in*	**sans**	*without*
avec	*with*	**chez**	*at*	**sous**	*under*
de	*from/of*	**pour**	*for/in order to*	**sur**	*on/on top of*

Il est parti sans moi*.   *He left without me.*

*Note: The forms for other pronouns would be **sans toi, sans lui, sans elle, sans nous, sans vous, sans elles,** or **sans eux.**

3 MORE EXAMPLES OF THE SUBJUNCTIVE

There are two examples in the conversation. Did you find them?

Tu veux que j'aille la rejoindre à l'hôpital?*   *Would you like me to meet her at the hospital?*

Encore heureux que tu aies téléphoné!   *Just as well you phoned!*

In the first example, the verb is **aller**. In the second example, the verb is in the past subjunctive, formed with **avoir** in the present subjunctive and the past participle of **téléphoner.** Study the chart to learn more about subjunctive forms.

Three essential verbs in the present subjunctive			
	ALLER	**AVOIR**	**ETRE**
Il faut que	j'aille	j'aie	je sois
Il faut que	tu ailles	tu aies	tu sois
Il faut que	elle aille	elle ait	elle soit
Il faut que	nous allions	nous ayons	nous soyons
Il faut que	vous alliez	vous ayez	vous soyez
Il faut que	ils aillent	ils aient	ils soient

4   DIRECT OBJECTS IN FRONT OF VERBS.

You will only need to recognize this when you see it for now, but look at what happens when a direct object is placed in front of the verb. Look at the question and answer below.

Tu as entendu la chanson?   *Have you heard the song?*

Oui, je l'ai entendue.   *Yes, I've heard it.*

Notice that in the answer there is an e at the end of entendue to reflect the fact that the direct pronoun is now placed before the verb.

 # Practice

 19.07 *Vous passez beaucoup trop de temps au téléphone! You have been telephoning all the people in the box on the same day.* **Listen to the recording and fill in the grid.**

Names and times called	You hear...	You say...
a Nadine (11.30)	A quelle heure avez-vous téléphoné à Nadine?	Je lui ai téléphoné à onze heures trente.
b Mathieu (12.00)		
c Chantal et Marc (17.15)		
d Votre sœur (18.45)		
e Vos parents (20.10)		
f Votre fiancé(e) (22.45)		

PRONUNCIATION

19.08 **Read the explanation. Then listen and repeat the words in bold.**

The words **la, là, l'a**, and **l'as** all sound the same **la, la, la**, and la but they all mean something different. Read the explanations and note the differences in meaning.

la   Definite article: **la voisine** *(the neighbor)*

là   An adverb: **Marie-Claire n'est pas là** *(means there but frequently used to mean here)*

l'a   Pronoun **le** or **la** in front of the verb **avoir**: **La voisine l'a emmenée à l'hôpital.** *(The neighbour took her to the hospital.)*

l'as   Same as above but with avoir in the second person singular: **Tu l'as vue?** *(Have you seen her?)*

LISTENING

19.09 **Listen to eight young people at the hospital casualty department. Link their names to what they say is wrong with them.**

Nom	Qu'est-ce qui ne va pas?
1 Marie-José	**a** infected mosquito bites
2 Alain	**b** toothache
3 Adrienne	**c** a hand burnt with an iron
4 Benoît	**d** headache
5 Elise	**e** hurt knees
6 Julien	**f** probably a broken arm
7 Cécile	**g** a backache
8 Didier	**h** a foot cut walking on a broken bottle

Read the poster and answer the questions.

PLONEOUR-LANVERN
LE MAL DE DOS

RÉUNION - DÉBAT

Animée par le Docteur FRIAT, Médecin
Service de rééducation fonctionnelle du C.H.U.* de BREST

Mercredi 21 MARS 2007, à 20H30
Salle Polyvalente, Plonéour-Lanvern
CAMPAGNE DE PRÉVENTION MENÉE PAR:

Mutualité
Sociale Agricole
Finistère

GROUPAMA
BRETAGNE

Le Télégramme

*Note: **C.H.U. (Centre Hospitalo-Universitaire)** means *Hospital.*

a When is there a meeting at Plonéour-Lanvern? _____

b Who is leading the debate? _____

c What is the debate about? _____

d Where is the meeting taking place? _____

e Where does Dr. Friat normally work? _____

Go further

1 **19.10** 'Jacques a dit' is a game similar to 'Simon Says'. Do what Jacques says if Jacques' name appears before the command. Familiarize yourself with the commands. Then listen and respond by doing the correct actions.

2 Now, write which actions you did.

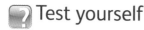

J'ai levé ...

> **INSIGHT: NEW WORDS**
> Commands
> **levez** *raise*
> **baissez** *lower*
> **grattez** *scratch*
> **touchez** *touch*
> **frappez** *hit*

Test yourself

1 Choose the correct answer to complete each of the sentences. There may be more than one correct option.

a **Marie-Christine s'est ...**
   a blessée
   b coupé avec un couteau
   c blessés

b **Son médecin traitant ...**
   a a conduit l'ambulance
   b lui a coupé le pied
   c lui a fait un bandage

c **Vincent Van Gogh s'est coupé ...**
   a une oreille
   b les deux oreilles
   c le nez

d **Mon père s'est ... en se rasant.**
   a coupée
   b coupé
   c coupés...

e **Mes deux frères sont...**
   a tombées de moto
   b tombés d'un arbre
   c tombé dans les pommes.

2 Complete the answers to the questions with the correct pronouns from the box.

> l'   les (2)   lui   leur   la   vous   le

a Qui a attaqué ma sœur, c'est Pierre? Oui, c'est ____ qui ____ a attaquée.

b Tu as donné les fleurs à ta mère? Non, je ____ ai données à ma fiancée.

c Vous avez invité vos parents? Bien sûr nous ____ avons invité. Nous ____ avons envoyé une invitation.

d Tes grands-parents sont-ils invités au mariage? Evidemment ils ____ sont!

e Tu connais la mariée? Non, je ne ____ connais pas.

3 Complete the sentences below using the verb aller in the correct form

a Quand il avait douze ans il ____ à l'école à vélo.

b Il faut que vous ____ la voir.

c Demain je ____ visiter le Musée d'Orsay.

d Je regrette que tu n' ____ pas en vacances avec elle.

e L'été dernier ils sont ____ aux Jeux Olympiques de Londres.

SELF CHECK

I CAN...
○ ...talk about public transport.
○ ...express myself at a hospital if I have a minor injury.
○ ...recognize indirect object pronouns.
○ ...use the subjunctive in more situations.

20 On prend le métro
Catching the métro

In this unit you will learn how to:
▶ *make apologies.*
▶ *talk about the Paris métro.*
▶ *use more of the perfect tense.*

CEFR: *Can scan a longer text to locate desired information (B1); Can understand the main point on standard speech on familiar matters (B1); Can understand text that consist mainly of high frequency language.*

 Sightseeing in Paris

In Paris you can do a lot for next to nothing or just for **le prix d'un ticket de métro** (*the cost of a metro ticket*) **ou le prix de location d'un Vélib'** (*or the cost of hiring a Vélib', part of the free bicycle share system*). You can sit **à la terrasse d'un café**, or on the rooftop terrace of a grand-magasin. le *BHV* or le *Printemps Haussman* and enjoy the best views of the city.

One of the most historically symbolic sights in Paris is the axis from **La Grande Arche de la Défense**, completed in 1989 as President Mitterand's legacy to Paris. From the top, **par temps clair** (*on a clear day*), **la vue sur Paris et l'Île de France est spectaculaire** (*the view over Paris and l'île de France is spectacular*) in itself, but also because of its location which lines it up with **l'Avenue de la Grande Armée** (*Napoleon's army*), **L'Arc de Triomphe** (planned by Napoleon in 1806), **les Champs-Elysées et l'Obélisque de Louxor sur la Place de la Concorde**, site of the guillotine during **la Révolution** (*the French Revolution*).

Le bus et le métro (*the bus and the tube or subway*) are run by la **R.A.T.P.** (Réseau Autonome des Transports Parisiens) *and* le R.E.R. (Réseau Express Régional).

 a **What are the three best ways of getting around Paris?**

Vocabulary builder

EXPRESSIONS WITH THE VERBS **DÉPLACER, DÉBROUILLER,** *AND* **PENSER**

> **INSIGHT: LANGUAGE**
>
> The verb **déplacer** means *to move* or *to get about*. **Se déplacer** is the reflexive form meaning to travel. **Se débrouiller** is also reflexive and means *to manage* or *to sort things out*. The verb **penser** is not reflexive and means *to think*.
> Remember to place the appropriate pronoun **(me, te, se, nous, vous)** in front of the verb when using **se déplacer**.

20.01 **Listen and match the French expressions to their meaning.**

a	Je pense donc je suis. (Descartes, 1637)	**1** *Sort yourselves out!*
b	Je me déplace partout pour mon travail.	**2** *He's resourceful, your son!*
c	Tant que j'y pense...	**3** *While I think about it...*
d	Débrouillez-vous!*	**4** *I doubt it!*
e	Je suis souvent en déplacement.	**5** *How do you get about in Paris?*
f	Je pense bien!	**6** *I should think so!*
g	Il est débrouillard**, ton fils!	**7** *I am often away.*
h	Penses-tu!	**8** *I think, therefore I am.*
i	Comment vous déplacez-vous dans Paris?	**9** *Don't worry! I'll manage on my own!*
j	Ne t'inquiète pas! Je me débrouillerai bien tout(e) seul(e)!	**10** *I travel all over the place for my work.*

*Note: This is usually said with an irritated tone.

**Note: Often used to describe someone who is resourceful.

NEW EXPRESSIONS

Look at the expressions that are used in the next conversations. Note their meanings.

Conversation 1

bouger	*to move*
Au fait...	*By the way...*
Eh bien dites-donc!	*You don't say!*
être bête	*to be silly*
se débrouiller	*to manage*
s'inquiéter	*to worry*
prévenir	*to inform/to warn*
Tout de même!	*All the same!*
Vous en avez de la chance!	*Aren't you the lucky ones!*

Conversation 2

demi-tarif	*half-fare*
un carnet de tickets	*a book of tickets (10)*
une station de métro	*a tube station*
une gare R.E.R./une gare S.N.C.F.	*an RER or SNCF train station*
un changement	*connection (on métro or railway line)*

Conversations

 1 20.02 *C'est mercredi matin. Marie-Claire est en congé de maladie. Elle bavarde avec sa sœur. Les enfants sont toujours en vacances.*

a **Listen to the conversation once and answer the questions.**

    1 What's the first thing Marie-Claire does? _____

    2 What has Sarah promised to do with Marie-Claire's children?

    _____

Conversation 1	
Sarah	Bonjour grande sœur, ça va mieux?
Marie-Claire	Oh écoute, je te prie de m'excuser pour hier soir!
Sarah	Mais tu n'y pouvais rien! Ce n'est pas de ta faute!
Marie-Claire	Non mais tout de même, je suis désolée!
Sarah	Ce que tu es bête! Ne t'inquiète pas pour cela! De toute façon je me suis bien débrouillée! Tu ne m'as pas dit si tu allais mieux.

Marie-Claire	Oui, ça va un peu mieux. On m'a fait six points de suture mais ça me fait encore mal quand je bouge la main. Je vais prendre trois jours de congé maladie et je reprendrai le travail lundi matin. Au fait, tu restes jusqu'à quand?
Sarah	Jusqu'à dimanche soir. Il faudra que je sois à Paris-Nord à dix-huit heures pour enregistrer mon billet pour l'Eurostar de dix-huit heures vingt-deux. Moi aussi je reprends le travail lundi matin. Au fait, Tante Eliane sait que je suis à Paris?
Marie-Claire	Oui, je l'ai prévenue. Elle nous invite tous à déjeuner dimanche midi. Je regrette mais je n'ai pas pu faire autrement.
Sarah	Non, cela ne fait rien, au contraire, je ne l'ai pas vue depuis Noël l'année dernière, ça me fera plaisir de la revoir.
Ariane	Maman, Tante Sarah a promis de nous emmener au zoo cet après-midi.
Pierre	Et puis aussi on va faire une grande balade dans le Bois de Boulogne, et si on a le temps, on s'arrêtera à Châtelet et on ira sur les quais voir les magasins d'animaux.
Marie-Claire	Eh bien dites-donc, vous en avez de la chance! Eh bien samedi soir on ira tous au cinéma.

b Listen to the recording several times or read, and make a note of Sarah's activities.

Calendar of events	What is Sarah doing / planning to do? Who with?
1 Wednesday a.m.	*off sick, chatting to her sister*
2 Wednesday p.m.	
3 Saturday p.m.	
4 Sunday lunch time	
5 Sunday 6.00 p.m.	
6 Sunday 6.22 p.m.	
7 Monday a.m.	

2 20.03 *Sarah, Ariane et Pierre sont en route pour leur promenade. Ils sont à la station de métro Nation. Ils se dirigent vers le guichet.*

a Listen to the conversation and answer the questions.

1 Does Sarah need to get tickets for the children? _____

2 What kind of tickets have they got? _____

> **INSIGHT: CULTURE**
> In the conversation Sarah promises Ariane and Pierre a stop **sur les quais** to have a look at pet shops. **Les quais de la Seine,** *the river banks throughout the centre of Paris,* have hundreds of little stalls where people sell old books, maps, stamps, postcards, etc.

b Now listen again and answer these questions.

    1 Who says that Sarah is a child? _____

    2 Why does Sarah say to the children she wants to think for a minute?
    _____

Conversation 2

Sarah	Attendez, les gamins! Il faut que j'achète des tickets.
Ariane	On en a, nous, des tickets.
Sarah	Ah oui? Bon, très bien, mais ce sont des tickets demi-tarifs pour les enfants et moi je ne suis plus une enfant!
Ariane	Si, tu es une enfant!
Sarah	Eh bien voilà! Je vous remercie, les petits! Sérieusement, est-ce que je prends une carte ou un carnet? Laissez-moi réfléchir une minute.
...	
Sarah	Pardon madame, c'est combien la carte Mobilis, Zone 1 et 2?
Employée	Cela dépend où vous allez et combien de voyages differents vous allez faire...
Sarah	Ah oui, je vois. Je vais prendre un carnet de tickets s'il vous plaît.
Ariane	Moi, je sais quelle ligne il faut prendre, c'est la ligne 1, en direction de la Grande Arche de La Défense. C'est facile, il n'y a même pas de changement.
Pierre	Et pour rentrer c'est la direction Château de Vincennes. A quelle station on descend?
Sarah	On a le choix entre la Porte Maillot et les Sablons. C'est plus ou moins la même distance pour le zoo. Si on descend aux Sablons on peut prendre le petit train du Bois de Boulogne.
Ariane et Pierre	Les Sablons!

---

c Now listen again or read to answer the questions.

    1 What does she get in the end? _____

    2 Which direction will they take to go back? _____

    3 Why do the children choose les Sablons as the station where they want to get off? _____

Language discovery

1 **Now link the following English phrases to the equivalent French expressions from Conversation 1.**

a *How silly you are!*

b *In any case I managed!*

c *I am feeling a bit better.*

d *I am going to take three days of sick leave.*

e *to register my ticket for Eurostar*

f *She is inviting us all for lunch.*

g *I shall be pleased to see her again.*

h *We are going to go for a long walk.*

1 Elle nous invite tous à déjeuner.

2 pour enregistrer mon billet pour l'Eurostar

3 Ce que tu es bête!

4 Ça me fera plaisir de la revoir.

5 De toute façon je me suis bien débrouillée!

6 On va faire une grande balade.

7 Ça va un peu mieux.

8 Je vais prendre trois jours de congé de maladie.

2 **Link the following English phrases to the French equivalent expressions from Conversation 2.**

a *Children, wait!*

b *I am no longer a child.*

c *Do I get a travel card or a book of tickets?*

f *I know which line we have to take.*

g *At which station do we get off?*

h *It's more or less the same distance to the zoo.*

1 A quelle station on descend?

2 Moi, je sais quelle ligne il faut prendre.

3 Attendez les gamins!

4 C'est plus ou moins la même distance pour le zoo.

5 Je ne suis plus une enfant.

6 Est-ce que j'achète une carte ou un carnet?

3 **Which is the most appropriate response in French?**

a You disagree with another person's point of view:
   Penses-tu!   **Je pense bien!**

b You tell a friend there is really no need to thank you:
   Ce que tu es bête!   **Ne t'inquiète pas!**

Learn more

1 HOW TO APOLOGIZE AND RESPOND TO AN APOLOGY

Review the lists of expressions to apologize and respond to an apology below. Note that most of the expressions are from Conversation 1 in case you want to see how they fit in context.

Excuses (Apologies)	
Je vous prie de m'excuser.*	*I must apologize.*
Excuse-moi/Excusez-moi.	*Excuse me.*
Je suis désolé(e)/Désolé(e)!	*I am sorry/Sorry!*
Je regrette mais...	*I am sorry but...*
Je n'ai pas pu faire autrement.	*I could not do anything different.*
Je vous demande pardon.**	*Please forgive me.*
Vous pardonnez!/Pardonnez!**	*'scuse!*

*__Note__: This expression is a bit formal, but not unusual in polite conversations.

**__Note__: This might be used for asking forgiveness when walking in front of someone.

***__Note__: This is matter of fact, bordering on rude – much is in the tone.

Réponses/Réactions (Responses)*	
Ne t'inquiète pas!	*Don't worry about it!*
Ne vous inquiétez pas!	*Don't worry about it!*
Ce n'est pas grave!	*Nothing serious!*
Cela/ça ne fait rien! **Ça n'a pas d'importance!** **Peu importe!**	*It doesn't matter!*
N'y pense/pensez plus!	*Forget it!*
Ce n'est pas de ta/votre faute.	*It's not your fault.*
Ne vous en faites pas.	*Don't worry.*
Il n'y a pas de mal!	*There is no harm done!*
Je vous en prie.	*Go ahead / don't mind me.*

*__Note__: Most of the responses apply to any of the apologies listed.

2 THE PERFECT TENSE AND AGREEMENT WITH THE DIRECT OBJECT*

As usual there are several examples of the perfect tense in the conversation.

dire *(to say)*: **Tu ne m'as pas dit.** *(You did not tell me.)*

promettre *(to promise)*: **Tante Sarah nous a promis.** *(Aunt Sarah promised us.)*

prévenir *(to inform)*: **Je l'ai prévenue.** *(I have informed her/Tante Eliane).*

You might need to go back to Unit 16 to remind yourself about the difference between verbs with **être** with the perfect tense and those with **avoir**. With **être** (including reflexive verbs) the number and the gender of the subject affect the ending of the past participle. In the first example, **allé** gains an **-e** because Marie-Claire is feminine. In the second example, **parti** gains an **-s** because there is more than one Dupont in the family.

Marie-Claire est <u>allée</u> à l'hôpital.

Les Dupont sont <u>partis</u> en Espagne.

With verbs with **avoir** in the perfect tense there is no agreement between the subject and the past participle of the verb. If the subject is feminine or plural it does not affect the ending of the past participle. Look at the two examples:

Elle a vu sa tante à Noël. *(She saw her aunt at Christmas.)*

Elle l'a vue. *(She saw her.)*

In the second example, when the direct object **(sa tante/l')** is placed before the verb, the past participle must 'agree' with the object. It must gain an **-e** if the object is feminine, an **-s** if it is plural and **-es** if it is feminine plural. Therefore, when the direct object pronoun (**l'**) is used instead of the direct object (**sa tante**) in example two, the past participle consequently gains an **-e** in agreement (**vue**).

In this next example, since Marie-Claire (the direct object of the sentence) follows the verbs, there is no agreement between the object and the verb.

La voisine a emmené Marie-Claire à l'hôpital. *The neighbour took Marie-Claire to the hospital.*

However, in the following example, the object must agree with the verb because it precedes the past participle as a direct object pronoun. Thus **emmené** gains an **-e** to agree with **l'** (standing for Marie-Claire).

La voisine l'a emmenée. *The neighbour took her.*

INSIGHT: LANGUAGE

Past participles: There is no audible difference between **emmené / emmenée / emmenés / emmenées** or between **vu / vue / vues / vus**. However, in some cases agreement of the past participle does make a difference to the sound of a verb so you'll need to pay attention!:

Mis sounds like [mi] and **mise** sounds like [miz]; **pris** sounds like [pri] and **prises** sounds like [priz].

Practice

1 **Répondre aux excuses. Say how you would respond to the following. There is more than one answer in each situation.**

a Someone bumps into you in the tube and says: **Oh excusez-moi!**

b Someone breaks a vase in your house (not a collection item) and says: **Oh je suis désolé, j'ai cassé le vase!**

c Someone is phoning you to let you know they are late and says: **Je regrette, je vais être en retard d'une heure. Je vous fais attendre…**

d Someone is saying why they were late (a problem at home) and explains: **Je n'ai pas pu faire autrement, il y avait un problème à la maison, alors…**

2 **Complete the sentences with the correct form of the verb in brackets.**

a Sandrine et Philippe _____ (partir) en vacances hier.

b Tu _____ (voir) le dernier film de Tarantino?

c Mes chocolats ! Tu les _____ (manger)?

d Ils _____ (prendre) le dernier métro.

e J' _____ (promettre) aux enfants de les emmener au Louvre.

f Alors Françoise, vous _____ (aller) à Londres hier.

g Ma mère _____ (prévenir) ta famille de ton arrivée.

READING

1 **Look at a leaflet describing travel pass options ni PAris and answer the questions.**

a Which of the three cards advertised is only a travel card? _____

b What do these three cards entitle tourists to do? _____

c Where can you buy your Passport for Disneyland Paris? _____

d Where can't you buy one? _____

e Which card has a half-fare tariff for children aged between 4 and 12? _____

f Can you buy a Carte Musées et Monuments for one day? For six days? _____

Et pour les touristes

A Paris Visite:

C'est la carte idéale pour voyager à volonté sur tous les réseaux de transports urbains d'Ile-de-France dans la limite des zones choisies pendant 1, 2, 3 ou 5 jours.

Une carte pour voyager malin: pas de perte de temps, les enfants de 4 à moins de 12 ans paient moitié prix, accès à la 1re classe en RER et sur les trains Ile-de-France.

Elle n'a que des avantages: 14 partenaires proposent réductions, offres exceptionnelles, en exclusivité.

En vente également

B Carte Musées et Monuments

Un laissez-passer de 1, 3 ou 5 jours pour visiter 70 musées et monuments de la région Ile-de-France.

C Passeport Disneyland® Paris

En même temps que votre titre de transport, vous pouvez acheter votre passeport Disneyland Paris dans toutes les gares RER de la RATP (sauf Marne-la-Vallée/Chessy), les principales stations de métro, les Agences Commerciales RATP, les terminus bus de la Gare de Lyon et de la Place d'Italie, le Carrousel du Louvre et les points RATP de l'aéroport Roissy Charles-de-Gaulle.

2 **Titres de transport: ticket ou carnet? Now read these two leaflets and answer the questions.**

   a Make a list of all the places where you can buy **Mobilis, Tickets, Ticket Jeunes.** _____

   b What kind of ticket can you buy for 6,65 €, and how many would you get for that price?

Les titres de transport

Mobilis: un seul ticket pour toute une journée.

Pendant une journée entière, Mobilis vous ouvre l'accès aux réseaux RATP, SNCF Ile-de-France, APTR et ADATRIF (à l'exception des dessertes aéroportuaires).

Muni de votre carte nominative et d'un coupon valable pour une journée, vous pouvez, à votre gré, combiner les trajets et vous déplacer dans les zones géographiques que vous avez choisies.

Economique, Mobilis propose un tarif forfaitaire en fonction des zones sélectionnées.

Ticket Jeunes: se déplacer partout le samedi, le dimanche ou un jour férié.

Pour tous les titulaires de la Carte Jeunes (française ou étrangère), le Ticket Jeunes permet de se déplacer partout pendant toute une journée, le samedi, le dimanche ou un jour férié. Le Ticket Jeunes est nominatif et permet de circuler en 2e classe sur les réseaux RATP (sauf Orlyval), SNCF Ile-de-France, APTR et ADATRIF dans la limite des zones choisies.

Points de vente Mobilis, Tickets, Ticket Jeunes:

- Toutes les stations de métro, gares RER.
- Terminus des lignes de bus.
- Commerces et bureaux de tabac signalés par le visuel RATP.
- Distributeurs automatiques pour les tickets.

Vous vous déplacez de temps en temps

Ticket ou Carnet: pour un ou plusieurs déplacements dans Paris et Ile-de-France.

Un ticket pour un seul voyage, c'est idéal pour un déplacement occasionnel. Il peut être vendu soit en carnet.

Dans le métro, et dans le RER à l'intérieur de Paris, un seul ticket suffit quelles que soient les correspondances effectuées et la longueur de votre parcours.

Dans le RER en banlieue, le tarif varie selon la longueur de votre parcours.

Dans le bus à l'intérieur de Paris, un ticket permet un seul trajet, sans correspondance, quelle que soit la longueur du parcours (sauf sur les lignes PC, Balabus et Noctambus).

Pour les Noctambus, une tarification spéciale est appliquée.

Dans le bus et le tram, en banlieue et pour tout trajet incluant un parcours hors des limites de Paris, un ou plusieurs tickets sont nécessaires selon le nombre de sections parcourues.

Dans le Funiculaire de Montmartre, un ticket permet d'effectuer un seul trajet (montée ou descente), sans correspondance possible avec le métro ou le bus.

Tickets	Plein tarif	Demi-tarif
A l'unité	1,70 €	
Carnet de 10 tickets	13,30 €	6,65 €

? Test yourself

1 **Match the likely response to the following apologetic statements.**

a **Votre sœur:** Oh je suis désolée ! j'ai cassé un verre.

b **Votre fils:** Oh pardon ! j'ai cassé ton vase avec mon ballon.

c **Une cliente au supermarché:** Excusez-moi mais j'étais là avant vous!

d **Un passager dans le métro:** Oh désolé ! je vous ai marché sur le pied, je vous ai fait mal ?

e **Une collègue de bureau:** Oh la la, je suis en retard !

1 ça alors! Pourquoi jouais-tu dans la maison

2 Ça n'a aucune importance Madame mais je suis sure que c'est vous qui étiez derrière moi !

3 Pas de problèmes, il n'y a pas de mal !

4 Ça ne fait rien mais essaie d'être à l'heure la prochaine fois !

5 Ça ne fait rien, j'en ai d'autres!

2 **Complete the answers to the following questions using a direct object pronoun. It will help if you note the underlined element of the question.**

a Tu as vu <u>ton oncle</u> à Noël ? Oui, je _____

b Vous avez regardé <u>les Jeux Olympiques</u> à la télé? Oui, nous _____

c Tu as prévenu <u>ta femme</u>? Non, je ne _____

d Ils ont lu <u>le journal</u>? Oui, ils _____

e Elle t'a dit la vérité ? Oui, elle _____

3 **Read the sentences below and say what you think they mean.**

  a Elle se débrouille très bien en maths.
  b Mon père a 90 ans mais il se débrouille tout seul à la maison.
  c Je me déplace dans Paris en Vélib'.
  d Ma fille s'est blessée en tombant d'un arbre.
  e Elle ne se débrouillera pas sans moi.

SELF CHECK

I CAN...
... apologise.
... talk about the Paris métro.
... use the perfect tense.

Si on gagnait le gros lot...

If we won the jackpot...

In this unit you will learn how to:
▶ *talk about some places to visit in Paris.*
▶ *discuss where to go and what to visit.*
▶ *express what you would like to do in certain conditions.*

CEFR: *Can describe dreams and hopes (B1); Can understand the essentials of reports (B2); Can identify speakers' viewpoints and attitudes (B2); Can ask someone to clarify what he/she just said (B1); Can write about feelings and opinions (B1).*

Paris

Paris is full of famous landmarks.

Le Louvre, un immense musée d'art et d'histoire sur la rive droite (*right bank*) of La Seine used to be **la résidence des rois de France** (*the residence of French kings*) before Louis XIV's decision to move to Versailles in 1678. It became a museum in 1793. En 1989, **une grande pyramide de verre et de métal** (*a large glass and metal pyramid*) was added to it as a large atrium for the underground reception area.

Le Musée d'Orsay, sur la rive gauche, was **l'ancienne gare du Paris-Orléans** (*the old Paris-Orleans station*) **jusqu'à** (*until*) 1939. **Depuis** (*since*) 1986 it has been **un musée d'art et un centre culturel** which houses many works **des Impressionistes** (*of the Impressionnists*).

 a   The Seine divides Paris into **rive droite** and **rive gauche**. This is consistent with the fact that the river flows westward. Other cities have a north/south divide. How would you say *south bank* and *north bank* in French?

Vocabulary builder

NEW EXPRESSIONS

Look at the expressions that are used in the next conversations. Note their meanings.

Conversation 1

être de bonne humeur	*to be in a good mood*
de meilleure humeur	*in a better mood*
se sentir mieux	*to feel better*
douloureux/se	*painful*
Cela ne me dit rien.	*I don't fancy it.* (colloquial)
au lieu de	*instead of*
une telle queue	*such a queue*
les gosses*	*kids*
Que je suis bête!	*How silly of me!*
C'est dommage!**	*It's a pity!*

*Note: This is similar to les gamins but slightly pejorative.

**Note: This can be a free-standing expression of regret.

Conversation 2

sans tricher	*no cheating*
C'est dingue.*	*It's crazy.* (colloquial)

*Note: You can also use **dingo**. For example **Il est dingo**. *(He is mad.)*

Conversations

1 21.01 *C'est vendredi matin. Marie-Claire est toujours en congé de maladie mais elle se sent beaucoup mieux. Sarah et Marie-Claire font des projets pour la journée. Les deux sœurs s'entendent très bien.*

INSIGHT: LANGUAGE

C'est dommage + que requires the use of the subjunctive with the verb which follows.

C'est dommage que nous ne puissions plus aller à la Samaritaine. *(It's a pity that we can't go to the Samaritaine any more.)*

C'est dommage que tu n'aies pas le temps de visiter le Louvre. *(It's a pity that you don't have time to visit the Louvre.)*

---

a **Listen to the conversation. Tick what things Sarah and her sister have agreed to do.**

1 go to the Louvre _____
2 go to the Musée d'Orsay _____
3 go and see paintings by Monet at L'Orangerie _____
4 go to the Bazar de l'Hôtel de Ville _____
5 go to the Samaritaine _____
6 go for a cup of tea _____

Conversation 1

Sarah	*Toi ça va mieux, cela se voit! Tu es de meilleure humeur ce matin! Si tu allais mieux on pourrait peut-être sortir.*
Marie-Claire	*Oui, je me sens beaucoup mieux, et puis les gosses sont chez la mère de Guillaume jusqu'à ce soir, le mari au travail ... À nous la liberté!*
Sarah	*Tu veux venir avec moi, je pensais faire une balade dans Paris?*
Marie-Claire	*Mais pourquoi pas? Ma main est encore douloureuse mais je ferai bien attention. Tu n'aurais pas envie d'aller au Louvre?*
Sarah	*Le Louvre ... non, ça ne me dit rien et puis nous n'aurions pas assez de temps, il y a toujours une telle queue!*
Marie-Claire	*Oui, je sais, si j'avais le temps ... et l'argent ... je sortirais beaucoup plus souvent.*
Sarah	*Écoute, si on allait au Musée d'Orsay on pourrait juste aller voir les Impressionnistes, non? Et après si on voulait, on aurait assez de temps pour faire les grands magasins: le Bazar de l'Hôtel de Ville ou je ne sais pas, moi...ou bien alors, on pourrait aller à L'Orangerie qui vient d'être rénovée.*
Marie-Claire	*Génial! J'adore Monet et je n'ai pas encore vu la nouvelle salle aux Nymphéas...mais au lieu du Bazar de L'Hôtel de Ville on pourrait aller à la Samaritaine ...mais non! Que je suis bête! La Samaritaine est fermée pour rénovations.*
Sarah	*Ah oui c'est vrai! C'est dommage! Mais ça ne fait rien, on ira prendre une tasse de thé à la terrasse du BHV.*

---

b **Now listen again or read to answer these questions.**

1 Considering that Marie-Claire is still on sick leave, why do the two young women decide to go out? _____
2 What does Marie-Claire wish for? _____

2 21.02 **What would you do?** *Sarah et Marie-Claire sont assises à la terrasse d'un grand magasin. Elles se relaxent un peu en jouant un jeu.*

a **Listen to the conversation, and answer the questions.**

    1 What game are they playing? _____

    2 What would Marie-Claire have if it happened and why? _____

b **Listen to the conversation again and answer the questions.**

    1 Why would Marie-Claire live in Paris? _____

    2 Would she carry on working? _____

Conversation 2	
Sarah	*Dis-moi Marie-Claire, honnêtement et sans tricher, ce que tu ferais vraiment si tu gagnais le gros lot au Loto?*
Marie-Claire	*Alors d'accord … euh … Eh bien j'aurais un grand appartement à Paris, parce que j'adore vivre à Paris, et une maison sur la Côte d'Azur parce que j'aime bien le soleil.*
Sarah	*Tu continuerais à travailler?*
Marie-Claire	*Euh, non! Comme cela j'aurais plus de temps pour moi.*
Sarah	*Et qu'est-ce que tu ferais avec tout ce temps?*
Marie-Claire	*J'irais à la piscine tous les jours, je lirais tous les livres que je voudrais, j'irais au cinéma, au théâtre, à l'Opéra, dans de très bons restaurants. Et puis de temps en temps je ferais des petits voyages quelque part, aux sports d'hiver par exemple. C'est dingue tout ce qu'on pourrait faire!*
Sarah	*Tu serais toute seule dans ton paradis?*
Marie-Claire	*Non, je serais avec toute ma famille, toi y compris!*
Sarah	*Merci, ma chère, c'est très aimable à toi!*

c **Now read the conversation and answer the questions.**

    1 When would Marie-Claire swim? _____

    2 What would she do in Paris? (List three things) _____ _____

        _____

    3 Who would be with her in her paradise? _____

💡 Language discovery

1 **Link the following English phrases to the French from Conversation 1.**

a It shows!

b The kids are at Guillaume's mother's.

c Do you fancy going to the *Louvre?*

d We would not have enough *time.*

e We would have time to go to *the department stores.*

f We'll go for a cup of tea at the terrace at the top.

1 **Nous n'aurions pas assez de temps.**

2 **Cela se voit.**

3 **On ira prendre une tasse de thé tout en haut à la terrasse.**

4 **Les gosses sont chez la mère de Guillaume.**

5 **Tu as envie d'aller au Louvre?**

6 **On aurait assez de temps pour faire les grands magasins.**

2 **Look at the verb forms in these two phrases from the conversations. Which one indicates an action that may or may not happen?**

a Je ferai bien attention

b Je ferais des petits voyages quelque part

Learn more

1 FAIRE

Faire can mean a lot more than *to make* or *to do.*

> **faire les grands magasins** *to go window-shopping (Lit. to do the shops)*

> **faire du lèche-vitrine** *to go window-shopping (Lit. to do window licking)*

> **faire une balade** *to go on an outing*

> **faire une balade en voiture** *to go out for a drive*

Faire is also used to express that someone has done it all.

> **Il a fait la Chine, l'Afrique, l'Amérique du Sud...** *He's done China, Africa, South America...*

> **Ça ne fait rien.** *It does not matter (Lit. It does nothing)*

2 THE CONDITIONAL AND THE IMPERFECT

You have already met and used the conditional (see Unit 7). It conveys the notion that if conditions were fulfilled, something would happen. It is used frequently in conversational French, especially with a few verbs which you are now familiar with. Here are two verbs in the conditional and the conditional verb ending pattern and some examples with other verbs.

Aller	Finir	Ending pattern for all verbs in the conditional	
j'irais	je finirais	je	-rais
tu irais	tu finirais	tu	-rais
elle irait	elle finirait	elle	-rait
nous irions	nous finirions	nous	-rions
vous iriez	vous finiriez	vous	-riez
ils iraient	ils finiraient	ils	-raient

Base form	Conditional sentence	Meaning
vouloir	**Je voudrais faire une balade.**	*I would like to...*
devoir	**Je devrais rentrer chez moi.**	*I ought to...*
pouvoir	**On pourrait aller au cinéma.**	*We could...*
falloir	**Il faudrait partir avant la nuit.**	*We should...*

You may have noticed that within one short conversation, people may use many different tenses. The imperfect tense and the conditional are often used together to convey the notion that if the condition <u>were</u> (imperfect) right something <u>would</u> (conditional) happen.

Look at the examples from Conversation 1. First of all note that **si** (*if*) together with a verb in the imperfect is often used with the conditional.

Si ça allait mieux on pourrait peut-être sortir.	*If you were better we could go out.*
Si j'avais le temps et l'argent je sortirais beaucoup plus souvent.	*If I had more time and money I would go out more often.*
Si on allait au Musée d'Orsay on pourrait aller voir...	*If we went to the Musée d'Orsay we could go and see...*

The emerging pattern here is therefore:

si + verb in the imperfect + verb in the conditional

or

verb in the conditional + si + verb in the imperfect

21 *Si on gagnait le gros lot... If we won the jackpot...*   257

It is also possible to have the conditional on its own with the condition unspoken but present in the mind of the speaker and understood by the listener.

Nous n'aurions pas assez de temps. *We would not have enough time.*

Note that when the doubt is lifted or when the condition is fulfilled the future tense is used instead of the conditional.

On ira prendre une tasse de thé...   We'll go for a cup of tea...

See below for a review of the ending patterns for the future tense.

Ending pattern for the future tense			
Personal pronoun	Verb ending	Personal pronoun	Verb ending
je	**-rai**	**nous**	**-rons**
tu	**-ras**	**vous**	**-rez**
elle	**-ra**	**ils**	**-ront**

Uses of the conditional

▶ The conditional is also used with the word **sans** *(without).* **Sans l'aide de leurs parents ils ne pourraient pas continuer leurs études.** *(Without their parents' help they wouldn't be able to continue their studies.)*

▶ The conditional can also be used to imply a duty or a necessity. **Tu devrais chercher du travail.** *(You ought to look for work.)*

▶ When the conditional is used with the verb **valoir** *(to be worth),* it is always used in an impersonal form.: **Il vaudrait mieux rentrer ce soir.** *(It would be best to return tonight.)*

🔓 Practice

Match both halves of the sentences.

a Si je savais son numéro de téléphone je...

b Si j'étais riche je ...

c Si Corinne travaillait mieux elle ...

d Si vous aviez le temps qu'est-ce que vous...

e S'il conduisait moins vite il ...

f Si tu lisais le journal tu ...

g S'ils étaient malades ils ...

h Si on allait au cinéma, ça ...

1 réussirait à ses examens.

2 iraient à l'hôpital.

3 n'aurait pas d'accidents.

4 ferais un voyage autour du monde.

5 saurais* ce qui se passe.

6 nous changerait les idées.

7 lui téléphonerais.

8 feriez?

* **Note**: This is a form of **savoir** (to know).

READING

Un peu de littérature. **Read an extract from *Dora Bruder*, a novel by the contemporary French writer Patrick Modiano. First, read what the Larousse dictionary says about Modiano. Then read the extract and answer the questions below.**

> **MODIANO (Patrick), écrivain français né à Boulogne-Billancourt en 1945. Ses romans forment une quête de l'identité à travers un passé douloureux et énigmatique.**

> **Elle allait certainement le dimanche retrouver ses parents qui occupaient encore la chambre du 41 boulevard Ornano. Je regarde le plan du métro et j'essaye d'imaginer le trajet qu'elle suivait. Pour éviter de trop nombreux changements de lignes, le plus simple était de prendre le métro à Nation, qui était assez proche du pensionnat. Direction Pont de Sèvres. Changement à Strasbourg-St-Denis. Direction Porte de Clignancourt. Elle descendait à Simplon, juste en face du cinéma et de l'hôtel.**
>
> **(Editions Gallimard 1997, page 46)**

a What did Dora most certainly do on Sunday? _____

b Where did her parents live? _____

c What is the author imagining? _____

d At which station would she catch the métro? Where would she get out? _____

e How many changes did she have to make? _____

f What was there next to the hotel? _____

g What is Modiano's date of birth? _____

h What are his novels mainly about? _____

WRITING

21.03 **Qu'est-ce que vous feriez si vous gagniez le gros lot au Loto? Write the suggested responses in French, then write on of your own. Listen to the recording to hear suggested answers for items a and b.**

a Write that you would have a big house in Brittany, that you would have a boat, that you would go fishing and watch TV in the evening.

b Write that you would take a trip round the world.

c Write what you would likely do.

INSIGHT: NEW WORDS

trajet	route
roman	novel (book)
éviter	avoid
quête	enquiry
pensionnat	boarding school
à travers	through
écrivain	writer
douloureux	painful

> J'aurais une grande ....

Go further

1 Vous avez acheté une carte jeux instantanés *(scratch cards)*. Vous l'avez grattée (gratter-*to scratch*). Est-ce que vous avez gagné? Look at the scratch card and answer these three questions.

a What is the rule of the game? _____

b What is the cost of this scratch card? _____

c What happens if you find 3 stars on your card? _____

> Gagner, cela n'arrive pas qu'aux autres
>
> (Lit. *Winning does not happen only to others.*)

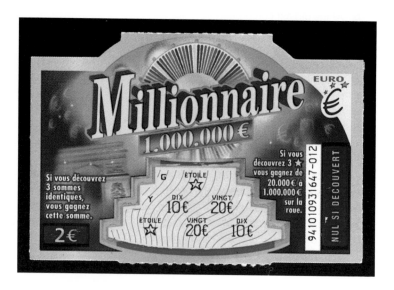

2 Avez-vous gagné au Loto? Look at the grid on the Loto card. Notice that there are two days of the week when the Loto is drawn and on each of these days there are two draws within a few minutes of one another. Answer the questions below.

a On which days is the lottery drawn each week? _____

b How much would you pay if you opted for eight numbers on only one of the two days? _____

c How much would you pay if you opted for eight numbers on both days? _____

d How many numbers would you be able to tick for 252 €? _____

e Up to how many weeks could you have a subscription for? _____

f How much would you pay for four weeks, having ticked eight numbers for both days? _____

21.04 **Vous avez coché?** Tick eight numbers on the Loto card. (You must get three and six numbers correct to win!) **Écoutez et voyez si vous avez gagné! Ne trichez pas! Pas de chance? Mais si vous aviez choisi les bon numéros, vous auriez gagné le gros lot...**

 Test yourself

1 Match the sentence halves, paying attention to the correct verb form (this is testing what you have learnt about the subjunctive, the imperfect and the conditional).

a Si j'avais assez de temps
b Avec du temps et de l'argent on
c C'est dommage qu'
d Il faudrait que vous
e Ce garçon aurait de meilleurs résultats à ses examens
f Si je n'étais pas diabétique
g Il faudrait faire beaucoup plus d'efforts pour
h Si mes parents gardaient les enfants
i Il faudrait partir plus tôt
j Si vous gagniez à la loterie

1 nous pourrions aller au cinéma
2 ferait le tour du monde
3 j'irais voir mes amis plus souvent
4 que feriez-vous avec votre argent ?
5 puissiez voyager ensemble
6 s'il travaillait plus au collège
7 elle ne puisse par sortir ce soir
8 pour gagner le marathon
9 pour arriver à temps
10 je mangerais des gâteaux au chocolat.

2 Find out the meaning of the following sentences:

   a C'est bien triste qu'il soit mort si jeune.
   b Il faudrait qu'elle finisse ses devoirs si elle veut sortir ce soir.
   c Je sortirais quand je voudrais.
   d Dommage qu'on ne puisse pas voir l'arrivée du Tour de France.
   e Sans nourriture on ne pourrait pas survivre.

Try to work out the meaning on your own or match the sentences to the translations.

   1 I 'll go out when I want to.
   2 Shame we can't see the arrival of the Tour de France.
   3 It's so sad he died so young.
   4 without food we couldn't survive.
   5 She would need to finish her homework if she wants to go out tonight.

SELF CHECK

	I CAN...
⚪	. . . talk about places to visit in Paris.
⚪	. . . discuss where to go and what to visit.
⚪	. . . express what I'd like to do if I had more time and money.

Les grèves
Strikes

In this unit you will learn how to:
▶ *talk about the French media.*
▶ *use possessive adjectives and pronouns.*
▶ *talk about strikes and French trade unions.*

CEFR: *Can cope with less routine situations (B1); Can read articles about contemporary problems in which writers adopt particular attitudes or viewpoints (B2).*

On strike

France has a reputation for **ses grèves** (*its strikes*), yet the rate of workers belonging to **un syndicat** (*a trade union*) is very low. This quote from **l'OCDE** (Organisation de Coopération et de Développement Économiques) shows that « **Avec 7% à 8% de salariés** (*workers*) **syndiqués** (*unionized*), **la France a le plus faible taux** (*weakest rate*) **de syndicalisation** (*unionisation*) **des pays de l'OCDE. En 2010, l'Allemagne en comptait 18,6%, le Royaume-Uni 26,5%, l'Italie 35% et la Finlande 70%.** ».

However **les français** have a very strong sense of **justice sociale** (*social justice*), especially when livelihood issues are at stake: **licenciements** (*redundancies*), **retraites** (*pensions*), **réformes de l'Education Nationale** (*National Education reforms*), **de la Sécurité Sociale** (*equivalent to the NHS*) **ou de la Justice**.

a **For French people what is the strong motivation for going on strike?**

Vocabulary builder

EXPRESSIONS WITH METTRE

22.01 **The verb mettre** *(to put)* **is frequently used in idiomatic expressions in the reflexive form, se mettre. Listen and choose the correct English translations to the expressions. Then listen and repeat.**

a **Les pêcheurs se sont mis en grève pour protester contre les quotas.**
1 *The fishermen went on strike to protest against the quotas.*
2 *At what time are we setting off?*

b **Nous nous mettons à table à une heure.**
1 *The fishermen went on strike to protest against the quotas.*
2 *We sit down to eat at one o'clock.*

c **On se met en route à quelle heure?**
1 *They moved in together.*
2 *At what time are we setting off?*

d **Ils se sont mis en ménage.**
1 *They moved in together.*
2 *We sit down to eat at one o'clock.*

NEW EXPRESSIONS

Look at the expressions that are used in the next conversations. Note their meanings

Conversation 1

un cri*	*a shout*
crier	*to shout*
un coup de pied	*a kick*
menteuse/menteur	*liar*
ni ... ni...	*neither ... nor...*
Ça suffit!	*That's enough!*

*****Note: Cri** is another faux-ami; the verb for *to cry* is **pleurer**.

Conversation 2

le journal (d'information)/	*the news*
les informations/les infos	
France Inter	*part of Radio France**
les routiers (short for **chauffeurs routiers**)	*lorry drivers*
mots-croisés**	*crosswords*
VF: **Version Française**	*dubbed*
VO: **Version Originale**	*with subtitles*

*Note: Radio France is the French national radio organization. **Radio France** broadcasts many other radio stations such as **France Musique**, **France Culture**, **France Info**.

Note: Here, on **France 2, it is the name of a televised political debate between politicians. The title plays on the expression **mots croisés**.

Conversations

1 22.02 *C'est vendredi soir. Les enfants sont tous les deux dans la chambre d'Ariane. Soudain on entend des cris: ils se disputent. Leur père va voir ce qu'il se passe.*

a Listen to the conversation once and answer the questions.
1 *Why are the children fighting?*
2 *Where is Pierre's game?*
3 *Whose game has he got now?*

b Listen to the conversation again and answer these questions.
1 *Who shouted?*
2 *What does Pierre claim he can prove?*
3 *What does Guillaume tell them to do?*

Conversation 1

Ariane	Donne-moi ça! C'est à moi!
Pierre	Non, c'est le mien!
Ariane	Mais non, tu as laissé le tien chez Bonne Maman et tu le sais bien!
Guillaume	Qu'est-ce que c'est que tout ce bruit? Qui a crié?
Ariane	C'est Pierre, il a pris mon jeu et il dit que c'est le sien!
Pierre	Mais elle est complèment dingue! C'est le mien, je peux te le prouver!
Ariane	Je te dis que ce n'est pas le tien!
Guillaume	Bon, ça suffit! Vous allez venir vous asseoir avec nous dans la salle de séjour et vous allez regarder la télé tranquillement. Il y a un programme très intéressant sur les animaux.
Ariane	J'aime pas les animaux!
Pierre	Menteuse! Aïe!! Elle m'a donné un coup de pied dans la jambe!
Guillaume	Bon, c'est terminé pour ce soir. Ni jeux, ni télé mais le lit! Immédiatement!

---

c Now listen again or read to answer the questions.
1 *Why does Pierre call Ariane a liar?*
2 *How does she retaliate?*
3 *What does Guillaume tell them to do?*

2 *22.03 Les enfants sont couchés. Marie-Claire regarde le programme de télévision.*

a Look at the TV listings for this evening and listen to the recording. Then answer the questions.

TELEVISION

TF1 F2 F3 C+ 5e ARTE M6 Câble et satellite

TF1 20.45	F2 20.55	F3 20.50	C+ 20.35	5e ARTE 20.45	M6 20.45	Câble 20.30

TF1 — 20.45

LA BELLE VIE
Téléfilm humoristique français de Gérard Marx (2/2) (1997). 120 min. VF. Avec : Jean Yanne (Julius), Danièle Evenou (Linda), Paulette Dubost (Mamé), Vanessa Devraine (Fanny), Christian Rauth (Gaspard). Une famille d'origine modeste devient milliardaire et rachète un château pour y habiter.

22.55
LE DROIT DE SAVOIR
Magazine présenté par Charles Villeneuve. «Un enfant à tout prix». Un reportage réalisé par Cathelyne Hemery, David Gosset et Philippe Véron en 1997. L'adoption d'enfants à l'étranger, en particulier au Viêt-nam et en Russie.

F2 — 20.55

URGENCES
Série médicale américaine. Deux épisodes : Se voiler la face. – Boomerang. VF. 90 min.

22.35
MOTS CROISÉS
Magazine présenté par Arlette Chabot et Alain Duhamel. «Quelle école pour nos enfants ?» Invités : Claude Allègre, Alain Madelin
23.50 La fin de compte.
23.55 Journal

MOTS CROISES
le magazine politique mensuel de la rédaction présenté par
Arlette CHABOT Alain DUHAMEL
ce soir
22h35

F3 — 20.50

LES CONQUÉRANTS DE CARSON CITY
Film américain d'André De Toth (1952). Western. 84 min. VF. Avec : Randolph Scott (Jeff Kincaid), Lucille Norman (Susan Mitchell), Raymond Massey (Big Jack Davis). Un ingénieur se bat pour l'ouverture d'une ligne de chemin de fer.
22.20 La dernière séance. Au sommaire : Actualités. - Tex Avery.
22.50 Soir 3.

23.15
TERREUR A L'OUEST
Film américain d'André De Toth (1954). Western. 80 min. VO. Avec : Randolph Scott (Jim Kipp), Marie Windsor (Alice Williams), Dolorès Dorn (Julie). Un justicier solitaire poursuit trois criminels dont il ignore encore le signalement.
0.35 La dernière séance. Tex Avery.

C+ — 20.35

RIDICULE
Film français de Patrice Leconte (1966). Comédie. 102 min. VF. En 16/9. Redif le 30. Avec : Charles Berling Fanny Ardant. Un jeune noble naïf et passionné découvre les artifices et les dangers de la cour de Versailles.
22.15 Flash infos.

22.20
PARTY
Film franco-portugais de Manoel de Oliveira (1996). 90 min. VF. 1ère diff. Redif le 28. Avec : Michel Piccoli, Irène Papas. Un séducteur impénitent s'efforce de charmer sa jeune hôtesse, lors d'une garden-party.
23.55 Caméléone. Film de Benoît Cohen (1996). Policier. 92 min. VF. En 16/9. Dern. diff.

5e ARTE — 20.45

LA LEÇON DE PIANO
Film de Jane Campion (1992). 125 min. VO. En 16/9. Avec : Holly Hunter (Ada), Harvey Keitel (Baines). Une jeune pianiste muette entre deux hommes, en Nouvelle-Zélande.
22.40 Kinorama.

22.55
L'ARGENT
Film de Robert Bresson (1983). 85 min. VF. Avec : Christian Patey (Yvon), Sylvie van den Elsen.
0.15 Court circuit - Bon voyage. Court-métrage d'A. Hitchcock.
0.45 La rate. Téléfilm de Martin Buchhorn.
2.15 Tracks.

M6 — 20.45

D.A.R.Y.L.
Film américain de Simon Wincer (1985). Science-fiction. 100 min. VF. Avec : Barret Oliver (Daryl), Mary Beth Hurt (Joyce Richardson), Kathryn Walker (Ellen Lamb). Un robot rêve de devenir un humain.

22.40
COUPS POUR COUPS
Film américain de Deran Sarafian (1990). Policier. 90 min. VF. Avec : Jean-Claude Van Damme (Louis Burke), Robert Guillaume (Naylor). Pour enquêter sur une série de meurtres inexpliqués dans un pénitencier, un inspecteur de police endosse l'identité d'un gangster.

Câble et satellite — 20.30

M. HIRE
Film français de Patrice Leconte (1989). Drama. 90'. En 16/9. **21.50** La main gauche du seigneur. Film américain d'Edward Dmytryk (1955). Aventures. VO. 85'. En 16/9. **23.20** La femme secrète. Film français de Sébastien Grall (1986). Comédie dramatique. 90'. En 16/9. **0.55** Secret mortel. Film américain de Michael Scott (1995). Policier. 88'.

CINÉ CINÉFIL
20.30 Arsène Lupin. Film américain de Jack Conway (1932). Policier. NB. VO. 86'. **22.00** Fanny Elssler. Film allemand de Paul Martin (1937). Romanesque. NB. VO. **23.25** Fabiola. Film italien d'Alessandro Blasetti (2/2) (1949). Aventures. NB. 90'. **0.45** L'empereur de Californie. Film allemand de Luis Trenker (1936). Western. NB. VO. 90'.

1 Guillaume has heard on the news that lorry drivers might go on strike. When is the strike likely to start? _____

2 Why is he telling Sarah? _____

3 What is Sarah's first reaction? _____

Conversation 2

Guillaume	Sarah, je viens d'écouter le journal de dix-neuf heures à France Inter, les routiers menacent de se mettre en grève à partir de dimanche, ça pourrait affecter ton voyage de retour!
Sarah	Super! Comme cela je resterai à Paris! Sérieusement parlant, je ne pense pas que l'Eurostar soit affecté par le blocage des routes mais on ne sait jamais. On verra bien!
Marie-Claire	Au fait il y a *Ridicule* qui passe à Canal+. Ça fait presque une demi-heure que cela a commencé.
Sarah	Parce que vous avez Canal+ maintenant?
Marie-Claire	Oui, c'est surtout pour les nouveaux films puisque nous ne sortons presque pas.
Sarah	Eh bien c'est bien! Alors on regarde le film?
Guillaume	Oui mais je voulais voir *Mots Croisés* après.
Marie-Claire	Ah oui, c'est vrai. Toi qui aimes la politique, Sarah, ça t'intéressera sûrement.

---

c Now listen again or read to answer the questions.

   1 What has already started on Canal+? _____

   2 Which programme would Guillaume like to watch after the film? _____

   3 Why should it interest Sarah? _____

d Look at the TV listings again and answer the questions. There may be more than one correct answer.

   1 Which channel would you watch and at what time...

     a if you wanted to watch a film in English? _____

     b if you wanted to watch a medical comedy? _____

     c if you wished to see the late night news? _____

     d if you wanted to watch a political debate? _____

     e if you wanted to watch a programme on the adoption of children from other countries? _____

     f if you fancied watching a science-fiction film? _____

     g if you wanted to see Monsieur Hire, a film you have been meaning to see for a long time? _____

2 On which condition would you be able to watch it? _____

3 Look at the small ad for Mots Croisés. Can you find the word which indicates that it is a monthly programme? _____

4 What is the theme of this month's debate? _____

💡 Language discovery

1 **Link the following English phrases to the equivalent French expressions from Conversation 1.**

a *Give me that!*

b *You left yours at Grandma's.*

c *What's all this noise?*

d *It's mine and I can prove it to you!*

e *That's enough!*

f *She kicked me in the leg.*

g *You are going to come and sit with us.*

h *No games, no TV but bed!*

1 **Ça suffit!**

2 **Elle m'a donné un coup de pied dans la jambe.**

3 **Vous allez venir vous asseoir avec nous.**

4 **Donne-moi ça!**

5 **Ni jeux, ni télé mais le lit!**

6 **Tu as laissé le tien chez Bonne Maman.**

7 **Qu'est-ce que c'est que tout ce bruit?**

8 **C'est le mien, je peux te le prouver!**

2 **Link the following English phrases to the equivalent French expressions from Conversation 2.**

a *I have just listened to the news.*

b *It could affect your return journey.*

c *We'll see.*

d *You can never tell.*

e *The lorry drivers are threatening to go on strike.*

f *Since we hardly ever go out.*

1 **On ne sait jamais.**

2 **Les routiers menacent de se mettre en grève.**

3 **Puisque nous ne sortons presque jamais.**

4 **On verra.**

5 **Ça pourrait affecter ton voyage de retour.**

6 **Je viens d'écouter le journal.**

3 **Use what you know to answer these questions:**

a What expression means *mine?*   **le tien**   **le mien**

b What expression means *yours?*   **le tien**   **le mien**

c Which expression means *your?*   **tien**   **ton**

Learn more

1 DEMONSTRATIVE ADJECTIVES AND PRONOUNS

Demonstrative adjectives are for pointing out specific places, people, and objects. Look at the chart for examples of *this* and *these* for masculine and feminine singular, and masculine and feminine plural.

	Masculine	Feminine
Singular	**ce ballon** (this ball)	cette voiture (this car)
Plural	**ces DVDs** (these DVDs)	ces cigarettes (these cigarettes)

Demonstrative pronouns are for referring to what has already been identified. Here we refer to the same objects as above:

	Masculine	Feminine
Singular	**celui-ci** (this one)	**celle-ci** (this one)
Plural	**ceux-ci** (these ones)	**celles-ci** (these ones)

2 POSSESSIVE ADJECTIVES AND PRONOUNS

Possessive adjectives and pronouns are used to say that something belongs to someone. The following examples show three different ways of saying something belongs to '*me*':

C'est à moi
C'est mon jeu / C'est le mien
C'est ma chambre / C'est la mienne
Ce sont mes chaussures / Ce sont les miennes
Ce sont mes crayons / Ce sont les miens

To express possession you can choose between the following:

1 *an emphatic pronoun:* **c'est à moi**, *when you are talking about something you can point to.*
2 *a possessive adjective: used before a noun:* **mon jeu, mes chaussures**. *Remember, the adjective agrees with the gender and number of the noun it accompanies.*
3 *a possessive pronoun: used to replace the noun altogether:* **le mien, les miennes**. *Here the form of the pronoun depends on the number and gender of the noun it replaces.*

Study the following table showing the whole range of possessive adjectives and pronouns and also the use of the emphatic pronoun following a preposition (in this case **à**).

Emphatic pronouns	Possessive adjectives	Possessive pronouns
C'est à moi	C'est mon/ma... Ce sont mes...	C'est le mien / la mienne Ce sont les miens / les miennes
C'est à toi	C'est ton/ta... Ce sont tes...	C'est le tien / la tienne Ce sont les tiens / les tiennes
C'est à lui/ à elle	C'est son/sa... Ce sont ses...	C'est le sien / la sienne Ce sont les siens / les siennes
C'est à nous	C'est notre... Ce sont nos...	C'est le nôtre / la nôtre Ce sont les nôtres
C'est à vous	C'est votre... Ce sont vos...	C'est le vôtre / la vôtre Ce sont les vôtres
C'est à elles/ à eux	C'est leur... Ce sont leurs...	C'est le leur / la leur Ce sont les leurs

3 INTERROGATIVE PRONOUNS

You can use interrogative pronouns to ask *which is/are yours?* The forms of interrogative pronouns are **lequel, laquelle, lesquel**, and **lesquelles**. Imagine a teacher is asking individual pupils about their possessions she has in her office.

Dans le bureau du prof il y a... *In the teacher's office there are...*

Look at the responses and notice which interrogative pronouns are used with which form and gender.

	Masculine noun	Which is / are yours?	Feminine noun	Which is / are yours?
Singular	des mobiles	Lequel est le tien?	des cagoules *(hood)*	Laquelle est la tienne?
Plural	des chewing gums	Lesquels sont les tiens?	des lunettes de soleil	Lesquelles sont les tiennes?

Practice

SPEAKING

1 **Maintenant vous êtes au bureau des objets trouvés** (*lost property office*). **Report that you have lost seven items in the following order:** *an umbrella, roller skates, reading glasses, a wallet, keys, a bag* and *a watch.* **Work through the list and say if the object shown to you is yours or not.**

Exemple:

Vous	*J'ai perdu mes lunettes de soleil.*
Employée	*Ce sont les vôtres?*
Vous	*Non, ce ne sont pas les miennes.*

Employée du bureau des objects trouvés	**Vous**
a **C'est votre parapluie?** (masc.)	**Non, ce n'est pas...**
b **Ce sont vos patins à roulettes?** (masc.)	**Oui, ce sont...**
c **Ce sont vos lunettes?** (fem.)	**Oui...**
d **C'est votre portefeuille?** (masc.)	**Non...**
e **Ce sont vos clefs?** (fem.)	**Oui...**
f **C'est votre sac?** (masc.)	**Oui...**
g **C'est votre montre?** (fem.)	**Non...**

2 22.04 **This time four of the items are yours. Listen to the recording and claim your property. Then continue listening to check your answers.**

Exemple:

Employée	*Ce sont vos lunettes de soleil?*
Vous	*Oui, ce sont les miennes.*

READING

French people have always been keen on reality TV shows. **Loft Story** was a **Télé Réalité** game that was very successful for a few years. It is no longer on French TV but seems to have taken by storm the province of Quebec. Read about the program and answer the questions below.

Les six gars et les sept filles qui participent à LOFT STORY circulent dans des locaux d'une superficie de 7000 pieds carrés sur deux étages. En plus des pièces comme les chambres, la salle à manger et le salon, les lofteurs et les lofteuses pourront se tenir en forme dans une salle de conditionnement physique ultramoderne.

Le confessionnal, cette pièce où les participants peuvent s'isoler pour s'adresser en privé aux téléspectateurs, sera situé au deuxième étage du loft, au-dessus des chambres. Dans chacune des pièces, on retrouvera des fenêtres-miroirs, permettant aux caméramans de filmer les allées et venues des lofteurs et des lofteuses.

Vingt-deux caméras robotisées seront installées un peu partout afin de ne rien manquer des échanges entre les gars et les filles... Cinquante-cinq microphones seront dissimulés dans chaque pièce afin de bien comprendre ce qui se dira et se tramera entre les participants.

Dans ce loft d'une dizaine de pièces, les six gars et les sept filles disposeront de tout l'espace nécessaire pour nous faire partager leurs états d'âme et s'adonner à de nombreuses activités.

   a *How many participants are there?* _____

   b *Make a list of all the rooms in the house.* _____

   c *What is the most private room in the house?* _____

   d *Where is it situated? What is its use?* _____

   e *List the different pieces of equipment used to record the participants' every utterance and action.* _____

   f *What can the participants do to keep in good shape?* _____

   g *What is the use of the two-way mirrors?* _____

   h *In square feet, what is the size of the Loft?* _____

Go further

1 Read the following newspaper article and answer the questions.

La grève dans les écoles de la Seine–Saint-Denis va-t-elle faire boule de neige?

Les syndicats d'enseignants de quinze établissements scolaires de la région de Créteil ont appelé à la grève pour protester contre «les graves insuffisances pour faire face aux besoins et lutter contre l'échec scolaire». Le ministre de l'Education Nationale avait proposé des réformes scolaires «pour donner aux élèves le goût d'apprendre et de se cultiver tout au long de la vie avec des itinéraires de découvertes». Les enseignants disent que «ces itinéraires prétendent résoudre l'échec scolaire. Or pour leur faire place dans l'emploi du temps on a été obligé de diminuer les horaires de français, mathématiques et histoire-géographie de deux heures par semaines.» Les professeurs réclament aussi la création de 6000 postes supplémentaires dans le 93*.

*Note: Ninety-three is the number for the area of **La Seine–Saint-Denis**. In France each **département** has a number which is linked to its alphabetical order, except for those used for Paris suburbs, which all have numbers in the 90s.

1 *What question is raised in the title of the article?* _____
2 *How many schools are facing strike action?* _____
3 *Where are these schools?* _____
4 *What new initiatives does the Minister wish to introduce?* _____
5 *What are teachers protesting against? Why?* _____
6 *What else do teachers want for this particular area?* _____

INSIGHT: NEW WORDS	
les enseignants	*teachers*
établissements scolaires	*schools*
lutter	*to fight*
l'échec scolaire	*school failure*
résoudre	*to resolve*
une boule de neige	*snowball*

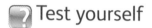

1 **Complete the following sentences with the correct possessive pronouns**

Exemple:

Ce vélo est à toi ? *Oui, c'est le mien !*

> la leur   le sien (x2)   les miennes (x2)   les leurs
> la sienne   la nôtre   les siennes   le mien

   a Ces fleurs sont à toi ? Oui ce sont _____!

   b Ce vélo est à ton père ? Oui c'est _____!

   c Et celui-ci est à toi ? Oui c'est _____!

   d Ces tickets sont à tes parents ? Oui, ce sont _____.

   e Monsieur et Madame Dupont, cette maison est à vous ? Oui, c'est _____.

   f Ce sac est à elle ? Oui, c'est -- ---- !

   g Cette balle de tennis est à Andy Murray ?!! Oui je te jure* que c'est _____!

   h Ces lunettes sont à Nicole ? Oui, ce sont _____!

   i Et celles-ci sont à vous? Oui ce sont _____.

   j Cette voiture est à eux ? Oui, c'est _____

*Note: I swear

2 **The teacher has confiscated items throughout the day. She gives them back at the end of school but cannot tell whose they are. Complete her questions with the words from the box.**

> lequel   lesquels   laquelle   lesquelles   le tien   la tienne
> les tiens   les tiennes   ceux-ci   celui-ci   celles-ci   celle-ci

Exemple: Sophie, ton bracelet? *Lequel* est *le tien? Celui-ci?*

   a Pierre, ta cagoule? _____ est _____? _____?

   b Laurent, ton iPod jeu vidéo? _____ est _____? _____?

   c Isabelle, tes baskets blanches? _____ sont _____? _____?

   d Lise, tes bracelets? _____ sont _____? _____?

23

La vie de famille
Family life

In this unit you will learn how to:
▶ *talk about cinema.*
▶ *talk about sport in France.*
▶ *use the pluperfect.*

CEFR: *Can invite others to give their views on how to proceed (B1); Can connect phrases in a simple way to describe things (B1).*

 Sport in France

Les Français adorent le sport (*the French love sports*), especially watching it **à la télé** (*on TV*) and discussing it **dans les bars et les cafés**. The attitude to sport, though, has changed over the years. Most French towns now have **une salle omnisports** (*a multi-sports centre*) or even **un Palais des Sports**. The largest one being **Le Palais Omnisports de Paris-Bercy** – a vast centre with a 17,000 spectators capacity, built **pour des manifestations sportives** (*sporting events*) **en salle couverte** (*indoor events*) and **pour la compétition internationale**.

French people are also moving away from beach holidays and spending more time **à pratiquer la marche** (*walking*), **le cyclisme** (*cycling*) **sur les routes** (*on roads*) and through the countryside on their **VTTs (–Vélos Tous Terrains** (*mountain bikes*). **Le ski et tous les sports de glisse** (*board sports*) **à la montagne et à la mer** are very popular with the younger generations.

a **Un exemple de sport de glisse est la planche à voile (*wind surfing*). Which word in the French name means *board*?**

Vocabulary builder

MORE DEMONSTRATIVE ADJECTIVES CE, CET, CETTE, CES

 23.01 **Match the demonstrative adjectives for this and these with the correct translations. Then listen to check your answers as you repeat.**

a	ce matin	**1**	*this week*
b	cet après-midi	**2**	*these last few weeks*
c	cette semaine	**3**	*this morning*
d	ces derniers jours	**4**	*this afternoon*
e	ces dernières semaines	**5**	*these last few days*

ADVERBS

 23.02 **Many adverbs are created from an adjective + -ement, which is equivalent to adjective + -*ly* in English. Complete the chart. Then listen and repeat the bolded words.**

> **INSIGHT: LANGUAGE**
> Notice that the odd one out here is **cet après-midi**. Just as the adjectives **nouveau** and **beau** become respectively **nouvel** and **bel** in front of a masculine noun starting with a vowel, **ce** becomes **cet**.

Adjectives		Adverbs	
malheureux	*unhappy*	**malheureusement**	*regrettably*
gratuit	a _____	**gratuitement**	*free of charge*
évident	*obvious*	**évidemment**	b _____
inlassable	*tireless*	**inlassablement**	c _____
particulier	d _____	**particulièrement**	_____

SPORTING EUPHEMISMS

 23.03 **Read the text. Then match the English translations to the French expressions. Listen to check your answers as you repeat.**

> **INSIGHT: LANGUAGE**
> Here is an exception to the rule:
> **vrai** *(true)* → **vraiment**

> Les Français sont fous (mad) de sport. Dans les bars les discussions tournent inlassablement autour du ballon rond, du ballon ovale, de la petite reine et de la grande boucle.

a	**le ballon rond** *(the round ball)* _____	**1**	*rugby*
b	**le ballon ovale** *(the oval ball)* _____	**2**	*football*
c	**la grande boucle** *(the big loop)* _____	**3**	*a bicycle*
d	**la petite reine** *(the little queen)* _____	**4**	*the Tour de France*

NEW EXPRESSIONS

Look at the expressions that are used in the next conversations. Note their meanings.

Conversation 1

débordée	*snowed under*
aider	*to help*
le ménage	*housework*
en avoir ras-le-bol	*to be fed up (lit. up to the brim)*
la rentrée	*start of the new school year*
ranger	*to tidy up*
Moi, j'en ai ras-le-bol!	*I'm fed up!*

Conversation 2

je te laisse choisir	*I let you choose*
la version sous-titrée	*subtitled version*
de toutes façons	*in any case*
déçues/déçu(e)	*disappointed*

Conversations

1 23.04 *C'est samedi matin et Marie-Claire est débordée!* **Listen to the conversation. Concentrate on what the various people in the family are planning to do and complete the grid.**

Saturday	Marie-Claire	Guillaume	Sarah	Ariane	Pierre
Morning	Housework Shopping	**a** _____	**b** _____	**c** _____	**d** _____
Afternoon	**e** _____	Football match	Cinema	**f** _____	**g** _____
Evening	Cinema	**h** _____	**i** _____	At home	**j** _____

Conversation 1

Ariane	Maman, c'est aujourd'hui que tu nous emmènes au cinéma? Tu avais dit qu'on irait voir Azur et Asmar...
Marie-Claire	Oui ma chérie, mais nous n'avons pas encore décidé ce que nous allons faire aujourd'hui.
Pierre	Tu nous avais promis!
Marie-Claire	Oui je sais, mais c'est un peu compliqué
Guillaume	Marie-Claire, je t'avais prévenue qu'aujourd'hui c'est le sport toute la journée. Je pars dans cinq minutes, là.
Marie-Claire	Quoi? Mais où vas-tu?
Guillaume	Mais je te l'ai dit avant-hier! Ce matin je vais à Bercy faire une partie de tennis avec les copains du bureau et cet après-midi je vais au foot avec Lionel. On va voir Paris-Saint Germain. C'est le premier match de la saison, on ne peut pas rater ça!
Marie-Claire	Il est possible que tu me l'aies dit mais j'avais complètement oublié. Moi j'en ai ras-le-bol! Je comptais sur toi pour m'aider à faire le ménage et les courses pour la semaine prochaine. Tu as sans doute oublié que c'est mardi, la rentrée!
Sarah	Bien, moi je vous propose une solution: Guillaume tu vas à Bercy et à ton match de foot, les enfants, ce matin on va tous aider Marie-Claire avec le ménage et les courses, et si vous avez bien travaillé, je vous emmènerai voir Azur et Asmar cet après midi. Maman profitera du calme pour se reposer.
Ariane	Super! Je vais ranger ma chambre. Tu viens Pierre?
Guillaume	Et moi, ce soir je garderai les enfants et vous deux vous pourrez aller au cinéma si vous en avez envie.

2 23.05 *Sarah et Marie-Claire ont finalement décidé d'aller au cinéma. Elles ont acheté L'Officiel des Spectacles (a weekly guide to what's on in Paris) et cherchent des films qu'elles aimeraient voir.*

a Listen and look at the list of films to answer the questions.

La liste de Sarah et Marie-Claire (par ordre alphabétique)

Arthur et les Minimoys (1h35) Aventure et animation de Luc Besson: comme tous les enfants de son âge Arthur est fasciné par les histoires que lui raconte sa grand-mère pour l'endormir. Mais..si ces histoires étaient vraies?

Azur et Asmar (1h39) Animation de Michel Ocelot: il y a bien longtemps, deux enfants étaient bercés par la même femme. Elevés comme deux frères, les enfants sont séparés brutalement…

Hors de Prix (1h43) Comédie de Pierre Salvadori avec Audrey Tautou et Gad Elmaleh. Jean, serveur timide d'un grand hôtel, passe pour un milliardaire aux yeux d'Irène, une aventurière intéressée. Quand elle découvre qui il est réellement elle le fuit aussitôt. Mais Jean, amoureux, se lance à sa poursuite et la retrouve sur la Côte d'Azur.

Les Infiltrés (VO) (2h30) Film américain de Martin Scorsese avec Leonardo Di Caprio, Matt Damon et Jack Nicholson: le 'parrain', Lou Costello règne en maître sur Boston. Pour le démasquer la police locale charge un jeune flic, Billy Costigan, d'infiltrer le gang du vieux malfaiteur.

Marie-Antoinette (2h03) Film américain de Sofia Coppola. Drame historique où la jeune Marie-Antoinette découvre un monde hostile et codifié, un univers frivole où chacun observe et juge l'autre…

Paris je t'aime (1h50) Film à sketches collectifs: voyages dans différents arrondissements de Paris à travers une série d'anecdotes amoureuses. Avec Fanny Ardant, Juliette Binoche, Steve Buscemi, Sergio Castellitto, Willem Dafoe, Gérard Depardieu, Marianne Faithfull, Ben Gazzara, Bob Hoskins, Nick Nolte, Natalie Portman, Gena Rowlands et Ludivine Sagnier.

1 Why does Sarah say she will let Marie-Claire choose the film? _____
2 What does Marie-Claire say about *Paris je t'aime*? _____
3 Which film do they choose to see? _____

Conversation 2

Sarah	Je te laisse choisir parce que je sors beaucoup plus souvent que toi quand je suis à Londres. De toutes façons j'aimerais certainement ton choix.
Marie-Claire	J'ai coché Azur et Asmar mais en fait tu l'as vu samedi avec les enfants. Je les emmènerai sans doute voir Arthur et les Minimoys samedi prochain.
Sarah	Les Infiltrés c'est la version originale sous-titrée en français je crois. Le titre anglais est The Departed. J'aime bien les films de Scorsese mais je le verrai certainement à Londres.
Marie-Claire	Paris Je t'aime vient de sortir en DVD, je te l'offre pour ton anniversaire si tu veux. C'est formidable, c'est plein d'acteurs connus et ce sont des histoires qui se passent dans chaque arrondissement de Paris.
Sarah	Bon eh bien il nous reste le choix entre Marie-Antoinette et Hors de Prix. Qu'est ce que tu préfères?
Marie-Claire	Moi j'adore Audrey Tautou, tu as vu Amélie?
Sarah	Bien sûr, j'ai adoré, bon alors c'est décidé on va voir Hors de Prix! Je suis sûre que nous ne serons pas déçues.

 b Look at the list of films. Then express these opinions in French.

a Say you would like to see *Paris je t'aime* because you love Paris.

b Say you would like to see *Arthur et les Minimoys* because you love films directed by Luc Besson.

c Say you would like to see *Marie-Antoinette* because it is interesting to see an American film about French history.

d Say you would like to see *Azur et Asmar* because the story, the animation and the music are beautiful.

 Language discovery

1 Link the English phrases to the equivalent French expressions from Conversation 1.

a *You had said we would go and see!*

1 On va tous aider.

b *I was counting on you to help with the shopping.*

c *I told you the day before yesterday.*

d *I shall look after the children.*

e *We are all going to help.*

f *We can't miss that!*

2 On ne peut pas rater ça!

3 Je garderai les enfants.

4 Tu avais dit qu'on irait voir!

5 Je te l'ai dit avant-hier.

6 Je comptais sur toi pour les courses.

Learn more

1 THE PLUPERFECT

This is another past tense, used for an action that took place prior to something else happening. Look at these examples from Conversation 1. In each, the person is referring to something that happened or was said prior to today.

Tu avais dit qu'on irait voir Azur et Asmar.	*You had said that we would go and see Azur et Asnar.*
Tu nous avais promis.	*You had promised.*
Je t'avais prévenue.	*I had warned you.*
J'avais oublié.	*I had forgotten.*

We may use the pluperfect in the following situations:

▶ a 'then and now' situation:

J'avais adoré Audrey Tautou dans *Amélie* mais dans le rôle de Coco Chanel elle est sublime. *I'd loved Audrey Tautou in 'Amélie' but in the role of Coco Chanel she is sublime.*

▶ a 'before and then' situation:

Marion Cotillard était peu connue mais avec *La Môme* cela a été une révélation. *Marion Cotillard had been little known but with 'La Môme' this was a revelation.*

▶ With an implicit pre-existing condition:

Isabelle Adjani était préprogrammée pour son rôle de professeure dans 'La Journée de la jupe'. *Isabelle Adjani had been preprogrammed for her role as a schoolteacher in 'La Journée de la jupe'.*

There is very little difference between the structures of the pluperfect and the perfect tense.

Perfect: **avoir** or **être** in the present tense + past participle

Pluperfect: **avoir** or **être** in the imperfect tense + past participle

Perfect		Pluperfect	
J'ai dit.	I have said.	**J'avais dit.**	I had said.
Elle est partie.	She has left.	**Elle était partie.**	She had left.

Note that in many cases the pluperfect and the perfect are used in the same sentence. They may occur in the following cases:

▶ Something was planned, said or done but more recent events altered the situation:

Michael Schumacher, deux fois champion du monde, avait voulu gagner mais à Jerez il a tout perdu dans un accrochage avec Jacques Villeneuve. *(Michael Schumacher, twice world champion, had wanted to win but at Jerez he lost everything in a collision with Jacques Villeneuve.)*

The following example is from a 1997 newspaper article. The old affinity between France and Canada meant that, at the peak of his career, francophone Jacques Villeneuve received support and full media attention in France.

Et Schumacher? En tout il a été sept fois champion du monde. Jacques Villeneuve ne l'a été qu'une seule fois, en 1997!

▶ something is done as a consequence of a prior state of things:

Le garçon a volé des pommes parce qu'il n'avait pas mangé depuis deux jours. *(The boy stole some apples because he hadn't eaten for two days.)*

Check that you know your past participles:

Verb	Past participle
prendre	**pris**
pouvoir	**pu**
devoir	**dû***
boire	**bu**
pleuvoir	**plu**
perdre	**perdu**
avoir	**eu**

*Note: The past participle of **devoir** *(to have to)* is **dû**. The circumflex on the **û** is used to differentiate between **dû**, the past participle, and **du**, the indefinite article (as in **du pain, du vin et du fromage**).

 # Practice

Terminez les phrases. Find a suitable end for each of the sentences.

a Sylvie avait beaucoup travaillé...

b Les Durand avaient gagné le gros lot;

c J'avais pris mon parapluie;

d Loïc avait dit qu'il viendrait à Paris...

e Les jeunes avaient trop bu...

f Laurent était allé en Angleterre pour les vacances...

g Il a appelé la police

h Le voleur est entré sans effort;

1 mais malheureusement il n'a pas pu.

2 pour déclarer qu'on lui avait volé sa voiture.

3 on avait dû laisser la porte ouverte.

4 et elle a réussi son examen.

5 et il a décidé d'y rester.

6 malheureusement ils ont tout perdu.

7 alors il n'a pas plu.

8 et ils ont eu un accident.

Go further

 1 Look at the list of sporting events in Paris and answer the questions.

a How many types of sporting events are listed? _____

b What are they? _____

c When is the barmen and women's race? _____

d Where does it take place? _____

e When is the **Prix du Président de la République?** _____

f What race starts and finishes at the Eiffel Tower? _____

Dates et Évènements sportifs	Lieux: où dans Paris
Dernier dimanche de janvier Prix d'Amérique (course de chevaux)	Hippodrome de Vincennes
Février – mars Tournoi des Six Nations (rugby)	Parc des Princes
Avril Marathon de Paris; Festival d'Arts Martiaux	À travers Paris; Palais Omnisports de Bercy
Première quinzaine d'avril (un dimanche) Prix du Président de la République	Hippodrome d'Auteuil
Fin mai / début juin Internationaux de France de Tennis	Stade Roland-Garros
Juin Finale de la coupe de France de Football; Course des serveuses et garçons de café	Stade de France; Des Champs-Elysées à la Bastille
Troisième dimanche de juin Grand Steeple-Chase	Hippodrome d'Auteuil
Dernier dimanche de juin Grand Prix de Paris	Hippodrome de Longchamp
Mi-juillet Arrivée du Tour de France Cycliste	Champs-Elysées
Mi-septembre (un samedi) Prix d'été	Hippodrome de Vincennes
Premier dimanche d'octobre Prix de L'Arc de Triomphe	Hippodrome de Longchamp
Octobre Les Vingt Kilomètres de Paris (course à pied)	Tour Eiffel
Deuxième dimanche d'octobre Course de côte de voitures anciennes (uphill race)	Rue Lepic (Montmartre)
Fin octobre Tennis: Le Tournoi de Paris (Paris Open)	Paris-Bercy

2   **Est-ce que vous connaissez bien les deux meilleurs footballeurs français?** How well are you acquainted with these two famous footballers? Use the information from the box to complete their profiles.

Marseille   française   Zidane   1,88m   Paris   23 juin 1972
milieu de terrain   Zinédine   1,85m   attaquant   française
17 août 1977   Henry

Player A	Player B
1. Prénom:	1. Prénom: Thierry
2. Nom:	2. Nom:
3. Nationalité:	3. Nationalité:
4. Date de naissance:	4. Date de naissance:
5. Lieu de naissance:	5. Lieu de naissance:
6. Taille:	6. Taille:
7. Poste:	7. Poste:

 READING

Et si vous aimez vraiment le cinéma abonnez-vous! The form below is for a year's subscription to Les Cahiers du Cinéma, the oldest and most famous cinema magazine.

Look at the form and answer these questions.

   a   *What was the special offer?* _____
   b   *How many issues would you receive for that price?* _____
   c   *How can you pay?* _____

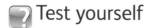 Test yourself

1 **Complete the following sentences with the correct past participle of the verbs in brackets.**

   a J'avais tranquillement (prendre) l'Eurostar à 20h13 à la gare du Nord.

   b Elle avait (vouloir) voyager en avion pour arriver plus rapidement à Paris.

   c Malheureusement il avait trop (boire) et il n'aurait pas (devoir) conduire.

   d Quand l'ambulance est (arriver) il avait déjà (perdre) connaissance *(to lose consciousness)*.

   e Il avait beaucoup (pleuvoir) pendant la nuit

   f Ils étaient déjà (partir) quand nous sommes arrivés.

   g Je sais qu'elle avait (avoir) de gros problèmes sentimentaux.

   h On lui avait toujours (dire) de ne pas parler à des inconnus.

   i J'avais complètement (oublier) que j'avais (prendre) un rendez-vous chez le dentiste.

   j Ils avaient parfaitement (comprendre) ce que je leur avais (dire).

2 **Say the following in French:**

   a They had taken a taxi to arrive faster.

   b She had wanted to work in Paris to earn more money.

   c Unfortunately I had lost my bag.

   d I had not eaten for 2 days.

3 **Go back to exercise 1 and see how many adverbs ending in –ment you can find. Say what they mean.**

SELF CHECK

I CAN. . .

⬤ . . . talk about cinema.

⬤ . . . talk about sport in France.

⬤ . . . use the pluperfect.

24 *Un repas familial*
A family meal

In this unit you will learn how to:
▶ *talk about French meals.*
▶ *understand recipe vocabulary.*
▶ *talk about family.*
▶ *talk about travelling.*
▶ *use the relative pronouns* qui *and* que.

CEFR: *Can understand specialized vocabulary (B2); Can narrate a story (B1); Can understand clearly written instructions (B1).*

 French cooking and meals

La cuisine familiale française (*home cooking*) is not quite as traditional as it used to be. The influence of world cuisine such as **la cuisine nord-africaine** (*North-African cooking*) with couscous-based dishes is integrated into what people eat at home.

There is a slight attempt to eat **moins de viande** (*less meat*). For many families, the pattern of an everyday meal remains **une entrée** (*a starter*), **un plat principal** (*a main course*), **puis la salade** (*then the lettuce*) after the main course, then **le fromage** (*the cheese*) **et pour finir, le dessert** (*and to finish, dessert*).

Les grandes réunions de famille often take place around the table and often last for hours. **Le grand repas gastronomique**, popularly known as **'la grande bouffe'** (*the big eat*), is exemplified in **La Grande Bouffe**, a 1973 French–Italian film starring Marcello Mastroianni.

La cuisine de tous les jours (*everyday cooking*), although more modest, is still enjoyed: people enjoy **se mijoter** (*preparing with care*) **des bons petits plats** (*tasty dishes*).

 If a **grande bouffe** is a formal meal, what do you think **une petite bouffe** is?

a a low-calorie meal,
b a two-course meal,
c a casual meal between friends

Vocabulary builder

IN THE KITCHEN

 24.01 **This vocabulary can be divided into four categories: ingredients, processes/utensils, adjectives of condition and instructions. In each of the four boxes, match the equivalent French and English expressions. Then listen to check your answers.**

Qu'est-ce qu'il faut?			
Les ingrédients			
a	échalotes _____	1	mushrooms
b	beurre _____	2	salt and pepper
c	champignons _____	3	shallots
d	jaunes d'œufs _____	4	fresh dill leaves
e	feuilles d'aneth fraîches _____	5	butter
f	sel et poivre	6	egg yolks
Les procédés et les ustensiles de cuisine			
g	le temps de cuisson _____	7	boiling point
h	ébullition _____	8	cooking time
i	la lèchefrite _____	9	cooking pan (in oven)
j	le four _____	10	the oven
Comment sont nos ingrédients?			
k	épluché(e)(s) _____	11	peeled
l	lavé(e)(s) _____	12	heated
m	vidé(e)(s) _____	13	gutted (emptied)
n	haché(e)(s) _____	14	chopped
o	chauffé(e)(s) _____	15	washed

Maintenant que faut-il faire?			
p	parsemer _____	16	to sprinkle
q	faire cuire _____	17	to remove (the skin)
r	arroser _____	18	to water
s	mouiller _____	19	to wet, dampen
t	ajouter _____	20	to season
u	mélanger _____	21	to cook
v	ôter (la peau) _____	22	to add
w	épaissir _____	23	to thicken
x	verser _____	24	to pour
y	assaisonner _____	25	to mix
z	napper _____	26	to cover with a sauce

COOKING AND TABLE EXPRESSIONS

 24.02 **Cooking and table expressions are often used figuratively with a derogatory meaning. Listen and choose the correct meaning for each expression. Then listen and repeat.**

a Je ne sais pas ce qu'il mijote!
   1 in the sense of plotting to do something
   2 a person who loses his/her temper easily
   3 to make an effort to please or impress

b Elle met les petits plats dans les grands.
   1 in the sense of plotting to do something
   2 a person who loses her temper easily
   3 to make an effort to please or impress

c Il est soupe au lait.
   1 in the sense of plotting to do something
   2 a person who loses his temper easily
   3 to make an effort to please or impress

NEW EXPRESSIONS

Look at the expressions that are used in Conversation 2. Note their meanings.

un ordinateur	a computer
célibataire	*single (applies to men or women)*
ma belle-sœur	*my sister-in-law*
à cause de	*because of*

Conversations

1 24.03 *La famille se retrouve chez tante Eliane, Rue du Docteur Blanche, à Passy dans le seizième arrondissement de Paris. Bruno, un de ses fils, est enseignant à Lyon mais en ce moment il est en vacances chez sa mère. Son autre fils, Daniel, travaille à l'étranger.*

a Listen and answer the questions.

1 What does aunt Eliane ask the children to do? _____

2 What does she ask them to be careful with? _____

3 What does she give them to take to Bruno? _____

4 What will they drink with the meal? _____

Conversation 1

Tante Eliane	Vous venez avec moi dans la salle à manger, les petits, vous allez m'aider à mettre le couvert.
Ariane	Moi, je sais mettre le couvert.
Pierre	Et moi aussi je sais.
Tante	Alors faites bien attention à ma vaisselle, surtout les verres. Alors vous faites comme cela. La petite assiette sur la grande assiette, la fourchette à gauche, le couteau à droite et la cuillère à dessert devant le verre. Voilà, c'est bien!
Pierre	On a fini!
Tante	Bon, tu veux demander à Bruno de m'ouvrir la bouteille de vin blanc qui est au frigo? Tiens, donne-lui le tire-bouchon.
Ariane	Qu'est-ce qu'on mange? J'ai faim!
Tante	Ah! J'aime bien que les enfants aient de l'appétit! Je vous ai préparé un très bon menu. Alors comme entrée on a du bon melon, et après je vais vous servir une truite au champagne et raisins avec des pommes de terre sautées.
Pierre	Et pour le dessert?
Tante	Ah mais avant le dessert il y a de la salade et du bon fromage et pour le dessert ... une tarte aux pommes!
Pierre et Ariane	Miam-miam!

b Find the French words in the conversation which mean:

1 a glass _____
2 a plate _____
3 a knife _____
4 a fork _____
5 a spoon _____
6 crockery/dishes _____
7 a corkscrew _____

c Listen again or read. Then write down Tante Eliane's menu in French and say what it means.

> Menu de Tante Eliane
> Dimanche 31 août
> _____
> _____
> _____
> _____

d Read Tante Eliane's recipe for *La grande truite au champagne et aux raisins frais (trout in champagne with fresh grapes)* opposite and answer the questions.

1 This recipe is for how many persons? _____
2 How long will it take to cook? _____
3 How much champagne is used? _____
4 What must be done to the champagne before pouring it on the trout? _____
5 When do you need to add the champagne? _____
6 What needs to be done to the trout's tail and head? _____

UNE ENVIE DE VRAI

à découvrir la truite de France
et ses recettes
mode et tradition

AU FOUR,
EN FÊTE, LA GRANDE TRUITE
AU CHAMPAGNE ET RAISINS FRAIS

Ingrédients

- *1 grande truite d'env. 2,5 kg*
- *3 échalotes*
- *100 g de beurre*
- *125 g de champignons de Paris*
- *1/2 bout. de champagne*
- *10 grains de raisin noir frais épluchés*
- *10 grains de raisin blanc frais épluchés*
- *Asperges*
- *125 g de crème fraîche*
- *2 ou 3 jaunes d'oeufs*
- *Baies de poivre rose*
- *Feuilles d'aneth fraîches*
- *Sel et poivre*

Temps de cuisson
Environ 45 minutes.

Préparation pour 6/8 personnes.

La truite étant vidée et lavée, saler et poivrer l'intérieur. Garnir le fond d'une léchefrite d'une feuille d'aluminium, la parsemer d'échalotes hachées et de champignons, y déposer la truite, après avoir enveloppé la tête et la queue de papier d'aluminium. Saler, poivrer, mouiller avec la moitié du champagne, couvrir le plat d'aluminium.

Faire cuire à 200ºC (thermostat 6) pendant 45 minutes environ. Une ou deux fois en cours de cuisson, arroser la truite de champagne chauffé en soulevant la feuille d'aluminium.

Sortir la truite et ôter la peau des deux côtés. Dresser sur un plat de service. Pour la sauce, à ébullition, verser le jus de cuisson dans une casserole, ajouter la crème mélangée aux jaunes d'oeufs. Assaisonner, faire épaissir, ajouter grains de raisins et baies de poivre rose et napper la truite.

2 24.04 *Tout le monde est encore à table, la truite au champagne est délicieuse, le vin est bon et on échange des nouvelles de la famille.*

a Listen to the recording and answer the questions.

1 Where is Daniel now? _____

2 When is he coming back to France? _____

b Listen again and answer these questions.

1 Does Daniel like it where he is? _____

2 Is he married? _____

Conversation 2

Sarah	Au fait, comment va Daniel?
Tante Eliane	Il va bien, il voyage beaucoup Euh en ce moment il est au Japon mais il rentrera en France à Noël.
Sarah	Ah bon! Ça fait combien de temps qu'il est là-bas?
Tante	Oh, à peu près trois mois. Il travaille pour une firme qui fabrique des ordinateurs et en ce moment il passe trois mois en France et trois mois au Japon.
Sarah	Ça lui plaît?
Tante	Ah oui, énormément. Et puis tant qu'il est célibataire il n'y a pas de problèmes. Oh mais je ne vous ai pas dit? Cette fois-ci c'est moi qui pars en voyage!
Marie-Claire	Ah bon! Et où vas-tu?
Tante	Au Canada! J'y vais avec ma belle-sœur qui habite à Nantes. C'est un voyage organisé. Ils avaient acheté les billets et maintenant son mari ne peut pas y aller à cause de son travail alors j'y vais à sa place.
Guillaume	Et quand est-ce que tu pars?
Tante	Eh bien le départ de Nantes est le 12 octobre et nous rentrons le 21.
Marie-Claire	Bon, alors on te souhaite un bon voyage et n'oublie pas de nous envoyer une carte postale, hein!

---

c Listen again or read to answer the questions.

1 Who is Tante Eliane going to Canada with? _____

2 Why is she going with her? _____

3 When are they leaving? From where? _____

4 When are they returning? _____

Names of countries or continents are masculine or feminine and singular or plural.

le Canada, la France, les Etats-Unis, les Pays-Bas, la Hollande

To say *in* we use either **en, au** or **à**.

au Canada, aux Etats-Unis, au Royaume-Uni / en Grande Bretagne, aux Pays-Bas / en Hollande, au Japon, en Australie, en Espagne

Language discovery

1 Link the following English phrases to the equivalent French expressions from Conversation 1.

a	*You are going to help to lay the table.*	**1 Donne-lui le tire-bouchon.**
b	*Mind my dishes.*	**2 Et pour le dessert ... une tarte aux pommes.**
c	*Do you mind asking Bruno to open the bottle of wine for me?*	**3 J'aime que les enfants aient de l'appétit.**
d	*Give him the corkscrew.*	**4 Vous allez m'aider à mettre le couvert.**
e	*I like it when children have an appetite.*	**5 Faites attention à ma vaisselle.**
f	*And for dessert ... an apple tart.*	**6 Tu veux demander à Bruno de m'ouvrir la bouteille de vin?**

2 Link the following English phrases to the equivalent French expressions from Conversation 2.

a	*How long has he been there?*	**1 C'est un voyage organisé.**
b	*He works for a firm which manufactures computers.*	**2 tant qu'il est célibataire**
c	*as long as he is single...*	**3 N'oublie pas de nous envoyer une carte postale.**
d	*I am going with my sister-in-law.*	**4 Ça fait combien de temps qu'il est là-bas?**
e	*Don't forget to send a postcard.*	**5 J'y vais avec ma belle-sœur.**
f	*It's a package tour.*	**6 Il travaille pour une firme qui fabrique des ordinateurs.**

3 Look at the examples below. What two similar words can be used to mean *that*?

J'aime que les enfants aient de l'appétit.

Il travaille pour une firme qui fabrique des ordinateurs.

Learn more

1 QUI *OR* QUE?

These are relative pronouns. Although similar, they have two different functions.

Qui is used to stand for *who* or *which* representing people or objects. It acts as the subject of the verb.

<u>une firme qui</u> fabrique des ordinateurs
c'est <u>**moi qui**</u> pars

In the two examples above **qui** represents the word which precedes it and which is the subject of the sentence. **Qui** links two sentences, making one longer and more elegant sentence:

C'est ma belle sœur. Elle habite à Nantes.
→ C'est ma belle sœur qui habite à Nantes.

Que/qu' stands for *which*, *that*, or *whom* and also links two sentences, but it represents the direct object of the sentence. It represents people or objects.

<u>**Le voyage que**</u> je vais faire est un voyage organisé.

In this type of sentence **que** is placed immediately before the subject. This should be more obvious in the next two examples.

Regarde, c'est le type que j'ai vu hier.   *Look, it's the guy I saw yesterday.*

Here **que** represents **le type** (the object of the sentence). **Que** precedes **j'** (the subject) who did the action of seeing the man (the object).

Regarde, c'est le type qui a vu l'accident.   *Look, it's the guy who saw the accident.*

In this sentence **qui** represents **le type** (the subject of the sentence) who saw the accident (the object).

Qui is always followed by a verb, sometimes preceded by an indirect pronoun.

C'est toi qui lui as donné les clefs! *It's you who gave her the keys!*

In the above example, **qui** represents the subject **toi**. In the following sentence que represents the object **les clefs** and precedes the subject **tu**.

Voici les clefs que tu lui as données. *Here are the keys you gave him.*

Note that as the object **les clefs** precedes the verb, the past participle agrees with the number and gender of the object (**données**).

Practice

Complete each of the sentences with qu', qui or que.

a Ce _____ j'aime ce sont les enfants _____ sont polis!

b La recette _____ je préfère c'est celle de la truite aux amandes.

c Le film _____ je voulais voir passe à la télé ce soir.

d Ce sont les années _____ j'ai passées en Angleterre à apprendre l'anglais _____ me seront les plus utiles.

e C'est toi _____ as les clefs?

f Pourquoi est-ce que ce sont toujours les mêmes _____ décident?

> **INSIGHT: CULTURE**
>
> If you're still in doubt whether to use **qui** or **que**, examine the sentence below. It may help your understanding.
>
> **Le seul magazine que j'achète régulièrement c'est le 'Nouvel Observateur', qui est un hebdomadaire.** *(The only magazine that I buy regularly is the 'Nouvel Observateur', which is a weekly magazine.)*

READING

1 Tante Eliane shows her family what she is going to see in Canada. Look at her schedule for Days 5, 6 and 7. Then decide whether the following statements are vrai ou faux (true or false).

a They will see skyscrapers in Tadoussac. _____

b Québec is one of two fortified towns north of Mexico. _____

c There is a lobster dinner at the end of day 7. _____

d The excursion to see the whales is optional. _____

e There will be some free time to see le Vieux Québec. _____

f Mont-Royal offers a window on the St Laurent. _____

g Montmorency Falls are one and a half times higher than Niagara Falls. _____

h There is a guided tour of Tadoussac. _____

i Québec is the cradle of French civilization in North America. _____

j L'Ile Ste Hélène is a church. _____

1400 €
Départ de Nantes

PROGRAMME

JOUR 5
MONTRÉAL-QUÉBEC
Petit déjeuner à l'hôtel. Départ pour la visite guidée, métropole cosmopolite, Montréal présente mille et un visages, mille et un éclats. Vous découvrirez le centre-ville et ses gratte-ciel, le Vieux Montréal et ses rues recouvertes de gros pavés, le Vieux Port qui offre une fenêtre sur St-Laurent, l'Eglise Notre-Dame, le Mont-Royal, l'Ile Ste-Hélène, le Jardin Botanique et le Stade Olympique. Départ pour Québec. Déjeuner à la Cabane à Sucre Chez Pierre. Dîner de homard au restaurant le Monte Carlo. 5e nuit Hôtel LE COTTAGE ou similaire.

JOUR 6
QUÉBEC
Petit déjeuner à l'hôtel. Départ de l'hôtel pour la visite guidée de la ville Québec, berceau de la civilisation française en Amérique du Nord. La seule ville fortifiée

au Nord du Mexique. Vous verrez le Vieux-Québec, le Château Frontenac, la Place Royale, la Colline Parlementaire et la Citadelle. Déjeuner et temps 'libre' dans le Vieux Québec pour découvrir ses boutiques et musées à pied. Dîner au restaurant La Cage aux Sports. 6e nuit Hôtel LE COTTAGE ou similaire.

JOUR 7
QUÉBEC-CHARLEVOIX
Petit déjeuner à l'hôtel. Départ pour la région de Charlevoix, nous ferons quelques arrêts, premier arrêt aux Chutes Montmorency (1 fois et demi la hauteur des Chutes du Niagara). Déjeuner à Tadoussac, suivi de temps libre pour visiter ce très beau petit village ou faire l'excursion des baleines (en option); pour les autres nous ferons la visite du Manoir Richelieu. Dîner à votre hôtel. 8e nuit au MANOIR CHARLEVOIX

---

2 Cherchez l'erreur. Attention: dans le texte pour le Jour 7 il y a une petite erreur d'imprimerie (a small printing error). L'avez-vous découverte?

INSIGHT: CULTURE

les gratte-ciel	*skyscrapers*
des baleines	*whales*
des pavés	*cobblestones*
un homard	*a lobster*

Go further

 1 Un peu de diététique. Avez-vous un bon équilibre alimentaire? Pour le savoir, testez-vous. Cochez les cases qui correspondent à vos habitudes alimentaires.

VOS HABITUDES ALIMENTAIRES	Toujours	Parfois	Jamais
1 Vous buvez de l'eau tout au long de la journée?			
2 Vous optez pour les fruits et légumes?			
3 Vous restez raisonnable avec le gras et le sucre?			
4 Vous consommez des fibres?			
5 Vous préférez le poisson et les volailles?			
6 Vous consommez des céréales?			
7 Vous utilisez des huiles végétales?			
8 Vous déjeunez copieusement et dînez légèrement?			
9 Vous limitez votre consommation d'alcool?			
10 Vous mangez avec plaisir et en bonne compagnie?			

2 **La solution.** Pour chaque question où vous avez coché la première colonne: accordez-vous 1 point; la deuxième colonne: 2 points; et la troisième: 3 points.

> **INSIGHT: NEW WORDS**
>
> | le gras | fat |
> | la volaille | poultry |
> | parfois | sometimes |

Et le verdict !

De 1 à 12 points: C'est bien! Vous avez un régime équilibré.

De 13 à 23 points: Encore un petit effort! Vous pouvez mieux faire et vous faire du bien.

De 24 à 30 points: C'est le désastre! Vous allez à la catastrophe à moins de faire quelque chose immédiatement.

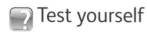 Test yourself

1 Complete tante Eliane's letter with either qui, que or qu'.

Une lettre de Québec

> Ma Chère Marie-Claire,
> Voici 1 _____ ma semaine au Québec touche à sa fin.
> Nous avons fait tellement de choses intéressantes 2 _____
> je n'ai pas le temps de dire tout ce 3 _____ nous
> avons fait sur cette carte postale mais je te raconterai
> tout en détails à mon retour. J'ai beaucoup aimé le vieux
> Montréal mais ce 4 _____ j'ai préféré ce sont tous les
> petits villages 5 _____ nous avons visités. J'ai surtout
> adoré Tadoussac 6 _____ est le village où Jacques Cartier
> a débarqué en 1535. Les villageois 7 _____ nous avons
> rencontrés nous ont fait fête. J'ai tellement aimé la façon
> 8 _____ ils ont de parler français avec leur accent
> chantant 9 _____ j'avais envie de parler comme eux.
> Hier soir nous sommes allés à un concert folklorique dans
> un vieux bar où il y avait un groupe de chanteurs 10 _____
> s'appellent 'La Bottine Souriante'. C'était drôle parce
> 11 _____ ça ressemblait un peu à de la musique bretonne.
> La personne 12 _____ était mon hôtesse, une femme très
> sympathique 13 _____ travaille à Radio Québec, m'a dit
> 14 _____ ils sont très connus partout dans le monde.
> J'espère 15 _____ tu vas bien et 16 _____ ta petite
> blessure ne te cause plus d'ennuis.
> Embrasse bien les enfants de ma part.
> A bientôt
> Tante Eliane

2 Read the postcard again and answer the questions.
   a What is it that Tante Eliane liked best during her trip?
   b What historical event does she mention in her letter?

   c At the folk concert who was Tante Eliane's hostess and where did she work?

   d Who are La Bottine Souriante? What do we know about them?

3 **Give a brief answer in French to the following questions.**

   a Qui est en vacances au Québec?

   b Qui a débarqué à Tadoussac en 1535?

   c Qu'est-ce que Tante Eliane pense de l'accent québécois?

   d Qu'est ce qu'elle avait envie de faire?

SELF CHECK

I CAN...
... talk about French meals.
... use vocabulary for recipes.
... talk about family.
... talk about travelling.
... use the relative pronouns **qui** and **que**.

25 Si on achetait une maison?

What if we bought a house?

In this unit you will learn how to:
▶ *express feelings of sadness.*
▶ *order pronouns.*
▶ *make plans to buy a house in France.*
▶ *better understand legal requirements when buying a property.*

CEFR: *Can identify speakers viewpoints and attitudes as well as information content (B2); Can keep up with an animated native speaker conversation (B2); Has sufficient vocabulary to express self on most topics (B1).*

 Buying a property in France

You have spent many happy holidays dans **un joli petit village** (*a pretty little village*) and you have just discovered that **la maison de vos rêves** (*your dream house*) is **à vendre** (*for sale*). However there are many formalities **la loi** (*the law*) demands you go through.

Une vente immobilière (*a property sale*) **est un long processus** (*is a long process*), **avec plusieurs étapes** (*with several stages*). Once all verifications have been carried out and **le prix du bien** (*the cost of the property*), **a été agréé** (*has been agreed*) **le vendeur et l'acquéreur** (*the seller and the would-be buyer*) **doivent le formaliser** (*must formalise it*). At this point there is **un engagement réciproque** (*a reciprocal engagement*) to complete the deal, **un compromis de vente or avant-contrat** (*pre-contract*).

On signing **le compromis de vente**, you engage yourself to buy the property by paying **le dépôt de garantie**, (*a deposit*), a sum of money **de 10% de la valeur de la propriété** (*10% of the value of the property*). It normally takes **trois mois** between **l'avant-contrat et l'acte authentique** (*completion*).

 a If all is in order, how long does it take between le compromis de vente and l'acte authentique for the house to be yours?

306

Vocabulary builder

DESCRIBING A DREAM HOME

 25.01 **Où situer sa maison? Quels sont vos critères?** *Where do you want your house situated? What are your criteria?* **Listen and match the descriptions. Then listen and repeat.**

a **en bord de mer**

b **entre mer et campagne**

c **en centre ville**

d **dans un quartier calme**

e **proche d'une plage**

f **sans vis-à-vis**

g **avec vue sur... la mer/la montagne...**

1 *with an open outlook*

2 *in a quiet area*

3 *in the centre of town*

4 *by the sea*

5 *near a beach*

6 *with a view of... the sea/ the mountains...*

7 *between the sea and the countryside*

GETTING A HOUSE BUILT

 25.02 **How do you go about getting a house built? Look at the tasks. Then listen and choose the correct translation for each.**

Il faut...

a **aller sur le site internet du Ministère de l'Écologie de l'Aménagement et du Développement durable.**

1 Fill in a form on line or hand it in at the Town Hall.

2 You have to... go to the ministry's website.

b **se conformer à la loi du 1er octobre 2007.**

1 Sign a building contract.

2 Comply with the law of 1 October 2007.

c **remplir un formulaire en ligne sur internet ou bien déposer le formulaire à la mairie.**

1 Fill in a form on line or hand it in at the Town Hall.

2 You have to... go to the ministry's website.

d **vérifier que le terrain est constructible.**
  1 Sign a building contract.
  2 Check that the site can be built on.

e **signer un contrat de construction.**
  1 Sign a building contract.
  2 Comply with the law of 1 October 2007.

TASKS FOR A NOTAIRE

 1 *25.03 Un notaire (notary) is a lawyer who deals specifically with property and family transactions such as wills, donations, etc.* **Look at the tasks a notaire usually handles. Then listen and choose the correct translation for each.**

a **se renseigner sur la propriété et les propriétaires actuels**
  1 to find out about the property and current owners
  2 to organize a visit to the property

b **recueillir des renseignements d'urbanisme**
  1 to gather the town planning information
  2 to prepare the draft sales contract

c **organiser une visite de la propriété**
  1 to find out about the property and current owners
  2 to organize a visit to the property

d **préparer le compromis de vente**
  1 to write or draft the sales contract
  2 to prepare the draft sales contract

e **rédiger le contrat de vente**
  1 to write or draft the sales contract
  2 to prepare the draft sales contract

Look at the expressions that are used in the next conversations. Note their meanings.

Conversation 1

Il a le cafard/Il est déprimé	*feeling depressed*
Il n'a pas la pêche*/Il n'a pas le moral	
triste	*sad*
faire part de	*to inform about*
un faire-part de naissance/mariage/décès	*announcement of birth/wedding/death*
Gallimard	*an important French publisher*

*Note: This is a colloquial expression.

Conversation 2

Maître (abbreviation **Me**)	*a notaire's title*
l'état civil	*civic status*
l'urbanisme	*town planning department*
recueillir des renseignements	*to gather information/to do a search*
le compromis de vente: l'avant-contrat	*the pre-contract*

Conversations

1 25.04 *Toute la famille accompagne Sarah à la gare du Nord d'où elle doit repartir pour Londres.*

a Listen to the recording once, and answer these questions.

   1 Why is Sarah feeling a bit low? _____

   2 How does Ariane feel about Sarah's departure? _____

b Now listen again and answer these questions..

   1 Is Sarah looking forward to going back to work? _____

   2 Who is Marie-Claire going to phone tonight? _____

   3 Why tonight? _____

Conversation 1

Sarah	Ah là là, je n'ai pas envie de rentrer!
Guillaume	Eh bien reste!
Sarah	Non … je ne peux pas, seulement j'ai toujours un peu le cafard quand je quitte la France.
Ariane	Moi non plus je ne veux pas que tu partes. On est triste quand tu t'en vas!
Marie-Claire	Tu regrettes de ne pas avoir accepté l'offre d'emploi chez Gallimard?
Sarah	Non, pas du tout, je n'y pensais même plus. Non, ce n'est pas grave, je suis un peu déprimée mais ce n'est tout de même pas la grosse dépression! C'est tout simplement que je n'ai pas la pêche quand il s'agit de reprendre le travail!
Marie-Claire	En fait de déprime il ne faut pas que j'oublie de téléphoner à Maman ce soir. C'est la rentrée pour elle aussi demain et, en général, elle non plus elle n'a pas le moral avant de reprendre les cours.
Sarah	Alors fais bien attention. Elle va sûrement te faire part de ses projets: elle voudrait prendre sa retraite à cinquante-cinq ans et s'acheter une petite maison dans le Midi.
Marie-Claire	Oui je sais, elle m'en a déjà parlé. Elle dit que cette idée, c'est toi qui la lui as donnée!
Guillaume	Et si on achetait une maison entre nous tous! On pourrait peut-être trouver quelque chose de pas trop cher à rénover …
Marie-Claire	Ah oui! Dis, Guillaume, et qui est-ce qui les ferait, ces rénovations?

c Listen again or read to answer the questions.

1 What is Mrs Burgess planning to do? (name two things) _____
_____

2 What does Guillaume suggest? _____

3 Does Marie-Claire think it is a good idea? _____

 2 25.05 *Depuis plusieurs mois déjà, Dominique et son copain Gildas ont décidé d'acheter une petite maison dans le Finistère. Ils en ont trouvé une qu'ils aiment beaucoup mais avant de faire les démarches nécessaires ils ont décidé de s'adresser à Maître Le Corre, leur notaire.*

a Listen to the conversation once and answer the questions.

    1 Why are Gildas and Dominique consulting a lawyer? _____

    2 What would they like to find out? _____

b Listen to the conversation again and answer these questions.

    1 How did they find the house? _____

    2 Have they contacted the owner? _____

    3 Have they seen the house? _____

Conversation 2

Gildas	Nous avons trouvé une petite maison que nous aimerions acheter. Nous avons pensé qu'il serait peut-être préférable de nous adresser à vous d'abord.
Me Le Corre	Vous avez eu tout à fait raison. Il vaut toujours mieux s'adresser à un notaire puisque c'est obligatoirement le notaire qui se chargera de rédiger l'acte de vente.
Dominique	Comment pouvons-nous être certains qu'il n'y a aucun problème avec la propriété et les propriétaires actuels?
Me Le Corre	C'est le rôle du notaire de le découvrir. Mais comment avez-vous trouvé la maison en question?
Dominique	Nous avons vu une petite annonce dans le journal, tout simplement.
Gildas	Oui, nous sommes allés voir la maison et nous pensons que c'est exactement ce que nous cherchions. Jusqu'ici c'est tout.
Me Le Corre	Et vous n'avez pas pris contact avec les propriétaires?
Gildas	Non, pas encore. Nous avons préféré venir en discuter avec vous d'abord.
Dominique	Vous pourriez organiser une visite de la maison parce que pour le moment nous ne l'avons vue que de l'extérieur?
Me Le Corre	Oui bien sûr, mais la mission du notaire va beaucoup plus loin que ça: si vous me chargez de l'affaire, je vous informe, je vous conseille, je vérifie l'état civil du vendeur, je peux aussi recueillir des renseignements d'urbanisme ...
Gildas	Pour vérifier s'il n'y a pas d'autoroute ou autres constructions en projet?
Me Le Corre	Exactement. Je vous préparerais le compromis de vente, c'est-à-dire un avant-contrat, et ensuite le contrat si tout va bien.
Gildas	Eh bien nous allons réfléchir mais de toute façon nous reviendrons vous voir.

c **Listen or read once more to answer the questions.**

1 What would they like the lawyer to do? _____

2 Who would check the present owner's civic status? _____

3 What are Gildas and Dominique going to do? _____

d **Now decide if the following statements are vrai ou faux (true or false).**

1 Dominique and Gildas have visited the house and they like it. _____

2 They saw the advert in a newspaper. _____

3 They have been in contact with the vendor. _____

4 They have found exactly what they were looking for. _____

5 They have asked the lawyer to start the search as soon as possible. _____

6 She can get information from the planning department. _____

7 By law the deed of sale has to be prepared by a lawyer. _____

8 The notary's mission is to inform and to advise. _____

Language discovery

1 **Link the following English phrases to the equivalent French expressions from Conversation 1.**

a *Do you regret turning down Gallimard's job offer?* _____

b *I was no longer thinking about it.* _____

c before going back *to school* _____

d *She has already spoken to me about it.* _____

e *She would like to retire at 55.* _____

1 **Elle m'en a déjà parlé.**

2 **Elle voudrait prendre sa retraite à 55 ans.**

3 **Je n'y pensais même plus.**

4 **avant de reprendre les cours**

5 **Tu regrettes de ne pas avoir accepté l'offre d'emploi chez Gallimard?**

2 **Link the following English phrases to the equivalent French expressions from Conversation 2.**

a *It would be preferable to consult you first.* _____

b *You were absolutely right.* _____

c *The lawyer will take care of drawing up the deeds of sale.* _____

d *We've only seen it from the outside.* _____

e *if you ask me to take care of the business* _____

f *We are going to think about it.* _____

1 **Vous avez eu tout à fait raison.**

2 **si vous me chargez de l'affaire**

3 **Nous ne l'avons vue que de l'extérieur.**

4 **Nous allons réfléchir.**

5 **Il serait peut-être préférable de nous adresser à vous d'abord.**

6 **Le notaire se chargera de rédiger l'acte de vente.**

Learn more

1 *ORDER OF PRONOUNS:* LE, LA, LES *AND* LUI

In the following sequence, the nouns in the sentences are replaced by pronouns:

Tu as donné cette idée à Maman.

Tu lui as donné cette idée. (**lui** represents **à Maman**)

Tu l'as donnée à Maman. (**la/l'** represents **cette idée**)

Tu la lui as donnée.

Word order, especially the order of pronouns, may appear difficult, but there is a simple principle that can help: **le, la** and **les** are weaker pronouns, in terms of sound, than **lui** and **leur**. They are always placed before **lui** or **leur**:

J'ai donné mon billet au contrôleur: Je le lui ai donné.

J'ai donné mon permis de conduire aux gendarmes: Je le leur ai donné.

In a negative sentence there are even more words to line up. The same principle applies:

Je ne le lui ai pas donné.

Je ne le leur ai pas donné.

In more slovenly speech there is a tendency to rush all the pronouns together and to drop **ne** (which is weaker than **pas**) and also **le**:

J'lui ai pas donné.

and in the affirmative too there is a tendency to drop **le**:

J'lui ai donné.

The two examples above are not what you are advised to say but you will hear them frequently.

2 MOI AUSSI *ME TOO* / MOI NON PLUS *ME NEITHER*

These two expressions are frequently used. They are strictly direct responses, agreeing with something someone else has said:

Statements	Responses
Je n'aime pas les départs!	Non, moi non plus.
Elle adore les voyages!	Oui, moi aussi.

 ## Practice

 25.06 **Vous êtes d'accord. Listen to the recording and react to what is being said. You agree with everything said.**

Exemples:

Je n'ai jamais aimé le football.   Moi non plus!

Nous avons souvent visité la Bretagne.   Moi aussi! / Nous aussi!

 READING

Acheter ou vendre dans les meilleures conditions. A leaflet details the desirable and necessary stages that apply if you sell or buy a property. Read it carefully.

ACHETER OU VENDRE DANS LES MEILLEURES CONDITIONS

La transaction immobilière notariale s'adresse à tous les particuliers, acquéreur ou vendeur d'un bien immobilier. En neuf étapes, le notaire vous assure un service rigoureux et professionnel, dans les meilleures conditions financières et de délai.

L'acquisition en 9 étapes

1. Conseils sur l'opportunité de l'achat.
2. Recherche des biens à vendre dans la région.
3. Organisation de la visite du bien.
4. Avis sur le prix et conseil personnalisé.
5. Evaluation des frais.
6. Information sur les meilleures conditions de crédit.
7. Mise au point de l'avant-contrat.
8. Elaboration et signature de l'acte authentique de vente.
9. Conseils patrimoniaux.

La vente en 9 étapes

1. Conseils sur l'opportunité de la vente.
2. Evaluation proposée du bien.
3. Examen des conditions de la vente.
4. Signature d'un mandat avec ou sans exclusivité.
5. Publicité de l'offre.
6. Accueil des acquéreurs potentiels et organisation de la visite du bien.
7. Mise au point de l'avant-contrat.
8. Elaboration et signature de l'acte authentique de vente.
9. Conseils patrimoniaux.

On the leaflet, the first nine points can be referred to as A for acquisition *(buying)* and the next nine V for vente *(selling)*. Indicate which stage of the proceedings the following statements refer to.

Exemple: Advice on opportunity to buy 1A

   a Advice on the price of the property _____
   b Cost evaluation (including legal cost) _____
   c Advertising the offer _____
   d Property evaluation _____
   e Organization of the visit to the property _____
   f Preparation of the pre-contract _____
   g Preparation of the deed of sale _____
   h Search for suitable property in the area _____

Go further

You too have decided to buy a small house in Brittany. Look at today's newspaper offering 13 properties for sale. Find which properties would suit you if you were looking for the requirements below. (More than one advert may apply)

   a a small house by the sea _____
   b a four-bedroom house _____
   c ruins to renovate _____
   d a secluded garden _____
   e preferably a stone house in the centre of a small town or a village _____
   f a house with potential for extension _____
   g vacant property _____
   h reduced legal costs _____

VENTES MAISONS

1) Vends GRANGE à démolir, petite et grande portes + escalier en pierre de taille. Tél. 02.98.66.39.41

2) PONT-DE-BUIS, maison pierres, 2 niveaux, terrain permis agrandissement, meublée. 202.200 € Libre. Tél. 02.98.77.31.66.

3) Particulier vend GUISCRIFF, maison, cuisine, chambre, sanitaires, grenier aménageable, terrain, dépendances. 90.500 € à débattre. Bon état. Tél. 02.97.44.61.37

4) PONT-CROIX place de l'Eglise, maison pierre 4 chambres, grenier aménageable, jardinet, dépendances à rénover, possibilité commerce. 257.000 € à débattre. Tél. 02.98.71.39.81

5) Vends maison SAINT-MARTIN-DES-CHAMPS, quartier calme, jardin clos, cave, garage extérieur, 6 CHAMBRES, chauffage gaz. 294.400 € Tél. 01.60.66.31.71.

6) Idéal pour loisirs et retraite, MOËLAN-SUR-MER, aur cœur d'un village proche plage, commerce et port, maison traditionnelle, jardin et parking privés, 3 chambres, séjour, kitchenette équipée, belles prestations, frais notaires réduits. 230.000 € Tél. 02.98.37.69.75

7) A saisir entre mer et campagne, dans un cadre exceptionnel, 200 m plage, entre CONCARNEAU ET LA

POINTE DE TRÉVIGNON, maison plus terrain, chambres, séjour, cuisine, belle prestation, frais de notaire réduits, 310.000 € Tél. 02.98.27.69.39.

8) FOREST-LANDERNEAU, maison T5, 5 chambres, salon, séjour, cuisine, cheminée, grand sous-sol, jardin 1.300 m², chauffage électrique. Tél. 02.98.77.66.33.

9) Vends maison CHATEAULIN, 4 chambres, salon, séjour, cuisine, cheminée, grand sous-sol, 1er étage à aménager, terrain arboré. 319.500 € Tél. 02.98.96.66.71

10) LESCONIL, sur plage, grande maison, standing, confortable, toute l'année, jardin clos, dépendances, 450.500 € Particulier. Tél. 02.98.44.65.66.

11) Vends maison CHATEAULIN, 3 CHAMBRES, salon-séjour, cuisine, grand sous-sol, 1er étage à aménager, terrain arboré, 290.000 € Tél. 02.98.74.75.45

12) Vends région PRIZIAC, 2 maisons ruines superbes, encadrements fenêtres, portes, terrain à proximité. Tél. 02.98.75.63.20.

13) PONT-L'ABBÉ centre-ville, vends maison pierre, jardin clos, calme, 255.500 € accès direct jardin public. Tél. 02.98.78.91.49 (heures repas).

INSIGHT: NEW WORDS

à aménager/ aménageable	to modernize/convert convertible	démolir	to pull down
agrandissement	extension	un grenier	an attic/loft
une grange	a barn	de la pierre	stone
		jardin clos	enclosed garden/ secluded

2 25.07 **Imagine that you are the four different customers listed below. Using the adverts above for guidance, Listen and answer Me Le Corre's question (she asks everyone the same thing). Continue listening for the correct answers.**

Me Le Corre: Qu'est-ce que vous recherchez exactement?

Client(e) 1   You are looking for a small stone house close to the coast.

Client(e) 2   You are looking for a five-bedroom house with a cellar.

Client(e) 3   You are looking for a small house with a secluded garden.

Client(e) 4   You are looking for a small house with a convertible loft.

3 **Trouvez les intrus. *Find the odd ones out.* Read the adverts in Part 1 and find the properties described below.**

 a Which is never going to be liveable in? _____

 b Which is the only one mentioning a fireplace? _____

 c Which property has direct access to the park? _____

 d Which property could be developed for commercial purposes? _____

 e Which is the only one which already has building permission for an extension? _____

 # Test yourself

1 **Version moderne des Trois Petits Cochons *The Three Little Pigs - retold***

> Il était une fois trois petits cochons qui voulaient construire leur maison: le premier avait décidé de bâtir une maison de paille, le deuxième, une maison de bois et le troisième, une maison de brique. Malheureusement les terrains qu'avaient choisis le premier et le deuxième petits cochons n'étaient pas constructibles et ils n'avaient ni permis de construire ni contrats de construction et le grand méchant loup, invoquant la loi du 1er octobre 2007, leur a fait démolir leurs deux maisons. Le troisième petit cochon, qui avait procédé selon le règlement, vit heureux dans sa maison et il a beaucoup d'enfants.

Find the expressions from the text that mean:

 a The land they had chosen was not suitable for development

 b He made them pull down their houses

 c He had decided to build a wooden house

d They neither had building permits or building contracts

e He had proceeded in accordance with the regulations.

2 Use the pronouns <u>le, la, les, lui</u> and <u>leur</u> in your answers where required.

Exemple :

On a donné [*le permis de construire*] [au troisième petit cochon]?

Non, on ne le lui a pas donné.

a On a fait démolir [*la maison*]?

Oui,....

b Ils avaient choisi [les terrains non constructibles]?

Oui,...

c Vous aviez présenté [*votre permis de construire*] [aux autorités]?

Oui, nous...

d On n'avait pas demandé [au maire] [*ce qu'il en pensait*]?

Si, ...

e On ne lui avait pas donné [les clefs de la maison]?

Si, ...

SELF CHECK

I CAN. . .
. . . express feelings of sadness.
. . . order pronouns.
. . . talk about planning to buy a house.
. . . understand some legal requirements when buying a property.

Revision unit

1 Profils
Profiles

 R.01

Listen to the recording several times. You will hear information which should allow you to complete the profiles of two friends. Make your notes in French. You may need to revise what you have learnt so far.

1
Nom:
Prénom:
Âge:
Adresse:
Numéro de téléphone:
Nationalité:
Nationalité du père:
Nationalité de la mère:
Profession:
Lieu de travail:
Aime:
N'aime pas:

2
Nom:
Prénom:
Âge:
Adresse:
Numéro de téléphone:
Nationalité:
Nationalité du père:
Nationalité de la mère:
Profession:
Lieu de travail:
Aime:
N'aime pas:

(Unités 1 à 5)

2 Une promenade à Saint Malo
A walk in St Malo

Follow the directions on the map and say what your starting point is and where you are going.

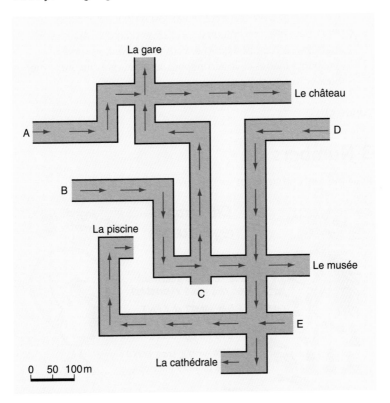

Exemple: Alors pour aller au musée vous allez vers la droite. Après cent cinquante mètres vous tournez à droite. Continuez sur cent mètres et vous tournez à gauche et le musée est à deux cents mètres.

Réponse: From **B** to the museum

1   Pour aller à la gare vous allez tout droit. Après deux cents mètres vous tournez à gauche. Vous continuez encore sur cent mètres, puis vous tournez à droite et la gare est à cent mètres environ.

2 Pour aller à la piscine vous allez vers la gauche, vous allez tout droit sur deux cent cinquante mètres. Vous tournez à droite. Vous continuez sur cent mètres et vous tournez encore à droite. La piscine est à cinquante mètres.

3 Pour aller à la cathédrale? Vous allez vers la gauche. Vous tournez à gauche après cent mètres. Vous continuez sur trois cents mètres et vous tournez à droite. La cathédrale est à cinquante mètres.

4 Alors, pour aller au château vous allez vers la droite. Après cent mètres vous tournez à gauche. Vous tournez à droite après cinquante mètres et vous continuez sur deux cent cinquante mètres pour arriver au château.

(Unité 5)

3 Numbers

Read the card and say what spelling rule applies for 20 and 100.

(Unités 4 et 5)

4 Grand jeu-concours

At 45 you are the managing director of a company from Rennes (Ille-et-Vilaine). You are representing your firm at an annual four-day conference in St Malo. Your firm has always favoured St Malo as a venue for this conference because of the excellent facilities and the range of activities available. You enjoy going to the swimming pool and going on your own around museums in your free time. You are staying in the conference centre hotel.

YOUR TASK:

Fill in the questionnaire on the next two pages as if you were the person described above and win the main prize in the competition.

1 What is the main prize?
2 What is the deadline for entering the competition?
3 Who are the organizers of the competition?

Grand JEU-CONCOURS

JUSQU'AU 14 SEPTEMBRE

Bienvenue
á SAINT-MALO

Vous êtes de passage ou en vacances à SAINT-MALO, nous souhaitons mieux vous connaître, recueillir vos attentes et vos appréciations. C'est pourquoi **LA VILLE et L'OFFICE DU TOURISME** vous proposent de remplir ce questionnaire pour participer au **JEU-CONCOURS**.

Chaque semaine, GAGNEZ UN ALLER-RETOUR pour l'Angleterre pour 2 personnes et de nombreux autres lots.

Voir au dos

---

1 – COMMENT AVEZ-VOUS CONNU SAINT-MALO?

☐ Bouche à oreille

☐ Foires ou salons

☐ Reportages TV ou presse

☐ Guides touristiques ou Agences de voyage

☐ Office du Tourisme

☐ Excursions précédentes

☐ Déplacements professionnels

2 – FIDÉLISATION

☐ Premier séjour à Saint-Malo

☐ Visites occasionnelles à Saint-Malo

☐ Visites régulières à Saint-Malo

3 – ACTIVITÉS PRATIQUÉES

(Plusieurs réponses possibles)

☐ Culturelles　　　　　☐ Autres: préciser

☐ Découvertes

☐ Nautiques

☐ Sportives

☐ Animations gratuites

☐ Thermalisme

☐ Déplacements professionnels et congrès

4 – SATISFACTION:

Êtes-vous satisfait de votre séjour à Saint-Malo?

☐ Pas du tout　　　　Justifier votre réponse _____

☐ Plutôt pas　　　　_____

☐ Plutôt satisfait　　_____

☐ Très satisfait

5 – DURÉE DU SÉJOUR:

☐ La journée　　　☐ 2 à 3 jours　　　☐ 4 à 8 jours

☐ 9 à 15 jours　　☐ 16 jours et plus

6 – MODE D'HÉBERGEMENT

☐ Hôtel   ☐ Camping-car   ☐ Camping

☐ Location meublée   ☐ Résidence secondaire   ☐ Bateau

☐ Amis – Famille – Parents   ☐ Gîtes – chambres d'hôtes   ☐ Famille d'accueil

7 – ÂGE

☐ - de 25 ans   ☐ 25/34 ans   ☐ 35/44 ans

☐ 45/54 ans   ☐ 55/65 ans   ☐ + de 65 ans

8 – ACCOMPAGNEMENT

(Êtes-vous venu à Saint-Malo…?)

☐ Seul   ☐ En couple

☐ En famille   ☐ Avec des amis

9 – CATÉGORIE SOCIO-PROFESSIONNELLE

☐ Agriculteur   ☐ Chef d'entreprise

☐ Cadre et profession libérale, commerçant, artisan

☐ Employé   ☐ Cadre moyen

☐ Retraité   ☐ Ouvrier

☐ Autres   ☐ Scolaire et étudiant

10 – ORIGINE GÉOGRAPHIQUE

☐ Ille-et-Vilaine

☐ Autre département: (n° du département) _____

☐ Étranger (Préciser la nationalité et la région) _____/_____

Pour participer au JEU CONCOURS,

n'oubliez pas d'indiquer vos coordonnées ci-dessous:

NOM: .... PRÉNOM: ....

Adresse ....

Lieu d'hébergement à Saint-Malo ....

Tél.: ....

Toutes les rubriques du questionnaire doivent être remplies pour valider votre participation au JEU CONCOURS.

DÉPOSEZ VOS BULLETINS DANS L'URNE

NB: ━━━

Les renseignements font l'objet d'un traitement automatisé. Conformément aux prescriptions de la loi nous vous informons que:

• les informations recueillies sont destinées à l'Office du Tourisme et au service économique de la Ville de Saint-Malo.

• l'intéressé a la possibilité de consulter sa fiche informatisée auprès du service concerné.

(Unités 6 à 9)

5 Quelle attitude!

In Unit 9 the boy and the girl express their wishes differently:

Jeune garcon	Moi je veux...
Jeune fille	Je voudrais...

1 What verbs and tenses do they use to express their respective wishes?

2 What do you think the difference indicates?

3 A boy asks for an ice cream. He might say **a Je veux une glace** or **b *Je voudrais une glace*.** To which request are you more likely to reply **Mais oui bien sûr!**

6 Aujourd'hui c'est samedi

Cochez les cases – *Tick the boxes*

Go back to Unit 9, Conversation 2 and read the dialogue once more. Tick the correct boxes below, to make a meaningful sentence, in accordance with the dialogue.

Dimanche matin ☐ Lundi matin ☐   Aujourd'hui ☐

les parents et les trois enfants □ les parents □
toute la famille □ vont □ va □ au Mont Saint Michel □
à la plage □ au barrage de la Rance □

Now write down your complete sentence.

7 La voiture idéale

Neuf personnes (ou couples) avec des goûts bien individuels

Look at the cars below and think about the personality of the person who might own each one.

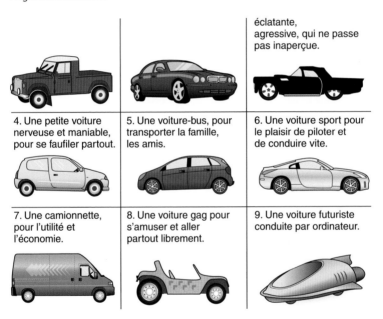

éclatante,
agressive, qui ne passe
pas inaperçue.

4. Une petite voiture nerveuse et maniable, pour se faufiler partout.

5. Une voiture-bus, pour transporter la famille, les amis.

6. Une voiture sport pour le plaisir de piloter et de conduire vite.

7. Une camionnette, pour l'utilité et l'économie.

8. Une voiture gag pour s'amuser et aller partout librement.

9. Une voiture futuriste conduite par ordinateur.

Now turn to the grid and, in column 2, match the cars with the people most likely to own them. 1Columns 3 nad 4 are jumbled. Choose where the 9 people are mostly likely to live and what is likely to be their favourite eating place.

Neuf caractères très différents	La voiture de leurs rêves	Où habitent-ils?	Où mangent-ils?/qu'est-ce qu'ils aiment?
1 André Morin a trente-cinq ans, célibataire. Il vient d'être nommé Directeur d'une grande banque parisienne. Il aime la vitesse, les avions, le ski, le ski nautique, etc. Quelle est la voiture de ses rêves?		**a** À Lyon dans une grande maison avec une piscine et un grand jardin.	**j** Ils adorent les pique-niques à la campagne.
2 Gérard Duigou a tout juste dix-huit ans. Il aime la mer, la plage et s'amuser avec ses copains. Quelle sera sa première voiture?		**b** Une petite maison dans la campagne pas loin de Toulouse.	**k** Elle aime surtout les bons couscous de sa mère.
3 M. et Mme Dumas ont cinq enfants. Ils vont souvent chez leurs parents dans le Midi. Quelle voiture viennent-ils d'acheter?		**c** Dans une grande propriété à Deauville.	**l** À la cantine universitaire.
4 Jean-Yves et Florence Beaumont habitent à Toulouse où ils sont tous les deux enseignants dans un collège. Ils adorent passer leurs week-ends à explorer les Pyrénées. Leur rêve est d'aller en Afrique. Quelle est leur voiture?		**d** Dans un élégant appartement du seizième arrondissement de Paris.	**m** Chez Maxime ou à la Tour d'Argent, les deux restaurants les plus chers de Paris.
5 Etienne Vaillant a habité à Grenoble toute sa vie. Il est maintenant chercheur à l'université de Grenoble où il travaille sur un prototype de voiture futuristique.		**e** Dans un studio avec vue sur le vieux port.	**n** À McDonald's aussi souvent que possible!
6 Bernard Fargeon est fermier. Il a une ferme d'élevage de poulets dans le Finistère. Il y a cinq ans il a acheté un véhicule pratique pour transporter la nourriture pour la volaille et aussi pour transporter sa mère qui est Bigoudène.		**f** Il partage un appartement avec des copains.	**o** Chez Maxime ou à la Tour d'Argent, les deux restaurants les plus chers de Paris.

7 Olivier Dubois est le PDG (Président Directeur Général) d'une chaîne d'hypermarchés. Il aime le confort, le luxe et tout ce qui est solide. Quelle voiture a-t-il choisi?		**g** Il habite toujours chez ses parents. Sa chambre a un décor de science-fiction.	**p** Dans les restaurants chics du quartier de l'Opéra Garnier.
8 Laurent Dubois, le fils de M. Dubois, ne travaille pas mais avec l'argent de son père il s'est acheté une vieille Cadillac rouge, remise à neuf.		**h** Une ferme dans un village sur la Baie d'Audierne.	**q** Une soupe bien chaude après une longue promenade en montagne.
9 Adidja Ahmed est docteur à Marseille. Elle a choisi une petite voiture rapide et pratique pour aller visiter ses patients. Quelle est sa voiture?		**i** Il habite à Paris avec son amie qui est chanteuse à l'Opéra.	**r** Il aime un bon poulet rôti cuit à la ferme.

(Unités 10 à 16)

8 Les jeunes et l'emploi

Read carefully this short newspaper article about three young students.

1 ÉTUDIANTES STAGIAIRES

VIE QUOTIDIENNE
«Il ne suffit pas de cocher des cases»
Étudiants stagiaires

Que faisiez-vous du 28 août au 25 octobre? Et bien, pendant que certains profitaient encore de leurs dernières semaines de vacances, Jenny, Maria et Nathalie bossaient. Etudiantes en maîtrise A.G.E. (traduisez Administration et Gestion d'Entreprise), elles ont effectué durant huit semaines un stage non rémunéré à la Caisse d'Allocations Familiales (CAF) de Brest. Premier contact avec le monde du travail.

elles bossaient *they worked*

bosser *to work* (slang)

cocher des cases *to tick boxes* (as in multiple choice questions)

Now answer these questions.

    a What did the three students do from 28 August to 25 October?

    b What is their area of study?

c Were they paid for their work?

d Was the work experience carried out in term time?

e What did this type of work do for them in terms of experience?

2 LA CHASSE AUX JOBS

Read the article below about the search for a part-time job. Then turn to the grid opposite and fill in the jobs in the order in which they appear in the article. The contents of the grid are jumbled so match each list of points with the correct job category and the correct heading. (Don't worry if you can't understand it all – just try to get the gist of the article.)

LA CHASSE AUX JOBS

Maigres bourses ou parents compréhensifs ne suffisent plus à subvenir à vos besoins? La chasse aux jobs est ouverte toute l'année. La concurrence est rude et mieux vaut se pointer devant votre employeur avec une bonne dose de motivation et une idée précise de ce que vous voulez. Conseils et idées en vrac.

Fast-foods et cafétérias

C'est payé tout juste le SMIC et les pourboires sont interdits. Cadences infernales, patrons omniprésents et cuisines aseptisées. Les grandes chaînes recrutent également assez régulièrement et le rythme y est légèrement plus supportable. Pour postuler, présentez-vous directement dans chaque restaurant (mais pas au moment du rush) ou envoyez lettre de candidature et CV avec photo. Un conseil: écumez les centres commerciaux. Il est rare qu'ils ne contiennent pas un ou deux points de restauration. Pour les emplois de serveur(se), les jobs sont mieux payés en général, pourboires aidant.

Télémarketing et sondages

Les horaires sont très modulables. Il vous suffit de faire preuve d'amabilité au téléphone et de ne pas être allergique à la répétition. Les sociétés de télémarketing préfèrent que le premier contact s'établisse par téléphone. Un excellent moyen pour elles de mesurer vos capacités et d'opérer une première sélection.

Distribution de prospectus

Lisez les journaux gratuits pour trouver une annonce. Avoir le pied solide et posséder une voiture sont deux atouts. L'étudiant est payé au nombre de journaux ou tracts distribués.

Pensez aussi aux grandes surfaces, parkings, gardiennages, livraisons à domicile...

3 main job categories (List them in the order they appear in the article)	Requirements to secure a job	Advantages (if any)	Disadvantages (if any)
1)	**a** • Flexitime	**b** • Large fast food firms recruit regularly • Serving jobs are better paid • Tips allowed	**c** • Go and introduce yourself directly • Send a letter of application + CV • Check all the shopping centres
2)	**d** • Only paid minimum wage • Tips are not allowed • Fast rhythm of work • Bosses always present	**e** • Paid according to number of newspapers or leaflets distributed	**f** • Good if you have two assets: solid feet and a car
3)	**g** • Selection over the telephone • Need a good telephone manner	**h** • Read the free press for job adverts	**i** • Very repetitive job

(Unités 17 à 20)

9 Paris et le tourisme

 R.02

Vrai ou faux? Ecoutez le débat à la radio et dites si les phrases suivantes sont vraies ou fausses:

1 On a besoin d'un seul billet pour tout déplacement.
2 Il n'y a pas de transport la nuit.
3 Les enfants de dix ans doivent payer plein tarif.
4 On peut voyager jusqu'à Disneyland.
5 On peut choisir un seul billet pour la zone 1 à 6.

6 Il ne faut pas de photo d'identité.

7 La carte Paris-Visite n'est pas valable pour le funiculaire de Montmartre.

8 On peut acheter un billet valable 4 jours.

(Unité 20)

10 Les loisirs et vous: sondage d'opinion
Leisure activities and you: opinion poll

This is a real French opinion poll. For part A pretend you are Stéphane Jacquelin:

▶ You like science-fiction films and psychological drama

▶ You enjoy TV programmes on classical music, religion and philosophy. You also like TV games shows

▶ You regularly read history magazines

Put a circle around **1** (**oui**) for all the activities mentioned above and circle **2** (**non**) for all the others.

A *Aimez-vous?*

Une réponse par ligne. Entourez le 1 ou le 2.

		oui	non
a	Les films d'arts martiaux (karaté, kung fu ...).	1	2
b	Les films de science-fiction.	1	2
c	Les films musicaux, disco, rock...	1	2
d	La musique pop, le rock.	1	2
e	Les variétés, les chansons.	1	2
f	Les livres érotiques ou suggestifs.	1	2
g	Je suis intéressé(e) par les émissions TV et les magazines sur la musique classique.	1	2
h	Je suis intéressé(e) par les émissions TV sur la religion, la philosophie.	1	2
i	J'aime les journaux sur la santé, les informations médicales.	1	2
j	J'aime les émissions de jeux à la télévision.	1	2
k	Je lis régulièrement un ou des magazines (revues) d'histoire.	1	2

B *Les sports*

Answer part B for yourself: circle as many answers as you like to find out if you are sporty, or a TV sports fan.

Parmi les sports suivants, lesquels pratiquez-vous et lesquels aimez-vous regarder? Répondez à chaque colonne. Autant de réponses que vous voulez.

	Je pratique	Je regarde
Tennis, autres sports à raquettes.	1	2
Cyclisme.	1	2
Courses de voiture et de motos.	1	2
Jogging ou athlétisme.	1	2

Vous totalisez entre 7 et 8 points: vous êtes un fanatique de sport!

11 Encore une bonne recette, simple et rapide à réaliser

Another good recipe: simple and quick to make

Read the recipe and answer the questions.

Couscous pilaf

PRÉPARATION: 20 minutes
CUISSON: 5 minutes
POUR 2 PERSONNES

▶ 1 petite pomme évidée, épluchée et coupée en dés
▶ 50 g de céleri blanc en petits morceaux
▶ 50 g de jeunes oignons en fines rondelles
▶ 1 cuillère à soupe de raisins secs blancs
▶ 2 moitiés d'abricot sec en petits morceaux
▶ 30 g de pignons de pin grillés
▶ 2 cuillères à café de margarine, 175 ml d'eau
▶ 75 ml de nectar d'abricots ou de poires
▶ ½ cuillère à café de curry en poudre
▶ 40 g de couscous
Pour la garniture: un brin de menthe

RÉALISATION
Mettez la pomme, le céleri, les oignons, les raisins, les abricots, les pignons de pin et la margarine dans le plat et mélangez. Placez le plat à couvert au four à micro-ondes pendant 2 minutes. Ajoutez l'eau, le nectar et le curry au mélange et remettez le plat, à couvert, 3 minutes au four. Incorporez le couscous au mélange aux fruits, couvrez le plat et laissez gonfler le couscous pendant 5 minutes. Disposez le couscous pilaf sur un plat et garnissez avec la menthe.

en dés *diced*

des pignons de pin *pine kernels*

un brin de menthe *a leaf of mint*

un four à micro-ondes *microwave oven*

    a How long does it take to prepare from beginning to end?
    b How much liquid is required in all?
    c How do you prepare the onions?
    d How much curry powder is needed?
    e What can you use if you don't have apricot juice?
    f How many raisins do you need?
    g What is the mint for?
    h What do you add the water and juice to?
    i At what stage do you add the couscous?
    j How long does the dish need to rest before serving?

(Unités 21 à 25)

Transcripts of listening exercises

Only the scripts of listening comprehension or other listening exercises which are not already printed in the units are to be found in this section.

UNIT 2

02.02 *Le Loto*

Et maintenant voici le tirage du Loto. Les numéros gagnants sont le 21, le 45, le 53, le 65, le 9, le 50, le 11, le 24 et le 37.

02.09 *Quel âge avez-vous?*

1 J'ai 21 ans. 2 Il a 38 ans. 3 Elle a 69 ans. 4 Il a 40 ans.

UNIT 4

04.07 *C'est combien?*

Dominique	C'est combien les cigarettes?
Sarah	Euh... c'est 48 € les dix paquets.
Dominique	Et le whisky?
Sarah	C'est 22 €.
Dominique	Et le gin?
Sarah	C'est 16 €.
Dominique	Et le Cognac?
Sarah	C'est 27 €.

UNIT 5

05.05 *Répondez aux touristes*

   a Pour aller à la piscine s'il vous plaît? C'est à droite.

   b Le musée s'il vous plaît? C'est à 200 m.

   c La cathédrale, c'est loin? Non, c'est tout près.

   d Pour aller à l'office de tourisme s'il vous plaît? C'est tout droit.

   e Pour aller au château? C'est à gauche.

UNIT 6

 06.05 *Quelle heure est-il?*

a Il est dix-sept heures cinq. b Il est midi et demi. c Il est huit heures cinquante-six. d Il est sept heures moins le quart. e Il est une heure vingt. f Il est trois heures. g Il est onze heures quinze. h Il est minuit moins le quart.

 06.06 *Matin ou après-midi?*

Jean-Pierre	Allô oui?
Martine	Salut Jean-Pierre, c'est Martine.
Jean-Pierre	Tu sais quelle heure il est? Il est quatre heures du matin ici!
Martine	Oh pardon! Il est deux heures de l'après-midi ici en Australie!

UNIT 8

 08.04 *Comment ça s'épelle?*

1 Sylvie Lécaille: Je m'appelle Mademoiselle Sylvie Lécaille. Lécaille ça s'épelle L-é-c-a-i-l-l-e.

2 Gaétan Leberre: Alors mon nom c'est Gaétan Leberre. Gaétan ça s'épelle G-a-é-t-a-n et Leberre L-e-b-e-r-r-e.

3 Yannick Tanguy: Je m'appelle Yannick Tanguy. Yannick ça s'épelle Y-a-n-n-i-c-k et Tanguy T-a-n-g-u-y.

UNIT 9

 09.05 *J'ai besoin de … / Je voudrais …*

1 Je voudrais du jambon et du pâté.
   Vous: Allez à la charcuterie!

2 J'ai besoin de médicaments
   Vous: Allez à la pharmacie!

3 Je voudrais acheter des journaux
   Vous: Allez à la Maison de la Presse!

4 J'ai besoin de timbres poste
   Vous: Allez à la poste!

5 Je voudrais du pain et des gâteaux
   Vous: Allez à la boulangerie-pâtisserie!

6 J'ai besoin d'un plan de la ville
   Vous: Allez à l'Office de Tourisme!

UNIT 10

10.04 *La cuisine française*

Pierre	Je crois que la cuisine française est la meilleure du monde.
Lionel	Oui, moi je suis tout à fait d'accord avec vous. Nous avons les meilleurs chefs et les meilleurs restaurants.
Pierre	Vous avez raison et la preuve c'est que nos chefs sont demandés partout dans le monde.
Pascale	Eh bien moi je ne suis pas d'accord avec vous. Je crois qu'il y a de la bonne cuisine partout dans le monde. Qu'est-ce que vous pensez de la cuisine chinoise ou de la cuisine italienne par exemple? Moi je pense que c'est une question de goût, c'est tout!

10.05 *Le souper marin*

Michel	C'est quel jour le souper marin?
Vous	Le 15 août.
Michel	C'est à quelle heure?
Vous	C'est à partir de 19h30.
Michel	Qu'est-ce qu'il y a au menu?
Vous	Soupe de poissons, moules, frites et dessert.
Michel	C'est combien?
Vous	10 € .

UNIT 11

11.05 *Où sont-ils en vacances?*

1 Bonjour, je m'appelle Fabienne. Dans la ville où je suis le temps est couvert et les températures sont entre 15 et 21 degrés.

2 Bonjour, je m'appelle Jérôme. Dans la ville où je suis il fait de l'orage et les températures sont entre 21 et 29 degrés.

3 Bonjour, je m'appelle Stéphanie. Dans la ville où je suis il fait de l'orage et les températures sont entre 7 et 12 degrés.

4 Bonjour, je m'appelle Alexandre. Dans la ville où je suis il fait de l'orage et les températures sont entre 12 et 23 degrés.

UNIT 12

12.04 *Bon appétit!*

Serveuse	Monsieur-dame, qu'est-ce que vous avez choisi?
Florence	Moi j'adore les fruits de mer. Je prends le menu à 45 € .
Serveuse	Excellent! Et pour Monsieur?
Luc	Alors moi je vais prendre le menu à 20 € .
Serveuse	Oui ... et qu'est-ce que vous prendrez comme entrées?
Luc	Alors, comme entrée je prends la Coquille St Jacques à la Bretonne et puis comme plat principal je prends la Brochette de joues de Lotte à la Diable avec salade de saison.
Serveuse	Très bien. Vous prendrez le plateau de fromage ou un dessert?
Luc	Je vais prendre un dessert ... une glace si vous en avez.
Serveuse	Certainement Monsieur.

12.05

Une autre table ... vous, un autre client	
Serveuse	Vous avez choisi? Qu'est-ce que vous allez prendre?
Vous	Je vais prendre le menu à 25 € .
Serveuse	Et qu'allez-vous prendre comme entrée?
Vous	Je vais prendre les six huîtres chaudes avec cocktail d'algues.
Serveuse	Oui, et comme plat principal?
Vous	Je vais prendre la Brochette de St Jacques au beurre blanc.
Serveuse	Et après le plateau de fromage vous prendrez un dessert?
Vous	Oui, une glace à la fraise, s'il vous plaît.

UNIT 13

13.06 *À la station service*

Marc	Le plein de gazole pour la camionnette SVP.
Sandrine	Mettez vingt litres de super dans ma vieille voiture de sport SVP.
Martine	Trente litres d'essence sans plomb SVP.

13.07 *un weekend meurtrier sur les routes françaises*

'Le weekend du quinze août a été marqué par de nombreux accidents de la route. L'accident le plus grave s'est produit sur la route nationale dix lorsqu'un car portugais a percuté un camion débouchant d'une route privée. Sur les 42 passagers huit ont été tués et 24 autres ont été blessés.

À St Nazaire un cycliste a été tué dans une collision avec une voiture et sur la D 940 entre Calais et Boulogne huit personnes ont été blessées dans un accident impliquant quatre voitures.'

UNIT 14

 14.06 *Un coup de téléphone*

	Propriétaire	Allô, j'écoute!
1	**Vous**	J'ai vu une annonce pour un studio dans Libé. C'est bien ici?
	Propriétaire	Oui, c'est bien cela.
2	**Vous**	C'est à quel étage?
	Propriétaire	C'est au sixième.
3	**Vous**	Il y a un ascenseur?
	Propriétaire	Euh, non mais monter et descendre les escaliers est excellent pour la santé!
4	**Vous**	Il y a le chauffage central?
	Propriétaire	Non, le chauffage est électrique.
5	**Vous**	Il y a une cuisine?
	Propriétaire	Oui il y a une cuisine moderne toute équipée.
6	**Vous**	C'est bien 400 € toutes charges comprises?
	Propriétaire	C'est bien cela. Vous pouvez visiter aujourd'hui?
7	**Vous**	Je viendrais cet après-midi si vous êtes disponible.

UNIT 16

 16.05 *À votre tour de poser des questions*

a	**Vous**	Vous êtes allée au Maroc avec le groupe?
	Adidja	Oui, j'y suis allée.
b	**Vous**	Combien de jeunes sont allés au Maroc?
	Adidja	Dix-huit. Huit filles et dix garçons.
c	**Vous**	Vous êtes restés combien de temps?
	Adidja	Nous sommes restés trois semaines.
d	**Vous**	Ils ont rencontré des jeunes marocains?
	Adidja	Oui, beaucoup. C'était formidable.

UNIT 17

17.07 *À Pôle- emploi*

a	**Employé**	Quel genre de métiers vous intéresse?
	Vous	Je m'intéresse aux métiers de l'hôtellerie.
b	**Employé**	Qu'est-ce qui vous intéresse?
	Vous	Je m'intéresse aux métiers de la photographie.
c	**Employé**	Qu'est-ce qui vous intéresse?
	Vous	Je m'intéresse aux métiers de la restauration.
d	**Employé**	Quel genre de métiers vous intéresse?
	Vous	Je m'intéresse aux métiers de la santé.
e	**Employé**	A quoi vous intéressez-vous?
	Vous	Je m'intéresse aux métiers de l'habillement.

UNIT 18

18.06 *À vous de réserver un billet*

a	**Vous**	Je voudrais réserver un billet pour Paris SVP.
	Employée	Vous voyagez aujourd'hui?
b	**Vous**	Non, je voyage demain.
	Employée	Vous prenez le train de quelle heure?
c	**Vous**	Je prends le train de 7h 05.
	Employée	Vous prenez un billet aller-retour?
d	**Vous**	Non, je prends un billet simple. C'est combien?

18.07 *Ça prend combien de temps...?*

Exemple:

Question	Ça prend combien de temps pour aller de Paris à Marseille par le TGV?
Vous	Ça prend deux heures cinquante-cinq.

a Ça prend combien de temps pour aller à Nantes?
Ça prend deux heures.

b Ça prend combien de temps pour aller à Toulouse?
Ça prend cinq heures.

c Ça prend combien de temps pour aller à Lyon?
Ça prend une heure cinquante-cinq.

d Ça prend combien de temps pour aller à Lille?
Ça prend exactement une heure.

UNIT 19

19.07 *Vous passez beaucoup trop de temps au téléphone!*

a À quelle heure avez-vous téléphoné à Nadine?
Je lui ai téléphoné à onze heures trente.

b À quelle heure avez-vous téléphoné à Mathieu?
Je lui ai téléphoné à midi.

c À quelle heure avez-vous téléphoné à Chantal et à Marc?
Je leur ai téléphoné à 17h15.

d À quelle heure avez-vous téléphoné à votre sœur?
Je lui ai téléphoné à 18h45.

e À quelle heure avez-vous téléphoné à vos parents?
Je leur ai téléphoné à 20h10.

f À quelle heure avez-vous téléphoné à votre fiancé(e)?
Je lui ai téléphoné à 22h45.

19.09 *Les maux et blessures*

Marie-José	J'ai mal au dos.
Alain	Je suis blessé aux genoux.
Adrienne	J'ai mal à la tête.
Benoît	J'ai mal aux dents.
Elise	Je crois que je me suis cassé le bras.
Julien	Je me suis brûlé la main avec le fer à repasser.
Cécile	Je me suis coupé le pied en marchant sur une bouteille cassée.
Didier	J'ai des piqûres de moustiques infectées.

19.10 *Jacques a dit…*

1 Jacques a dit 'levez le bras droit'
2 Baissez le bras
3 Grattez la tête
4 Jacques a dit 'touchez la bouche avec la main gauche'
5 Jacques a dit 'baissez le bras droit'
6 Levez le pied droit
7 Frappez le nez
8 Dansez
9 Jacques a dit 'chantez'

10 Jacques a dit 'touchez le pied gauche'

11 Jacques a dit 'levez la main droite'

12 Asseyez-vous

UNIT 21

21.03 Qu'est-ce que vous feriez?

a Qu'est-ce que vous feriez si vous gagniez le gros lot au Loto?
J'aurais une grande maison en Bretagne, j'aurais un bateau, j'irais à la pêche et le soir je regarderais la télé.

b Est-ce que vous feriez des voyages?
Je ferais un voyage autour du monde.

21.04 Vous avez coché?

Et voici les numéros gagnants pour le deuxième tirage du Loto: le 35, le 8, le 15, le 28, le 13, le 45, le 11, le 25, et le 12 est le numéro complémentaire.

UNIT 22

22.04 Oui, c'est le mien

1 Ce sac, c'est à vous?
Oui, c'est le mien.

2 Ce sont vos clefs?
Oui, ce sont les miennes.

3 C'est votre montre?
Oui, c'est la mienne.

4 Ce sont vos patins à roulettes?
Oui, ce sont les miens.

UNIT 25

25.06 Vous êtes d'accord

1 J'adore la cuisine française.
Moi aussi.

2 Je n'aime pas les voyages organisés.
Moi non plus.

3 Nous aimons beaucoup la Bretagne.
Moi aussi.

4 Je n'aime pas la rentrée.
Moi non plus.

5 Je déteste prendre l'avion.
Moi aussi.

6 Je préfère rester chez moi.
Moi aussi.

25.07 *Le notaire vous pose des questions*

Me Le Corre	Qu'est-ce que vous recherchez exactement?
1	Je cherche une petite maison de pierre près de la côte.
2	Je cherche une maison de cinq chambres avec cave.
3	Je cherche une petite maison avec un jardin clos.
4	Je cherche une petite maison avec un grenier aménageable.

UNITÉ DE RÉVISION

R.01 *Profils*

1 Je m'appelle Sarah Burgess. J'ai 28 ans. J'habite 12 Stella Avenue, Londres SW2. Mon numéro de téléphone est le 020 8476 5656. Je suis de nationalité britannique, mon père est de nationalité britannique, ma mère est de nationalité française. Je suis éditrice chez Hodder & Stoughton. J'aime les voyages, le cinéma, la lecture. Je n'aime pas le sport à la télévision. 2 Je m'appelle Dominique Périer. J'ai 36 ans. J'habite 5 Avenue de la Vieille Ville à St Nazaire en France. Mon numéro de téléphone est le 02 40 45 18 11. Je suis de nationalité française, mon père et ma mère sont de nationalité française. Je suis professeur de philosophie au lycée de St Nazaire. J'aime beaucoup les chats, l'opéra et les musées d'art. Je n'aime pas la télévision. Je n'aime pas les voitures.

R.02 *Paris et le tourisme*

Présentateur du programme	Et vous pensez que Paris est accessible à tous nos visiteurs?
Représentante de la RATP	Mais certainement avec Paris-Visite les touristes peuvent allez partout dans Paris et la région parisienne.
Présentateur	C'est quoi Paris-Visite?
Représentante	Eh bien c'est un seul et unique billet qui permet de voyager à volonté sur tous les modes de transport: métro, bus, tram, funiculaire de Montmartre, Noctambus pour voyager la nuit...
Présentateur	Ça c'est bien mais pour ce qui est de la banlieue qu'est-ce que vous leur proposez aux touristes?
Représentante	Eh bien toujours avec ce même billet ils peuvent prendre les trains de banlieue, suivant les zones qu'ils ont choisis soit zone 1 à 3 ou bien la zone 1 à 8. Ils peuvent se rendre avec le même billet jusqu'à Disneyland, Versailles et jusqu'aux aéroports parisiens.

Présentateur	Il faut acheter un nouveau billet tous les jours?
Représentante	Non, pour une visite de cinq jours ont peut acheter un billet qui sera valable cinq jours, en fait il y a quatre possibilités: un billet pour un jour, deux, trois ou cinq jours.
Présentateur	Il y a des réductions pour les enfants?
Représentante	Bien sûr, il y a un tarif réduit pour les enfants de 4 à 11 ans.
Présentateur	Et cela est compliqué comme démarche? Ça prend beaucoup de temps?
Représentante	Pas du tout! Vous voyagez sans perdre de temps, un seul achat et pas besoin de photo!
Présentateur	Alors j'espère que les touristes seront nombreux dans la capitale!
Représentante	Merci!

Key to the exercises

Unit 1

Hello and goodbye: a bonjour **b** going to bed **Vocabulary builder:**
3 c good **d** good **4 a** Bonjour Madame Corre! **b** Au revoir Marie-Claire.
c Bonne nuit Paul! **d** Bon après-midi Mademoiselle! **e** À tout à l'heure /
À bientôt Monsieur Jarre. **5 a** 3 **b** 1 **c** 5 **d** 6 **e** 4 **f** 2 **Conversations:**
1 a daytime **b** 1 Monsieur Blanchard is feeling fine **b** Monsieur Lebrun is
feeling so-so **2 a** giving good wishes **b** 1 the New Year **2** a birthday
3 a wedding **3 Conversation 5** c **Conversation 6** b **Conversation 7** c
4 a un kilo de pommes **b** cinq euros **c** un sandwich au fromage **d** une bière
e la gare **Language discovery: a** Bon **b** Bonne **c** Bonnes **Practice a** bon
b bonne **c** bonnes **d** bon **Go further 2 a** the post office **b** the tourist office
c the supermarket **d** the Citroën garage

Test yourself: 1 a 3 **b** 1 **c** 2 **d** 4 **2** 1 **c** 2 **b** 3 a **4** a **5** a **3 a** fêtes
b appétit/pain **c** appétit/pain **d** bière **e** fruits

Unit 2

French etiquette: a tu **b** vous **Vocabulary builder: 2 a** vingt-quatre
b trente-neuf **c** quarante-trois **d** quarante-cinq **e** cinquante-deux
f cinquante-sept **g** soixante-six **h** soixante-huit **3 a** Between 2 and 10
b Twenty numbers for each draw **c** 3 € for two draws and 1,5 € for one
4 The winning numbers are: 21, 45, 53, 65, 9, 50, 11, 24, 37. **The Family:**
2 a Grand-mother **b** Father **c** Aunt **d** Cousin **e** Brother **Conversations:**
1 a Alain **b** 1 Claire 2 Paris 3 Marseille **2 a** She's Isabelle's mother
b 1 David's 2 No 3 Mark Thompson 4 England **3 a** 12 years old **4 a** English
and French **b** 1 J'ai douze ans. **2** Mon frère, il a quatorze ans. **3** Je n'ai pas
de frère. **4** Moi aussi! **5** Tu as quel âge? **4 a** English and French **b** 1 French
and English 2 French **c** 1 Il est professeur de français. **2** Cela dépend.
3 Je parle français ou anglais. **4** Je parle français à la maison.
5 Les enfants parlent couramment les deux langues. **6** Il parle bien le
français. **Language discovery: 1 a** Je suis de Paris. **b** Enchanté de faire
votre connaissance. **2 a** J'habite en Angleterre. **b** La tante de David.
c Je vous présente Madame ... **d** Mon fils **e** Ma fille **3 a** Je suis **b** voici
Practice: a 3 **b** 5 **c** 4 **d** 1 **e** 2 **Listening:** 5 is the odd one out – *mon oncle* is
the only male.

Test yourself 2 1 Sophie, un **2** David, parlent **3** M. Norbert, s'
4 Lucien, suis **5** Camille, pas **6** Hélène Lejeune, ma **7** Mark Thompson, de
8 Danielle, j' **9** David, sont **10** Anne Thompson, êtes

Unit 3

Work and leisure a 38 hours **b** football **Vocabulary builder: Expressing
likes b** like, like; **c** I **d.** I **Expressing dislikes a** like **b** like; I; **Introductions:
1 a 1** 36 **2** yes **3** two **4** Yes **5** cinema, travelling, reading, photography
b 1 Je suis professeur d'histoire. **2** J'aime voyager. **3** J'habite à Vannes en
Bretagne. **4** J'aime aller au cinéma. **5** Je n'aime pas faire le ménage.
2 a 1 29 **2** Paris **3** German **4** watching films and sports on TV, photography
and travelling **b 1** Je demeure à Paris. **2** J'aime bien regarder des films à la
télé. **3** J'ai horreur des voitures. **4** Je vais au travail à vélo. **3 a 1** 45 **2** her
husband **3** at the post office **4** a little **5** She hates it. **b 1** Je travaille à la
poste. **2** Je parle un peu l'anglais. **3** Je n'ai pas d'enfants. **4** J'apprends le
vietnamien. **5** Il est au chômage. **4 a 1** 52 **2** Monique **3** at Renault **4** In
Dijon **b 1** Ma mère est veuve. **2** Je travaille chez Renault. **3** Elle habite chez
nous. **4** J'adore les voyages et la lecture. **5** Je n'aime pas la télé sauf les
documentaires. **6** Je comprends un peu l'anglais. **Language discovery:
a** so **b** therefore

Practice: 1 Je m'appelle Anne-Marie Pélerin. J'ai quarante-cinq ans.
J'habite à Boulogne. Je suis dentiste. Je parle français, anglais et
allemand. J'adore le football et la photographie. **2:**

NAMES	QUESTIONS	ANSWERS
Natalie		Je m'appelle Natalie
Antoine		J'ai vingt-neuf ans
Natalie	Quelle est votre profession?	
Monique		Je travaille à la poste
Pierre	Où habitez-vous?	
Antoine	Quelles langues parlez-vous?	
Monique	Vous aimez le sport?	
Pierre		Oui, je suis marié avec Monique

3 a Faux **b** Faux **c** Vrai **d** Vrai **e** Vrai **f** Faux **Listening** Martin

Test yourself 1 a travaille, Antoine **b** ans, Natalie **c** utilise, Antoine **d** mon,
Monique, **e** avec, Pierre **2 a** soixante-cinq **b** veuve, vivent **c** pharmacien,
son **d** regarder **e** apprends

Unit 4

Saying you a le douzième siècle **b** mille neuf-cent quatre-vingt-dix; mille neuf-cent quatre-vingt-dix-sept

Vocabulary builder, On the boat: 1 a 6 **b** 11 **c** 12 **d** 2 **e** 4 **f** 1 **g** 13 **h** 17 **i** 7 **j** 15 **2 2** Pont 8 **4** Pont 7 **6** Pont 9 **7** Pont 7 **11** Pont 8 **12** Pont 7 **13** Pont 7 **15** Pont 9 **17** Pont 7 **Conversations: 1a** Au pont cinq **b** 1 eight **2** Information desk **3** It's in the evening (they say bonsoir) **5** 017 **2 a** the cinema **b 1** Le Come-back **2** 22.30 **3** 10 € **Language discovery: 1 a** 4 **b** 5 **c** 1 **d** 2 **e** 3 **2 a** 3 **b** 4 **c** 1 **d** 2 **3 a** Où est...? **b** au **c** à **Go further: 2 a** 27 € **b** 22 € **c** 48 € for 10 packets **d** 16 €

Test yourself: 1 bar; bateau; pont; six **2** bureau; sais; équipage; une; pardon **3** commence; allons-y; pas; alors; voudrais

Unit 5

Discovering France a le nord de la France **b** le drapeau anglais
Vocabulary builder: directions a 4 b 2 c 5 d 1 e 3 **Ordinal numbers**
2 a dixième **b** quinzième **c** trente-quatrième **d** vingt-troisième **e** centième
Conversations: 1 a 2 **b** 1 **b** 2 **c** 2 **a** Dominique **b 1** a passer-by **2** no **3** no
Language discovery: 1 a 5 **b** 3 **c** 1 **d** 6 **e** 4 **f** 2; **2 a** 6 **b** 7 **c** 1 **d** 2 **e** 3 **f** 4
g 5 **3 a** prenez **b** s **c** connais **Practice: 1 a** Et toi tu connais? **b** Vous allez/ vous tournez **2** 1c 2a 3c **Speaking: 1 Q1:** Le petit aquarium SVP?
Q2: La cathédrale SVP? **Q3:** Le Musée SVP? **Go further: 2 a** cent dix
b cent soixante **c** deux cent quatre-vingt **d** sept cent vingt-deux **e** huit cent cinquante **f** mille un **g** mille trois cents **h** deux mille trente **i** dix mille cent **j** dix mille six cent trente-quatre

Test yourself 5 1 le **2** la **3** la **4** les / la **5** le **6** la **7** la **8** l' **9** le **10** le **11** le **12** les **13** l' **14** les **15** le **16** la **17** la **18** le **19** le **20** l'

Unit 6

France for free! a to advise **b** oui **Vocabulary builder Parking expressions 1 b** parking **c** parking **2 a** 2 hours and 30 minutes **b** 24 hours **c** from 19.00 to 9.00 **3 a** 2 hours **b** no **c** the ticket **Days, months, and seasons 1 a** Wednesday **b** Saturday **c** February **d** May **e** August **f** November **g** summer **h** winter **Conversations 1 a** 1 **b 1** 4 hours **2** 4 € **3** change **4 a** 1 **b** 1 **c** 1 **d** 2 **e** 1 **2 a** 1 femme 2 midnight **b**

b	Q1	Q2	Q3
Femme		12.30	11.00
Homme	7.00		about midnight
Fille	7.15		10.00
Garçon		12.30	9.00

Language discovery: 1 a 1 **b** 4 **c** 6 **d** 1 **e** 3 **f** 2 **2 a** combien **b** on
3 a votre déjeuner; ton déjeuner **b** 1 **Practice 1** e **2** h **3** a **4** b **5** c **6** g **7** f
8 d **2 a** monnaie **b** me repose **c** reste **d** argent **e** argent **3 a** 5th channel
b Saturday 9 August at 2.30 p.m. and Wednesday 13 August at 12.30 p.m.
c At what altitude do giant pandas live?

Listening a 4 a.m. **b** 2 p.m. **c** le matin **d** l'après-midi **Reading a** 1 July
to 31 August **b** No, there are no guided tours at the weekend between 1
September and 30 June **c** 10 a.m. to 11.30 and 2.30 to 6 p.m. **d** From 10
a.m. to 3 p.m. **e** School parties and groups of 10+ if they pre-book **f** It's
free **g** Musée ouvert toute l'année, Tous les jours du 1er juillet au 31 août
h In French, unless names for the days of the week and the months of
the year are at the beginning of a sentence, they are spelt without capital
letters.

Test yourself 1 a Combien ça coûte pour deux heures? **b** Tu as de la
monnaie? **c** Quelle heure est-il? **d** À quelle heure est-ce que tu manges le
petit déjeuner? **e** À quelle heure est-ce que tu te réveilles le dimanche?
f Tu as un billet de 10 €? **g** On reste/Nous restons combien de temps?
h Tu aimes la vieille ville? **i** Le musée est ouvert tout l'année? **j** Tu voudrais
te reposer? **2 a** toute **b** toutes **c** tous **d** tout **e** tous **f** toutes

Unit 7

Where to stay a Je suis en vacances. **b** Je suis en voyage d'affaires.

Vocabulary builder: Hotel expressions 1 a 3 **b** 5 **c** 6 **d** 2 **e** 1 **f** 4
2 a 8 **b** 10 **c** 11 **d** 13 **e** 2 **f** 3 **g** 14 **h** 1 **i** 9 **j** 4 **k** 5 **m** 7 **m** 6 **n** 12

Conversations 1 a 2 **b** 1 One room for two people for one night, in a
three-star hotel with sea view **2** A hotel where he/she can take a small dog
3 One room for one person in a not too expensive hotel with restaurant
and swimming pool **4** A large room for three people in a hotel with a lift
(disabled daughter in wheelchair) **2 a** yes **b** 1 no **2** yes **3** no **Language
discovery 1 a** Cela devrait être possible. **b** Pouvez-vous nous renseigner?
c Vous vous chargez des réservations? **d** Non, je suis désolé madame!
e Nous passons quelques jours dans la région. **2 a** devrait **b** chargez
Practice 1 Je voudrais une chambre pour une personne avec vue sur la

mer. **b** Je voudrais une chambre double dans un hôtel. **c** Nous cherchons un hôtel avec piscine. **d** On voudrait une chambre d'hôtel pour le week-end **2 a** dentifrice **b** chauffe biberon **c** sèche-cheveux **d** brosse à dents **e** crème à raser **f** télécopie **Reading 1 a** Chez des agriculteurs **b** Pour une ou plusieurs nuits **c** Un petit déjeuner campagnard **d** Vos hôtes vous serviront **Go further a** (inside the old town) **b** 18 **c** Yes, they have English TV channels **d** a lift **e** between 45 € and 79 €

Test yourself Nous voudrions une chambre d'hôtel avec deux lits. **2** À quelle heure sert-on le petit déjeuner ? **3** Est-ce que l'office de tourisme se charge des réservations? **4** Est-ce que l'hôtel accepte des animaux? **5** Puis-je louer un vélo? **6** Pouvez-vous servir le petit déjeuner dans ma chambre à 9h? **7** It's more expensive with a sea view. **8** We don't accept cheques. **9.** The pool is shut in winter. **10.** The lift is reserved for disabled people. **11** There are only rooms without bathrooms available. **12** You should phone the police.

Unit 8

Choosing a hotel la gastronomie **Conversations 1a** l'Hôtel de la Gare **b 1** It's convenient, easy with luggage and it's the cheapest **2** near the station **3** Madame Olivier **4** more comfortable **2 a** yes **b 1** two nights **2** third floor **3** 25 **4** from 8 to 10 a.m. **5** at 11 p.m. **Language discovery 1 a** 3 **b** 1 **c** 6 **d** 5 **e** 2 **f** 7 **g** 4 **2 a** 5 **b** 4 **c** 1 **d** 6 **e** 7 **f** 3 **g** 2 **3 a** plus **b** moins **Practice 1 a** Faux **b** Faux **c** Faux **2 a** Café des Amis **b** Café du Port **c** Café de la Vieille Ville **d** Café de l'Europe **3 a** Je prends/peux, **b** Tu peux/prends, **c** Il prend/ Il peut, **d** Elle prend/Elle peut **e** On prend/On peut **f** Nous prenons **g** Vous prenez **h** Ils peuvent/prennent **i** Elles peuvent/prennent **4 a** s'épelle, **b** prendre, **c** voudrais, **d** est, **e** on, **f** moins, **g** ont, **h** sortez, **i** avons

Exercise 5

C	Q	A	D	H	B	G	T	I	C	R	V
H	A	P	D	E	O	U	Y	T	N	H	I
S	Q	F	X	G	L	T	W	T	T	Y	E
H	O	T	E	L	D	U	P	O	R	T	
R	E	G	T	D	F	M	E	D	A	W	L
T	G	H	W	A	E	F	P	F	M	F	L
A	N	G	L	A	I	S	V	I	L	L	E
A	M	G	L	B	I	S	Q	C	R	U	P
B	C	V	N	F	T	H	W	A	Q	S	F

Pronunciation 3 1 Lécaille **2** Gaétan Leberre **3** Yannick Tanguy
Go further 1 dogs, cats and rabbits **2** He has a diploma **3** When a dog owner collects his/her dog and leaves the salon proud of the dog.

Test yourself 1 Pour le petit déjeuner je voudrais des croissants, du pain, de la confiture, de l'eau minérale bien fraîche, du café au lait, et des yaourts aux fruits. **2 a** j **b** l **c** i **d** g **e** k **f** h

Unit 9

French cities: a le plus **b** son **Vocabulary builder Asking questions**
a Où **b** Quand **c** après demain/la semaine prochaine/bientôt **d** Comment
e en voiture/par le train/à vélo **Conversations: 1 a** Try to find a post office
b 1 Yes (PTT) **2** A tour of the ramparts **3**b **c a** Faux **b** Vrai **c** Faux **d** Faux
e Faux **2a** Mum **b 1** The girl **2** Take the little train in St Malo **4** Dad
4 What they will do tomorrow **Language discovery 1a** 5 **b** 1 **c** 6 **d** 8 **e** 7
f 3 **g** 4 **h** 2 **2 a** 4 **b** 5 **c** 1 **d** 2 **e** 6 **f** 3 **3 a** tu vas **b** je vais **c** amusant
Practice 1 a la bibliothèque municipale **b** la boulangerie-pâtisserie
c la Maison de la Presse **d** la boucherie **e** la banque **f** la pharmacie
g la charcuterie

	A	B	C	D
1	M & Mme Olivier	vont	choisir	des cartes postales
2	Tu	vas	téléphoner	à ton frère
3	Sarah Burgess	va	prendre	le petit déjeuner au lit
4	Vous	allez	visiter	la vieille ville
5	Je	vais	rester	à St Malo
6	On	va	chercher	du travail
7	Les enfants	vont	faire	une promenade
8	Nous	allons	voir	le dernier film de Spielberg

Speaking: a Allez à la charcuterie! **b** Allez à la pharmacie! **c** Allez à la Maison de la Presse! **d** Allez à la Poste! **e** Allez à la boulangerie-pâtisserie! **f** Allez à l'Office de Tourisme! **Reading a** St Malo **b** arrival and departure **c** no

Test yourself 1 a vais, fatigant **b** allons, intéressant **c** vont, amusant
2 a Qu'est-ce que **b** faire **c** Où **d** allons, réservé **e** as, Quand **f** prochaine, toi **g** pas **h** pourrais, voiture, y **i** valise

Unit 10

Where to eat? a tasting **b** plat du jour **Vocabulary builder Meal times**
1 a 5 **b** 4 **c** 2 **d** 6 **e** 3 **f** The Times of the Day **1 a** 4 **b** 3 **c** 2 **d** 5 **e** 1

Conversations 1 a a picnic **b 1** the other side of the street **2** 10,50 € all included **Reading 1 a 1** Chauvinism **2** When it is a question of cuisine/cookery **b 1** two **2** the chefs and French restaurants **3** China and Italy

4 one **Reading 2** Fine food and good meals **a** Christening, communion or confirmation, a wedding, an exam result, a birthday, Christmas and the New Year. **2** 7 to 8 p.m. **3** Children **4** *Souper* is later than *dîner* and it is also a lighter meal. **5** At the canteen, cafeteria, restaurant or at home if they live close to their work place. **Language discovery a** 7 **b** 5 **c** 1 **d** 6 **e** 2 **f** 8 **h** 4 **i** 3 **2 a** a envie d'aller, **b** avez envie de manger **Reading a** orchards and cider making **b** apple juice or cider **c** jams or preserves **d** every afternoon from 1 May to 15 September **e** You need to book. **Go further a** 1, 4, 6 **b** 1, 5 **c** 3 **d** 4, 7 **e** 7 **f** 3 **g** 5

Test yourself 1 a 4, **b** 2, **c** 1, **d** 5, **e** 3 **2 a** meilleur, **b** goût, **c** meilleures, **d** dégoûtant, **e** mieux **3 a** Les vins de Bordeaux sont meilleurs. **b** Il y a une réduction si on en achète six. **c** J'ai soif! **d** J'ai envie de boire une bonne bière belge.

Unit 11

Rain and shine a quotidien **b** la météo **Vocabulary builder Directions** le nord 7; le nord-est 2; l'est 6; le sud-est 4; le sud 5; le sud-ouest 1; l'ouest 3; le nord-ouest 8 **Weather proverbs a** 2; **b** 1; **c** 1; **d** 2; **e** 1; **f** 2; **g** 2; **h** 1

Conversation: 1 a in the afternoon **b** 1 to listen to the weather forecast **2** the Pyrenees, the Alps and Corsica **c** 1c 2c 3b 4b 5b and c **Language discovery: 3 a** fait; **b** va faire; va changes the expression to *It's going to...* **Listening 1 a** à Dublin **b** à Athènes **c** à Genève **d** à Oslo **2 a** A Varsovie le temps est ensoleillé. **b** Il fait de l'orage. **Reading 1 a** Poitou-Charentes, Centre, Limousin, Aquitaine, Midi-Pyrénées, Auvergne, Rhône-Alpes **b** Bretagne, Pays de la Loire, Normandie, Nord-Picardie, Ile-de-France, Nord-Est, Bourgogne, Franche-Comté **c** The same as the areas with thunderstorms **d** & **e** Nord-Picardie, Ile de France **f** Pourtour méditerranéen, Corse **g** Nord-Est, Bourgogne, Franche-Comté **h** Pays de la Loire **2 a** 1 **b** 1 **c** 2 **d** 2 **e** 1 **f** 2 **g** 2

Test yourself 1 b **2** b **3** a **4** b **5** a **6** b **7** b **8** b **9** b **10** a **11** b **12** a

Unit 12

French cafés a le patron **b** no **c** smokers **Vocabulary builder Restaurant expressions a** 10 **b** 5 **c** 12 **d** 2 **e** 4 **f** 11 **g** 7 **h** 1 **i** 9 **j** 6 **k** 3 **l** 8 **m** 13 **Conversations 1** 1b 2c 3a 4c 5b **2 a** No, Sarah orders a draft beer and Dominique a shandy. **b** 1 ice cream **2** Because she is on a diet **3** Sarah **4** Dominique. Sarah paid last time **5** 9,50 € Yes 50c **3 a** a table by the window **b** 1 No, they ask for the menu. **2** a children's menu **3** yes **4** It's only available at lunch time **5** two menus at 20 €, two children's menus and a bottle of Muscadet **Language discovery 1 a** Je vous apporte la carte. **b** Prends un sorbet; il y a moins de calories. **c** une glace à la fraise et un sorbet au citron **d** Tu as payé la dernière fois. **e** quelques minutes plus tard **f** un peu plus tard **Practice** 1.1 Je viens d'arriver à Paris. **2** Tu viens de finir tes examens. **3** Jean-Paul vient de gagner le gros lot au Loto. **4** Nous venons de visiter St Malo. **5** Vous venez de choisir un menu. **6** Elles viennent de voir un bon film. **2.1** J'ai écouté les infos à la radio. **2** Tu as fini ton travail. **3** On a mangé des moules-frites. **4** Nous avons choisi un hôtel pas trop cher. **5** Vous avez posté vos cartes postales. **6** Sarah et Dominique ont réservé une cabine. **Go further 1**

	Menus (prix)	First course	Second course	Cheese	Dessert
Luc	20 €	Scallops	Monkfish	No	Ice cream
Florence	45 €	Sea food platter	Lobster	Cheese	Choice of dessert
Vous	25 €	6 huîtres chaudes avec cocktail d'algues	brochette de St Jaques au beurre blanc	fromage	glace à la fraise

Test yourself 1 ab ba cb da ec fb 2 a J'ai appris à surfer. **b** Je n'ai pas lu une seule ligne. **c** J'ai nagé pendant des heures. **d** J'ai goûté à la délicieuse cuisine locale. **3 a** Tu m'as prêté un livre. **b** Josiane a pris 3 semaines de vacances. **c** Je viens de visiter l'île. **d** On a nagé tous les jours. **e** J'ai appris à cuisiner.

Unit 13

Rules of the road a since **Vocabulary builder Parts of a car a**1 **b**2 **c**3 **d**4 **e**5 **f**6 **g**7 **h**8 **i**9 **Driving rules a** 2; **b** 1; **c** 1; **d** 2; **e** 2; **f** 2 **f** 1 **g**1 **Les principales couleurs: a**6 **b**3 **c**2 **d**7 **e**5 **f**4 **g**1 **Conversations 1 a** There is a diversion in 500 m. **b 1** 50 km/hour **2** service station **3** on the right **Language discovery 1 a**5 **b**8 **c**7 **d**2 **e**6 **f**1 **g**3 **h**4 **2 a** and **c** refer to an obligation to stop; **b** refers to the intention to stop. **Practice 1 a** 1 or 3 **b**5 **c**4 **d**2 **e**6 **f** 1 or 3 **2 3** vérifier la pression des pneus **Listening 1 a**3, **b**1, **c**2, **2 a** full tank of diesel, 20 litres of leaded 4 star petrol, 30 litres of unleaded petrol **Exercise 2**

Accidents	Type of vehicle involved in the accident	Place where accident occurred	No. of people killed	No. of people injured
1	Portuguese coach and lorry	RN10	8	24
2	Bicycle and a car	St Nazaire	1	–
3	Four cars	D940 Calais–Boulogne	0	8

Reading 1 32: 8 dead and 24 injured **2** c, d, f, g, i, j **Go further 1 a** the end of the area where the signs apply **b** blue **c** red **d** a blue square **2** 1f **2**g **3**a **4**d **5**e **6**c **7**b

Test yourself 1 a Non je n'ai pas acheté de lait. / Non, je n'en ai pas acheté. **b** Non, il n'a pas lu de livre / Non, il n'en a pas lu. **c** Non, ils n'ont pas mangé de pommes. / Non, ils n'en ont pas mangé. **2 a** Il en faut. **b** Il y en a. **3 a** Si, j'en bois assez! **b** Si, il en reste! **4 a** Il faut manger. **b** Il faut le visiter. **c** Il faut que je les poste.

Unit 14

Searching for a flat a no **Vocabulary builder Getting an Appartment a** 10 métro **b** 7 douzième arrondissement **c** 4 deuxième étage, dernier étage **d** 8 charges comprises **e** 12 salle de bain/wc (WC pronounced both les double v c and wouataires) **f** 1 cuisine équipée **g** 2 ascenseur **h** 3 chambre personnelle **i** 9 10 m² environ **j** 11 refait neuf **k** 5 chauffage électrique **l** 6 répondeur automatique **Around the house 1** balcon **2** porte d'entrée **3** bureau **4** fenêtre **5** salle de séjour **6** toilettes **7** couloir **8** escaliers **9** cambre **10** cuisine **11** coin salle à manger **12** salle de bain **Conversations 1 a** fourth floor **b 1** no **2** Yes, the view is great, it's cheap and the neighbours are quiet. **3** There is no lift. **4** going up and down stairs **5** Dominique and her boyfriend **6** the sea **2 a** her mother **b 1** a room in the university campus **2** rent a studio flat or share a flat with one or two girl friends **3** She is going to find a holiday job. **Language discovery 1 a**8 **b**5 **c**7 **d**11 **e**2 **f**3 **g**4 **h**6 **i**10 **j**1 **k**9 **2 a**4 **b**6 **c**1 **d**5 **e**3 **f**2 **3 1 b** je le loue; **c** si, les voilà; **d** l'a décoré; **e** tu la vois? **Reading 1 a** 2, 3 **b** 2, 3, 4, 6 **c** 1, 5, 7, 8 **d** 3 **Go further 1** 2, b and j **2** b **3** g (although **g** is too expensive for her) and k, **4** 400–550 € **5** a

Test yourself 1 a la regardons **b** je l'achète **c** Il la prévient **d** Non, je ne le finis pas. **e** On ne la connaît pas. **2 a** On va lui donner un livre. **b** Il m'a offert un bracelet. **c** Elle lui offre une voiture. **d** Je vais t'offrir un billet de théâtre. **3** (answers vary)

Unit 15

Shopping in France a affaires de la semaine **b** fréquemment

Vocabulary builder Shopping expressions a 6 **b** 3 **c** 5 **d** 1 **e** 4 **f** 2 **Clothing 1 a** 13 **b** 6 **c** 4 **d** 5 **e** 11 **f** 10 **g** 8 **h** 3 **i** 2 **j** 1 **k** 7 **l** 9 **m** 12 **Store departments 1 a** 14 **b** 22 **c** 28 **d** 26 **e** 3 **f** 23 **g** 25 **h** 36 **i** 26 **j** 21 **k** 3 **l** 24 **m** 40 **n** 33 **o** 28 **Conversation 1 a** (any four) lait, fromage, yaourts, beurre, pain, poisson, fruits et légumes, liquide lave-vaisselle, sans oublier des boîtes pour Papaguéno! **b 1** her cat **2** her neighbour **3** film for her camera, batteries for her torch, white wine and a cake **4** for Sarah and Dominique's evening meal **5** a pair of shoes and a pullover **6** No **7** green **8** fish counter **c** Sarah has just told Dominique that red does not suit her. In reply Dominique suggests that they move on to the fish counter, saying that she hopes they don't sell goldfish. The French word for goldfish is *poisson rouge* (lit. red fish). **Language discovery** 1 a5 b6 c8 d2 e3 f1 g4 h7 **2 a** en **b** mieux **Practice** a5 b6 c1 d2 e4 f3 **Listening** Bayonne ham: six slices; garlic sausage: 12 slices; farmhouse pâté: 250 g; Greek mushrooms: 200 g; scallops: 4

Reading a white nectarines **b** 1 to 3 August **c** A Sunday **d** in the town centre on Tuesday 12 and Wednesday 13 August **e** bedding **f** 4800 € **g** Wednesday 6 August **h** furniture **Go further 1**

P	A	C	C	D	M	N	G	H	I	L	P	K
A	D	S	E	A	P	O	M	M	E	S	O	D
M	S	Q	R	D	S	A	T	E	E	G	M	H
P	E	T	I	T	S	P	O	I	S	K	M	K
L	R	G	S	F	T	Y	M	S	E	L	E	H
E	A	P	E	B	A	N	A	N	E	S	S	A
M	I	O	S	D	C	E	T	A	P	A	D	R
O	S	I	Z	A	H	R	E	T	O	L	E	I
U	I	R	C	V	O	B	S	M	I	A	T	C
S	N	E	R	H	U	S	G	D	R	D	E	O
S	C	A	R	O	T	T	E	S	E	E	R	T
E	T	U	Y	U	H	N	F	D	S	V	R	S
S	F	X	J	V	B	C	A	S	W	R	E	M

Test yourself 1i **2**j **3**a **4**h **5**c **6**d **7**f **8**b **9**g **10**e

Unit 16

Diversity in France a to help people develop through leisure and social and cultural activities

Vocabulary builder Possessive adjectives 2 a son **b** sa **c** ses **d** leurs **e** sa **f** votre **g** mes **Conversations 1 a1 b 1** in France **2** his parents and sisters **3** about ten times **4** Arabic **5** three: Arabic, French and English **Language discovery a**8 **b**6 **c**5 **d**7 **e**1 **f**2 **g**4 **h**3 **2 a** rencontré **b** resté **Practice a**4 **b**1 **c**6 **d**5 **e**2 **f**3 **Reading a** 50%: cinquante pour cent **b** 48%: quarante-huit pour cent **c** 65%: soixante-cinq pour cent **d** 32%: trente-deux pour cent

Test yourself 1 aa **b**c **c**b **d**a **e**a **2 a** Je t'enverrai un mail. **b** Tout va bien. **c** Il s'est cassé la figure en faisant l'idiot. **d** rien de grave **e** ils ont maintenant rejoint le groupe. **3 a** Ils sont partis visiter leurs familles. **b** elle la ramènera ici **c** Ils sont restés quelques jours. **d** Nous sommes arrivés samedi. **e** Elle s'est installée chez sa tante.

Unit 17

Employment, unemployment and apprenticeship a 1 to 3 years
Vocabulary builder Professions a 6 **b** 3 **c** 2 **d** 5 **e** 4 **f** 1 **Tasks for the** Pôle emploi **a** 1 welcoming and registering the unemployed **b** 2 unemployment insurance **c** 2 professional training and job-hunting **Conversations 1 a 1** It's very good **2** Sarah is bilingual. **b 1** her mother and her father **2** He died. **3** five years ago **4** fine **5** because he is tiring Sarah out with his questions **6** her room **7** two years ago **c a**1 **b**4 **c**5 **d**3 **e**6 **f**2 **2a 1** He does not know. **2** He was a baker's apprentice. **3** He works full-time as a baker. **b 1** Go out to clubs in the evening **2** 5 a.m.
3 In a pharmacy **Language discovery** 1 **a**4 **b**6 **c**1 **d**3 **e**2 **f**5 **2 a** no **b** était **Practice 1 a** Je dansais. **b** Je skiais/je faisais du ski. **c** Je faisais du basket. **d** J'allais à la pêche. **e** Je faisais de la planche à roulettes. **f** Je jouais du piano. **Speaking a** Je m'intéresse aux métiers de l'hôtellerie. **b** Je m'intéresse à la photographie. **c** Je m'intéresse aux métiers de la santé. **d** Je m'intéresse aux métiers de l'habillement. **Reading a** between 16 and 26 **b** two years **c** It can be extended to three and reduced to one. **d** two months **e** The contract can be broken. **f** five weeks **g** six weeks before the date of birth and ten afterwards **h 1** four days **2** three days **i** general and technical **j** between one and two weeks per month **Go further a** job offers **b** You can look up all adverts for the last fortnight. **c** You can send your CV immediately via the Internet. **d** sales assistants, doorman, confectioner, waitresses, apprentice (in a delicatessen), home helps **e** secretarial jobs or accountancy, sales, electrician **f** at least 26 **g** You must be dynamic, motivated and interested in information technology. **h** maths, physics, chemistry, economics or management

Test yourself 1 aa **b**c **c**a **d**ac **e**b **f**ab **2 a** prenais, a sonné **b** voulions, avait **c** était **d** était, travaillait **e** enseignait, adorions **f** fallait, prendre **3 a** nagions **b** commençait **c** mangeaient

Unit 18

Travelling by train a towards the west, southwest, and Spain **b** la Gare du Nord **Vocabulary builder Additional expressions for times of day a** une journée **b** un matin **c** une soirée **d** un an **Expressions for self-service a** self-service laundrette **b** self-service restaurant **c** ATM / cashpoint **d** ticket machine **Conversations 1 a 1** She has to go back to work **2** She likes it a lot **b 1** to Paris **2** by train (TGV) **3** 3 hours **c 1** 3 hours **2** 12 hours **3** to make her train reservation **4** between 3 and 4 p.m. **5** her sister **6** Bordeaux and Les Landes, the wines and the region **2 a 1** 1h45 **2** return tickets **b 1** on Thursday **2** 10.09 **c 1** 10.37 **2** It arrives at Poitiers just in time for lunch. **3** No **4** book her ticket at the ticket machine **Language discovery 1 a**4 **b**6 **c**1 **d**7 **e**2 **f**3 **g**8 **h**5 **2 a**4 **b**5 **c**2 **d**8 **e**1 **f**3 **g**6 **h**7 **3 a** c'est comme tu veux **b** Ça prend combien de temps ? **c** nous ne savons pas encore **d** il faut que je réfléchisse **Practice 1 a**2 **b**3 **c**4 **d**1 **e**6 **f**5 **2 a** une soirée **b** ans **c** jours **d** ans **Listening a** Ça prend deux heures. **b** Ça prend cinq heures. **c** Ça prend une heure cinquante-cinq. **d** Ça prend exactement une heure. **Reading a** Vrai **b** Faux **c** Vrai **d** Vrai **e** Faux **f** Faux **g** Vrai **Go further**

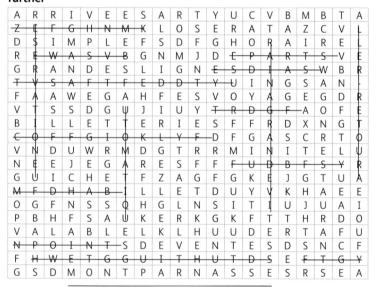

Test yourself 1 ab **b**a **c** a and c **d**c **e** a **f** a and c **2 a** sans **b** à **c** pour **d** de, sans **3 a** pris **b** prenions **c** prendrez **d** prendre **e** prenais

At the GP or at the pharmacy? **a** la Sécurité Sociale **Vocabulary builder: Body parts and health problems 1 a** la tête **b** l'œil, les yeux **c** l'oreille, les oreilles **d** le nez **e** la bouche **f** le cou **g** le dos **h** le bras **i** le ventre **j** la main **k** le genou **l** la jambe **m** le pied **2 a**1 I have a headache. **b**8 I have a stomachache. **c**4 I cut myself. **d**5 I burnt myself. **e**7 I am injured. **f**9 I have sun stroke. **g**3 I have got sunburnt. **h**10 I have got a high temperature. **i**6 I can't breathe properly. **j**2 I've broken my leg. **Pharmacist tasks: a** 1 They give advice **b** 2 They give information **c** 1 They treat minor ailments and wounds with medicines and bandages. **Expressions with une garantie (guarantee): a** garantie **b** garantie **c** garantis **Conversations 1 a** 1 19.15 **2** 19.05 **3** No, she will not get compensation-her train was less than 30 minutes late. **4** to telephone her sister **5** a mobile phone **2 a** 1 her mobile phone **b** 2 01 48 05 39 1 **b** 1 at the hospital **2** opening a tin of cat food **3** not really **c** 1 Marie-Claire's children **2** get a taxi **3** a taxi would be more convenient if she has a lot of luggage **3 a** 1 she has a stomachache **2** her stomach **b** 1 38.2C, yes **2** She is worried it's appendicitis. **c** 1 nothing **2** breakfast **3** this morning at 10 a.m. **4** She should stay overnight for observation. **Language discovery 1a**4 **b**7 **c**5 **d**8 **e**2 **f**3 **g**1 **h**6 **2 a**3 **b**1 **c**4 **d**5 **e**6 **f**2 **3** a lui **b** l'a **Practice**

Names	Questions on the recording	Your answer
Nadine	A quelle heure avez-vous téléphoné à Nadine?	Je lui ai téléphoné à onze heures trente
Mathieu	... à Mathieu?	Je lui ai téléphoné à midi
Chantal et Marc	... à Chantal et Marc?	Je leur ai téléphoné à dix-sept heures quinze
Votre sœur	... à votre sœur?	Je lui ai téléphoné à dix-huit heures quarante-cinq
Vos parents	... à vos parents?	Je leur ai téléphoné à vingt heures dix
Votre fiancé/e	... à votre fiancée?	Je lui ai téléphoné à vingt-deux heures quarante-cinq

Listening a7 **b**5 **c**4 **d**2 **e**6 **f**3 **g**8 **h**1 **Reading a** Wednesday 21 March 2007 at 8.30 p.m. **b** Dr Friat **c** backache **d** salle polyvalente (village hall) **e** C.H.U. of Brest **Go further 1 1** lift right arm **2** nothing **3** nothing **4** touch mouth with left hand **5** lower right arm **6** nothing **7** nothing **8** nothing **9** sang **10** touch left foot **11** lift right arm **12** nothing

Test yourself 1 aa **b**c **c**a **d**b **e**b **2 a** lui, l' **b** les **c** les, leur, **d** le **e** la **3 a** allait **b** alliez **c** vais **d** ailles **e** allés

Unit 20

Sight-seeing in Paris a on the Vélib', or via the bus or métro **Vocabulary builder Expressions with the verbs déplacer, débrouiller, and penser: a** 8 **b** 10 **c** 3 **d** 1 **e** 7 **f** 6 **g** 2 **h** 4 **i** 5 **h** 9 **Conversations 1 a 1** chatting to her sister **2** will take the children out to the Bois de Boulogne zoo and go for a walk **b 1** visit her sister **2** go to the zoo **3** all go to the cinema **4** lunch at Tante Eliane's **5** gare du Nord: register train ticket **6** takes Eurostar back to London **7** starts work in London **2 a 1** No they have got some. **2** half-fare **b 1** Ariane **2** She needs to think which kind of ticket she needs to buy. **c 1** a carnet of tickets **2** direction Porte de Vincennes **3** because they may be able to have a ride on the little train at the Bois de Boulogne **Language discovery 1 a**3 **b**5 **c**7 **d**8 **e**2 **f**1 **g**4 **h**6 **2 a**3 **b**5 **c**6 **d**8 **e**2 **f**2 **g**1 **h**4 **3 a** Penses-tu! **b** Ce que tu es bête! **Practice 2 a** sont partis **b** as vu **c** as mangés **d** ont pris **e** ai promis **f** êtes allée **g** a prévenu **Reading 1 a** card A **b** B is for museums and monuments, C is for Disneyland **c** in all RER and RATP stations, Marne-la-Vallée/Chessy (Disneyland station) **d** At Disneyland station **e** card A **f** for 1, 3 or 5 days **2 a** all RATP stations, bus stations, tabaconists displaying an RATP sign, ticket machines **b** 10 half-fare tickets

Test yourself 1 a5 **b**1 **c**2 **d**3 **e**4 **2 a** Je l'ai vu. **b** Oui, nous les avons regardés. **c** Je ne l'ai pas prévenue. **d** Ils l'ont lu. **e** Elle me l'a dite. **3 a** She does well in maths. **b** My father is 90, but he manages well by himself in the house **c** I move around Paris on the Vélib' **d** My daughter hurt herself falling from a tree. **e** She would never manage without me.

Unit 21

Paris a rive sud, rive nord **Conversations 1 a** 3, 4, 6 **b 1** Marie-Claire is feeling much better and she will be careful. **2** more time and money **2 a 1** Marie-Claire is imagining what she would do if she won the jackpot. **2** a large apartment in Paris and a house on the Mediterranean **b 1** She loves living in Paris. **2** no **c 1** Every morning. **2** She would go to the cinema, theatre, opera, and fine restaurants. **3** all her family including Sarah **Language discovery 1 a**2 **b**4 **c**5 **d**1 **e**6 **f**3 **2 a** is the future verb form of faire; **b** is the conditional form – it may or may not happen. **Practice 1 a**7 **b**4 **c**1 **d**8 **e**3 **f**5 **g**b **h**6 **Reading a** She would go and meet her parents. **b** in a hotel room at 41 Boulevard Ornano **c** her journey **d** Nation; Simplon **e** One **f** a cinema **g** 1945 **h** a quest for the identity of people and their painful and enigmatic past **Go further**

1 a three identical sums of money on the card and you win that amount **b** 2 € **c** you win 20 000–1 000 000 € on the wheel **2 a** Wednesdays and Saturdays **b** 16,8 € **c** 33,6 € **d** 10 **e** 5 **f** 134,40 € **Winning numbers:** 35, 8, 15, 28, 13, 45, 11, 25; bonus number is 12

Test Yourself 1 a3 **b**2 **c**7 **d**5 **e**6 **f**10 **g**8 **h**1 **i**9 **j**4 **2 a**3 **b**5 **c**1 **d**2 **e**4

Unit 22

On strike a They are concerned with social justice issues. **Vocabulary builder Expressions with mettre: a** 1 The fishermen went on strike to protest against the quotas. **b** 2 We sit down to eat at one o'clock. **c** 3 At what time are we setting off? **d** 1 They moved in together. **Conversations 1 a 1** over a game **2** He left it at his grandmother's. **3** Ariane's **b 1** Pierre **2** That it is his game. **3** to go and sit down in the living-room and watch TV **c 1** because she says she does not like animals **2** She kicks Pierre. **3** go to bed **2 a 1** from Sunday **2** It might affect her return journey. **3** Good, she can stay in Paris! **c 1** a film called *Ridicule* **2** *Mots-Croisés* **3** because she is interested in politics **d 1 a** Channel 5 (ARTE) at 20.45 **b** F2 at 20.55 **c** F2: 23.55/F3: 22.50/C+: 22.15 **d** F2: 22.35 **e** TF1: 22.55 **f** M6: 20.45 **g** Cable TV: 20.30 **2** if you had cable TV **3** mensuel **4** 'Which school for our children?' **Language discovery 1 a**4 **b**6 **c**7 **d**8 **e**1 **f**2 **g**3 **h**5 **2 a**6 **b**5 **c**4 **d**1 **e**2 **f**3 **3 a** le mien **b** le tien **c** ton **Speaking 1 a** Non, ce n'est pas le mien. **b** Oui, ce sont les miens. **c** Oui, ce sont les miennes. **d** Non ce n'est pas le mien. **e** Oui ce sont les miennes. **f** Oui c'est le mien. **g** Non, ce n'est pas la mienne. **2 Q1**: Ce sac est à vous? **R1**: Oui, c'est le mien **Q2**: Ce sont vos clefs? **R2**: Oui, ce sont les miennes. **Q3:** C'est votre montre? **R3**: Oui, c'est la mienne. **Q4:** Ce sont vos patins à roulettes? **R4**: Oui, ce sont les miens. **Reading a** 13 **b** bedrooms, dining rooms, sitting room, a gym and the « confessional » **c** the confessional **d** it is on the second floor and is used for individuals to address TV audience **e** 22 cameras and 55 microphones **f** use the gym **g** the filming of the competitors **h** 7000 **Go further 1** Will this strike snowball to the other towns in France? **2** 15 **3** in La Seine-Saint-Denis **4** personal itineraries/programmes to motivate pupils and give a taste for lifelong learning **5** The new initiatives, because changes have had to be made to the timetable. They object to French, Maths, History and Geography having to be cut by two hours a week. **6** They want an extra 6000 teachers for La Seine–Saint-Denis.

Test yourself 1 a les miennes **b** le sien **c** le mien **d** les leurs **e** la nôtre **f** le sien **g** la sienne **h** les siennes **i** les miennes **j** la leur **2 a** laquelle, la tienne, celle-ci **b** lequel, le tien, celui-ci **c** lesquelles, les tiennes, celles-ci **d** lesquels, les tiens, ceux-ci

Unit 23

Sport in France a la planche **Vocabulary builder**: **More demonstrative adjectives a**3 **b**4 **c**1 **d**5 **e**2 *Adverbs:* **a** free **b** obviously **c** tirelessly **d** particular *Sporting euphemisms:* **a**2 **b**1 **c**4 **d**3

Conversations 1

Saturday	Marie-Claire	Guillaume	Sarah	Ariane	Pierre
Morning	Housework Shopping	**Bercy Sports centre, playing tennis with his office friends**	**Housework and shopping**	**Housework and shopping**	**Housework and shopping**
Afternoon	**Having a rest at home**	Football match	**Cinema**	**Cinema**	**Cinema**
Evening	Cinema	**At home looking after the children**	**Cinema**	At home	**At home**

2 a 1 when she is in London she gets more opportunities to go to the cinema than Marie-Claire. **2** *Paris je t'aime* has just come out on DVD and Marie-Claire will give a copy to Sarah for her birthday **3** Hors de Prix **b a** Je voudrais voir *Paris je t'aime* parce que j'adore Paris. **b** J'aime beaucoup les films de Luc Besson. **c** C'est intéressant de voir un film américain sur l'histoire de France **d** l'histoire, l'animation et la musique sont très belles. **Language discovery 1 a**4 **b**6 **c**5 **d**3 **e**1 **f**2 **2** Tu avais dit qu'on irait voir **Practice a**4 **b**6 **c**7 **d**1 **e**8 **f**5 **g**2 **h**3 **Go further 1 a** around 10 **b** car rally, horse racing, rugby, running (marathon and 20 km), martial arts, tennis, football, waiters' races, cycling: Tour de France, vintage cars race **c** in June **d** from the Champs-Elysées to Bastille **e** on a Sunday during first two weeks of April **f** a 20 km run **2**

1	Prénom: Zinédine	1	Prénom: Thierry
2	Nom: Zidane	2	Nom: Henry
3	Nationalité: française	3	Nationalité: française
4	Date de naissance: 23 juin 1972	4	Date de naissance: 17 août 1977
5	Lieu de naissance: Marseille	5	Lieu de naissance: Paris
6	Taille: 1,85 m	6	Taille:1,88 m
7	Poste: milieu de terrain	7	Poste: attaquant

Reading a 40% discount **b** 5 issues for 17€ **c** cheque, postal order or credit card

Test yourself 1 a pris **b** voulu **c** bu, dû **d** arrivée, perdu **e** plu
f partis **g** eu **h** dit **i** oublié, pris **j** compris, dit **2 a** Ils ont pris un taxi
pour aller plus vite. **b** Elle avait voulu travailler à Paris pour gagner plus
d'argent. **c** Malheureusement j'avais perdu mon sac. **d** Je n'avais pas
mangé depuis **2** jours. **3** tranquillement (calmly, leisurely), rapidement
(quickly), malheureusement (unfortunately), complètement (completely),
parfaitement (perfectly)

Unit 24

French cooking and meals a c **Vocabulary builder In the kitchen:**
Ingredients:1c **2**e **3**a **4**f **5**d **6**b **Utensils: 7**h **8**g **9**i **10**j **Preparation of**
ingredients: 11k **12**o **13**m **14**n **15**l **What to do: 16**p **17**u **18**r **19**s **20**v
21y **22**q **23**w **24**x **25**t **26**z **Cooking and table expressions: a**1 **b**3 **c**2
Conversations 1a 1 to help her lay the table **2** her crockery and her
glasses **3** the corkscrew **4** white wine **b** 1 un verre **2** une assiette **3** un
couteau **4** une fourchette **5** une cuillère **6** la vaisselle **7** un tire-bouchon **c**
Menu de Tante Eliane: Melon, Melon, Truite au champagne et raisins, Trout
in Champagne with grapes, Pommes de terre sautées, Sauté potatoes,
Salade, Salad, Fromage, Cheese, Tarte aux pommes, Apple Tart **d 1** 6 to 8
2 45 minutes **3** half a bottle **4** heated **5** once or twice during the cooking
time **6** They need to be wrapped in aluminium paper. **2 a 1** in Japan **2**
for Christmas **b 1** Yes **2** No, he is single. **c 1** her sister-in-law **2** because
her brother-in-law cannot go **3** 12 October, from Nantes **4** 21 October
Language discovery 1 a4 **b**5 **c**6 **d**1 **e**3 **f**2 **2 a**4 **b**6 **c**2 **d**5 **e**3 **f**1 **3** qui and
que **Practice a** que, qui **b** que **c** que **d** que, qui **e** qui **f** qui **Reading 1**
a Faux **b** Faux **c** Faux **d** Vrai **e** Vrai **f** Faux **g** Vrai **h** Faux **i** Vrai **j** Faux **2**
Printing error: In the last sentence for Day 7 of the visit it refers to la 8e
nuit instead of 7e.

Test yourself 1 que **2** que **3** que **4** que **5** que **6** qui **7** que **8** qu' **9** que
10 qui **11** que **12** qui **13** qui **14** qu' **15** que **16** que **2 a** the little villages
b Jacques Cartier landing at Tadoussac in 1535 **c** a woman who works for
Radio Quebec **d** a group of singers, their music ressembles that of Brittany
3 a Tante Eliane **b** Jacques Cartier **c** C'est charmant **d** raconter tout ce
qu'elle a fait

Unit 25

Buying a property in France a 3 months **Vocabulary builder:**
Describing a dream home: a4 **b**7 **c**3 **d**2 **e**5 **f**1 **g**6 **Getting a house built:**
a 2 **b** 2 **c** 1 **d** 2 **e** 1 **Tasks for a notaire: a** 1 **b** 1 **c** 2 **d** 2 **e** 1 **Conversations**
1 a 1 because she is leaving **2** sad **b 1** No **2** their mother **3** because she

too is going back to work tomorrow **c 1** retire at 55 and buy a small house in the South of France **2** all buy a house together and renovate it **3** not really **2 a 1** because they intend to buy a house **2** whether there are any problems **b 1** an advert in a newspaper **2** no, not yet **3** Yes **c 1** arrange a visit **2** the lawyer **3** think about it **d 1** Vrai **2** Vrai **3** Faux **4** Vrai **5** Faux **6** Vrai **7** Vrai **8** Vrai **Language discovery 1 a**5 **b**3 **c**4 **d**1 **e**2 **2 a**5 **b**1 **c**6 **d**3 **e**2 **f**4 **Practice 1** S: J'adore la cuisine française R: Moi aussi **2** S: Je n'aime pas les voyages organisés R: Moi non plus **3** S: Nous aimons beaucoup la Bretagne R: Nous/moi aussi **4** S: Je n'aime pas la rentrée R: Moi non plus **5** S: Je déteste prendre l'avion R: Moi aussi **6** S: Je préfère rester chez moi R: Moi aussi **Read a** 4A **b** 5A **c** 5V **d** 2V **e** 3A **f** 7A **g** 8A and 8V **h** 2A **Go further 2 C1**: Je cherche une petite maison de pierre près de la côte. **C2**: Je cherche une maison de cinq chambres avec cave. **C3:** Je cherche une petite maison avec un jardin clos. **C4:** Je cherche une petite maison avec grenier aménageable. **2 a** 1 **b** 8 **c** 13 **d** 4 **e** 2

Test yourself 1 a Les terrains qu'ils avaient choisis n'étaient pas constructibles. **b** Il leur a fait démolir leurs maisons. **c** Il avait décidé de bâtir une maison de bois. **d** Ils n'avaient ni permis de construire ni de contrats de construction. **e** Il avait procédé selon le règlement. **2 a** On l'a fait démolir. **b** Ils les avaient choisis. **c** Nous l'avions présenté. **d** On le lui a demandé. **e** On les lui avait données.

Unité de révision

1 **Profiles 1** Nom: Burgess; Prénom: Sarah; Âge: 28 ans; Adresse: 12 Stella Avenue, Londres SW2; Numéro de téléphone: 020 8476 5656; Nationalité: britannique; Nationalité du père: britannique; Nationalité de la mère: française; Profession: éditrice, Lieu de travail: Hodder & Stoughton, Londres, Aime: les voyages, le cinéma, la lecture; N'aime pas: le sport à la télévision 2 Nom: Périer; Prénom: Dominique; Âge: 36 ans; Adresse: 5 Avenue de la Vieille Ville; St Nazaire; France; Numéro de téléphone: 02 40 45 1811; Nationalité: française, Nationalité du père: française; Nationalité de la mère: française; Profession: professeur de philosophie; Lieu de travail: lycée de St Nazaire; Aime: les chats, l'opéra, les musées d'art; N'aime pas: la télévision, les voitures

2 **Une promenade à St Malo** (1) from c to the station, (2) from e to the swimming pool, (3) from d to the cathedral, (4) from a to the castle

3 **Orthographe des nombres** *vingt* and *cent* only have s in the plural if they come at the end of the number e.g. *deux cents*, *quatre vingts*, but *deux cent trois*, *quatre-vingt-cinq*

4 **Grand jeu-concours** 1 A trip to England for two 2 14 September 3 The town and the tourist office.

5 **Quelle attitude!** 1 They both use the verb *vouloir*: *je veux* is the present tense and *je voudrais* is the conditional. 2 The difference shows two different attitudes: *je veux* is likely to be perceived as impolite 3 To b)

6 **Aujourd'hui c'est samedi** Aujourd'hui les parents et les trois enfants vont au barrage de la Rance. /Aujourd'hui toute la famille va au barrage de la Rance.

7 **La voiture idéale** 1 6-d-m/o 2 8-f-n 3 5-a-j 4 1-b-q 5 9-g-l 6 7-h-r 7 2-c-m/o 8 3-i-p 9 4-e-k

8 **Les jeunes et l'emploi** 1 a Work experience b Administration and management c No d It was eight weeks of their holidays e It gave them their first contact with the world of work 2 1 Fast food and cafeteria: c b d 2 Telephone marketing and opinion polls: g a i 3 Leaflet distribution: h f e

9 **Paris et le tourisme** 1 V 2 F there is a night bus, 3 F children of 4 to 11 pay a reduced rate, 4 V 5 F the zones are 1 to 3 and 1 to 8 6 V 7 F 8 F tickets are for 1, 2, 3 or 5 days

10 **Les loisirs et vous** 1A Oui: b g h j l Non: a c d e f i

11 **Encore une bonne recette** a 25 minutes b 175 cl of water + 75 cl of juice c Thin slices d Half a teaspoon e Pear juice f One soup spoon g Garnish h The mixture i After the fruit mixture is cooked j Five minutes

A quick guide to French pronunciation

A language is primarily something that you hear and something that you speak. When learning a new language the most important thing to do is to listen to it. Reading about the way it sounds is not really satisfactory but I shall attempt to describe the sounds comparing them with English sounds where possible and giving a very simple description of the position of the tongue in relation to the palate and the position of the lips and jaws. In order to describe it, it is necessary to divide the tongue into three broad areas: the tip of the tongue, the front of the tongue (more or less the centre of the blade) and the back of the tongue.

There is an important difference between the hard palate and the soft palate. You need only feel the roof of your mouth with your tongue in order to discover the difference between the two.

Reading through the list of words and practising how to say them, taking into account the position of the lips, tongue, palate and jaws should give you awareness of how sounds are formed. And try to listen to French as often as you can.

VOWELS

French examples	Similar English sounds	Characteristic position of tongue (T), lips (L), jaw (J)
idée *(idea)* ami *(friend)* ici *(here)*	be, meet (the French sound is shorter)	T: The whole tongue is raised towards the hard palate, as high as possible, L: spread, J: together
été *(summer)* assez *(enough)* aller *(to go)* et *(and)*	ready, play (with a Scottish accent)	T: The front of the tongue is raised towards the middle of the hard palate, L: neutral, J: nearly together
mais *(but)* sept *(seven)* même *(even)* béret rester *(stay)* scène les *(the)*	men set maim ray Seine lay	T: The front of the tongue is slightly lifted towards the hard palate, L: neutral, J: slightly open

là *(there)* la *(the)* malade *(sick)*	cap, pat,	T: Front is only very slightly lifted (passage between tongue and palate is wide), L: neutral, J: wide.
pâté là-bas *(over there)* pas *(not)*	dark, father	T: The tip is kept against the lower teeth. The back part is slightly raised towards soft palate, L: not rounded, J: wide open.
rue *(street)* plus *(more)* futur	there is no very similar sound in English: 'dew' with very rounded lips	T: Very similar to i, L: rounded and pouting. Try practising i and u, first li, then lu, keeping the same tongue position, but rounding your lips for lu (like in 'Lully'), J: not far apart
deux *(two)* peu *(little)* heureux *(happy)* œufs *(eggs)*	no satisfactory comparison: 'adieu' with very rounded lips	T: Stretched but not raised, L: rounded and pouting, but open wider than for u, J: not far apart
heure *(hour)* seul *(alone)* œuf *(egg)*	something between the 'ur' in 'turn' and 'er' in 'butter'	T: Stretched but not raised, L: rounded but not pouting.
ouvert *(open)* sous (under) où *(where)*	hoot, two, do	T: Back is raised towards the soft palate, L: rounded and closed, as for u, J: not far apart
gros *(big)* beau *(beautiful)* rôle chaud *(hot)*	as in 'go', but very much shorter	T: Back is retracted towards the pharynx, L: very rounded, J: not far apart
homme *(man)* mort *(dead)*	hot, dog	T: Back slightly raised towards the larynx, L: rounded as for o, but with a wider opening, J: not far apart

NASALISED VOWELS

These are very common in French. The **m** or **n** is swallowed, and the preceding vowel is pronounced in a nasal fashion (i.e. through the nose).

French examples	Similar English sounds	Characteristic position of tongue (T), lips (L), jaw (J)
camp grand *(tall)* emblème	calm, part (pronounced in a nasal fashion)	T: Back slightly raised towards the larynx, L: not rounded, J: wide apart. The soft palate is lowered
fin *(end)* pain *(bread)* plein *(full)* simple	pet (nasalised)	T: Back slightly raised towards the larynx, L: spread, J: wide apart. The soft palate is lowered
brun *(brown)* lundi *(Monday)* humble	turn (nasalised)	T: Back slightly raised towards the larynx, L: rounded, J: apart. The soft palate is lowered.
bon *(good)* nom *(name)* long	song (nasalised)	T: Back slightly raised towards the larynx, L: closely rounded, J: not far apart. The soft palate is lowered

SEMI-VOWELS

French examples	Similar English sounds	Characteristic position of tongue (T), lips (L), jaw (J)
briller (shine) travail (work) pied (foot) mayonnaise	yellow, young	T: Back moves towards the hard palate, sides touch the upper teeth each side of the mouth, L: neutral, J: not far apart
lui (him) puis (then) bruit (noise)		T: It is stretched and raised toward the hard palate, L: rounded, J: not far apart.
oui (yes) ouest (west)	'w' as in 'walk', 'west'	T: The back forms a narrow passage against the soft palate, L: very rounded, J: not far apart.
loi (law) moi (me) quoi (what) poële (frying pan)	the 'wo' sound in 'wonder'	T: similar to 'wonder', L: rounded, J: Not far apart

CONSONANTS

Although there are some differences between French and English, it is not difficult to produce the correct sounds, even if you have never heard them before. (The position of the tongue, lips and jaw are only mentioned if relevant.)

French examples	Similar English sounds	Characteristic position of tongue (T), lips (L), jaw (J)
port papier (paper)	port, bump	not aspirated (no puff of air after the 'p')
bon (good) beau (beautiful)	boy, bat	
tout (all) porte (door)		not aspirated (no puff of air after the 't')
dans (in) monde (world)	day, pad	
quai (platform) carotte	cup, cook	not aspirated (no puff of air after the 'c/qu')
gauche (left) vague	go, gag	
moment mère (mother)	man, jam	
noir (black) fini (finished)	new,	
digne (dignified) agneau (lamb)	onion, Tanya	

lourd *(heavy)* ville *(town)* pluriel *(plural)*	let, little	a tight sound, like the first, not the last 'l' in 'little'
café photo	telephone, friend	
vert*(green)* avant *(before)*	virus, have	
savoir *(to know)* ça (this) passé *(past)*	save, place	
maison *(house)* rose zone	zany, roses	's' between two vowels has the sound 'z'
chat *(cat)* chercher *(to look for)*	shine, fresh	
jeune *(young)* mangeons *(we eat)* garage	's' in 'pleasure', or 'Jane' in English without the 'd' sound at the beginning	there is no hard 'dj' sound in French
rouge *(red)* nourriture *(food)* amour *(love)*	difficult to compare with an English 'r'	There are many varieties of r. The sound varies according to individuals and regions. In a Parisian r, the back of the tongue is raised to form a narrow passage against the soft palate.

Although many words have the same spelling in both French and English, the pronunciation is usually entirely different. When trying to pronounce a word, it is important to bear the following points in mind:

1 Final consonants are usually silent (except for *c, f, l, r*). *h* is not normally pronounced. *e* is silent at the end of a word, except for words of one syllable.

2 Stress mainly falls on the last syllable of a word.

3 The written accents in French are:
   é acute, *ê* circumflex, *è* grave
   ë tréma is used to separate the sounds of 2 consecutive vowels, e.g. in 'Noël'.
   cedilla *ç*, which changes the sound /k/ into /s/ before *u, a* and *o*.

Accents may be omitted when capital letters are used.

LINKING WORDS

Two consecutive words can be pronounced as one by linking the last letter of the first word to the first letter of the second when the first word ends in a consonant and the second words begins with a vowel or **h**.

Examples:

mes amis	**mezami**	*my friends*
tout est fini	**tutay fini**	*it's all over*
vous habitez à Paris	**vuzabitezapari**	*you live in Paris*
	vuzabite apari	
un œuf	**unœf**	*an egg*
des œufs	**dezeu**	*eggs*

These expressions are pronounced as if they were one word:

jmappelle (je m'appelle – *my name is*)
jai (j'ai – *I have*)
jabite (j'habite – *I live*)
jaime (j'aime – *I love / like*) / j**nai**me pas (je n'aime pas – *I don't like*)
ilya (il y a – *there is*)

Try these three examples of **liaison**: two words linked together because of the last letter of the first one:

Je suis amoureux / amoureuse (*I am in love*). This should be pronounced: je **suiza**moorer / je **suiza**moorerze

Bonjour mes amis (*hello my friends*), pronounced bonjour **meza**mi (the **s** at the end of **amis** is silent)

Bon appétit, pronounced **bona**ppeti (the **t** at the end of **appétit** is silent)

INTONATION

Intonation (variation in the tone of voice), for example when raising your voice in order to ask a question, reveals the intentions and feelings of the speaker. The same sentence can be uttered differently according to circumstances.

Grammar summary

ADJECTIVES

Adjectives are used to provide more information about nouns. In English they can appear in front of a noun or they can stand on their own after a verb such as to *be/to look/to seem*:

The new school opens today.   *It looks good.*

In French, adjectives have the same function but their spelling is affected by the noun they are linked with. Also they stand either before or after the nouns and in some cases the meaning of the adjective changes slightly according to where it is placed. The two factors which affect the spelling of adjectives are the gender and number of the noun:

un joli petit village   *a pretty little village*

une jolie petite ville   *a pretty little town*

In French, village is masculine and town feminine. **-e** indicates the feminine form except if the adjective finishes with an **-e** in its generic form:

un quartier tranquille   *a quiet district*

une région tranquille   *a quiet area*

Adjectives linked to plural nouns tend to take an **-s** but in some cases (as for the feminine) there are more drastic changes. If there is already an **-s** at the end of the adjective, it does not change in the plural form:

J'aime un bon verre de cidre   *I like a good glass of fresh cider*
frais avec des moules   *with very fresh mussels.*
bien fraîches.

J'aime une bonne bière bien   *I like a good cool beer with very*
fraîche avec des fruits de   *fresh seafood.*
mer bien frais.

Examples of a few adjectives which change more drastically:

Quel beau château!   *What a beautiful castle!*

Quelle belle journée!   *What a beautiful day!*

Quels beaux enfants!   *What beautiful children!*

C'est le tarif normal.	*It's the normal price.*
Ce sont des gens normaux.	*They are normal people.*
Ils mènent une vie normale.	*They lead a normal life.*
Ce sont des attitudes tout à fait normales.	*These are perfectly normal attitudes.*

Possessive adjectives: For the full list of words such as **mon**, **ma**, **mes** *my*, **son**, **sa**, **ses**, *her/his*, **votre** *your*, see Unit 22.

ADVERBS

Just as adjectives provide more information about nouns, so adverbs tend to provide more information about verbs or adjectives:

Il marche vite.	*He walks fast.*
Le voyage s'est bien passé.	*The journey went well.*
Ils ne sont nullement fatigués.	*They are not at all tired.*

For easy recognition of a large number of French adverbs you need to note the following pattern: adjective in feminine form + **-ment** (equivalent of **-ly** in English):

| Heureusement qu'il fait beau. | *Luckily the weather is good.* |
| Les gendarmes sont arrivés rapidement. | *The policemen arrived rapidly.* |

An adverb can also provide information about another adverb:

| Ils conduisent trop vite. | *They drive too fast.* |

ARTICLES

The definite article

This term is given to *the* in English and to **la**, **le**, **l'** and **les** in French. **Le** is used in front of masculine nouns, **la** with feminine nouns, **l'** if a noun starts with a vowel or a mute **h**; **les** is used in front of nouns in the plural form:

| À la naissance d'un enfant il faut déclarer la date, le lieu de naissance, le nom et les prénoms de l'enfant et les noms des parents. | *When a child is born you have to declare the date, the place of birth, the surname and first names of the child and the names of the parents.* |

The indefinite article

This is the term given to the words *a* and *an* in English and to **un, une, des** in French:

Il y a des jours où un rien me donne un mal de tête ou une migraine.	*There are some days when nothing much can give me a headache or a migraine.*

AUXILIARY VERBS

Auxiliary verbs are used as a support to the main verb, for example, I *am* working, you *are* working. Here *am* and *are* are used to support the verb *work*. By its very nature an auxiliary verb does not normally stand on its own, because it is the main verb which carries the meaning. *Working* gives us the information as to what activity is going on. **Avoir** to have and **être** to be are the main auxiliary verbs in the two languages and are mainly used to form past tenses. Others are **pouvoir** *can*, **venir de** ... *to have just* ..., also *to do* in English.

Est-ce que vous travaillez le samedi?	*Do you work on Saturdays?*
Je viens de voir un très bon film.	*I have just seen a very good film.*
J'ai perdu ma montre.	*I have lost my watch.*
Pourriez-vous m'indiquer la bonne route?	*Could you show me the right way?*
Ils sont partis de bonne heure.	*They left early / They have left early.*

COMPARATIVES

When we make comparisons, we need the comparative form of the adjective. In English this usually means adding **-er** to the adjective or putting more, less or as in front of it. In French you add plus, **moins** or **aussi** in front of adjectives:

Tu es plus fort que moi.	*You are stronger than me.*
Il est plus intelligent que son frère et beaucoup moins beau. Mais ils ont aussi mauvais caractère.	*He is more intelligent than his brother and less good-looking but they are just as bad tempered.*

CONJUNCTIONS

Conjunctions are words such as *and* and *although*. They link words, or clauses or sentences:

Nous sommes allés à Paris mais nous n'avons pas vu la tour Eiffel.	*We went to Paris but we did not see the Eiffel Tower.*
Nous avons fait une promenade bien qu'il pleuve.	*We went for a walk although it was raining.*
Je vous téléphonerai plus tard si vous voulez.	*I'll call you later if you want.*

GENDER

In English, grammatical gender is only used for male and female persons or animals, so for example we refer to a man as *he* and a woman as *she*. Objects of indeterminate sex are referred to as having *neuter* gender. So a table is referred to as *it*. In French all nouns have a gender which is either masculine or feminine and although the gender of the word is linked to the sex of the person or the animal in most cases, there are very few guidelines to help you guess whether other nouns are feminine or masculine.

Le vélo de Paul et **la bicyclette** de Pierre: both words mean *bike* although one is masculine and the other feminine. In this case it is likely that **bicyclette** is feminine because it ends with **-ette** and words ending with **-ette** are usually feminine words e.g **une fillette** *a little girl.* It is not normally so easy to rationalize the reason for the gender of words. It is important to remember that it is the word which is feminine or masculine, not the object it refers to.

IMPERATIVE

The imperative is the form of the verb used to give orders, commands or advice:

Viens ici!	*Come here! (order)*
Roulez à droite.	*Drive on the right. (command)*
Faites attention en traversant la rue.	*Be careful when you cross the road. (advice)*
Écoutons les informations.	*Let's listen to the news.*
Regarde la télé.	*Watch TV.*
N'attrape pas froid!	*Don't catch a cold!*

The imperative is used for notices everywhere to direct or guide our actions:

Poussez!	*Push!*
Tirez!	*Pull!*
Cochez les cases.	*Tick the boxes.*
Ralentissez!	*Slow down!*

INFINITIVE

The infinitive is the basic form of the verb. This is the form that you will find in the dictionary. In English the infinitive is usually accompanied by the word *to*, e.g. *to go, to play*.

In French the infinitive form of a verb is noticeable by its ending. There are three major groups of verbs: **-er** verbs (ending in **-er**: **chercher**, **regarder**, **manger**), **-ir** verbs (ending in **-ir**: **choisir**, **finir**) and **-re** and **-oir** verbs (ending in **-re**: **prendre**, **attendre** or **-oir**: **vouloir**, **pouvoir**).

Verbs are used in the infinitive in two particular types of circumstances:

Je vais acheter du fromage.   *I am going to buy some cheese.*

A second verb is always in the infinitive, except when the first verb is **avoir** or **être**. A verb following a preposition such as **à**, **de**, **sans**, etc is always in the infinitive form.

J'ai passé toute la journée à ranger mes placards.   *I spent the whole day tidying up my cupboards.*

NOUNS

Nouns are words like **maison** *house*, **pain** *bread*, **beauté** *beauty*. A useful test of a noun is whether you can put **le**, **la** or **les** *the* in front of it.

OBJECTS

The term 'object' expresses the 'receiving end' relationship of a noun and a verb. So, for instance, **le facteur** *the postman* is said to be the object at the receiving end of the biting in the sentence:

Le chien a mordu le facteur.   *The dog bit the postman.*

J'ai donné des fleurs à ma mère.   *I gave flowers to my mother.*

In this particular example **des fleurs** is referred to as the direct object because there is nothing between it and the verb, and **ma mère** is referred to as the indirect object because it is linked to the verb with a preposition (**à**, **de**, etc).

It is important to know whether a noun is a direct or indirect object when it comes to using a pronoun to replace the noun.

Some verbs don't need an object:

Le chien a aboyé. *The dog barked.*

PAST PARTICIPLE

This is the name for the part of the verb which follows the auxiliary verbs **avoir** and **être** in the perfect and pluperfect tenses. Verbs ending with **-er** in the infinitive tend to have a past participle ending with **-é**. Other endings for past participles are **-i** for most **-ir** verbs, **-u** for most **-oir** verbs and **-is** for most **-re** verbs:

J'ai regardé la télé.	*(regarder, to watch)*
Yannick a fini son travail.	*(finir, to finish)*
Les garçons ont voulu partir en Angleterre.	*(vouloir, to want)*
Ariane a mis le couvert.	*(mettre, to put / to set the table)*

PREPOSITIONS

Words like **à** *at*, **avec** *with*, **de** *of*, **dans** *in*, **chez** *at someone's house*, **pour** *for*, **sans** *without*, **sous** *under*, **sur** *on* are called prepositions. Prepositions often tell us about positions or relationships. They are normally followed by a noun or pronoun:

Ton livre est sur la table.	*Your book is on the table.*
Il a laissé son parapluie dans le train.	*He left his umbrella in the train.*
Voici un cadeau pour toi.	*This present is for you.*
Elle est sortie avec son copain.	*She went out with her boyfriend.*

PRESENT PARTICIPLE

The part of a French verb which is often equivalent to *-ing* in English:

Ils sifflent en travaillant.	*They whistle while working.*
En réfléchissant bien...	*Thinking about it...*
La chance aidant il a réussi son examen.	*With the help of luck he has passed his exam.*

PRONOUNS

Pronouns fulfil a similar function to nouns and often stand in the place of nouns which have already been mentioned:

La maison a plus de 200 ans.   *The house is over 200 years old.*

Elle est très belle.   *It is very beautiful.*

(*House* is the noun and *it* is the pronoun.)

TABLE OF PRONOUNS				
Subject pronouns	Reflexive pronouns	Direct object pronouns	Indirect object pronouns	Emphatic pronouns
je	me/m'	me/m'	me/m'	moi
tu	te/t'	te/t'	te/t'	toi
il	se/s'	le/l'	lui	lui
elle	se/s'	la/l'	lui	elle
on	se/s'			soi
nous	nous	nous	nous	nous
vous	vous	vous	vous	vous
ils	se/s'	les	leur	eux
elles	se/s'	les	leur	elles

For more explanations of pronouns, please refer to the following sections of the book: Unit 12 (emphatic pronouns), Unit 19 (indirect object pronouns), Unit 22 (possessive pronouns) and Unit 25 (order of pronouns). For relative pronouns see relative clauses.

REFLEXIVE VERBS

When the subject and the object of a verb are one and the same, the verb is said to be reflexive:

Jean se lève à 6 heures.   *John gets (himself) up at 6 a.m.*

Je me lave bien.   *I wash myself thoroughly.*

Florence s'est blessée.   *Florence hurt herself.*

In French nearly all verbs can be reflexive if they are preceded by a reflexive pronoun:

Il a lavé sa chemise.   *He has washed his shirt.*

Il s'est lavé les mains.   *He has washed his (own) hands.*

Je regarde la télé.   *I watch TV.*

Je me regarde dans le miroir.   *I look at myself in the mirror.*

When reflexive verbs are used in the perfect tense, they are always used with **être**. But when the same verb is not in its reflexive form, it takes **avoir** in the perfect tense.

Hélène a coupé du bois.	*Helen cut some wood.*
Hélène s'est coupé la main avec la scie.	*Helen cut her hand with the saw.*
J'ai vu la télé.	*I saw the TV.*
Je me suis vue à la télé.	*I saw myself on TV.*

RELATIVE CLAUSES AND RELATIVE PRONOUNS

A relative pronoun such as **que** *which/that* or **qui** *who* can be used to provide more information about a noun which has just been mentioned. The resulting clause is called a relative clause:

Je connais la personne qui habite à côté de chez toi.	*I know the person who lives next door to you.*
La voiture que je conduis a presque dix ans.	*The car (which) I drive is nearly ten years old.*

(In French it is not possible to omit the relative pronoun **que**.) See Unit 24 for more about relative pronouns.

SUBJECT

The term 'subject' expresses a relationship between a noun and a verb. The subject is the person or thing doing the action, as here for instance:

Le chien a mordu le facteur.	*The dog bit the postman.*

Because it is the dog that does the biting, the dog is said to be the subject of the verb **mordre** *to bite*.

SUPERLATIVES

The superlative is used for the most extreme version of a comparison:

Ce magasin est le moins cher de tous.	*This shop is the cheapest of all.*
C'est la plus belle femme du monde.	*She is the most beautiful woman in the world.*
Le champion du monde de Formule Un, c'est le meilleur pilote du monde.	*The Formula One champion is the best driver in the world.*

TENSE

Most languages use changes in the verb form to indicate an aspect of time. These changes in the verb are referred to as 'tense', and the tense may be present, past or future. Tenses are often reinforced with expressions of time:

Past: **Hier je suis allé à Londres.** *Yesterday I went to London.*

Present: **Aujourd'hui je reste à la maison.** *Today I am staying at home.*

Future: **Demain je prendrai l'avion pour Berlin.** *Tomorrow I'll be flying to Berlin.*

The course introduces verbs in the present tense. This includes the subjunctive – a verbal form referred to as a 'mood', mostly used in the present to express regrets, doubts and uncertainties. Several past tenses are used throughout the course: the perfect tense, the imperfect and the pluperfect. The future tense also features in the course.

The conditional is used to indicate that if certain conditions were fulfilled something else would happen.

VERBS

Verbs often communicate actions, states and sensations. So, for instance, the verb **jouer** *to play* expresses an action, the verb **exister** *to exist* expresses a state and the verb **voir** *to see* expresses a sensation. A verb may also be defined by its role in the sentence or clause. It usually has a subject:

Je	**nage**		*I swim*
subject	*verb*		
Ma fille	**joue**	**au tennis**	*My daughter plays tennis*
subject	*verb*	*object*	

IRREGULAR VERBS

Life would be easier if all verbs behaved in a regular fashion. Unfortunately, all European languages have verbs which do not follow a set pattern and which are therefore commonly referred to as irregular verbs.

There are 30 useful verbs in the verb table which follows. Most are irregular but, all the same, most can be used as a pattern for a few other verbs.

Verb tables

Trente verbes utiles *(Thirty useful verbs)*

1 Four regular verbs (with subject pronouns: *je, tu, il, elle, on, nous, vous, ils, elles*)

Parler *to speak, to talk Past participle:* **parlé** *Present participle:* **parlant**

Present indicative Présent de l'indicatif	Perfect Passé composé	Imperfect Imparfait	Conditional Conditionnel	Future Futur	Present subjunctive Présent du subjonctif	Imperative Impératif
je parle	j'ai parlé	je parlais	je parlerais	je parlerai	(que) je parle	
tu parles	tu as parlé	tu parlais	tu parlerais	tu parleras	tu parles	parle
il/elle parle	il a parlé	il parlait	il parlerait	il parlera	il parle	
nous parlons	nous avons parlé	nous parlions	nous parlerions	nous parlerons	nous parlions	parlons
vous parlez	vous avez parlé	vous parliez	vous parleriez	vous parlerez	vous parliez	parlez
ils/elles parlent	ils ont parlé	ils parlaient	ils parleraient	ils parleront	ils parlent	

Remplir *to fill Past participle:* **rempli** *Present participle:* **remplissant**

Present indicative Présent de l'indicatif	Perfect Passé composé	Imperfect Imparfait	Conditional Conditionnel	Future Futur	Present subjunctive Présent du subjonctif	Imperative Impératif
je remplis	j'ai rempli	je remplissais	je remplirais	je remplirai	(que) je remplisse	
tu remplis	tu as rempli	tu remplissais	tu remplirais	tu rempliras	tu remplisses	remplis
il/elle remplit	il a rempli	il remplissait	il remplirait	il remplira	il remplisse	
nous remplissons	nous avons rempli	nous remplissions	nous remplirions	nous remplirons	nous remplissions	remplissions
vous remplissez	vous avez rempli	vous remplissiez	vous rempliriez	vous remplirez	vous remplissiez	remplissez
ils/elles remplissent	ils ont rempli	ils remplissaient	ils rempliraient	ils rempliront	ils remplissent	

Vendre to sell Past participle: **vendu** Present participle: **vendant**

Present indicative	Perfect	Imperfect	Conditional	Future	Present subjunctive	Imperative
je vends	j'ai vendu	je vendais	je vendrais	je vendrai	(que) je vende	
tu vends	tu as vendu	tu vendais	tu vendrais	tu vendras	tu vendes	vends
il/elle vend	il a vendu	il vendait	il vendrait	il vendra	il vende	
nous vendons	nous avons vendu	nous vendions	nous vendrions	nous vendrons	nous vendions	vendons
vous vendez	vous avez vendu	vous vendiez	vous vendriez	vous vendrez	vous vendiez	vendez
ils/elles vendent	ils ont vendu	ils vendaient	ils vendraient	ils vendront	ils vendent	

Se lever to get up Past participle: **levé** Present participle: **levant**

*Note that there is an accent on the first e of lever when the following syllable has a neutral sound, e.g. **je me lève, je me lèverai**.*

Present indicative	Perfect	Imperfect	Conditional	Future	Present subjunctive	Imperative
je me lève	je me suis levé(e)	je me levais	je me lèverais	je me lèverai	(que) je me lève	
tu te lèves	tu t'es levé(e)	tu te levais	tu te lèverais	tu te lèveras	tu te lèves	lève-toi
il/elle se lève	il(elle) s'est levé(e)	il se levait	il se lèverait	il se lèvera	il se lève	
nous nous levons	nous nous sommes levés(es)	nous nous levions	nous nous	nous nous lèverons	nous nous levions	levons-nous
vous vous levez	vous vous êtes levé(s)(es)(e)	vous vous leviez	vous vous lèveriez	vous vous lèverez	vous vous leviez	levez-vous
ils/elles se lèvent	ils se sont levés elles se sont levées	ils se levaient	ils se lèveraient	ils se lèveront	ils se lèvent	

2 Twenty-six irregular verbs

Present indicative	Perfect	Imperfect	Conditional	Future	Present subjunctive	Imperative

Aller to go Past participle: allé Present participle: allant

Present indicative	Perfect	Imperfect	Conditional	Future	Present subjunctive	Imperative
je vais	suis allé(e)	allais	irais	irai	aille	
tu vas	es allé(e)	allais	irais	iras	ailles	va
il/elle va	est allé(e)	allait	irait	ira	aille	
nous allons	sommes allés(e)	allions	irions	irons	allions	allons
vous allez	êtes allé(e)(s)(es)	alliez	iriez	irez	alliez	allez
ils/elles vont	sont allés(es)	allaient	iraient	iront	aillent	

S'asseoir to sit assis – asseyant

Present indicative	Perfect	Imperfect	Conditional	Future	Present subjunctive	Imperative
je m'assieds	me suis assis(e)	m'asseyais	m'assiérais	m'assiérai	m'asseye	
tu t'assieds	t'es assis(e)	t'asseyais	t'assiérais	t'assiéras	t'asseyes	assieds-toi
il/elle s'assied	s'est assis(e)	s'asseyait	s'assiérait	s'assiéra	s'asseye	
nous nous asseyons	nous sommes assis(es)	nous asseyions	nous assiérions	nous assiérons	nous asseyions	asseyons-nous
vous vous asseyez	vous êtes assis (e)(es)	vous asseyiez	vous assiériez	vous assiérez	vous asseyiez	asseyez-vous
ils/elles s'asseyent	se sont assis(es)	s'asseyaient	s'assiéraient	s'assiéront	s'asseyent	

Present indicative	Perfect	Imperfect	Conditional	Future	Present subjunctive	Imperative

Avoir to have: **eu – ayant**

Present indicative	Perfect	Imperfect	Conditional	Future	Present subjunctive	Imperative
j'ai	ai eu	avais	aurais	aurai	aie	
tu as	as eu	avais	aurais	auras	aies	aie
il/elle a	a eu	avait	aurait	aura	ait	
nous avons	avons eu	avions	aurions	aurons	ayons	ayons
vous avez	avez eu	aviez	auriez	aurez	ayez	ayez
ils/elles ont	ont eu	avaient	auraient	auront	aient	

Boire to drink: **bu – buvant**

Present indicative	Perfect	Imperfect	Conditional	Future	Present subjunctive	Imperative
je bois	ai bu	buvais	boirais	boirai	boive	
tu bois	as bu	buvais	boirais	boiras	boives	bois
il/elle boit	a bu	buvait	boirait	boira	boive	
nous buvons	avons bu	buvions	boirions	boirons	buvions	buvons
vous buvez	avez bu	buviez	boiriez	boirez	buviez	buvez
ils/elles boivent	ont bu	buvaient	boiraient	boiront	boivent	

Commencer to begin: **commencé – commençant**
(ç is necessary to keep the sound /s/ before a, o or u)

Present indicative	Perfect	Imperfect	Conditional	Future	Present subjunctive	Imperative
je commence	ai commencé	commençais	commencerais	commencerai	commence	
tu commences	as commencé	commençais	commencerais	commenceras	commences	commence
il/elle commence	a commencé	commençait	commencerait	commencera	commence	
nous commençons	avons commencé	commencions	commencerions	commencerons	commencions	commençons
vous commencez	avez commencé	commenciez	commenceriez	commencerez	commenciez	commencez
ils/elles commencent	ont commencé	commençaient	commenceraient	commenceront	commencent	

Conduire to drive: **conduit – conduisant**

Present indicative	Perfect	Imperfect	Conditional	Future	Present subjunctive	Imperative
je conduis	ai conduit	conduisais	conduirais	conduirai	conduise	
tu conduis	as conduit	conduisais	conduirais	conduiras	conduises	conduis
il/elle conduit	a conduit	conduisait	conduirait	conduira	conduise	
nous conduisons	avons conduit	conduisions	conduirions	conduirons	conduisions	conduisons
vous conduisez	avez conduit	conduisiez	conduiriez	conduirez	conduisiez	conduisez
ils/elles conduisent	ont conduit	conduisaient	conduiraient	conduiront	conduisent	

Present indicative	Perfect	Imperfect	Conditional	Future	Present subjunctive	Imperative

Connaître *to know:* connu – connaissant

Present indicative	Perfect	Imperfect	Conditional	Future	Present subjunctive	Imperative
je connais	ai connu	connaissais	connaîtrais	connaîtrai	connaisse	
tu connais	as connu	connaissais	connaîtrais	connaîtras	connaisses	connais
il/elle connaît	a connu	connaissait	connaîtrait	connaîtra	connaisse	
nous connaissons	avons connu	connaissions	connaîtrions	connaîtrons	connaissions	connaissons
vous connaissez	avez connu	connaissiez	connaîtriez	connaîtrez	connaissiez	connaissez
ils/elles connaissent	ont connu	connaissaient	connaîtraient	connaîtront	connaissent	

Croire *to believe:* cru – croyant

Present indicative	Perfect	Imperfect	Conditional	Future	Present subjunctive	Imperative
je crois	ai cru	croyais	croirais	croirai	croie	
tu crois	as cru	croyais	croirais	croiras	croies	crois
il/elle croit	a cru	croyait	croirait	croira	croie	
nous croyons	avons cru	croyions	croirions	croirons	croyions	croyons
vous croyez	avez cru	croyiez	croiriez	croirez	croyiez	croyez
ils/elles croient	ont cru	croyaient	croiraient	croiront	croient	

Devoir *to have to (I must):* dû – devant

Present indicative	Perfect	Imperfect	Conditional	Future	Present subjunctive	Imperative
je dois	ai dû	devais	devrais	devrai	doive	
tu dois	as dû	devais	devrais	devras	doives	dois
il/elle doit	a dû	devait	devrait	devra	doive	
nous devons	avons dû	devions	devrions	devrons	devions	devons
vous devez	avez dû	deviez	devriez	devrez	deviez	devez
ils/elles doivent	ont dû	devaient	devraient	devront	doivent	

Dire *to say:* dit – disant

Present indicative	Perfect	Imperfect	Conditional	Future	Present subjunctive	Imperative
je dis	ai dit	disais	dirais	dirai	dise	
tu dis	as dit	disais	dirais	diras	dises	dis
il/elle dit	a dit	disait	dirait	dira	dise	
nous disons	avons dit	disions	dirions	dirons	disions	disons
vous dites	avez dit	disiez	diriez	direz	disiez	dites
ils/elles disent	ont dit	disaient	diraient	diront	disent	

Present indicative	Perfect	Imperfect	Conditional	Future	Present subjunctive	Imperative

Entendre *to hear:* **entendu – entendant**

Present indicative	Perfect	Imperfect	Conditional	Future	Present subjunctive	Imperative
j'entends	ai entendu	entendais	entendrais	entendrai	entende	
tu entends	as entendu	entendais	entendrais	entendras	entendes	entends
il/elle entend	a entendu	entendait	entendrait	entendra	entende	
nous entendons	avons entendu	entendions	entendrions	entendrons	entendions	entendons
vous entendez	avez entendu	entendiez	entendriez	entendrez	entendiez	entendez
ils/elles entendent	ont entendu	entendaient	entendraient	entendront	entendent	

Envoyer *to send:* **envoyé – envoyant**

Present indicative	Perfect	Imperfect	Conditional	Future	Present subjunctive	Imperative
j'envoie	ai envoyé	envoyais	enverrais	enverrai	envoie	
tu envoies	as envoyé	envoyais	enverrais	enverras	envoies	envoie
il/elle envoie	a envoyé	envoyait	enverrait	enverra	envoie	
nous envoyons	avons envoyé	envoyions	enverrions	enverrons	envoyions	envoyons
vous envoyez	avez envoyé	envoyiez	enverriez	enverrez	envoyiez	envoyez
ils/elles envoient	ont envoyé	envoyaient	enverraient	enverront	envoient	

Être *to be:* **été – étant**

Present indicative	Perfect	Imperfect	Conditional	Future	Present subjunctive	Imperative
je suis	ai été	étais	serais	serai	sois	
tu es	as été	étais	serais	seras	sois	sois
il/elle est	a été	était	serait	sera	soit	
nous sommes	avons été	étions	serions	serons	soyons	soyons
vous êtes	avez été	étiez	seriez	serez	soyez	soyez
ils/elles sont	ont été	étaient	seraient	seront	soient	

Faire *to do, to make:* **fait – faisant**

Present indicative	Perfect	Imperfect	Conditional	Future	Present subjunctive	Imperative
je fais	ai fait	faisais	ferais	ferai	fasse	
tu fais	as fait	faisais	ferais	feras	fasses	fais
il/elle fait	a fait	faisait	ferait	fera	fasse	
nous faisons	avons fait	faisions	ferions	ferons	fassions	faisons
vous faites	avez fait	faisiez	feriez	ferez	fassiez	faites
ils/elles font	ont fait	faisaient	feraient	feront	fassent	

Present indicative	Perfect	Imperfect	Conditional	Future	Present subjunctive	Imperative

Falloir *to be necessary (impersonal only): Past participle:* **fallu** *No present participle*

il faut	il a fallu	il fallait	il faudrait	il faudra	(qu')il faille	

Manger *to eat:* **mangé – mangeant**
(**e** is added after the **g** in order to keep the soft sound before **a**, **o** and **u**)

Present indicative	Perfect	Imperfect	Conditional	Future	Present subjunctive	Imperative
je mange	ai mangé	mangeais	mangerais	mangerai	mange	
tu manges	as mangé	mangeais	mangerais	mangeras	manges	mange
il/elle mange	a mangé	mangeait	mangerait	mangera	mange	
nous mangeons	avons mangé	mangions	mangerions	mangerons	mangions	mangeons
vous mangez	avez mangé	mangiez	mangeriez	mangerez	mangiez	mangez
ils/elles mangent	ont mangé	mangeaient	mangeraient	mangeront	mangent	

Mettre *to put:* **mis – mettant**

Present indicative	Perfect	Imperfect	Conditional	Future	Present subjunctive	Imperative
je mets	ai mis	mettais	mettrais	mettrai	mette	
tu mets	as mis	mettais	mettrais	mettras	mettes	mets
il/elle met	a mis	mettait	mettrait	mettra	mette	
nous mettons	avons mis	mettions	mettrions	mettrons	mettions	mettons
vous mettez	avez mis	mettiez	mettriez	mettrez	mettiez	mettez
ils/elles mettent	ont mis	mettaient	mettraient	mettront	mettent	

Ouvrir *to open:* **ouvert – ouvrant**

Present indicative	Perfect	Imperfect	Conditional	Future	Present subjunctive	Imperative
j'ouvre	ai ouvert	ouvrais	ouvrirais	ouvrirai	ouvre	
tu ouvres	as ouvert	ouvrais	ouvrirais	ouvriras	ouvres	ouvre
il/elle ouvre	a ouvert	ouvrait	ouvrirait	ouvrira	ouvre	
nous ouvrons	avons ouvert	ouvrions	ouvririons	ouvrirons	ouvrions	ouvrons
vous ouvrez	avez ouvert	ouvriez	ouvririez	ouvrirez	ouvriez	ouvrez
ils/elles ouvrent	ont ouvert	ouvraient	ouvriraient	ouvriront	ouvrent	

Present indicative	Perfect	Imperfect	Conditional	Future	Present subjunctive	Imperative

Pleuvoir to rain (impersonal only): plu – pleuvant

Present indicative	Perfect	Imperfect	Conditional	Future	Present subjunctive	Imperative
il pleut	il a plu	il pleuvait	il pleuvrait	il pleuvra	(qu')il pleuve	

Pouvoir to be able to (I can): pu – pouvant

Present indicative	Perfect	Imperfect	Conditional	Future	Present subjunctive	Imperative
je peux	ai pu	pouvais	pourrais	pourrai	puisse	
tu peux	as pu	pouvais	pourrais	pourras	puisses	
il/elle peut	a pu	pouvait	pourrait	pourra	puisse	
nous pouvons	avons pu	pouvions	pourrions	pourrons	puissions	
vous pouvez	avez pu	pouviez	pourriez	pourrez	puissiez	
ils/elles peuvent	ont pu	pouvaient	pourraient	pourront	puissent	

Prendre to take: pris – prenant

Present indicative	Perfect	Imperfect	Conditional	Future	Present subjunctive	Imperative
je prends	ai pris	prenais	prendrais	prendrai	prenne	
tu prends	as pris	prenais	prendrais	prendras	prennes	prends
il/elle prend	a pris	prenait	prendrait	prendra	prenne	
nous prenons	avons pris	prenions	prendrions	prendrons	prenions	prenons
vous prenez	avez pris	preniez	prendriez	prendrez	preniez	prenez
ils/elles prennent	ont pris	prenaient	prendraient	prendront	prennent	

Savoir to know: su – sachant

Present indicative	Perfect	Imperfect	Conditional	Future	Present subjunctive	Imperative
je sais	ai su	savais	saurais	saurai	sache	
tu sais	as su	savais	saurais	sauras	saches	sache
il/elle sait	a su	savait	saurait	saura	sache	
nous savons	avons su	savions	saurions	saurons	sachions	sachons
vous savez	avez su	saviez	sauriez	saurez	sachiez	sachez
ils/elles savent	ont su	savaient	sauraient	sauront	sachent	

Present indicative	Perfect	Imperfect	Conditional	Future	Present subjunctive	Imperative

Sortir *to go out*: **sorti – sortant**

Present indicative	Perfect	Imperfect	Conditional	Future	Present subjunctive	Imperative
je sors	suis sorti(e)	sortais	sortirais	sortirai	sorte	
tu sors	es sorti(e)	sortais	sortirais	sortiras	sortes	sors
il/elle sort	est sorti(e)	sortait	sortirait	sortira	sorte	
nous sortons	sommes sortis(es)	sortions	sortirions	sortirons	sortions	sortons
vous sortez	êtes sorti(e)(s) (es)	sortiez	sortiriez	sortirez	sortiez	sortez
ils/elles sortent	sont sortis(es)	sortaient	sortiraient	sortiront	sortent	

Venir *to come*: **venu – venant**

Present indicative	Perfect	Imperfect	Conditional	Future	Present subjunctive	Imperative
je viens	suis venu(e)	venais	viendrais	viendrai	vienne	
tu viens	es venu(e)	venais	viendrais	viendras	viennes	viens
il/elle vient	est venu(e)	venait	viendrait	viendra	vienne	
nous venons	sommes venus(es)	venions	viendrions	viendrons	venions	venons
vous venez	êtes venu(e)(s) (es)	veniez	viendriez	viendrez	veniez	venez
ils/elles viennent	sont venus(es)	venaient	viendraient	viendront	viennent	

Voir *to see*: **vu – voyant**

Present indicative	Perfect	Imperfect	Conditional	Future	Present subjunctive	Imperative
je vois	ai vu	voyais	verrais	verrai	voie	
tu vois	as vu	voyais	verrais	verras	voies	voie
il/elle voit	a vu	voyait	verrait	verra	voie	
nous voyons	avons vu	voyions	verrions	verrons	voyions	voyons
voys voyez	avez vu	voyiez	verriez	verrez	voyiez	voyez
ils/elles voient	ont vu	voyaient	verraient	verront	voient	

Vouloir *to want*: **voulu – voulant**

Present indicative	Perfect	Imperfect	Conditional	Future	Present subjunctive	Imperative
je veux	ai voulu	voulais	voudrais	voudrai	veuille	
tu veux	as voulu	voulais	voudrais	voudras	veuilles	veuille
il/elle veut	a voulu	voulait	voudrait	voudra	veuille	
nous voulons	avons voulu	voulions	voudrions	voudrons	voulions	veuillons
vous voulez	avez voulu	vouliez	voudriez	voudrez	vouliez	veuillez
ils/elles veulent	ont voulu	voulaient	voudraient	voudront	veuillent	

French–English vocabulary

à *prep to; at; with*
abonné *nmf subscriber; season ticket holder*
abonnement *nm subscription; season ticket*
d'abord *phr first*
absolument *adv absolutely*
accident *nm accident; hitch; mishap*
accompagner *vtr to accompany, to go with*
accord *nm agreement;* **je suis d'~** *I agree*
accueil *nm welcome, reception; reception desk*
accueil *adj* **page d'** *– home page (computer)*

accueillant, -e *adj hospitable, welcoming*
accueillir *vtr to welcome; to receive; to greet*
acheter *vtr to buy*
acheteur, -euse *nmf buyer, purchaser*
acquéreur *nm buyer, purchaser*
acquérir *vtr to acquire; to purchase*
acquisition *nf purchase*
acteur, -trice *nmf actor/actress*
actif, -ive *adj active;* **la vie active** *working life*
activité *nf activity*
actuel, -elle *adj present, current*
addition *nf bill*

adieu *goodbye, farewell*

adorer *vtr to adore*

adresse *nf address*

s'adresser à qn *v refl (+ v être) to speak to sb*

aéroport *nm airport*

affiche *nf poster*

agaçant, -e *adj annoying, irritating*

âge *nm age*

agence *nf agency;* ~ **immobilière** *estate agents*

agglomération *nf town; (smaller) village*

agir *to act;* **s'agir de** *v impers* **de quoi s'agit-il?** *what is it about?; what's the matter?*

agréable *adj nice, pleasant*

aider *vtr to help*

ail, *pl* ~**s** *or* **aulx** *nm garlic*

ailleurs *adv elsewhere* **d'ailleurs** *phr besides*

aimable *adj pleasant; kind; polite*

aimer *vtr to love; to like, to be fond of*

ainsi *adv thus*

ajouter *vtr to add (***à** *to)*

alcool *nm alcohol*

alentour *adv* **la ville et la région** ~ *the town and surrounding area*

alimentation *nf food;* **magasin d'** ~ *food shop, grocery store*

Allemagne *nf Germany*

allemand, ~**e** *adj German; nm (lang) German*

aller *vi to go; v aux* **je vais apprendre l'italien** *I'm going to learn Italian* **comment ça va?** *how are you? to go;* **s'en aller** *v refl (+ v être) to go, to leave*

allumer *vtr to light*

alors *adv then*

améliorer *vtr* **s'améliorer** *refl (+ v être) to improve*

aménagement *nm development*

aménager *vtr to convert; to do up [house, attic]*

amener *vtr to accompany, to bring sb*

américain *adj American*

ami, -e *nmf friend*

amitié *nf friendship*

amusant, ~**e** *adj entertaining; funny*

amuser *vtr to entertain;* **s'amuser** *v refl (+ v être) to have fun, to play;* **pour s'**~ *for fun*

an *nm year*

ancien, -ienne *adj old*

anglais, ~**e** *adj English*

Anglais, ~**e** *nmf Englishman/ Englishwoman*

Angleterre *nf England*

animal, ~**e,** *mpl* -**aux** *animal*

animateur, -trice *nmf coordinator*

animer *vtr to lead*

année *nf year*

anniversaire *nm birthday*

août *nm August*

apercevoir *vtr to make out; to catch sight of*

apéritif *nm drink*

à-peu-près *nm inv approximation*

appareil *nm appliance; telephone;* ~ *photo camera*

appartement *nm flat*

appeler *vtr to call*

s'appeler *v refl (+ v être)* **comment t'appelles-tu?** *what's your name?*

appétit *nm appetite*

apprendre *vtr to learn*

apprenti ~**e** *nmf apprentice*

apprentissage *nm apprenticeship*

après *adv afterward(s), after; later*

après-midi nm/nf inv afternoon

argent *nm money; silver*

arrêter *vtr to stop*

arrière *adj inv back*

arriver *(+ v* **être***) vi to arrive*

arrondissement *nm administrative division*

s'asseoir *v refl (+ v* **être***) to sit down*

assez *adv enough*

attendre *vtr to wait for*

au *prep (=* **à le***) see* **à**

auberge *nf inn;* **~ de jeunesse** *youth hostel*

aujourd'hui *adv today*

aussi *adv too, as well, also*

aussitôt *adv immediately*

auteur *nm author*

autocar *nm coach*

automne *nm autumn*

autoroute *nf motorway*

autour de *phr around*

autre *other*

avant *adv before*

avant-hier *adv the day before yesterday*

avec *prep with*

avenir *nm future*

averse *nf shower (rain)*

avion *nm plane*

avis *nm inv opinion*

avocat *nm lawyer*

avoir *vtr to have*

avril *nm April*

bagage *nm piece of luggage*

baguette *nf French stick*

bain *nm bath*

balcon *nm balcony*

banlieue *nf suburbs*

bar-tabac *nm café (selling stamps and cigarettes)*

bas, basse *adj low*

bateau *nm boat, ship*

bâtonnier *nm president of the Bar*

bavarder *vi to talk to, to chatter*

beau, belle *adj beautiful; handsome; good; fine*

beaucoup *adv a lot*

beau-frère *nm brother-in-law*

Belgique *nf Belgium*

belle-mère *nf mother-in-law*

belle-sœur *nf sister-in-law*

besoin *nm need* **avoir ~ de** *to need*

bête *adj stupid, silly*

beur *nmf second-generation North African (living in France) (slang)*

beurre *nm butter*

bibliothèque *nf library*

bicyclette *nf bicycle*

bien *adj inv good; adv well*

bien que *phr although*

bière *nf beer*

bijou *nm piece of jewellery*

bilan *nm outcome, result*

bilingue *adj bilingual*

blanc, blanche *adj white*

blessé, ~e *nmf injured or wounded man/ woman*

blessure *nf injury*

bleu ~e *adj blue*

bois *nm inv wood*

boisson *nf drink*

boîte *nf box; tin*

bon, bonne *adj good*

bonne-maman *nf grandma*

bord *nm* **le ~ de la mer** *the seaside*

bouche *nf mouth*

bouche-à-oreille *nm inv* **le ~** *word of mouth*

boucher, -ère *nmf butcher*

boucherie *nf butcher's shop*

bouchon *nm cork*

bouillir *vi to boil*

boulanger, -ère *nmf baker*

boulangerie *nf bakery*

bout *nm end; tip*

briser *vtr to break*

brouillard *nm fog*

bruit *nm noise*

brûler *vtr to burn*

bureau *nm office*

ça *that; this*

caisse *nf cash desk*

carrefour *nm crossroads*

carte *nf card;* **~ à puce** *smart card*

en tout cas *phr in any case*

case *nf box (on form)*

casserole *nf saucepan, pan*

cave *nf cellar*

céder *vtr* **~ le passage** *to give way*

celui / celle / ceux / celles *pron the one(s)*

celui-ci / celle-ci / ceux-ci / celles-ci *this one; these*

celui-là *pron that one*

cent *adj a hundred*

chacun, -e *each*

chambre *nf bedroom; room*

champignon *nm mushroom*

change *nm exchange rate*

chaque *each, every*

charcuterie *nf pork butcher's*

se charger *v refl (+ v* **être***)* **se ~ de** *to take responsibility for*

chat *nm cat*

château *nm castle*

chaud *adj hot*

chaussure *nf shoe*

chauvin ~e *adj chauvinistic*

cher, chère *adj dear*

chercher *vtr to look for*

cheveu *nm hair*

chèvre *nm goat('s cheese)*

chez *prep* **~ qn** *at sb's place*

chien *nm dog*

chiffre *nm figure*

chinois, ~e *adj Chinese*

chômage *nm unemployment*

chose *nf thing*

chou *nm cabbage*

ciel *nm sky*

clos *adj closed*

cocher *tr to tick*

coffre *nm (of car) boot*

coin *nm corner*

collège *nm secondary school*

combien de *how many, how much*

comme *conj as*

comment *adv how*

comprendre *vtr to understand*

compter *vtr to count*

concours *nm inv competition*

conduire *vtr to drive*

conduite *nf (of vehicle) driving*

confiture *nf jam*

connaître *vtr to know*

conseil *nm advice*

contre *prep against*

convenu, -e *adj agreed*

copain, copine *nmf friend; boyfriend/ girlfriend*

corps *nm inv body*

à côte *phr nearby*

se coucher *v refl (+ v* **être***) to go to bed*

coup *blow;* **donner un ~ de pied** *to kick*

couper *vtr to cut;* **se couper** *to cut oneself*

couramment *adv fluently*

courir *vi to run*

courriel *nf e-mail*

court ~e *adj short*

couteau *nm knife*

coûter *vtr to cost*

couvert *adj [sky] overcast;* **mettre le ~** *to lay the table*

crêpe *nf pancake*

crever *vtr puncture*

croire *vtr to believe*

cuillère *nf spoon*

cuillerée *nf spoonful*

cuire *vtr to cook*

cuisine *nf kitchen; cooking*

dans *prep in*

déboucher *vtr to uncork*

début *nm beginning; start*

découvrir *vtr to discover*

défense *nf* **'~ de fumer'** *'no smoking'*

défi nm challenge

dehors adv outside

déjà adv already

déjeuner vi to have lunch; nm lunch

demain adv tomorrow

demander vtr to ask for

déménagement nm moving house

déménager vtr to move (furniture)

demeurer to reside, to live

demi, ~e nmf half

demi-heure nf half an hour

demi-tarif adv half-price

dent nf tooth

dentifrice nm toothpaste

dépanner vtr to fix [car, machine]

départ nm departure

déprimer vtr to depress; vi to be depressed

depuis adv since

dernier, -ière adj last

derrière prep behind

dès que phr as soon as

descendre vtr (+ v **avoir**) to go down, to come down sth; vi to go down (+ v **être**)

désolé pp adj sorry

dessous adv underneath; **en dessous** phr underneath

dessus adv on top

devant prep in front of

devenir vi (+ v **être**) to become

deviner vtr to guess

devoir v aux to have to

diététique adj dietary; nf dietetics

dingue adj (person) crazy (slang)

dire vtr to say

doigt nm finger

donc conj so, therefore

donner vtr to give

dormir vi to sleep

dos nm inv back; **mal de ~** backache

douche nf shower

droit, -e adj straight

droite nf right; **tourner à ~** to turn right

dur, -e adj hard

durée nf length

eau nf water

ébullition nf boiling

école nf school

écrire vtr to write

éditeur, -trice nmf editor, publisher

en effet phr indeed

église nf church

embouteillage nm traffic jam

embrasser vtr to kiss

embrumé, ~e adj misty

emmener vtr to take

emploi nm job; employment

employé, ~e nmf employee

emporter vtr to take [object]; **pizzas à** takeaway pizzas

en prep in; into

encore adv still; again

endroit nm place

enfant nmf child

enfin adv finally

ennuyeux, -euse adj boring

enregistrer vtr to check in (baggage)

enseignant, ~e nmf teacher

enseigner vtr to teach

ensoleillé adj sunny

ensuite adv then

entendre vtr to hear

entier, -ière adj whole

entre prep between

entrée nf entrance; starter

entrer vi to come in

envie nf **avoir ~ de qch** to feel like sth

envoyer vtr to send

épais, épaisse adj thick

épicerie nf grocer's (shop)

éplucher vtr to peel

époux nm inv husband

équilibre nm balance

équipage nm crew

équipe nf team

escalier nm staircase; stairs

Espagne nf Spain

espagnol, -e adj Spanish nm **l'** Spanish

espérer vtr to hope

essayer vtr to try

essence nf petrol

essuie-glace nm windscreen wiper

étage nm floor

été nm summer

être vi (+ v avoir) to be

étudiant, -e nmf student

extrait nm (from book, film) extract

fabriquer vtr to make

en face de phr **en ~ de l'église** opposite the church, across from the church

facile adj easy

façon nf way; **de toute ~** anyway

faim nf hunger **avoir ~** to be hungry

faire vtr to make

faire-part nm inv announcement

faisable adj **c'est ~** it can be done

au fait phr by the way

falloir v impers **il faut qch/qn** we need sth/sb

familial, -e adj (meal, life, firm) family

famille nf family

fatigant, ~e adj tiring

fatiguer vtr to make [sb/sth] tired

fauteuil nm armchair; **roulant** wheelchair

faux, fausse adj wrong

féliciter vtr to congratulate

femme nf woman

fenêtre nf window

fer nm iron; **~ à repasser** iron

ferme nf farm, farmhouse

fermer vtr to close

fête nf public holiday; name-day

feu nm fire

février nm February

fille nf daughter; girl

fillette nf little girl

fils nm inv son

fin, fine adj fine; [slice, layer] thin

finir vtr to finish

fois nf inv (with numerals) **une ~** once; **deux ~** twice

fort, ~e adj strong

fou, folle adj mad

four nm oven

fourchette nf fork

frais, fraîche adj cool; cold; fresh

fraise nf strawberry

framboise nf raspberry

frère nm brother

frigo nm fridge

froid, -e adj cold

fromage nm cheese

gagner vtr to win

galette nf pancake

Galles nf pl **le pays de ~** Wales

gamin, -e nmf kid

garçon nm boy

gâteau, pl **-x** nm cake

gauche nf left

genou, pl **-x** nm knee

genre nm sort, kind, type

gens nm pl people

gestion nf management

gîte nm shelter; **~ rural** self-catering cottage

gonflé, -e adj inflated

gonfler vtr to inflate [tyre]

goût nm taste; palate

goûter nm snack

grand, -e adj [person, tree, tower] tall

grand-mère nf grandmother

grand-père nm grandfather

gras, grasse adj [substance] fatty

gratter vtr to scratch

gratuit, -e adj free

grave adj [problem, injury] serious

gris, -e adj grey

gros, grosse adj big, large; thick

habiller vtr to dress; **s'habiller** v refl (+ v être) to get dressed

habitation *nf house*

halle *nf covered market*

haricot *nm bean;* **~ vert** *French bean*

haut, **-e** *adj high; tall*

hébergement *nm accommodation*

héberger *vtr to put [sb] up*

heure *nf hour;* **l'~ d'arrivée** *the arrival time;* **~s d'ouverture** *opening times*

hier *adv yesterday*

histoire *nf history*

hiver *nm winter*

homme *nm man*

hors-d'œuvre *nm inv starter*

humide *adj damp*

ici *adv here*

immatriculation *nf registration*

immeuble *nm building*

immobilier *nm* **l' ~** *property*

imprimerie *nf printing*

incendie *nm fire*

infirmier *nm male nurse*

infirmière *nf nurse*

information *nf* **écouter les ~s** *to listen to the news*

inquiet, **-iète** *adj anxious; worried.* **s'inquiéter** *v refl (+ v* **être***) to worry*

interdit, **-e** *pp adj prohibited, forbidden*

intéresser *vtr to interest* **ça ne m'intéresse pas** *I'm not interested*

irlandais, **-e** *adj Irish nm Irish*

italien, **-ienne** *adj Italian nm Italian*

jamais *adv never*

jambe *nf leg*

jambon *nm ham*

jardin *nm garden*

jaune *adj yellow*

je *(***j'** *before vowel or mute* **h***) I*

jeu, *pl* **-x** *nm game*

jeu-concours *nm competition*

jeudi *nm Thursday*

jeune *adj young*

jeunesse *nf youth*

joli **-e** *adj (gen) nice; [face] pretty*

jouer *vtr to play*

jour *nm day*

journal, *pl* **-aux** *nm newspaper*

journée *nf day*

juillet *nm July*

jus *nm inv juice*

jusque-là *adv until then, up to here*

juste *adv right, just*

justement *adv precisely*

là *adv there; here*

là-bas *adv over there*

laisser *vtr to leave*

lait *nm milk*

lancer *vtr to throw*

large *adj broad; wide*

lavabo *nm washbasin, washbowl*

laver *vtr to wash* **se laver** *v refl (+ v* **être***) to wash;* **se ~ les mains** *to wash one's hands*

le, **la** *(***l'** *before vowel or mute* **h***), pl* **les** *the*

lecture *nf reading*

léger, **-ère** *adj light*

lent, *-e adj slow*

lequel / laquelle / lesquels / lesquelles *adj who; which*

se lever *v refl (+ v être) to get up*

liaison *nf link*

librairie *nf bookshop*

libre-service *adj inv self-service*

lieu *nm place;* **au lieu de** *phr instead of*

lire *vtr to read*

livre *nm book*

locataire *nmf tenant*

location *nf renting*

logement *nm accommodation*

loin *adv a long way,* **c'est trop ~** *it's too far*

loisir *nm spare time; leisure*

Londres *n London*

longtemps *adv a long time*

louer *vtr [owner, landlord] to let; to rent out*

lourd, -e *adj heavy*

lumière *nf light*

lundi *nm Monday*

lune *nf moon*

lunettes *nf pl glasses;* **~ de soleil** *sunglasses*

lycée *nm secondary school (school preparing students aged 15-18 for the Baccalauréat)*

madame, *pl* **mesdames** *Mrs; a woman whose name you do not know*

mademoiselle, *pl* **mesdemoiselles** *Miss; a woman whose name you do not know*

magnétophone *nm tape recorder*

magnétoscope *nm video recorder, VCR*

maigre *adj [person] thin; [cheese] low-fat*

main *nf hand*

mairie *nf town council*

mais *conj but*

maison *nf house; home*

mal, *pl* **maux** *adj bad, wrong; nm pain;* **avoir ~ partout** *to ache all over;* **avoir ~ à la tête** *to have a headache*

malade *adj [person] ill, sick*

malgré *prep in spite of, despite*

malheureusement *adv unfortunately*

Manche *nf the Channel;* **le tunnel sous la ~** *the Channel tunnel*

manger *vtr to eat;* **il n'y a rien à ~ dans la maison** *there's no food in the house*

manière *nf way;* **d'une ~ ou d'une autre** *in one way or another*

manoir *nm manor (house)*

manquer *vtr to miss*

manquer de *v + prep to lack;* **on ne manque de rien** *we don't want for anything*

manteau, *pl* **-x** *nm coat*

marcher *vi to walk; to work;* **ma radio marche mal** *my radio doesn't work properly*

mardi *nm Tuesday*

marée *nf tide;* **à ~ haute/basse** *at high/ low tide*

marémoteur, -trice *adj tidal;* **usine marémotrice** *tidal power station*

mari *nm husband*

marié, -e *pp adj married*

se marier *v refl (+ v* **être***) to get married (***avec qn** *to sb)*

mars *nm inv March*

matin *nm morning*

mauvais, -e *adj bad*

mécanicien, -ienne *nmf mechanic*

Méditerranée *nf la (mer) ~ the Mediterranean*

meilleur, -e *adj better; best;* **le ~ des deux** *the better of the two*

mélanger *vtr to mix*

même *adj same; adv even; phr* **agir** *or* **faire de** *~ to do the same*

ménage *nm household; housework;* **faire le ~** *to do the cleaning*

mensuel, -elle *adj monthly; nm monthly magazine*

menteur, -euse *nmf liar*

mentir *vi to lie, to tell lies*

mer *nf sea*

merci *nm thank you*

mercredi *nm Wednesday*

mère *nf mother*

météo *nf weather forecast*

métier *nm job; profession*

métro *nm underground*

mettre *vtr to put*

meuble *nm des ~s furniture*

meublé *nm furnished flat*

meubler *vtr to furnish*

miam-miam *excl yum-yum!*

micro-ondes *nm inv microwave*

midi *nm twelve o'clock, midday, noon; lunchtime;* **le Midi** *the South of France*

miel *nm honey*

le mien, la mienne, les miens, les miennes *mine*

mieux *adj inv* better; **le ~, la ~, les ~** the best

milieu *nm* middle; **au ~ de la nuit** in the middle of the night

mille *adj inv* a thousand, one thousand

milliard *nm* billion

mince *[person, leg]* slim, slender

minuit *nm* midnight

mi-temps *nm inv* part-time job; **elle travaille à ~** she works part-time

mobilier, -ière *adj* **biens ~s** movable property

mobylette® *nf* moped

moi I, me; **c'est ~** it's me

moi-même myself

moins minus; **il est huit heures ~ dix** it's ten (minutes) to eight; *adv (comparative)* less

à moins de *phr* unless

au moins *phr* at least

mois *nm inv* month

moitié *nf* half; **à ~ vide** half empty

môme *nmf* kid; brat *(slang)*

mon, ma *pl* **mes** my

monde *nm* world; people; **tout le ~** everybody

moniteur, -trice *nmf* group leader

monnaie *nf* currency; change

monsieur, *pl* **messieurs** *nm* Mr

montagne *nf* mountain

monter *vtr (+ v avoir)* to go up sth; *vi (+ être)*; **tu es monté à pied?** did you walk up?

montrer *vtr* to show

mordre *vtr* to bite

morsure *nf* bite

mort *nf* death

mort, -e *adj* dead; **je suis ~ de froid** I'm freezing to death

mot *nm* word

moule *nf* mussel

mourir *vi (+ v être)* to die

moyen, -enne *adj [height, size]* medium; medium sized; *[price]* moderate

municipal, ~e *adj [council]* local, town

mur *nm* wall

musée *nm* museum; art gallery

nager *vtr* to swim

nageur, -euse *nmf* swimmer

naissance *nf* birth

naître *vi (+ v être)* to be born; **elle est née le 5 juin** she was born on 5 June

naturellement *adv* naturally

né, -e *pp see* **naître**

nécessaire *adj* necessary

neige *nf* snow

neiger *v impers* to snow; **il neige** it's snowing

n'est-ce pas *adv* **c'est joli, ~?** it's pretty, isn't it?

net, nette *adj [price, weight]* net

nettoyage *nm* cleanup

neuf nine

neuf, neuve *adj* new

neveu, *pl* **-x** *nm* nephew

nez *nm* nose

ni *conj* nor, or

Noël *nm* Christmas; **'Joyeux ~'** Merry Christmas

noir *adj* black

nom *nm* name; **~ et prénom** full name

nombre *nm* number

nombreux, -euse *adj* numerous, many

non *adv* no

nord *adj inv* north; northern

nord-africain, -e *adj* North African

nord-ouest *adj inv* northwest

notaire *nm* notary public

notre, *pl* **nos** our

nourriture *nf* food

nous *(subject)* we; *(object)* us

nous-même, *pl* **nous-mêmes** ourselves

nouveau (nouvel before vowel or mute **h), nouvelle** *adj* new

nouveau-né *adj* newborn

nuage *nm cloud*

nuageux, -euse *adj [sky] cloudy*

nuit *nf night*

nulle part *phr nowhere*

nullement *adv not at all*

numéro *nm number* **~ de téléphone** *telephone number* ~ **d'abonné** *customer's number;* ~ **d'appel gratuit** *freefone number*

obligatoire *compulsory; inevitable*

occupant, -e *occupant*

occupé, ~e *[person, life] busy; [seat] taken; [phone] engaged*

s'occuper *v refl (+ v* **être**) **s'~ de** *to see to, to take care of [dinner, tickets]*

œil, *pl* **yeux** *nm eye*

offre *nf offer;* **répondre à une ~ d'emploi** *to reply to a job advertisement*

oignon *nm onion*

oiseau, *pl* **-x** *nm bird*

oncle *nm uncle*

onze *eleven*

orage *nm storm*

orageux, -euse *stormy; thundery*

ordinaire *adj ordinary*

ordinateur *nm computer*

oreille *nf ear*

oreiller *nm pillow*

organisateur, -trice *nmf organizer*

orthographe *nf spelling*

os *nm inv bone*

ou *conj or*

où *adv where*

oublier *vtr to forget [name, date, fact]*

ouf *phew!*

oui *yes*

outil *nm tool*

ouvert, -e *adj open*

ouvrable *adj [day] working; [hours] business*

ouvre-boîtes *nm inv tin-opener*

ouvrier, -ière *nmf worker; workman*

ouvrir *vtr to open*

paiement *nm payment*

pain *nm bread*

pancarte *nf notice*

panier *nm basket*

panneau *nm sign;* ~ **indicateur** *signpost*

pantalon *nm trousers*

papeterie *nf stationer's (shop), stationery shop*

papier *nm paper*

Pâques *nm, nf pl Easter*

par *prep* **elle est arrivée ~ la droite** *she came from the right;* **régler** *or* **payer ~ carte de crédit** *to pay by credit card*

paradis *nm inv heaven; paradise*

paraître *vi to appear, to seem, to look*

parapluie *nm umbrella*

parc *nm park*

parce que *phr because*

pardon *nm forgiveness; pardon;* **je te demande ~** *I'm sorry* ~! *sorry!*

pare-chocs *nm inv bumper*

pareil, -eille *adj similar*

paresse *nf laziness*

paresseux, -euse *adj lazy*

parfait, -e *adj perfect*

parfaitement *adv perfectly*

parfois *adv sometimes*

parier *vtr to bet*

parisien, -ienne *adj Parisian*

parler *vtr to speak*

parmi *prep among, amongst*

part *nf (of food) slice, helping*

partager *vtr to share*

partir *vi (+ v* **être**) *to leave*

partout *adv everywhere*

pas *adv* **je ne prends ~ de sucre** *I don't take sugar*

passager, -ère *nmf passenger*

passant, -e *nmf passer-by*

passer *vtr to cross; to go through*

patin nm skate; **~ à roulettes** roller skate

pâtissier, -ière nmf confectioner, pastry cook

patron, -onne nmf boss

pauvre adj poor

payer vtr to pay for

pays nm country

péage nm toll

peau nf skin

pêche nm peach; **avoir la ~** to be feeling great

pêcher vtr to go fishing for

peine nf sorrow, grief; **avoir de la ~** to feel sad or upset

pellicule nf film

se pencher v refl (+ v être) to lean

pendant prep for; **je t'ai attendu ~ des heures** I waited for you for hours

penser vtr to think

Pentecôte nf Whitsun

perdre vtr to lose

père nm father

permettre vtr ~ **à qn de faire** to allow sb to do

permis nm **~ de conduire** driver's licence

petit, -e adj small, little; short

petite-fille nf granddaughter

petit-fils nm grandson

petits-enfants nm pl grandchildren

peu adv not much

peut-être adv perhaps, maybe

phare nm headlight

pharmacie nm chemist's (shop)

pharmacien, -ienne nmf (dispensing) chemist

pièce nf room

pied nm foot

pierre nf stone

piéton, -onne adj pedestrianized; nmf pedestrian

piqûre nf injection, shot; sting; bite

placard nm cupboard

plage nf beach

plaisanter vi to joke

plan, nm map; (in building) plan, map

planche nf ~ **à voile** windsurfing board

plateau, pl **-x** tray (**de** of)

plein, -e adj full

pleurer vi to cry

pleuvoir v impers to rain; **il pleut** it's raining

pluie nf rain

la plupart nf inv most

plus adv more; **le ~** the most; **de plus** phr furthermore; **une fois de ~** once more, once again

plusieurs adj several

plutôt adv rather; fairly

pluvieux, -ieuse adj wet, rainy

pneu nm tyre

poids nm inv weight

poignée nf ~ **de main** handshake

point nm ~ **de suture** (Med) stitch; ~ **de vue** point of view

pointure nf shoe size

poire nf pear

pois nm **petit ~** (garden) pea

poisson nm fish

poivre nm pepper

poivrer vtr to add pepper to [sauce]

pôle emploi French employment agency

poli, -e adj polite

pomme nf apple; **~ de terre** potato; **~s frites** chips

pompe nf ~ **à essence** petrol pump

pompier, -ière nm fireman

pont nm bridge; deck

populaire adj working-class

portail nm gateway, portal (computer)

portefeuille nm wallet

porter vtr to carry

portugais adj Portuguese nm Portuguese

poulet nm chicken

pour prep to; **~ faire** to do; in order to do; for; **le train ~ Paris** the train for Paris

pourquoi *why*

pourtant *adv though*

pousser *vtr to push*

pouvoir *v aux to be able to;* **peux-tu soulever cette boîte?** *can you lift this box?*

pratique *adj practical; convenient*

pratiquer *vtr to play [tennis]; to practise*

préavis *nm inv notice;* **déposer un ~ de grève** *to give notice of strike action*

premier, -ière *adj; first*

prendre *vtr to take;* **je vais ~ du poisson** *I'll have fish;* **aller ~ une bière** *to go for a beer*

prénom *nm first name, forename*

près *adv close;* **à peu ~ vide** *phr practically empty*

presque *adv almost, nearly*

prêt, -e *adj ready*

preuve *nf proof*

prévenir *vtr to tell; to warn*

prévision *nf forecasting;* **~s météorologiques** *weather forecast*

printemps *nm inv spring*

prix *nm inv price*

prochain, ~e *adj next*

proche *adj nearby*

produit *nm product*

professeur *nm (in school) teacher*

profil *nm profile*

se promener *v refl (+ v* **être***) to go for a walk/drive/ride*

promettre *vtr* **~ qch à qn** *to promise sb sth*

prononcer *vtr to pronounce*

propos *nm inv* **à ~, je...** *by the way, I...*

propre *adj clean*

prouver *vtr to prove*

PTT *nf pl (abbr* = **Administration des postes et télécommunications et de la télédiffusion***) French postal and telecommunications service*

puis *adv then*

quai *nm quay; river bank*

quand *conj when*

quart *nm quarter*

quartier *nm area; district*

Québécois, -e *nmf Quebecois, Quebecker*

quel, quelle *who; what; which*

quelque *some; a few; any;*

quelquefois *adv sometimes*

quelqu'un *someone, somebody; anyone, anybody*

qui *who; whom*

quitter *vtr to leave [place, person, road]*

quoi *what;* **à ~ penses-tu?** *what are you thinking about?*

quotidien, -ienne *adj daily; nm daily (paper)*

raccrocher *vtr to hang [sth] back up* **~ le combiné** *to put the telephone down.*

raisin *nm grape*

raison *nf reason;* **~ d'agir** *reason for action*

ralentir *vtr, vi to slow down*

rallye *nm (car) rally*

ranger *vtr to put away; to tidy*

rapide *adj quick, rapid*

rapidement *adv quickly; fast*

se raser *v refl (+ v* **être***) to shave*

rasoir *nm* **~ électrique** *electric shaver*

rater *vtr to miss*

rayon *nm department*

recette *nf* **~ (de cuisine)** *recipe*

recevoir *vtr to receive, to get*

reconnaître *vtr to recognize; to identify*

réfléchir à *vtr + prep to think about*

réfrigérateur *nm refrigerator*

regarder *vtr to look at [person, scene, landscape]*

régime *nm diet;* **être au ~** *to be on a diet*

région *nf region; area;* **le vin de la ~** *the local wine*

regretter *vtr to be sorry about, to regret*

rejoindre *vtr to meet up with*

remarquer *vtr to point out*

remercier *to thank* (**de qch** *for sth*)

remplir *vtr to fill (up)* [container]; *to fill in or out* [form]

rencontre *nf meeting; encounter*

rencontrer *vtr to meet* [person]

rendez-vous *nm inv appointment*

renseignement *nm information*

renseigner *vtr* ~ **qn** *to give information to sb*

rentrée *nf (general) return to work (after the slack period of the summer break, in France)*

réparer *vtr to repair, to mend, to fix*

repasser *vtr to iron*

répétitif, -ive *adj repetitive*

répondre *vtr to answer, to reply*

réponse *vtr answer, reply*

repos *vtr rest*

reposer *vtr to rest;* **se reposer** *v refl (+ v être) to have a rest, to rest*

réserver *vtr to reserve, to book* [seat, ticket]

respirer *vtr to breathe in* [air]; *vi to breathe*

rester *vi (+ v être) to stay, to remain*

résultat *nm result*

retard *nm lateness;* **un ~ de dix minutes** *a ten-minute delay;* **avoir de ~** *to be late*

retour *nm return;* (**billet de**) ~ *return ticket*

retraite *nf retirement*

se retrouver *v refl (+ v être) to meet (again);* **on s'est retrouvé en famille** *the family got together*

réunion *nf meeting*

réussir *vtr to achieve* ~ **à un examen** *to pass an exam*

rêve *nm dreaming; dream*

se réveiller *v refl (+ v être) to wake up*

revoir *vtr to see again*

au revoir *phr goodbye, bye*

rien *nothing;* **se disputer pour un** ~ *to quarrel over nothing*

rire *vi to laugh*

rond, -e *adj* [object, table, hole] *round*

rond-point *nm roundabout*

roue *nf wheel*

rouge *adj red*

route *nf road, highway*

routier *nm lorry driver*

sage *adj wise, sensible; good, well-behaved*

saison *nf season*

salade *nf lettuce; salad;* ~ **verte** *green salad*

salaire *nm salary; wages*

salle *room; hall;* ~ **d'attente** *waiting room;* ~ **de bains** *bathroom;* ~ **de jeu(x)** *(for children) playroom* ~ **à manger** *dining room;* ~ **de séjour** *living room*

sans *adv without*

santé *nf health;* **à votre** ~! *cheers!*

saucisse *nf sausage*

saucisson *nm* ~ **à l'ail** *garlic sausage*

sauf *prep except, but*

savoir *vtr to know* [truth, answer]

sécurité *nf security;* **en toute** ~ *in complete safety*

selon *prep according to*

semaine *nf week*

sens *nm inv direction, way*

sentinelle *nf sentry*

sentir *vtr to smell*

serveur, -euse *nmf waiter/waitress*

servir *vtr to serve;* **qu'est-ce que je vous sers (à boire)?** *what would you like to drink?*

se servir *v refl (+ v être) (at table) to help oneself*

seul, -e *adj alone, on one's own*

seulement *adv only*

si *nm inv if; adv yes; so* **c'est un homme** ~ **agréable** *he's such a pleasant man*

siffler vtr to whistle [tune]

sinon otherwise, or else

skier vi to ski

sœur nf sister

soif nf thirst; **avoir** ~ to be thirsty

soir nm evening; night

soirée nf evening; **dans** or **pendant la** ~ in the evening

en solde phr **acheter une veste en** ~ to buy a jacket in a sale

soldes nm pl sales; sale

sommaire nm contents

sommeil nm sleep; **avoir** ~ to be or feel sleepy

son, sa, pl **ses** his/her/its

sondage d'opinion nm opinion poll

sortir vi (+ v **être**) to go out; to come out; **être sorti** to be out

sous prep under, underneath

souvent adv often

stage nm professional training; work experience

studio nm studio flat

sud adj inv south

suffire vi to be enough; **ça suffit (comme ça)!** that's enough!

suivant, ~e adj following; next; **le** ~ the following one; the next one

sur prep on; ~ **la table** on the table

sympathique adj nice; pleasant

syndicat nm trade union

tabac nm tobacco

taille nf size

tant adv (so) much

tante nf aunt

tard adv late; **plus** ~ later

tarif nm rate

tarte nf (food) tart; ~ **aux fraises** strawberry tart

tasse nf cup; ~ **à thé** teacup; ~ **de thé** cup of tea

tel, telle adj such; **je n'ai jamais rien vu de** ~ I've never seen anything like it

télécopieur nm fax machine, fax

tellement adv so

temps nm inv weather; time

tenir vtr to hold

terrain nm ground

terrasse nf terrace; **s'installer à la** ~ **d'un café** to sit at a table outside a café

tête nf head

tien, tienne, le tien, la tienne, les tiens, les tiennes yours

timbre nm stamp

tirer vtr to pull

toi pron you

toile nm fabric, web (computer) – **d'araignée** spider's web

tomber vi (+ v **être**) to fall

tonnerre nm thunder

tort nm **avoir** ~ to be wrong

tôt adv [start] early

toujours adv always

tourner vtr to turn

tout ~e mpl **tous** fpl **toutes** everything; all; anything

trafic nm traffic

tranquille adj [person, life, street, day] quiet

tranquillement adv quietly

travail nm work; **chercher du/ un** ~ to look for work/a job

travailler vtr to work

traverser vtr to cross

très adv very

triste adj sad

trop adv too; too much

trouver vtr to find

tutoyer vtr to address [sb] using the 'tu' form

université nf university

urgence nf urgency; **le service des ~s, les ~s** the casualty department

utile adj useful

utiliser vtr to use

vacances nf pl holiday

vache *adj* mean, nasty (slang) *nf* cow

vachement *adv* really; **il a ~ maigri** *he's lost a hell of a lot of weight*

valise *nf* suitcase

véhicule *nm* vehicle

vélo *nm* bike; **~ tout terrain, VTT** *mountain bike*

vendeur, -euse *nmf* shop assistant

vendre *vtr* to sell

vendredi *nm* Friday

venir *v aux* **venir de faire** *to have just done*; **elle vient de partir** *she's just left*; *vi* (+ *v* **être**) *to come*

vent *nm* wind

vente *nf* sale

ventre *nm* stomach; **avoir mal au ~** *to have stomach ache*

vérifier *vtr* to check

verre *nm* glass

vers *prep* toward(s)

vert, ~e *adj* green

vêtement *nm* piece of clothing

veuf, veuve *adj* widowed

viande *nf* meat

vide *adj* empty

vie *nf* life

vieux, vieille *adj* old

ville *nf* town; city

vin *nm* wine

virage *nm* bend

vite *adv* quickly; **~!** *quick!*

vitesse *nf* speed

vivre *vi* to live

voici *prep* here is, this is; here are

voilà *prep* here is, this is; here are

voir *vtr* to see

voisin, ~e *nmf* neighbour

volant *nm* steering wheel

vomir *vtr* to vomit

votre, *pl* **vos** your

vôtre: mes biens sont ~s *all I have is yours*

vouloir *vtr* to want

vous *you*

vous-même *yourself*

vouvoyer *vtr* to address [sb] using the 'vous' form

voyage *nm* trip; journey

voyager *vi* to travel

voyageur, -euse *nmf* passenger

vrai, ~e *true; real, genuine*

y *it*; **il ~ a** *there is/are*; **il ~ a du vin? il n'~ en a plus** *wine? there's none left*; **il n'~ a qu'à téléphoner** *just phone*

yaourt *nm* yoghurt

yeux *nm pl* see **œil**

zéro *nm* zero, nought

zone *nf* zone, area; **~ d'activités** *business park*

zut *damn!*

English–French vocabulary

Abbreviations:

a *adjective*
adv *adverb*
aux *auxiliary*
conj *conjunction*
excl *exclamation*
f *feminine*
i *intransitive*
m *masculine*
n *noun*

phr *phrase*
pl *plural*
prep *preposition*
pron *pronoun*
qch *quelque chose (something)*
rel *relative*
tr *transitive*
v *verb*

---

a, an **un, une**; *a man,* **un homme**; *an apple,* **une pomme**
able a. **capable, compétent, habile**
aboard **adv. à bord**; *to go a.,* **monter à bord**
about **adv. & prep. autour (de); au sujet de**
above **adv. & prep. au dessus (de)**
abroad **adv. à l'étranger**
accelerate **v.tr. accélérer**
accompany **v.tr. accompagner**
account **n. compte m**; *my bank a.,* **mon compte en banque**
accurate **a. exact, juste, précis**
ache **n. mal m, douleur f**
acquire **v.tr. acquérir**
across **adv. & prep. en travers (de)** *to walk a. (a street),* **traverser (une rue)**
acute **a. 1. aigu. 2. (douleur) aiguë**
add **v.tr. ajouter**
address **n. adresse f**
adequate **a. suffisant**
admit **v.tr. admettre**
adventure **n. aventure f**

advice **n. conseil(s) m**
advise **v.tr. conseiller**
aerial **n. antenne f**
afford **v.tr. (usu. with can) avoir les moyens**
afraid **a. effrayé**; *to be a.,* **avoir peur**
Africa **l'Afrique f**
African **a. & n. africain, -aine**
after **adv. après**; *the day a. tomorrow,* **après-demain**
again **de nouveau, encore**; *once a.,* **encore une fois**
against **prep. contre**
agenda **programme m (d'une réunion)**
ago **adv.** *ten years a.,* **il y a dix ans**
agree **v.i. & tr. consentir**
alas **excl. hélas!**
alcohol **n. alcool m**
alike **a. semblable, pareil**
alive **adj. vivant**
all **a., pron., & adv. tout**; *a. day,* **(pendant) toute la journée**; *a. men,* **tous les hommes**
allow **v.tr. (permit) permettre**

alone a. **seul**

along prep. **le long de;** *to go a. a street,* **suivre une rue**

aloud adv. **à haute voix**

already adv. **déjà**

also adv. **aussi**

altogether adv. (wholly) **entièrement, tout à fait;** *how much a.?* **combien en tout?**

always adv. **toujours**

America **l'Amérique f;** *North, South, A.,* **l'Amérique du Nord, du Sud**

American a. & n. **américain, -aine**

amiable a. **aimable**

amid(st) prep. **au milieu de; parmi**

among(st) prep. **parmi, entre**

and conj. **et**

anger n. **colère f**

angry a. **fâché, en colère**

animator n. **animateur, -trice (d'un groupe, d'un club)**

anniversary n. **anniversaire m**

another a. & pron. **encore;** *a. cup of tea,* **encore une tasse de thé;** *(a similar)* **une(e) autre, un(e) second(e)**

answer n. 1. **réponse f;** 2. **solution f (d'un problème)**

anxious adj. **inquiet**

anything pron. & n. **quelque chose**

anyway adv. & conj. **en tout cas, de toute façon**

anywhere adv. **n'importe où**

apartment **appartement m**

apple n. **pomme f**

apprentice n. **apprenti, -ie**

apricot n. **abricot m**

April n. **avril m**

area n. **région f**

arm n. **bras m;** *armchair,* n. **fauteuil**

around adv. **autour, à l'entour**

artichoke n. **artichaut m**

as adv. **aussi, si;** *you're as tall as I am, as me,* **vous êtes aussi grand que moi**

ash n. **cendre(s);** *ashtray* n. **cendrier m**

ask v.tr. & i. **demander**

asleep adv. & a. **endormi**

assault v.tr. **attaquer;** *to be assaulted,* **être victime d'une agression**

assist v.tr. **aider**

astonish v.tr. **étonner**

at **at table, at school, à table, à l'école**

August n. **août m**

aunt n. **tante f**

autumn n. **automne m**

average n. **moyenne f**

avoid v.tr. **éviter**

awake v.i. **s'éveiller, se réveiller**

away adv. **loin; au loin**

back n. **dos m**

bad a. **mauvais**

bag n. **sac m**

baggage n. **bagages mpl**

bake v.tr. **cuire, faire cuire (qch.)**

ball n. **balle f**

bank n. **banque f**

bargain n. **affaire f**

barrister n. **avocat m**

basket n. **panier m**

be v.i. **être**

beach n. **plage f**

bean n. **haricot m**

beautiful a. **beau, belle; magnifique**

because conj. **parce que**

become v.i. **devenir**

bed n. **lit m;** *twin beds,* **lits jumeaux;** *double b.,* **grand lit**

bee n. **abeille f**

beef n. **bœuf m**

beer n. **bière f**

beetroot n. **betterave f**

before adv. **avant; devant**

begin v.tr. & i. **commencer**

behind adv. **derrière**

Belgian a. & n. **belge (mf)**

Belgium **la Belgique**

believe v.tr. **croire**

bell n. **cloche f**

belly n. **ventre m**

belong v.i. appartenir

below adv. en bas, (au-)dessous

belt n. ceinture f

bench n. banc m

bend n. (of road) virage m; *bends for 3 miles,* virages sur 5 kilomètres

beneath adv. dessous, au-dessous, en bas

best a. & n. (le) meilleur, (la) meilleure; le mieux

better adj. meilleur

between prep. entre

beverage n. boisson f

big a. (large) grand; (bulky) gros

bill n. (in restaurant) addition f

black a. noir

blood n. sang m

blue a. bleu

boat n. bateau m

body n. corps m

boil v.i. bouillir

bone n. os m

book n. livre m

boss n. patron, chef m

bottle n. bouteille f

box n. boîte f

boy n. garçon m

brake n. frein m; *hand b.,* frein à main

bread n. pain m

break v.i. casser

breakfast n. (petit) déjeuner m

Britain, Great B., la Grande-Bretagne

British a. britannique

Brittany la Bretagne

broken a. cassé

brother n. frère m

brown a. brun; marron

build v.tr. bâtir (une maison)

burn v.tr. & i. brûler

business n. affaire f

busy a. affairé, occupé; actif

but conj. mais

butcher n. boucher m

butter n. beurre m

by prep. (near) (au)près de, à côté de

bye(-bye) au revoir!

cake n. gâteau m

call v.tr. appeler

can1 n. boîte f (de conserves, de bière)

can2 v. aux. pouvoir

car n. auto(mobile) f, voiture f; *rail:* voiture, wagon m

card n. carte f

carpet n. tapis m

carry v.tr. porter

cat n. chat

chair n. chaise f

Channel la Manche

cheap a. bon marché

child n. enfant mf

China la Chine

Christmas n. Noël m

church n. église f

clean a. propre, net

clear a. clair

clock n. *(large)* horloge f; *(smaller)* pendule f

close v.tr. fermer

clothes n.pl. vêtements mpl

cloud n. nuage m

code, the Highway C., le code de la route

coffee n. café m

coin n. pièce f de monnaie

cold a. froid

colour n. couleur f

come v.i. venir, arriver

computer n. ordinateur nm

construct v.tr. construire; bâtir

cook v.tr. (faire) cuire

cool a. frais, f. fraîche

cost v.i. coûter

count v.tr. compter

country n. pays m, région f

crash (car) accident m

cross v.tr. traverser (la rue)

crowd n. foule f
cry v.tr. pleurer
cup n. tasse f; c. of tea, tasse de thé
customs (bureaux de la) douane
cut v.tr. couper
dairy produce, produits laitiers mpl
dark a. sombre, obscur
day n. jour m
dead a. mort; he's d., il est mort
dear a. cher
death n. mort f
deep a. profond
Denmark le Danemark
depart v.i. s'en aller, partir
depth n. profondeur f
die v.i. mourir
dinner n. dîner m
discover v.tr. découvrir, trouver
do v. aux., v.i., v.tr. faire
dog n. chien m
door n. porte f
down adv. en bas; to go d., descendre
dozen n. douzaine f
dream n. rêve m
dress n. robe f
drive n. left-hand d., conduite f à
    gauche; v.tr. conduire (une auto)
drunk a. ivre
dry a. sec, f. sèche
duck n. canard m
duty n. devoir m
each a. chaque; e. day, chaque jour;
    tous les jours
ear n. oreille f
early a. de bonne heure
earth n. terre f; monde m
Easter n. Pâques m; E. Day, le jour de
    Pâques
easy a. facile
eat v.tr. manger
egg n. œuf m; boiled e., œuf à la coque
eight huit (m); to be e. (years old), avoir
    huit ans

elbow n. coude m
eleven onze (m)
e-mail n. courriel nm
emergency n. cas urgent m
end n. fin f
engine n. moteur m
England l'Angleterre f; in E., en
    Angleterre
English a. & n. anglais, -aise
enjoy v.tr. aimer, to e. oneself, s'amuser
enough a. assez
enter v.i. entrer
entrance n. entrée f
envelope n. enveloppe f
eve n. veille f; Christmas E., la veille de
    Noël
even adv. même
evening n. soir m; soirée f
event n. événement m
ever adv. jamais
every a. chaque
except prep. excepté; sauf
exhaust pipe, tuyau m d'échappement
exit n. sortie f
expense n. dépense f; expensive, a.
    coûteux, cher; to be e., coûter cher
explain v.tr. expliquer
eye n. œil m, pl. yeux; to have blue
    eyes, avoir les yeux bleus
fall v.i. tomber
false a. faux
family n. famille f
famous a. célèbre, renommé
far adv. (of place) loin
fare n. prix m du voyage, de la place
fast a. rapide; vite, not so f.! pas si vite!
    doucement
fasten v.tr. attacher
fat a. gros; gras
father n. père m
fault n. défaut m; imperfection f
fear n. peur f
February n. février m

feel **v.tr. toucher**

fetch **v.tr. aller chercher**

few **a. peu de;** *he has f. friends,* **il a peu
d'amis**

field **n. champ m**

fill **v.tr. remplir**

find **v.tr. trouver, rencontrer, découvrir**

finger **n. doigt m**

finish **v.tr. finir, terminer**

fire **n. feu m**

first **a. premier;** *the f. of April,* **le
premier avril**

fish **n. poisson m**

five **cinq (m)**

flag **n. drapeau m**

flat **a. plat; horizontal;** *f. roof,* **toit plat**

flight **n. vol m**

flower **n. fleur f**

flu **n. grippe f**

fly **v.i. voler**

fog **n. brouillard m**

follow **v.tr. suivre**

food **n. nourriture f; aliments mpl**

foot **n. pied m**

for **prep. pour**

forbid **v.tr. défendre, interdire;** *smoking
forbidden,* **défense de fumer**

forget **v.tr. oublier**

fork **n. fourchette f**

fortnight **n. quinzaine f; quinze
jours m**

forty **quarante (m)**

forward **adv. en avant**

four **quatre (m)**

free **a. & adv. libre;** *is this table f.?*
**est-ce que cette table est libre?;
gratuit**

French **a. français**

Friday **n. vendredi m**

fridge **n. réfrigérateur m**

friend **n. ami, f amie**

from **prep. de**

full **a. plein, rempli**

fun **n. amusement m**

furniture **n. meubles mpl**

further **davantage, plus;** *furthermore*
adv. de plus

gale **n. coup m de vent;** *it's blowing a
g.,* **le vent souffle en tempête**

game **n. jeu m**

garden **n. jardin m**

garlic **n. ail m**

gas **n. gaz m;** *g. cooker,* **cuisinière
f à gaz**

gate **n. porte f (de ville); portail m**

genuine **a. authentique, véritable**

Germany **l'Allemagne f.**

get **v.tr. obtenir;** *if I g. the time,* **si j'ai le
temps;** *to g. dressed,* **s'habiller**

gift **n. cadeau m**

girl **n.f. jeune fille;** *little g.,* **petite fille**

give **v.tr. donner**

glad **a. heureux, content**

glass **n. verre m**

go **v.i. aller;** *come and go,* **aller et venir**

gold **n. or m**

good **a. bon**

grape **n. raisin m;** *bunch of grapes,*
grappe f de raisin

grass **n. herbe f**

great **a. grand**

green **a. vert**

grey **adj. gris (m)**

grow **v.i.** *(of plant)* **pousser;** *(of pers.)*
grandir

guess **v.tr. deviner**

guest **n. invité**

habit **n. habitude f,** *to be in the h. of
doing...,* **avoir l'habitude de faire...**

hair **n.** *(of head)* **cheveu m;** *to do one's
h.,* **se coiffer**

half **n. moitié f**

ham **n. jambon m;** *h. and eggs,* **œufs
au jambon**

hand **n. main f**

happen **v.i. arriver; se passer**

happy **a. heureux**

hat **n. chapeau m**

have **v.tr. avoir, posséder;** *he has no friends,* **il n'a pas d'amis**

he **pron. il**

head **n. tête f;** *headache,* **n. mal m de tête;** *headlamp* **n. phare f**

hear **v.tr. entendre**

heat **n. chaleur f**

heavy **a. lourd**

height **n. hauteur f**

hello **excl. bonjour!**

help **n. aide f, assistance f, secours m;** *with the h. of a friend,* **avec l'aide d'un ami**

her **pron. la, lui, elle;** **adj. son, sa, ses**

here **adv. ici**

hers **pron. le sien, la sienne, les sien(ne)s**

herself **pron. elle-même**

hide **v.tr. cacher**

high **a. haut**

him **pron. le, lui**

himself **pron. lui-même**

hire **v.tr. louer (une voiture)**

his **a. son, sa, ses;** **pron. le sien, la sienne, les sien(ne)s**

hit **v.tr. frapper**

holiday **n. fête f; jour m férié;** *the holidays,* **les vacances;** *a month's h.,* **un mois de vacances f;** *where did you spend your h.?* **où avez-vous passé vos vacances?**

home **n. chez-soi m;** *at h.,* **à la maison, chez soi**

home page **n. accueil nm**

honey **n. miel m**

hope **v.i. espérer**

horse **n. cheval, -aux m**

hot **a. chaud**

hour **n. heure f;** *an h. and a half,* **une heure et demie;** *half an h.,* **une demi-heure**

house **n. maison f**

how **adv. comment**

however **adv. toutefois, cependant, pourtant**

huge **a. énorme**

hundred **cent (m)**

hunger **n. faim f;** *to be hungry,* **avoir faim**

hurry **v.tr. hâter, presser**

hurt **v.tr. blesser**

husband **n. mari m**

I **pron. je**

ice **n. glace f**

idea **n. idée f**

if **conj. si**

ill **a. mauvais; malade**

impede **v.tr. empêcher**

in **prep. en, à, dans;** *in Europe,* **en Europe;** *in Japan,* **au Japon;** *in Paris,* **à Paris;** *in the country,* **à la campagne**

include **v.tr. comprendre, renfermer;** *we were six including our host,* **nous étions six y compris notre hôte**

income **n. revenu m**

indeed **adv. en effet; vraiment**

India **l'Inde f**

indoor **n. intérieur m**

inside **n. dedans m; intérieur m**

instance **n. exemple m, cas m;** *for i.,* **par exemple**

instead **prep. phr. au lieu de**

interview **n. entrevue f**

into **prep. dans, en;** *to go i. a house,* **entrer dans une maison**

iron **n. fer m**

island **n. île f**

it **pron. il, f. elle**

Italian **a. italien**

Italy **l'Italie f**

its **adj. son, sa, ses**

itself **pron. lui-même, elle-même**

jam **n. confiture f;** *strawberry j.,* **confiture(s) de fraises**

jaw **n. mâchoire f**

jewel **n. bijou m**

job n. tâche f; travail m

joke n. plaisanterie f, farce f

juice n. jus m

July n. juillet m

June n. juin m

keep v.tr. garder

key n. clef f, clé f

kind a. bon, aimable, bienveillant; *kindness* n. bonté f

king n. roi m

kitchen n. cuisine f

knee n. genou m

knife n. couteau m

know v.tr. & i. connaître

lady n. dame f; *ladies and gentlemen!* mesdames, mesdemoiselles, messieurs!

lager n. bière blonde f

lake n. lac m

land n. terre f; *by l. and sea,* sur terre et sur mer

lane n. route f; voie f; *four l. highway,* route à quatre voies

large a. grand; gros; fort; *to grow l., larger,* grossir, grandir

last a. dernier; *the l. but one,* l'avant-dernier

late a. *I am l.,* je suis en retard

laugh n. rire m; v.i. rire

launderette n. laverie f automatique

law n. loi f

lawn n. pelouse f; gazon m

lazy a. paresseux

lean a. maigre

learn v.tr. apprendre

leather n. cuir m; *l. shoes,* chaussures f en cuir

leave v.tr. laisser; *to l. the door open,* laisser la porte ouverte; quitter

left a. gauche; *on the l. bank,* sur la rive gauche; adv. *turn l.,* tournez à gauche

leg n. jambe f

lemon n. citron m

length n. longueur f

less n. moins m; adv. *l. known,* moins connu; *l. and l.,* de moins en moins

life n. vie f; *it's a matter of l. and death,* c'est une question de vie ou de mort

light1 n. lumière f; *traffic lights,* feux de circulation

light2 a. *it is l.,* il fait jour

like1 a. semblable, pareil, tel; *l. father, l. son,* tel père, tel fils

like2 v.tr. aimer; *I l. him,* je l'aime bien

lip n. lèvre f

listen v.i. écouter

little a. petit

live a. vivant; en vie

lock n. serrure f

loft n. grenier m

look n. regard m; v.i. & tr. regarder; *to l. out of the window,* regarder par la fenêtre

lose v.tr. perdre

lot beaucoup

love n. amour m

low a. bas, basse; *l. tide,* marée basse

luck n. hasard m, chance f, fortune f; *good l.,* bonne chance

luggage n. bagage(s) m(pl)

mad a. fou

mail n. courrier m; la poste

main a. principal; premier, essentiel

make v.tr. faire; *to m. a noise,* faire du bruit

man n. homme m

manner n. manière f, façon f

manor n. *m. (house),* manoir m

map n. carte f

March n. mars m; *in M.,* au mois de mars

market n. marché m

marmalade n. confiture f d'oranges

may1 aux. might, *I m. do it with luck,*

avec de la chance je peux le faire;
he m. miss the train, **il se peut
qu'il manque le train;** *m. I?* **vous
permettez?**

May2 **n. mai m;** *in M.,* **en mai; au mois
de mai**

me **pron. me, moi**

meal **n. repas m**

mean **v.tr. vouloir dire; signifier**

meat **n. viande f**

medium **n. milieu m; a. moyen**

meet **v.tr. rencontrer**

meeting **n. réunion f;** *attend a
m.,* **assister à une réunion**

memory **n. mémoire f**

middle **a. du milieu;** *m. size,* **grandeur
moyenne;** *the m. class(es),* **la classe
moyenne**

milk **n. lait m**

mine **pron. le mien, la mienne, les
mien(ne)s**

mislay **v.tr. égarer (ses clefs, etc.)**

mispronounce **v.tr. mal prononcer**

mist **n. brume f**

mistake **n. erreur f; faute f**

Monday **n. lundi m**

money **n. monnaie f; argent m**

month **n. mois m**

moon **n. lune f**

more **a. plus;** *m. than ten men,* **plus
de dix hommes;** *some m. bread,*
encore du pain

Morocco **le Maroc**

most **a. le plus**

mother **n. mère f**

mountain **n. montagne f**

mouth **n. bouche f**

move **v.tr. déplacer; bouger**

much **a. beaucoup;** *with m. care,* **avec
beaucoup de soin**

mum **n. maman f**

must **modal aux.** *you m. hurry up,* **il
faut vous dépêcher**

my **adj. mon, f. ma, pl. mes**

myself **pron. moi(-même)**

name **n. nom m;** *full n.,* **nom et
prénoms**

near **adv. près, proche**

neck **n. cou m**

need **n. besoin m**

never **adv. jamais**

new **a. nouveau, nouvelle**

news **n. nouvelle(s) f(pl);** *n. (bulletin),*
informations fpl

next **a. prochain**

no **non**

nobody **pron. personne**

noise **n. bruit m**

none **pron. aucun**

nor **conj. (ne, ni...) ni;** *he has neither
father n. mother,* **il n'a ni père ni mère**

Normandy **la Normandie**

north **n. nord m**

nose **n. nez m**

not **adv. pas**

nothing **n. or pron. rien**

noun **n. substantif m, nom m**

November **n. novembre m**

now **adv. maintenant**

nowhere **adv. nulle part**

number **n. nombre m; numéro m**

nurse **n. infirmière f**

obvious **a. évident, clair, manifeste**

occur **v.i.** *(of event)* **avoir lieu; arriver;
se produire**

October **n. octobre m**

of **prep. de**

office **n. bureau m**

oil **n. huile f;** *olive o.,* **huile d'olive**

old **a. vieux; âgé**

on **prep. sur**

once **adv. une fois**

one **adj. & n. un**

only **a. seul, unique;** *o. son,* **fils unique;
adv. seulement;** *if o. I knew!* **si
seulement je le savais!**

open **a. ouvert**

opposite **a. en face**

other **a. autre;** *the o. one,* **l'autre;** *the o.*
   day, **l'autre jour**

our **poss.a. notre, pl. nos**

ours **pron. le/la nôtre, les nôtres**

ourselves **pron. nous-mêmes**

out **adv. dehors;** *to go o.,* **sortir**

outside **n. extérieur m**

outskirts **n. banlieue f**

outward, the o. voyage, **l'aller m**

oven **n. four m**

owe **v.tr. devoir**

own **v.tr. posséder**

oyster **n. huître f**

paint **n. peinture f**

pan **n. casserole f**

paper **n. papier m; journal m;** *weekly*
   p., **hebdomadaire m**

partner **n. associé, -ée; partenaire mf**

pay **v.tr. payer**

pea **n. pois m;** *green peas,* **petits pois**

peace **n. paix f**

pen **n. stylo m**

pencil **n. crayon m**

people **n. peuple m; habitants mpl**
   (d'une ville)

permit **v.tr. permettre**

petrol **n. essence f**

pig **n. porc m, cochon m**

pillow **n. oreiller m;** *p.-case,* **taie f**
   d'oreiller

pink **adj. & n. rose (m)**

plate **n. assiette f**

platform **quai m;** *departure p.,* **(quai**
   de) départ m; *arrival p.,* **(quai d')**
   arrivée f

play **n. jeu; v.i. jouer**

please (if you) p., **s'il vous plaît**

plum **n. prune f**

pool **n.** *swimming p.,* **piscine f**

poor **a. pauvre**

pork **(viande f de) porc m**

portal **n. portail nm**

poultry **n. volaille f**

prepay **v.tr. payer d'avance**

present **n. cadeau m**

pretty **a. joli; beau**

prevent **v.tr. empêcher**

previous **a. préalable**

price **n. prix m**

pronounce **v.tr. prononcer**

property **n. propriété f**

proprietor **n. propriétaire mf**

proud **a. fier, orgueilleux**

pub **n. bistro(t) m**

pull **v.i. & tr. tirer**

punish **v.tr. punir**

pupil **n. élève mf**

push **v.tr. pousser**

put **v.tr. mettre**

quarrel **n. querelle f, dispute f**

quarter **n. quart m**

query **n. question f**

quick **a. rapide**

quiet **n. tranquillité f, repos m, calme**
   m; a. tranquille, calme, silencieux;
   be q.! **taisez-vous!**

quite **adv. tout à fait; entièrement**

rabbit **n. lapin m**

rain **n. pluie f**

rather **adv. plutôt; un peu; assez;** *r.*
   pretty, **assez joli**

read **v.tr. lire;** *to teach s.o. to r.,*
   apprendre à lire à qn

ready **a. prêt**

real **adj. vrai**

rebate **n. rabais m**

receipt **n. reçu m, quittance f**

receive **v.tr. recevoir**

recipe **n. recette f**

recover, to r. one's health, **v.i. guérir**

red **a. & s. rouge (m)**

reduce **v.tr. réduire**

refrigerator **n. réfrigérateur m**

remain **v.i. rester**

remember v.tr. **se souvenir; se rappeler**
rent n. **loyer m**; v.tr. *(a) (let)* **louer (une maison)**; *(b) (hire)* **louer, prendre en location (une maison)**
repair n. **réparation f**
reply n. **réponse f**
report n. **rapport m**
request **demande f, requête f**
rescue n. **sauvetage m**
resort n., *seaside r.* **station balnéaire, plage f**
respond v.i. **répondre**
rest n. **repos m**
return n. **retour m**; *the r. to school,* **la rentrée (des classes)**
reward n. **récompense f**
rice n. **riz m**
ride n. **promenade f (à cheval, à vélo)**
right **à droite**
river n. **fleuve m; rivière f**
road n. **route f**
roast v.tr. **rôtir, faire rôtir**
rob v.tr. **voler**
rock n. **rocher m**
roof n. **toit m, toiture f**
rope n. **corde f**
round a. **rond, circulaire**
run v.i. **courir**
Russia **la Russie**
safe a. *s. and sound,* **sain et sauf; sans danger**
sale n. **vente f**
salt n. **sel m**
same a. & pron. **(le, la) même, (les) mêmes**; *he's the s. age as myself,* **il a le même âge que moi**
sand n. **sable m**
Saturday n. **samedi m**; *he comes on Saturdays,* **il vient le samedi**
sausage n. **saucisse f**
save v.tr. **sauver**
say v.tr. **dire**
school n. **école f**

Scot n. **Écossais, -aise**; *she's a S.,* **c'est une Écossaise**
screen n. **écran m**
sea n. **mer f**
season n. **saison f**
seat n. **siège m**
see v.tr. **voir**
seem v.i. **sembler, paraître**
sell v.tr. **vendre**
send v.tr. **envoyer**
seven a. & n. **sept (m)**
shave *to have a s.,* **se raser**; v.tr. **raser**
she pron. **elle**
sheet n. **drap m (de lit); feuille f (de papier)**
shoe n. **chaussure f**; *I shouldn't like to be in his shoes,* **je ne voudrais pas être à sa place**
shop n. **magasin m**
short a. **court**
show n. **spectacle m (de théâtre)**
shower n. **averse f**; *to take a s.,* **prendre une douche**
shriek n. **cri m**
shy a. **timide**
sick a. **malade**; *she's still s.,* **elle est toujours malade**
side n. **côté m**
sight n. **vue f**
silver n. **argent m**; *s. spoon,* **cuiller f d'argent**
similar a. **semblable, pareil**
since adv. **depuis**
single a. **seul, unique**
sink n. **évier m (de cuisine)**
sit v.i. **s'asseoir; être assis**
site n. **emplacement m**
size n. **dimension f; taille (de vêtements); pointure f (de chaussures)**
skin n. **peau f**
skirt n. **jupe f**
sleep n. **sommeil m**

slice n. tranche f
slow a. lent
small a. petit
smart a. élégant, distingué, chic
smell n. odeur f; parfum m
smile n. sourire m
smoke n. fumée f
snow n. neige f
so adv. si, tellement; tant, aussi
soap n. savon m
soft a. doux; s. voice, voix douce
solicitor n. notaire m
some a. quelque
somebody, someone n. or pron. quelqu'un
something n. or pron. quelque chose m
sometimes adv. quelquefois, parfois
somewhere adv. quelque part
son n. fils m
song n. chant m; chanson f
soon adv. bientôt, tôt
sore a. douloureux; to be s. all over, avoir mal partout
sound n. son m, bruit m; s. engineer, ingénieur m du son
south a. & n. sud (m)
space n. espace m, intervalle m
Spain l'Espagne f
Spanish a. espagnol
spare s. parts, pièces f de rechange, pièces détachées
speak v.i. parler
spectacles n. pl. lunettes f
speed n. vitesse f
spend v.tr. dépenser
spice n. épice f
spinach n. épinards mpl
spine n. colonne vertébrale; dos m
spoon n. cuiller f, cuillère f
spring n. printemps m; in (the) s., au printemps
staff n. personnel m; teaching s., personnel enseignant

stamp n. timbre m
stand v.i. être debout
star n. étoile f
starve I'm starving, je meurs de faim
state the United States of America, les États-Unis d'Amérique
station n. service s., station-service f; (railway) s., gare f
stay n. séjour m; visite f
steeple n. clocher m
step n. pas m
stomach n. estomac m; s. ache, douleurs fpl d'estomac
stop n. arrêt m; bus s., arrêt d'autobus
storey n. étage m (d'une maison)
storm n. orage m
story n. histoire f, récit m
straight a. droit; s. line, ligne droite
strawberry n. fraise f
street n. rue f
strike n. grève f
strong a. fort
subscribe to, s. to a newspaper, s'abonner, prendre un abonnement, à un journal
such a. tel, pareil, semblable
sudden a. soudain, subit
sugar n. sucre m
sum n. somme f
summer n. été m
sun n. soleil m
sure a. sûr, certain
surgeon n. chirurgien, -ienne
Sweden la Suède; Swede, n. Suédois, -oise
swim v.i. & tr. nager
switch n. interrupteur m
take v.tr. prendre
talk v.i. parler; to learn to t., apprendre à parler
tall a. grand
tap n. robinet; t. water, eau f du robinet

taste **n. goût m**

tax **n. impôt m;** *income t.,* **impôt sur le revenu**

tea **n. thé m;** *t. bag,* **sachet m de thé**

teach **v.tr. enseigner**

team **n. équipe f**

tell **v.tr. dire;** *to t. the truth,* **dire la vérité**

ten **a. & n. dix (m)**

term **n. trimestre m**

than **conj. que**

thank **n.pl.** *thanks,* **remerciement(s) m**

that1 **pron., pl.** *those;* **cela, ça;** *what's t.?* **qu'est-ce que c'est que ça?**

that2 **rel. pron. (for subject) qui; (for object) que**

that3 **conj. que**

the **le, la**

their **a. leur, pl. leurs**

theirs **pron. le/la leur, les leurs**

them **pron. les; eux**

themselves **pron. eux-mêmes**

then **adv. alors**

there **adv. là**

they **pron. ils, elles**

thick **a. épais**

thief **n. voleur, -euse**

thin **a. mince**

thing **n. chose f**

think **v.tr. & i. penser, réfléchir**

third **adj. troisième**

thirst **n. soif f**

thirsty **adv.** *to be thirsty* **avoir soif**

thirteen **a. & n. treize (m)**

thirty **a. & n. trente (m)**

this **pron. ceci; ce**

though **conj. quoique, bien que**

thought **n. pensée; idée f**

thousand **a. & s. mille (m)**

three **a. & n. trois (m)**

throat **n. gorge f;** *to have a sore t.,* **avoir mal à la gorge**

through **prep. à travers**

thunder **n. tonnerre m**

Thursday **n. jeudi m**

tide **n. marée f;** *high, low, t.,* **marée haute, basse**

till **prep. jusqu'à**

time **n. temps m**

tip **n. pourboire m**

to **prep. à**

together **adv. ensemble**

toll **n. péage m**

tomorrow **adv. & n. demain (m);** *t. night,* **demain soir**

tonight **adv. & n. cette nuit; ce soir**

too **adv. trop;** *t. much money,* **trop d'argent**

tooth **n. dent f;** *toothache,* **n. mal m de dents**

towel **n. serviette f (de toilette)**

town **n. ville f**

toy **n. jouet m**

traffic **n. trafic m**

travel **n. voyages mpl**

tree **n. arbre m**

trip **n. excursion f; voyage m**

trousers **n.pl. pantalon m**

true **a. vrai**

truth **n. vérité f**

try **v.tr. essayer;** *to t. a dish,* **goûter**

twelve **a. & n. douze (m);** *t. noon,* **midi m,** *t. midnight* **minuit m**

twenty **a. & n. vingt (m)**

twice **adv. deux fois**

twin **a. & n. jumeau, jumelle**

two **a. & n. deux (m)**

tyre **n. pneu m**

umbrella **n. parapluie m**

uncork **v.tr. déboucher (une bouteille)**

under **prep. sous; au-dessous de;** *to swim u. water,* **nager sous l'eau**

undo **v.tr. défaire**

unfair **a. (of pers.) injuste**

unhappy **a. malheureux, triste**

union **n. (trade) u.,** **syndicat m**

unknown **a. inconnu**

unless **conj. à moins que**

unpleasant **a. désagréable**

untidy **a.** *(of room)* **en désordre**

until **prep. jusqu'à**

up **adv. vers le haut;** *to go up,* **monter**

us **pron. nous**

use **n. emploi m, usage m**

vacuum **n. v.** *cleaner,* **aspirateur m**

van **n. camionnette f**

vanilla **n. vanille f**

vegetable **n. légume m**

vehicle **n. véhicule m, voiture f**

very **adv. très**

view **n. vue f**

voice **n. voix f**

wage **n. salaire m, paie f**

wait **v.i. attendre**

wake *to w. (up),* **se réveiller**

Wales **le Pays de Galles**

walk **v.i. marcher**

wall **n. mur m**

wallet **n. portefeuille m**

want **v.i. désirer, vouloir;** *he knows what he wants,* **il sait ce qu'il veut**

war **n. guerre f**

warm **a. chaud**

wash **v.tr. laver;** *to w. oneself,* **se laver**

watch **v.tr. observer; regarder;** *to w. television,* **regarder une émission de télévision**

water **n. eau f**

way **n. chemin m, route f**

we **pron. nous**

weak **a. faible**

wear **v.tr. porter (un vêtement)**

weather **n. temps m;** *in all weathers,* **par tous les temps**

web **n.** *(computer)* **toile nf**

Wednesday **n. mercredi m**

week **n. semaine f**

weep **v.i. pleurer**

welcome **v.tr. souhaiter la bienvenue**

well **adv. bien;** *to work w.,* **bien travailler**

Welsh **a. & n. gallois, du Pays de Galles**

west **n. ouest m**

wet **a. mouillé; humide**

what **a. (rel.) (ce) que, (ce) qui**

wheel **n. roue f**

when **adv. quand?** *w. will you go?* **quand partirez-vous?**

where **adv. où?** *w. am I?* **où suis-je?**

which **a. quel, f. quelle, pl. quels, quelles**

while **conj. pendant que, tandis que;** *w. you are at it,* **pendant que vous y êtes**

white **a. blanc, f. blanche**

who **pron. qui**

whole **a. entier; complet**

whom **pron. qui? (rel.) que**

why **adv. pourquoi?**

wide **a. large**

wife **n. femme f, épouse f**

win **v.tr. & i. gagner; a.** *winning number,* **numéro gagnant**

wind **n. vent m**

window **n. fenêtre f**

wine **n. vin m**

winner **n. gagnant, -ante**

winter **n. hiver m**

wish **v.i. désirer, souhaiter**

with **prep. avec**

within **prep. à l'intérieur de**

without **prep. sans**

woman **n. femme f**

wood **n. bois m**

wool **n. laine f**

word **n. mot m**

work **n. travail, -aux m**

worry **v.i. s'inquiéter**

worse **a. & n. pire**

worst **a. (le) pire**

wound **n. blessure f**
wrong **a. mauvais; faux, f. fausse**
Xmas **n. Noël m**
year **n. année f**
yellow **a. jaune**
yes **adv. oui**
yet **adv. déjà; jusqu'ici;** *not y.,* **pas encore**
you **pron. tu, te, toi, vous**

young **a. jeune**
your **adj. ton, ta, votre; pl tes, vos**
yours **pron. le/la tien(ne), le/la vôtre; pl les tien(ne)s, les vôtres**
yourself, yourselves **pron. toi-même, vous-même(s)**
youth **n. jeunesse f;** *y. hostel,* **auberge f de la jeunesse**
zip z. fastener, **fermeture f éclair**

Credits